Engaging Contradictions

Engaging Contradictions

Theory, Politics, and Methods of Activist Scholarship

Edited by
CHARLES R. HALE

Global, Area, and International Archive
University of California Press

BERKELEY   LOS ANGELES   LONDON

The Global, Area, and International Archive (GAIA) is an initiative of International and Area Studies, University of California, Berkeley, in partnership with the University of California Press, the California Digital Library, and international research programs across the UC system. GAIA volumes, which are published in both print and open-access digital editions, represent the best traditions of regional studies, reconfigured through fresh global, transnational, and thematic perspectives.

University of California Press, one of the most distinguished university presses in the United States, enriches lives around the world by advancing scholarship in the humanities, social sciences, and natural sciences. Its activities are supported by the UC Press Foundation and by philanthropic contributions from individuals and institutions. For more information, visit www.ucpress.edu.

University of California Press
Berkeley and Los Angeles, California

University of California Press, Ltd.
London, England

© 2008 by The Regents of the University of California

Library of Congress Cataloging-in-Publication Data

Engaging contradictions : theory, politics, and methods of activist scholarship / edited by Charles R. Hale.
  p. cm. — (Global, area, and international archive ; 6)
Includes bibliographical references and index.
ISBN 978-0-520-09861-9 (pbk. : alk. paper)
  1. Political activists. 2. Social action. 3. Scholars. I. Hale, Charles R., 1957–
JF799.E54 2008
322.4—dc22
                                        2007053060

17 16 15 14 13 12 11 10 09 08
10 9 8 7 6 5 4 3 2 1

For Michael Zinzun
in memoriam

Contents

Acknowledgments ix

A Note on Resources xi

Foreword, by Craig Calhoun xiii

Introduction 1
Charles R. Hale

PART I. MAPPING THE TERRAIN

1. Forgotten Places and the Seeds of Grassroots Planning 31
   Ruth Wilson Gilmore

2. Research, Activism, and Knowledge Production 62
   Dani Wadada Nabudere

3. Breaking the Chains and Steering the Ship: How Activism Can Help Change Teaching and Scholarship 88
   George Lipsitz

PART II. TROUBLING THE TERMS

4. Activist Groundings or Groundings for Activism? The Study of Racialization as a Site of Political Engagement 115
   Jemima Pierre

5. Globalizing Scholar Activism: Opportunities and Dilemmas through a Feminist Lens 136
   Jennifer Bickham Mendez

6. Activist Scholarship: Limits and Possibilities in Times of Black Genocide 164
   João H. Costa Vargas

7. Making Violence Visible: An Activist Anthropological Approach to Women's Rights Investigation   183
Samuel Martínez

PART III. PUTTING ACTIVIST SCHOLARSHIP TO WORK

8. Forged in Dialogue: Toward a Critically Engaged Activist Research   213
Shannon Speed

9. Community-Centered Research as Knowledge/Capacity Building in Immigrant and Refugee Communities   237
Shirley Suet-ling Tang

10. Theorizing and Practicing Democratic Community Economics: Engaged Scholarship, Economic Justice, and the Academy   265
Jessica Gordon Nembhard

PART IV. MAKING OURSELVES AT HOME

11. Crouching Activists, Hidden Scholars: Reflections on Research and Development with Students and Communities in Asian American Studies   299
Peter Nien-chu Kiang

12. Theoretical Research, Applied Research, and Action Research: The Deinstitutionalization of Activist Research   319
Davydd J. Greenwood

13. FAQs: Frequently (Un)Asked Questions about Being a Scholar Activist   341
Laura Pulido

Afterword: Activist Scholars or Radical Subjects? by Joy James and Edmund T. Gordon   367

Contributors   375

Index   377

Acknowledgments

This volume has been a collective project throughout, and I am deeply grateful to all those who contributed to its realization along the way. It was first conceived within the now defunct Committee of the SSRC-MacArthur Program on Global Security and Cooperation (GSC), which also provided core financial support. The two GSC Program Officers, Itty Abraham and John Tirman, supported the idea throughout, as did many of the Committee members, especially Dani Nabudere, Francis Loh, Daniel Garcia Peña, Mary Kaldor, and Yezid Sayigh. The workshop in Los Angeles during which the volume first took shape was graciously hosted at the offices of the Coalition Against Police Abuse (CAPA). Special thanks to João Vargas and especially Michael Zinzun, CAPA's director (now deceased), for making this possible. Abriendo Brecha, the annual conference on activist scholarship at the University of Texas, provided speaking venues for Ruthie Gilmore and George Lipsitz, who presented papers that grew into the chapters published here. I am especially grateful to Vivian Newdick, whose careful editorial hand helped immensely in the final preparation of the manuscript, and to Mariana Mora for her eleventh-hour work on the Appendix. Les Field and M. Brinton Lykes provided thoughtful and constructive feedback on every chapter, with a level of care that one always hopes for but rarely achieves in these endeavors. Elisabeth Magnus, our copy editor, toiled valiantly to make our prose read well, and in so doing, showed a keen understanding of the substantive contents of our work. Finally, we all have an enormous debt of gratitude to Nathan MacBrien, GAIA's publications director, for seeing the promise in this project early on and for providing sage advice at every stage that has helped us to fully realize its potential.

C. R. H.

A Note on Resources

We hope that this book will be used not only for its theoretical and empirical insights but also as a resource, for inspiration and for guidance, by those who are carrying out activist research or who aspire to do so. Toward this end, we have prepared an online appendix, meant to be a guide to organizations, networks, and the like that work in this field. Interested readers may find it alongside the online version of this book, at http://repositories.cdlib.org/gaia/gaia_books/6/.

The appendix is intended to provide activist scholars with the names and contact information of activist research centers in North America, Latin America, Asia, Africa, Oceania, and Europe, as well as to give a general sense of the types of areas in which research has been combined with concrete community action. The guide is not intended to be exhaustive but rather representative of the different types of activist research initiatives currently under way.

Foreword

Activist scholarship is as old as Machiavelli and Marx or indeed Aristotle. The social sciences developed partly in and through activist scholarship. The classical political economists of the early nineteenth century did not simply observe the effects of mercantilism, they campaigned for the repeal of the Corn Laws. Sociologists at Hull House and the University of Chicago not only studied migration, they pressed for changes in legislation and local administration and through the settlement house movement engaged in direct action. Anthropologists have lately engaged in much soul-searching over complicity in colonialism, but anthropology was also recurrently the basis for efforts to mitigate harmful colonial practices. If early anthropology was shaped by racial thinking, modern anthropologists have been widely committed not only to intellectual criticism of the use of the race concept but to action to end racism.

That knowledge is vital to social action—as to individual ethics—has long been recognized. Thinkers have been doers (contrary to stereotype). And reflection on successes, failures, and unexpected consequences of social action has been a vital source of new understanding.

Yet activist scholarship often seems an unusual or surprising idea. It isn't widely taught in textbooks. Tenure committees are unsure how to think about it. Why should this be so? Three reasons seem especially influential: (1) modern science (and modern epistemology more generally) has developed an ideal of knowledge based on detached, objective observation; (2) the university has come to contain a much larger proportion of scholarship than in the past (though perhaps not as big a proportion as academics believe), and thus scholarship is more contained with "academic" agendas and career structures; and (3) activism is widely understood as directly expressive of individual interests, or emotions, or ethical commitments rather than of a broader, more reflective, and more intellectually informed perspective on social issues.

Nonetheless, activist scholarship is of vital importance, as the chapters in this book suggest. The importance of social science to social action is not limited by discipline. Neither is the potential for improving social science by learning from and through activism.

The Social Science Research Council (SSRC) has for more than eighty years sponsored and organized projects to improve the quality and creativity of social science and to connect it better to public issues and concerns. Many SSRC projects have had little to do with broader social activism; they have focused on improving research methods or theories, on building better linkages across disciplinary boundaries, or on ensuring integrated scholarly attention to major world regions. But the SSRC has also mobilized academic experts to inform the policy process—helping, for example, to create the U.S. Social Security system and shaping approaches to economic development in the mid–twentieth century.

Occasionally SSRC projects have sought to put issues on the policy agenda that weren't yet the focus of policy makers' attention or to change the way issues were understood in public debates. In the 1990s, for example, the SSRC was active in developing new ways of thinking about "peace and security" that complemented previous concerns regarding conventional warfare and nuclear arms races with new attention to international immigration, environmental degradation, food supplies, ethnic conflicts and genocides, and gender-based violence as basic dimensions of "human security." Grasping the connections among these different topics required scholars from different disciplines to collaborate; making their knowledge effective required them to communicate not only with each other but with broader constituencies and actors in various practical domains. It was—and is—not enough simply to communicate social science knowledge to policy makers in government. It is important to foster collaboration and communication with those whose work in NGOs, social movement organizations, businesses, legal advocacy, and other arenas that can be improved by social science knowledge—and can challenge social scientists to keep improving their own understandings.

Engaging Contradictions is linked to this work on international peace and security. Charles Hale was among the advisors to a MacArthur Foundation–funded Global Security and Cooperation fellowship program. Discussions there and elsewhere led him to propose a more sustained look at activist scholarship. Most of the chapters are about the work of researchers in or with activist organizations and social movements. But it is important to see that their activism is addressed also to the academy. The contributors to this project seek a social science that continually renews itself through direct engagement with practical problems and efforts to create a better world. They wish to overcome tendencies to reproduce existing frameworks of knowledge in "ivory tower" settings cut off from practical human concerns. They try to encourage collaboration with nonacademics who are also actively engaged in the development of new knowledge.

Inevitably, activist scholars confront patterns of academic organization and reproduction at odds with these foci. In addition to the basic epistemological issue mentioned above—commitment to ideas separating theory and practice, observation and action, the universal and the particular—there are a variety of practical organizational challenges. Activist scholarship demands efforts to change universities, disciplines, and interdisciplinary fields. Universities, for example, are as committed as ever to internal academic hierarchies. Faculty members hold different ranks, and junior scholars compete for tenure. Departments are ranked by their research prestige. Disciplines compete for resources from central administrations concerned with capacity to bring in funding. Universities themselves are ranked in increasingly influential ratings schemes, not only nationally but globally, and often as though there were only a single dimension to "excellence," so that conformity is rewarded more than the attempt to make a distinctive contribution.

The academic hierarchy not only privileges certain sorts of intellectual work but encourages insulation of elite academics. These are likely to be educated and to work in a set of institutions constituting only a thin layer of the overall higher education system. They are likely to think of themselves as cosmopolitan in ways that reduce their ties to specific localities and indeed the social struggles and human issues in those localities. They are rewarded largely on the basis of the prestige their work can attract in specific disciplines (and increasingly on their ability to bring new financial resources into their universities). Thus, even while university presidents talk about interdisciplinarity and the social contributions of academic knowledge, many practical considerations for scholars trying to make careers militate against those goals.

This isn't all new, of course. Universities grew as elite institutions, training gentlemen for service to the state, the church, and as members of learned—and elite—professions. As universities became mass institutions in the twentieth century, the democratic impulse to provide higher education to as many citizens as possible contended with the interests of elites in maintaining their distinction. A growing emphasis on research and scientific knowledge—in one sense democratic because truth was a matter of logic and evidence, not aristocratic privilege—was harnessed to the production and reproduction of internal hierarchies. Some institutions would train PhDs, others would receive them. Some would do "basic" science; others would focus mainly on "application." Funds would be allocated on the basis of scientific merit and scholars attracted to elite academic centers in ways that encouraged what Robert Merton called the "Matthew effect," after the biblical observation that "unto every one that hath shall be given, and he shall have abundance: but from him that hath not shall be taken away even that which he hath."[1]

The social sciences grew up as the university system was transformed from its older focus on a "classical" curriculum through a new emphasis on research and as it expanded from its older elite bases to become a much larger and more important social institution. In the United States, universities like Chicago, Cornell, Columbia, and especially public universities like Michigan, Wisconsin, and Berkeley became centers for the development of new fields like anthropology, sociology, and economics. But it is worth recalling these fields had strong roots outside the universities as well—in social reform movements, social welfare projects, local efforts at poor relief, and international missionary activity. Before the twentieth century most social scientists worked outside universities.

Social science developed increasingly inside the university but also in some tension with the emerging structure of academia. Activist social scientists like the great economist Thorstein Veblen found themselves fired—in his case, from Stanford for supporting trade unions. Entire disciplines were shaped by these tensions, as when economics split off from history in the late nineteenth century partly because the economists were widely engaged in social activism, and sociology in turn split from economics in 1905 partly because the economists (shaped both by sensitivity to shifting politics and by the marginalist revolution) were increasingly distancing themselves from activism and from older social institutional concerns (like those of Veblen).

Activist social scientists strove to maintain connections with broader publics and practical work on social issues. Some found wider audiences in the Chautauqua movement. Some were pacifists (and many suffered reprisals). Some were committed to Christian social reform—whether in its more paternalistic versions or in more insurgent forms like the Catholic Worker movement. Some focused on integrating immigrants or overcoming racial divisions. Many published frequently in the broader, nonacademic press. Some indeed spent significant parts of their careers as journalists. Academic and nonacademic intellectuals collaborated on a range of small magazines such as (in the United States) *Partisan Review*, *New Republic*, and *Dissent*. But over the course of mid-twentieth century, the boundaries between academia and broader public discourse grew more rigid. Prominent social scientists like Margaret Mead or C. Wright Mills might write for broader publics, but for academic disciplinary elites this would seem increasingly déclassé, a matter of "popularization."

Rebellion against the complete "academicization" of social science was one thread in demands for "relevance" in the 1960s. More recently, across the social sciences there have been calls for more engagement with broader publics—public anthropology, for example, or public sociology. These are important trends. In the introduction to this book, Charles Hale connects the present enterprise to Michael Burawoy's account of what a more public sociology—and by extension a more public social science—might look like.[2] But as Hale notes, activism is not just a matter of publicity or reaching broader publics with a message from social science. It is a way of doing social science, often in collaboration with non–social scientists. And as I have elsewhere emphasized, giving social science more public importance is a matter of choosing important problems for research, not simply finding more effective means of communicating existing disciplinary knowledge (good though that may be).[3]

Activist scholarship is not simply the "application" of previously accumulated knowledge. Both sides of this widespread formulation are misleading. First, activist scholarship—like a variety of practical engagements—is part of the process of forming, testing, and improving knowledge. Social scientists should take heed of Donald Stokes's invocation of "Pasteur's Quadrant."[4] Invoking the great Louis Pasteur, Stokes notes how many advances in basic science have been stimulated—even made possible—by efforts to solve practical problems. "Pasteurization" was not simply an application of previously acquired knowledge but the result of a process that inextricably intertwined knowledge formation, practical problem solving, and the effort to actually make something work. Although the idea of applied science is much older—and was linked to activist scholarship by great nineteenth-century figures like Lester Frank Ward—in the post–World War II context it became part of the way in which the presidential science adviser Vannevar Bush and others sold funders on the value of basic science that had no immediate payoff: sooner or later, they suggested, such "blue sky" research would eventually yield truths that could be applied in more practical efforts. This may be true at one level—as famously space research yielded the capacity to make nonstick cooking surfaces—but it is misleading. It implies an order of discovery followed by application that is often not how knowledge develops in the real world. This may be especially true for the social sciences, where knowledge is especially embedded in culture and in dialogue between researchers and the rest of society. But even in the apparently more "objective" natural sciences it is true. And thinking otherwise encourages a hierarchical structure of scientific knowledge in which allegedly "pure" research is seen as more "basic" than "applied research." This sort of hierarchy is especially pernicious for activist research.

The commonplace notion of application is also misleading in its reliance on a notion of scientific knowledge as the accumulation of established truths. Not only are "pure" scientists believed to work most completely in the realm of these truths (no matter where their funding comes from), but the truths are held to be certain, settled, and independent of context or formulation. Especially since Thomas Kuhn's classic *Structure of Scientific Revolutions*, however, this presumption has been widely treated with skepticism or rejected. Even those who disagree with particulars of Kuhn's argument mostly recognize the importance of his central point: that "truths" are formulated and stabilized within scientific paradigms that allow for the "normal science" of effective testing of propositions and elaboration of theories but that revolutionary breakthroughs in science often derive from growing recognition of contradictions and aporias within these paradigms, which in turn they shatter and replace.[5] This is not an argument against truth or for an anything-goes relativism. But it is an argument for seeing science as a historical process, always open-ended in ways large as well as small. And this in turn is an argument for a more democratic vision of science, one in which possession of current "truths" is less of a trump card for certified experts to play in relation to laypeople.

Activist scientists need to offer truth. If scholarly knowledge has no authority, if it doesn't provide good reasons to believe that some courses of action are better than others, or riskier, or less reliable, then it doesn't have a distinctive value. But the authority of scholarly knowledge isn't and can't be perfect. Science is, after all, in large part a process of learning from errors, not just a process of accumulating truths. And especially in social science, truths are often highly contextual and conditional, predictions of what is more or less likely under certain circumstances, not statements of absolute and unvarying causal relationships. The truths of social science are, moreover, graspable in different ways. Anthropologists are particularly aware of the extent to which knowledge is part of culture, not easily and fully abstractable from the rest of culture. The knowledge social scientists bring to activism is of this sort. It is real knowledge, but it is also incomplete knowledge. It has to be communicated, and this always means rendering it in ways that foreground certain aspects more than others, that illuminate some dimensions and leave others in the shadows. Indeed, it is partly through the effort to communicate knowledge to nonspecialists that activists (like teachers) see new implications of what they know, new dimensions to issues they thought they understood fully, and sometimes limits to their own grasp of what they thought were established truths.

These considerations suggest humility and embedding knowledge in dialogue, not dicta. But they do not suggest abandoning the idea that some claims to knowledge are more authoritative than others. Social science really does offer useful knowledge, and the knowledge is useful because it is has what philosophers call "truth value." The truths may be partial, or qualified, or statable in different ways in different languages with somewhat different connections and implications. But *truth value* means that certain statements get things right more than others. They offer more accurate or better understanding of what is going on in the world.

But here a distinction needs to be made between science and the scientist. None of us has complete command of all the "truths" of social science. We need to watch out for confusing the authority of scientifically verified knowledge—which is very important, even if limited—with the authority of scientists as individual people. It may make sense for others to respect social scientists for their PhDs and the breadth of their knowledge. But it wouldn't make sense for this respect to turn into the belief that because a social scientist is smart, well-educated, and a member of a discipline with authoritative knowledge on some subjects everything this social scientists says is true or deserving of more respect than what others have to say. For after all, on many subjects—including some of the subjects of her or his own discipline—the social scientist knows little if anything more than the average layperson and often less than the laypeople who focus most on those subjects. Pierre Bourdieu, following Michel Foucault, expressed this point as the difference between "general" and "specific" intellectuals. General intellectuals use their prestige to claim the right to speak authoritatively on almost any subject, regardless of whether they have specialized, research-based knowledge of that subject. Specific intellectuals more modestly but also more rigorously claim the authority of research—and scholarly debate and testing of research findings—to speak on those subjects about which they have real expertise. But, suggested Bourdieu, the more general authority of science inheres in the collective work of many participants, not simply the personae of individuals.[6]

Moreover, as nearly all the chapters in this book point out, activist researchers learn an enormous amount from the activists with whom they work. They are not the only ones carrying knowledge, though they may be the only ones in the business of trying to formulate it as scientific propositions or write it up in books. Housing activists often know more about housing issues than academic researchers. The kind of expertise that academics offer will seldom be simply accumulated facts, and especially not about the domains in which activists work. But researchers may be able to analyze data in ways that reveal previously unseen or at least inadequately demonstrated patterns in the facts. They may be able to clarify understanding of some of the broader contexts that influence the specific domains in which activists work. They may be able to help activists reflect on their own movements and struggles, partly through knowledge of how other struggles have played out. They may bring knowledge of tactics to expand the repertoires of activists.

It shouldn't be thought that all potential constituencies for social science research are actively waiting for social scientists to show an interest. On the contrary, activists in particular commonly work on demanding short-term schedules and are apt to be impatient with the slow pace of social science. As many chapters in this book report, they are also apt to be distrustful of volunteers from outside their core community in general and all the more so if those volunteers arrive wanting to contribute "expertise." This distrust is not simply a result of experience with previous academic researchers whose commitments have been brief or who have given little back. It also reflects the more general disengagement of academic social science from practical social action. If activists a century ago were keen to see social science develop because they thought it would help their practical projects, many activists today see social science as turned inward on its own concerns, more interested in producing the next round of journal articles to benefit academics' own careers.

There is justice to this rebuke, but activists commonly underestimate the contributions research and scholarship could make. It is part of their habitus to focus on the problem at hand, but that doesn't mean longer-term perspectives wouldn't be helpful. A sense of urgency can detract from reflexivity that would be helpful. And working on practical problems in the frames of everyday cultural understanding can be limiting.

Activists sometimes think their work should be a direct expression of political or ethical values. But efforts to secure positive social change often thrive most as a combination of these values with strong commitments to improvements in knowledge and understanding. Many activist scholars emphasize appreciating the knowledge that nonscholars have developed, and that appreciation is important. But it is easy to elide the difference between contributing knowledge and analysis to social movements or other practical efforts and simply sharing in the general tasks of struggle. The latter may be important for access or credibility or equity, as many of the chapters in this book attest; it may be important simply in itself, for scholars are also individuals and citizens. But if activist scholarship is to contribute all that it really can (and if it is to be appreciated well in either scientific or practical realms), it has to do so through production and mobilization of knowledge.

Commitment to social action in pursuit of social change is one of the sources for a commitment to social science. Readers of this volume will see evidence throughout of the authors' passionate commitments—at once to various causes, to particular groups of people, and to the pursuit of knowledge that can matter. Readers will also find reports of personal experience and writing that defies the conventional impersonality academics sometimes associate with objectivity. The first-person voices are significant and valuable. They invite students and other readers to think about what it means to do activist research and to be an activist scholar. More conventional writing presents results of finished projects, often in ways that disguise the process through which they were carried out. But the first-person voice is also important in another way. It reminds us that activist engagement connects social scientists to different people, problems, and places in very particular ways. It is not just about universal truths—though these do matter—but about producing truth in particular contexts and making knowledge useful in particular projects. It is about the way the world looks from different particular perspectives.

For example, the discipline of anthropology has a long-standing engagement with helping readers see how the world looks from different vantage points. It has usually identified these different vantage points with different cultures, and there has been some justified criticism of the extent to which the concept of culture can be misleading, implying clearer boundaries and more internal homogeneity than it should and stabilizing phenomena that are changing and often conflictual. The activist perspectives reported here emphasize that differing perspectives are created by different practical circumstances and commitments, not only by differences of culture. They are created by being engaged in particular struggles—from resistance to racism to advocacy for women's rights. They are created by having certain resources—like community solidarity—and lacking others—like wealth. They are created by the ways in which people are marked—or marked off—by racial identities, by the ways they embrace or try to change the meaning of ethnic identities, and by the tensions between "host" and immigrant cultures, not just by culture as something everyone has. Yet the original anthropological insight about the importance of specific culturally informed perspectives remains vital, even if perspectives are informed by more than culture.

Activist research and scholarship also complements traditional anthropological and sociological thinking about participant observation. It makes explicit the tension in much traditional thought between "really participating" and "just observing," especially in settings where social conflicts and struggles shape what participating can mean. It demands that researchers be explicit about their collaboration with colleagues who are not professional researchers—not just thank their informants. When researchers are participants in activist movements or organizations, their informants are colleagues. Activist research also emphasizes a kind of reflexivity about the conditions for formulating knowledge of different kinds. This includes recognizing the privilege academics enjoy to spend time articulating and working through understandings that others engaged in immediate practical pursuits often necessarily leave more tacit. With the privilege, of course, comes responsibility. Activist scholars make contributions to the material work of activist movements and organizations. But they may also have responsibility to make more specifically scholarly contributions to knowledge that may matter to others engaged in other practical pursuits in the future.

There are thus a range of different kinds of expertise, and different sorts of roles for experts. One of the reasons why activist research helps advance social science is that it brings into scientific discussion the knowledge accumulated by practitioners in various practical domains—

including struggles for social justice. It is not just that academics are able to "debrief" practitioners. In addition, practitioners often have knowledge and perspectives that challenge the way academic researchers think about issues. This can be an important spur to intellectual innovation.

In this context, it is worth noting that in many contexts it should not be assumed that professional academics are a great deal more educated than the nonacademics with whom they may work. Historically, anthropological thinking commonly viewed "the natives" as not only of a different culture but without academic education. They might possess expertise in various roles within their culture, and thus knowledge of that culture—and anthropologists celebrated the remarkable knowledge of some of their informants. Similarly, sociologists and other social scientists often assumed that they were studying people who were less articulate about their lives, social projects, and practical agendas than themselves, not people educated in more or less the same way as themselves. But the greater extent of formal education in contemporary societies means that the anthropologist is not necessarily the most educated person in the village. Fieldworkers and interviewers commonly find themselves studying college and university graduates. Nor is the social scientist the only master of rendering practical knowledge discursive. When scholars work in activist organizations or movements, their collaborators and informants are likely to include lawyers, journalists, teachers, social workers, doctors, nurses, and others with substantial education and professional skills.

But there is still a further sense in which the relationship between theory and practice is not simply one between "pure" knowledge and application. This is emphasized in Davydd Greenwood's contribution to this book, with its focus on Aristotle's concept of *phronesis* as distinct from *tekne* and *episteme*. In the *Nichomachean Ethics*, Aristotle distinguishes two forms of moral intelligence. *Sophia* derives from the pursuit of universal truths, such as those of geometry. But in itself it does not yield the capacity to act to make the world—or one's individual life—better. Such constructive action is always a matter of particulars as well as universals. And one does not successfully make choices in a world of particulars simply by applying knowledge of universals. *Phronesis* is the capacity to think about practical choices (it is sometimes translated as "prudence," but this no longer has the right connotations in English). Knowing how to act in particular situations, however, is a kind of knowledge according to Aristotle and as crucial a moral virtue as *sophia,* the sort of abstract wisdom concerned with universals. A widespread error today is to regard only the latter as knowledge—and to think about it entirely on the model of science—while regarding *phronesis* a matter of mere intuition, or taste, or even luck. At best, practical knowledge is seen as derivative and inferior; this is what the typical notion of "application" of previously established "theory" suggests. But this is a distortion of a distinction better made between the knowledge of particulars and of universals, with both sorts of knowledge required for effective practical action.[7]

Greenwood emphasizes the importance of *phronesis* in relation not only to abstract knowledge of universal laws (*episteme,* a central dimension of wisdom or *sophia*), but also to *tekne,* the kind of purely instrumental knowledge that tells one how to do things but not why, that allows one to judge them in technical terms but not in terms of beauty, or morality, or justice.[8] This isn't the place to pursue this important theoretical as well as practical argument, but one point deserves emphasis specifically with regard to activist scholarship: the enlarged idea of action that is implied by Greenwood's (and Aristotle's) arguments. We might think of activists as people who insist on action, who pursue action in order to make the world better, and who thus necessarily draw on practical knowledge of particulars as well as abstract knowledge of universals.

To be committed to action is to be committed to acting in a world of particulars. One may learn of these particulars from experience as well as from books or conversations with others. As Bourdieu has emphasized, also drawing on Aristotle, one's knowledge of these particulars and of how to act may be tacit rather than explicit, embodied rather than discursive, a matter of habitus rather than propositions.[9] But practical actors may also be articulate. And practical action may be informed by discursive, propositional knowledge as well as experiential learning. It is important for social science to learn from the experience of activists. Activists may also learn from reflection on their experience and the experience of others that social scientists may help to make articulate. And social scientists may contribute knowledge from outside the particular realms of knowledge in which activists are already expert.

Crucially, activist social science may inform both activism and social science by pursuing critical knowledge. Critique is not the same thing as just objecting to the way things are; intellectual criticism is not mere complaint. Rather, as a crucial part of social science, critique is an effort to understand how things could be different and why existing frameworks of knowledge do not recognize all the actual possibilities. Critical theory is not just criticism of other theories, it is an orientation to the world that combines the effort to understand why it is as it is (the more conventional domain of science) and how it could be otherwise (the more conventional domain of action). Precisely because of attention to the possibilities of change, critical social science is often focused on the ways in which power, privilege, and self-interest as well as ideology and limited vision reinforce actually existing patterns in social life and limits on potentially positive change.[10] And precisely because it assumes the world as it is and neglects action to change it, more conventional social science commonly neglects these factors and ends up affirming the contemporary as the necessary.

So, in short, activist scholarship is a matter of critique, not just advocacy. It is part of a project of producing new knowledge, of integrating more abstract and universal sorts of knowledge with more concrete and particular sorts of knowledge, and of keeping action and its possibilities at the center of attention.

One reason for activist scholarship is obvious but worth restating: the world is in considerable need of improvement, and improvement comes in large part by means of social movements, struggles, and campaigns to change public agendas, not merely by the provision of technical expertise to those already in power. Activist scholarship can help movements have more success improving the world.

A second reason for activist scholarship is less immediately obvious but no less important: it is easy for social science to become too complacent, too affirmative of the existing order, and turned in on itself as though it were entirely self-justifying. Activist scholarship puts new issues on the research agenda as well as the public agenda. It encourages creativity and forces confrontation between different perspectives, explanations, and statements of fact. Such creativity and confrontation advance social science.

The primary purpose of activist scholarship thus may be to address public issues or help specific constituencies. Activist scholarship is one way to make social science useful. But activist scholarship can also make social science better, providing occasions for new knowledge creation, challenges to received wisdom, and new ways of thinking.

Craig Calhoun
President, Social Science Research Council

NOTES

1. Robert K. Merton, *The Sociology of Science* (1968; repr., Chicago: University of Chicago Press, 1973).
2. Michael Burawoy, "For Public Sociology," *American Sociological Review* 70, no. 1 (2005): 4–28.
3. Charles R. Hale, "Toward a More Public Social Science," *Items and Issues* 5, nos. 1–2 (2004): 12–14.
4. Donald Stokes, *Pasteur's Quadrant* (Washington, DC: Brookings Institute Press, 1997).
5. Thomas Kuhn, *The Structure of Scientific Revolutions* (Chicago: University of Chicago Press, 1962; rev. ed. 1970).
6. Pierre Bourdieu, "The Corporatism of the Universal: The Role of Intellectuals in the Modern World," *Telos* 81 (1989): 99–110.
7. Before modern science, philosophy (note the etymology) already tended to exalt *sophia* above *phronesis*, as a purer kind of knowledge. Aristotle differed from Plato partly in emphasizing the practical as much as he did. The dominant tendency was reinforced by Christian thinkers who viewed the study of universals as an approach to God and practical knowledge as more concerned with the mundane world.
8. Greenwood's efforts to revitalize anthropology—and the tradition of applied anthropology—through thinking about *phronesis* should be read together with Bent Flyvberg's similarly grounded *Making Social Science Matter* (Cambridge: Cambridge University Press, 2001) and Alasdair MacIntyre's effort in *After Virtue* (Notre Dame: Notre Dame University Press, 1984) and elsewhere to revitalize moral reason in a way that overlaps social science rather than remaining contained by philosophy.
9. See, e.g., Pierre Bourdieu, *Logic of Practice* (1980; repr., Stanford: Stanford University Press, 1990).
10. I have elaborated this way of thinking about critical theory in *Critical Social Theory: Culture, History and the Challenge of Difference* (Cambridge, MA: Blackwell, 1995) and elsewhere.

Introduction

Charles R. Hale

> Although this activity appeared to follow the standard "academic workshop" format of papers-discussion-conclusions, it also departed from that format in important, formative, at times radical ways. The Coalition Against Police Abuse (CAPA) offices, located in the heart of South Central, are a living museum of 30 years of ongoing community struggle for social justice, with a primary emphasis on the lives and struggles of African Americans. A mural on one wall depicts this history in Diego Rivera style; another on the adjacent wall memorializes the "gang truce" between the Crips and the Bloods, which CAPA helped to forge in 1992. Pictures, posters, and other artifacts of community activism fill every available space in the main conference room. Directly across from the table where we worked for the two days hangs a frame, with pictures of two Black men who the police shot down on the UCLA campus in the days of Black Panther activism. As our first session began on Friday morning, Ruthie Gilmore briefly remembered one of these men, John Huggins, her cousin, who had been like a brother to her. This moment of reflection drove home the deeply felt personal and political immediacy of the workshop, and set the tone for the discussions that followed.
>
> My own notes from the L.A. Workshop on
Activist Scholarship, CAPA, April 2003

> Strong passions are necessary to sharpen the intellect and help make intuition more penetrating.... Reality is a product of the application of human will to the society of things.... Only the man who wills something strongly can identify the elements which are necessary to the realization of his will.
>
> ANTONIO GRAMSCI, *Prison Notebooks*

The primary purpose of this volume is to provide a broad and grounded counterpoint to the standard admonition to students entering social science and humanities graduate training programs: "Welcome, come in, and please leave your politics at the door." Some aspects of our message are already conventional wisdom. It has long since become a truism, perhaps best illustrated in the biting satiric novels of authors such as David Small and Karin Narayan, that academic politics of the "small p" variety is rampant in our universities. More substantively, poststructuralist theorists of varying affinities have delivered the basic critique forcefully and persistently over the past three decades: all knowledge claims are produced in a political context; notions of objectivity that ignore or deny these facilitating conditions take on a de facto political positioning of their own, made more blatant and unavoidable by the very disavowal.[1] Further, if we consider the full spectrum of affiliations that the word *political* entails, we find politics in academe at every turn as high-level professors shuttle back and forth between the university and government or private sector pursuits. Nevertheless, graduate students and junior faculty members are regularly warned against putting scholarship in the service of struggles for social justice, on the grounds that, however worthy, such a combination deprives the work of complexity, compromises its methodological rigor, and, for these reasons, puts career advancement at risk.

This volume advances the opposite argument—that research and political engagement can be mutually enriching—and offers a wide range of disciplinary and interdisciplinary perspectives on how the two have been brought together. The essays collected here are meant to chart some paths taken and to inspire others to follow, not by glossing over difficulties and contradictions, but by confronting them head on. One of the principal reasons for the skeptical reception of activist scholarship within the academy in the past has been the tendency for proponents to make the case in terms that sound overly celebratory or sanguine. In contrast, by naming and confronting the contradictions from the outset, we deflect the common objection that activist scholars seek reductive, politically instrumental truths at the expense of social complexity. Another principal reason that activist scholarship of the type documented here has made only small inroads in our universities is that the institutional powers that be find it threatening. Such conflicts are real and at times daunting. Yet the essays here in general emphasize a different scenario, in which modest institutionalization of activist scholarship, as one option among many, can help universities resolve specific problems and can enrich the entire spectrum of scholarly and pedagogic goals that universities encompass. The fact that support for this volume came from the Social Science Research Council (SSRC) constitutes a resounding vote of confidence in this pluralist scenario; such support illustrates broader trends in the United States and internationally, to be revisited later in this introduction, that substantiate the steady increase in legitimacy and recognition of activist scholarship today.

At the same time, activist scholars, at least in North America and Europe, are still mainly located at the margins of mainstream academic institutions and often prefer to speak from these locations. The contributors to this volume, for example, are predominantly scholars of color, many of whom are associated with ethnic studies programs and have greater affinities with imagined political-intellectual communities revolving around feminist theory, critical race theory, and activist scholarship itself than with the disciplines in which they were trained. The preponderance of scholars of color in this volume stems neither from a superficial celebration of diversity nor from a facile elevation of experience as a privileged source of analytical insight and political authority. Rather, it is the expression of a basic principle: for people who feel directly and personally connected to broader experiences of oppression and to struggles for empowerment, claims of objectivity are more apt to sound like self-serving maneuvers to preserve hierarchy and privilege; and the idea of putting scholarship to the service of their own communities' empowerment and well-being is more apt to sound like a sensible, if not an inevitable, way to practice their profession. For those, like myself, who do not claim such experience-based connections, the move is one of active alignment, avoiding the righteous fervor of a convert/traitor while rejecting the privilege-laden option to remain outside the fray. Activist scholarship, in this sense, is inevitably (at least for the foreseeable future) a practice from the margins, undertaken for us all out of motives that variously combine necessity and choice.

The essays gathered here are intended to till a field, not to fill a container. A review of the literature on activist scholarship, known by an array of specific names (*action research, participatory action research, collaborative research, grounded theory, public intellectual work, engaged research,* and the like), yields a large number of works of the "container" variety: attempts first to stake out definitional ground and then to establish rules, procedures, and best practices, often in the tone of a "how-to" manual. Such texts have their place, but they can also be constraining. In contrast, the challenge here is to provide a general mapping of how people think about and practice activist scholarship, while leaving the research process fully open to contradiction, serendipity, and reflexive critique. The authors in this collection have met this challenge by taking a strongly experience-based approach: explaining what they do, what the consequences are, and how a certain kind of scholarship has emerged from their own particular blends of political commitments and research practice. Some of the essays are more general and programmatic, others more empirically focused, and taken together they constitute not a unified method but an open field with a fair amount of shared ground.

At the risk of unwarranted enclosure of the field, this introductory chapter attempts to identify the shared ground and briefly to explore some of the implications that follow. Each author makes her or his political alignments explicit, rejecting the assertion that this would somehow undermine scholarly rigor. Alignments with specific groups of people, in turn, foster a commitment to listen closely to them, to assign special importance to their agency and standpoint. This requires a certain practice of qualitative research methods, not as a sole defining feature, but as a necessary element to ensure that these people's voices are heard. The practice of qualitative research methods is not sufficient, however, given the further principle that the people who are subjects of research play a central role, not as "informants" or "data sources," but as knowledgeable, empowered participants in the entire research process. Once the research topic has been determined through horizontal dialogue of this sort, the participants assume a special responsibility for the validity of the research outcome, knowing that it is apt to have direct applicability in their own lives. For all the variation in discipline, empirical focus, and method represented here, this last feature stands out as fundamental: activist scholars work in dialogue, collaboration, alliance with people who are struggling to better their lives; activist scholarship embodies a responsibility for results that these "allies" can recognize as their own, value in their own terms, and use as they see fit. In this way, activist scholarship redefines, and arguably raises the stakes for, what counts as high-quality research outcomes; this, in turn, gives it the potential to yield knowledge, analysis, and theoretical understanding that would otherwise be impossible to achieve.

This summary is intended not to close discussion but to invite critical scrutiny and reformulation, some of which will come from these very pages. To make the invitation complete, the argument needs to be filled out, especially in relation to three assertions embedded in the preceding paragraph, regarding methodological rigor, scholarly privilege, and theoretical innovation. Each can be framed and explored in relation to a countervailing challenge. First, how can activist scholarship claim methodological rigor while rejecting the positivist notion of objectivity that has been the lynchpin of such claims throughout the twentieth century? Second, once political engagement has been established as a defining feature of one's scholarship, doesn't this mean relinquishing the control necessary to ensure a high-quality outcome? Third, isn't activist research more accurately portrayed as the "praxis" side of the theory-and-praxis combination, which in turn leaves it poorly suited to yield theoretical innovation? In the pages that follow, I briefly recount the genesis of this volume, from a proposal to the SSRC-sponsored International Peace and Security (IPS) program to its current state. I then draw on the essays in this volume to elaborate on the assertions and to address their countervailing challenges, devoting one section to each.

HOW THIS VOLUME CAME TO BE

For me the account begins in revolutionary Nicaragua. During the 1980s I worked for about five years with a Nicaraguan organization called the Center for Research and Documentation on the Atlantic Coast (CIDCA), which carried out research and analysis in critical support of the Sandinista revolution. Simultaneously, I carried out research on my dissertation, focused on conflict between the Sandinista state and Miskitu Indians, and on the eventual negotiated settlement, sealed when the central government granted rights to autonomy for indigenous and black inhabitants of the coastal region. From this experience I gained an introduction to activist scholarship, became convinced of its promise (even amid intense contradictions), and developed something of an expertise in the broader topic of "ethnic conflict," which would gain great prominence in global post–Cold War political and intellectual agendas. This expertise, combined with the practical, problem-solving orientation that activist research embodies, left me well suited to join the Global Security and Cooperation (GSC) program associated with the SSRC and funded by the MacArthur Foundation.[2] First as a postdoctoral fellow (1989–91), and later as a committee member, I maintained a thirteen-year association with this program, participating in many of the yearly fellows' conferences and later in the selection of fellows and, as the sole anthropologist on the committee, working with others to bring an anthropological and "human security" perspective to the program. Not until 2001, however, did the opportunity arise to make a direct connection between my activist research experience and the GSC program.

In 1999 the MacArthur Foundation renewed a five-year cycle of support for the GSC program, with a bold two-pronged methodological innovation. The new guidelines mandated a vigorous internationalization of peace and security studies and required fellowship research proposals to have a "collaborative" component, understood as research designed to cross the boundaries of distinct realms of knowledge production (i.e., academics in cooperation with nongovernmental organization [NGO], government, private sector, or social movement intellectuals). In keeping with the first objective of internationalization, the new thirteen-member committee had only two U.S.-born scholars and included a fascinating, dynamic roster of accomplished intellectuals who combined scholarly endeavors with political engagements of diverse sorts and sequences. In addition to fellowships and the yearly conferences, this GSC program allocated a certain portion of its budget to "field-building" projects, proposed by committee members, with the purpose of exploring and strengthening some facet of the program's new mandate. After long discussions with others on the committee, especially Dani Nabudere and Francis Loh, I submitted a proposal for a field-building project to explore the contributions of "activist scholarship" to the broader rubric of "collaborative research." This proposal, which included a workshop and commissioned essays for a volume, was finally approved in our biyearly committee meeting of early September 2001.

That turned out to be the last selection meeting that the GSC program ever had. Global turmoil in the months after the 9/11 attacks and new leadership in the MacArthur Foundation converged to produce an abrupt change of course in the foundation's nearly two-decade program of support for the progressive transformation of "security studies." While the pre-9/11 programmatic goals had included decentralization of U.S. dominance in security studies, methodological innovation, and distinctly plural notions of security, the post-9/11 MacArthur funding, we were informed, would shift (back) to terrorism, technology, weapons of mass destruction, and other U.S.-centered definitions of the field. While commitments already made would be respected, all remaining funding would be reallocated toward these new goals, and the GSC Committee would be disbanded. By the time of the activist scholarship workshop in Los Angeles (April 2003), the GSC program was closing accounts, and the audacious alternative vision of security studies, while arguably more urgently needed than ever before, had lost a major source of both economic backing and institutional legitimacy. The SSRC continued to support this book on activist scholarship, even though forces of global change had conspired to eliminate the stimulating programmatic setting from which the idea had originally emerged.

To plan the Los Angeles workshop and to gather the participants for this volume, I drew heavily on the activist scholarship communities taking shape at the University of Texas. My colleague João Costa Vargas had recently completed a long stint with the Coalition Against Police Abuse (CAPA) and offered to arrange for our workshop to be held at the CAPA offices in East Los Angeles, with the endorsement of CAPA director Michael Zinzun. CAPA turned out to be a uniquely stimulating locale for this workshop. The concrete and often urgent character of CAPA's work served as a constant grounding, and CAPA members, especially Zinzun himself, participated actively in our discussions, offering forceful reminders of how political practice and broader analysis could enrich one another. In the subsequent months we began planning at the University of Texas for the first annual "Abriendo Brecha" Activist Scholarship Conference (held in February 2004), which provided ample space for further discussion of these issues and keynote venues for early versions of the chapters of Ruth Wilson Gilmore (chapter 1) and George Lipsitz (chapter 3). Other authors were recruited to the volume with multiple goals in mind: diversity in disciplinary coverage, substantive focus, and methodological approaches to activist scholarship, as well as shared political sensibilities.

This last criterion merits further explanation. Although I have not inquired systematically about the authors' political principles and commitments, I suspect they vary widely in many ways; some of these differences surely announce themselves in this volume. By shared political sensibilities, I do not mean homogeneity, but rather a shared commitment to basic principles of social justice that is attentive to inequalities of race, gender, class and sexuality and aligned with struggles to confront and eliminate them. This volume makes no pretense of encompassing the full political spectrum in the name of equal coverage or balance, and indeed such an approach would not be viable. I contend that there is a strong elective affinity between the authors' shared political sensibilities and the activist research methods they employ and that the politics and the methods challenge and enrich one another. While it is possible in an abstract sense to speak of "activist research of the right," an explicit practice along these lines is unlikely to emerge for two reasons. First, to the extent that right-wing or conservative ideologies tend to uphold and justify social inequalities rather than contest them, the pretense of value neutrality is a much more effective means to this end than explicit political alignment with the powerful. Second, even if an "activist research of the right" could be aligned with the relatively powerless (e.g., conservative Christians, heartland antiabortion activists), the activist research methods (horizontal dialogue and broad-based participation in each phase of the research; critical scrutiny of the analytical frame; thorough critical self-reflection) would tend to be antithetical to the political goals and vision of the people in question. In short, activist scholarship methods themselves embody a politics, which the authors affirm and critically explore; this affirmation, in turn, far from an admission of "political bias," is a step toward deeper reflection on the entanglement of researcher and subject and, by extension, toward greater methodological rigor.

RECLAIMING METHODOLOGICAL RIGOR

> One can reduce biases and increase objectivity within social science. However, such cannot be achieved through repetition of the formula "I am objective," but through examination of the impact of ethical and political decisions upon social research.
> GIDEON SJOBERG, preface to *Ethics, Politics, and Social Research*

Any attempt to make the case for activist scholarship runs directly up against objections, encapsulated in three powerful words: positivism, objectivity, and rigor. In most essays of this volume, the authors acknowledge these critiques and hold their ground, often by advancing explicit counteranalysis. In part, this counteranalysis is fueled by the now-familiar deconstructive moves: against positivism as an apology for Western imperial reason; against objectivity as a smoke screen for alignment with the powerful; against methodological rigor as a fetishization of data in the absence of critical scrutiny of underlying social categories and precepts. Yet in part the authors' commitments to activist scholarship also engender a different strategy: endorsing deconstructive counteranalysis, while at the same time taking care not to throw out the baby with the bathwater. The impetus here is not some spurious notion of balance but rather a need to make sure that, when dialogue begins with an organization, social movement, or group of people in struggle, the activist scholar has concrete and potentially useful research skills to bring to the table. While the deconstruction of "bad" science will often have an important role to play, it is rarely enough. In the move from critique to alternative, the very terms being critiqued, especially *methodological rigor*, may need to be reclaimed.

For good reason, the term *positivism* has come to epitomize the social science tradition against which activist scholars must take a stand. But at first glance it is not completely clear why this should be so. The barebones elements of positivist research methods, especially in their twentieth-century "logical" variant, are partial and naive but otherwise disarmingly mild: pose only those questions that can be answered by marshaling verifiable (replicable) data; apply rationalist logic; seek parsimonious explanation.³ The twentieth-century history of professionalization of the social sciences can be recounted as a systematic process of harnessing these elements to sweeping precepts of societal organization, which can easily be shown to be profoundly ideological: that the natural sciences provide the best model for understanding and organizing human interaction; that value- and location-neutral data collection (the research equivalent of the market's "invisible hand") is the underpinning for just and valid societal decision making; that, correctly applied, these precepts will yield steady progress toward a good society. Standpoint theorists such as Sandra Harding (2005) and Patricia Hill Collins (2000) have been especially effective in exposing the noxious effects of these precepts, their barely concealed articulations with the enduring inequalities of our times. In chapter 10, Jessica Gordon Nembhard advances a closely parallel critique of neoclassical economics, perhaps the most well-defended safe haven of this positivist ideology in the social sciences. While decades of critique have made some headway in revealing the organic relationship between positivism and these inequalities—along the lines of gender and racial or cultural difference, for example—such arguments have achieved most traction when advanced in the language of science, showing, for example, that embedded assumptions of invisibility or inferiority are "bad science." The general result is small (if at times substantive) reformulations in the positivist repertoire that do not challenge its overall relationship to the reproduction of patriarchal and racial capitalism.

While it is tempting, and at times necessary, to present this full-throttle critique of positivism's noxious ideological affinities as the final word, a number of the essays in this volume suggest a more nuanced position. Unqualified endorsement of the deconstructive critique of positivism does not leave the activist scholar well positioned to carry forward his or her project for two distinct reasons. The first has to do with the kinds of knowledge production that the activist scholar's allies are carrying out, and asking for, to advance their struggles. The offices of CAPA, where Vargas worked, are filled with archives on cases of police abuse, each one carefully registered and correlated with other data on the LAPD. Samuel Martínez (in chapter 7) and Shannon Speed (in chapter 8) both describe research in conjunction with legal struggles that hinge upon positive evidence on rights and their violation. Gordon Nembhard, after her critique of neoclassical economics, turns to her own ambitious research agenda on "democratic community economics," which includes an effort to determine the conditions for success and failure of cooperative subaltern economic enterprises. Each of these examples also points to the second rationale for a distinct position: not only is there at times a need for knowledge with positivist attributes, but also positivist knowledge claims are hegemonic in most settings where our allies work and struggle. To defend or advance a given position, we often have no choice but to state the case in the language of science, even while harboring critical reservations about the dominant role that language often plays. Together, these two rationales add up to a dual stance, mildly contradictory but inevitably so, in which the Western positivist tradition is both thoroughly deconstructed and partially reclaimed. The particulars of this duality vary widely by project and, as Laura Pulido insightfully notes in chapter 13, by the temperament and training of the activist scholar; at times the requirements of the duality can best be met by a collective approach, whereby different individuals do different parts. Yet in general, Sandra Harding (2005, 349) seems right to suggest that full-throttle antipositivism can inadvertently lend support to the neopositivist camp by portraying the target of critique in such encompassing, homogeneous, and all-or-nothing terms. In good subaltern fashion, there may be more subversive potential in a strategic duality that both advances the critique and reclaims the assertions that connect data collection and analysis to notions of the good society, insisting that this chain of connections is something about which we have a lot to say.

A parallel, more specific recovery effort already has met with some success in the case of the term *objectivity*. The critiques are well known and well deserved. Over the years, notions of objectivity have been consistently deployed to keep women, African Americans, Latinos, and Asian Americans out of academic positions, to defend white privilege, and to conceal the specific power relations in which social science research is inevitably enmeshed. During the Cold War, persecution of left-leaning scholars was often justified with reference to supposed violations in the notion of objectivity, as David Price's (2004) new book on anthropology painstakingly documents. There is evidence to suggest that such persecution may again be on the rise; if so, objectivity is sure to be pressed into service once again. The problem, as João H. Costa Vargas pointedly argues in chapter 6, is the two-pronged disavowal that has turned the recourse to objectivity into a tendentious challenge: claiming objectivity has come to be equated with a refusal to acknowledge the intersubjective character of data collection in social science research; and speaking objectively has come to mean that the speaker has no history, identity, or social position that has shaped his or her perspective. This challenge is tendentious because it disguises a blatant political-ideological stance in methodological garb and then, in a perverse reversal, dismisses these methodological postulates (intersubjectivity and positionality) as political interventions that compromise good science.

One effective way to do battle against such tendentious uses of objectivity is to reclaim the term by giving it a new meaning. Many decades ago, in a pioneering examination of the ethics and politics of social science research, Gideon Sjoberg (1967) pointed in this direction, suggesting that greater objectivity could be achieved by a deepened awareness of the ethical-political context of research. More recently, Donna Haraway (1988) gave this alternative reading a more elaborated feminist grounding, advancing the explicit argument that "situated knowledge" is more insightful, complete, and accountable. Haraway's famous justification for positioned objectivity in feminist approaches to science—that otherwise we would be forced into the position "They're just texts anyway, so let the boys have them back"—seems equally applicable to activist research in general. The stakes are too high and the mantle of objectivity is too powerful for us to simply refuse association with the term; according to the resignified definition, after all, activist scholarship can plausibly be presented as more objective.

This recovery might even begin with Max Weber and his iconic text on objectivity in the social sciences (Weber 1949). Although Weber ultimately defends the ideal of objectivity, he does so while acknowledging that any given notion of objective social science will be culturally and historically particular, shaped by provisional societal consensus rather than by universal standards of validity. This leads him to admit that the "highest ideals" of Western societies, which "move us most forcefully" and frame "our" notions of objectivity, can prevail only through "struggle with other ideals which are just as sacred to others as ours are to us" (72). He defends this struggle, while acknowledging that "our" culturally and historically particular frame remains "perpetually in flux, ever subject to change in the dimly seen future of human culture" (111).

Weber's proposed resolution to this subjectivity problem sounds surprisingly convergent with Haraway's later intervention: any given evaluative frame on which notions of objectivity rest is historically given and must be subjected to critical analysis itself. Somewhere along the way Weber himself undermined this key insight by assuming that a certain variant of Western rationality was both ascendant and superior, an assumption that made full critical scrutiny of his own standpoint both difficult and unnecessary. (His latter-day interpreters may well have reinforced this abdication.) But the resignified notion of objectivity may draw even on Weber (along with the usual roster of activist scholar "ancestors") as a source of inspiration. This requires explicit critical reflection on one's own subjectivity as a researcher (as Martínez notes in chapter 7, not just where you stand, but where you come from; not just how you think about yourself, but how you are viewed and positioned in the social context of your work) and systematic monitoring of how our relationship to research subjects affects both the content and the meaning of the data we collect. Since activist research orients reflection and analysis precisely along these lines, we are well positioned to claim a resignified objectivity, while at the same time critiquing its hegemonic (mis)use.

The same argument applied to the term *methodological rigor* has an even more compelling rationale. It is crucial that activist scholars claim rigor because in practice our research requires precisely that. Given the collaborative character of activist research projects, getting it wrong means not only unfavorable reviews from academic peers or a delay in one's promotion schedule but, much more seriously, data and analysis that could harm or mislead our allies. Moreover, as Davydd Greenwood points out in chapter 12, activist research methods have a built-in test of validity that is much more demanding and stringent than conventional alternatives: Is it comprehensible to, and does it work for, a specific group of people who helped to formulate the research goals to begin with? The principal barriers here are the mainstream's association of methodological rigor with the scholar's ultimate and absolute control over the research process and its fetishization of large quantitative data sets as proof that findings are valid and incontrovertible. The question of control I take up in the following section; suffice it to say here that if rigor stands in direct contradiction to horizontal dialogue and egalitarian distribution of the benefits from research, then this highlights the parts of the term's baggage that we are well advised to stop carrying. The second barrier is less challenging: quantitative methods certainly have their place in activist scholarship so long as they are combined with the kind of qualitative research that generates healthy skepticism of the data and their categories and that opens a space for our allies to scrutinize and participate actively in pragmatic evaluation of the results. After taking these provisos into account, it seems both appropriate and necessary for activist scholars to endorse the canons of methodological rigor most applicable to their topic, to scrupulously follow them, and to assertively report this compliance, both in scholarly settings and in dialogue with allies, who will have their own abiding interest in getting the research right. Especially given that the criteria for rigor have been expanded and made more stringent in that they include systematic reflection on the positioned and intersubjective character of the research process, activist scholars would seem to be ideally situated to make this case.

If these arguments for reclaiming the very tools that have been used to delegitimate activist research are to be persuasive, the contradictions involved in such an effort cannot be denied or downplayed. In the first place, as already mentioned, to subvert the hegemonic meanings of terms like these inevitably involves a certain degree of compromise: the hegemonic power of the term *objectivity* must be partially endorsed for the full potential of its alternative—*positioned objectivity*—to be realized and for this struggle for rearticulation to be worth waging. Moreover, there are inherent contradictions between the two parts of the dyad of activism and scholarship that we cannot reasonably expect to eliminate and that have a direct bearing on the methodology: differences in the time frame for doing the analysis; long-standing institutionalized inequalities along the lines of race, class, gender, and sexuality among the bodies that populate academia and in the societies that we study; specific power differentials that derive from the relative privilege of advanced research training; the tension between scholars' conditioned drive for comprehensive knowledge and full disclosure and activists' more instrumental and selective proclivities—the list goes on. The point is that most of these tensions arise in mainstream social science research as well, especially when such research is focused on processes of social domination, mobilization, conflict, and change. Activist researchers may at times accentuate the tensions, but we also make an explicit commitment to name and confront them. Herein lies the principal basis for the claim to methodological rigor: a deeper and more sustained analysis of the sociopolitical conditions that frame the research question and the research process. Finally, amid the contradictions that activist scholarship brings to the fore, some constitute a proactive agenda for social change in the academic realm: against the unearned privilege embedded in mainstream forms of knowledge production, and for a democratization of research, to go hand in hand with the much more commonly advocated (though still only sporadically practiced) democratization of pedagogy and education. This productive contradiction is the focus of the following section.

CHALLENGING INEQUITY, UNLEARNING PRIVILEGE, AND FINDING A HOME

Not one of the authors in this collection feels completely at home in his or her discipline or in the university setting where he or she works. Many have found a more hospitable environment in interdisciplinary programs or ethnic studies departments; Dani Wadada Nabudere (chapter 2), who once worked in established African academic institutions, founded the Afrika Study Center, which allows him more fully to pursue his activist scholarship commitments. Even for those who have supportive immediate work environs, Shirley Suet-ling Tang's description, in chapter 9, of a "nepantla" space, a term borrowed from the late Gloria Anzaldua, is still apt to resonate. Commitments to activist scholarship can leave one feeling torn (if not mildly schizophrenic), stretched too thin, and resentful, especially toward the larger academic community, whose reaction generally ranges from indifference to outright hostility. Gordon Nembhard is hard at work studying what most reasonable people would agree are among the critical life-and-death societal problems of the twenty-first century, yet she finds her economics colleagues largely unreceptive; Greenwood's essay (chapter 12) expresses a cumulative frustration with anthropology's indifference to activist research, which he argues is rooted in the systematic, concerted banishment of collaborative knowledge production from the academy. Part of the project of activist scholarship, in light of these experiences, is to effect institutional change, creating more supportive space for the particular kind of research that we do.

Central to this agenda for institutional change, as many of the authors in this volume forcefully argue, is to challenge and unlearn the deeply embedded unearned privileges of social science and humanities research. The adjective *unearned* is crucial here, deployed with a meaning roughly parallel to the one invoked by critical race theorists who have urged us to think about unearned privilege in racial hierarchies (e.g., Lipsitz 1995; Frankenberg 1994; Fine et al. 1997). Many facets of a recent PhD's newfound expertise are well earned: skills, experience, and wisdom that form the basis of what activist scholars have to offer in the first place. In this sense Gilmore's admonition (in chapter 1) to would-be activist researchers who lament that they have nothing to offer to social movements is important. But other privileges associated with higher education almost everywhere have little or no rationale in relation to the basic goal of scholarly excellence. These begin with the race, class, and gender composition of our universities, as Jemima Pierre (chapter 4) forcefully argues. The reinforcement of white privilege, which inevitably occurs, for example, when predominantly white researchers study social processes in racially diverse societies, is not just ethically wrong; it also makes for parochial scholarship. As Pierre suggests, diversifying the cadre of scholars, especially in relation to certain key issues under study, is an indispensable first step in any effort to make an institutional home for activist research.

Challenges to other forms of privilege logically follow. Nearly all the authors in this volume report that a good part of their insight and analysis—not just their data—comes from the communities, organizations, and movements with which they are aligned. These long-term involvements, in Peter Nien-chu Kiang's narrative (chapter 11), have always been the primary source of inspiration and guidance for his work within the academy. In chapter 3, Lipsitz presents this relationship as a generalized feature of activist scholarship, with benefits that flow in both directions. This being the case, another, even more fiercely guarded privilege of mainstream academia is called directly into question: privilege associated with ultimate authority and control over the process of knowledge production. At each stage in this process—from the selection of the research topic to the ownership and dissemination of the results—if the subjects of research have an additional quota of real control, the researcher will have devolved some significant quota of her own. Tang, in chapter 9, makes this point especially powerfully in her narrative of her research experiences and their goals: her research is designed primarily to enhance the capacity of organized Khmer American communities to identify, analyze, and devise solutions to the key problems that they face. This goal directly challenges the standard privilege-laden alternative: for the researcher to produce original, innovative results that advance the frontiers of knowledge in a given area. Martínez, in chapter 7, expresses the same insight in a different way: conventional scholarship is designed to achieve maximum output (where *maximum* is variously defined in quantity and quality terms), while activist research seeks equitable returns. To acknowledge the privileges associated with "maximum output"—even when the output is social justice aligned, what Gilmore (1993) calls "luxury production" progressive scholarship—is to highlight the fundamental, age-old question that activist scholarship always brings to the fore: "Research for whom?" The answers that activist scholars give to this question are widely varying and often multifaceted, including but also adamantly reaching beyond the conventional monothematic response, "For other scholars like me."

This insistence on posing the "Research for whom?" question makes for a generally awkward relationship between activist scholarship and "luxury" knowledge production—even of the progressive variety. Proponents of the latter generate crucial data and critical analysis that can expose the workings of power inequities, help engender fresh understandings of complex analytical questions, and push us to ask new questions or forge new approaches to existing problems, all of which can have great practical and strategic value for a given organized group in struggle. Yet it is also very likely to remain one step removed, in accordance with its primary and explicit purpose: to speak to other scholars and scholars in the making who read the same work, engage one another in dialogue, and belong to the same imagined intellectual community. Within anthropology, I have suggested, this is the realm of "cultural critique" (Hale 2006); activist scholarship needs cultural critique (and presumably the converse is also true), but the two can be sharply differentiated on methodological grounds with regard to the relationship between the researcher and the political process under study. Pierre, in chapter 4, usefully points out that some activist research takes place in alignment with an imagined organized group in struggle before that struggle has explicitly emerged and that the activist scholar's political alignments—with the African diaspora in her case—call into question any neat dichotomy between inside and outside academia. The awkwardness follows: it seems important to defend these dichotomies (inside/outside; cultural critique/alignment with an organized group in struggle) and also to acknowledge that the resulting categories are fluid and fraught. The "Knowledge for whom?" question, as Pierre's essay demonstrates, rests on an implied concreteness and specificity that can be misleading. Yet if that question is not centrally posed, and the answer is not systematically probed, we can reasonably assume that the unearned privileges of conventional research methods are being left unchallenged.

A parallel complexity arises in relation to the question of institutionalization: How important is it for activist scholars to have a home? One could argue, with perhaps only a hint of irony, that one source of activist scholarship's integrity is that it has been practiced mainly by individuals and networks of scholars throughout the world in the relative absence of institutionalization. This may be especially true in the United States. Kiang's essay eloquently narrates this predicament in the case of Asian American studies: how the field has gradually drifted away from its "revolutionary origins," partly as a consequence of the protagonists' ability to negotiate with, and gain entry into, mainstream academia. Ironically, the skills, experience, and wisdom gained in the prior phase of community organizing and direct political action worked all too well. Greenwood's essay offers a political-institutional explanation for this outcome: the systematic suppression of an egalitarian and reciprocal mode of knowledge production—what he calls phronesis—that has occurred with the professionalization of one social science discipline after another.

A somewhat different caution against institutionalization comes from activist scholars with strong poststructuralist affinities, which engender an abiding skepticism of any organized effort that involves wielding (rather than simply contesting) power. The founding statement of the World Anthropology Network (2003), in general an inspiring, parallel effort to the ones documented here, vividly frames this tension. The goal, they argue, is to create a fluid network of "nonhegemonic" scholars who ask all the critical questions, practice anthropology differently in accordance with their answers, yet assiduously avoid anything that could even faintly resemble an alternative structure with its own ideologies, practices, and forms of governance (see also Ribeiro 2006). The principled consistency of this position is appealing, especially when understood in the spirit of the visionary projects of Third World feminists such as Chela Sandoval (2000), who challenge us to develop radically new ways of thinking and doing politics. The danger that Sandoval's challenge warns us against is depressingly familiar: organized struggles for social justice that, for a combination of reasons, end up taking on noxious features of their adversaries and oppressors. In my own reading of the essays collected here I sense a general, hearty endorsement of Sandoval's warning and vision, with perhaps a mild Gramscian corrective: we need to create and defend safe spaces from which to carry out activist scholarship within often inhospitable environments; this requires us to wage a struggle from within, to negotiate and even to wield the modest quotas of institutional power to achieve our goals, while remaining especially vigilant toward the destructive allure of the elitism and hierarchy that surround us.

While seeking this delicate balance within academia, to the extent that we continue to make our provisional homes there, the source of confidence that we are on the right track will come primarily not from academic validation or rewards but rather from the people with whom we build activist research relationships. As Martínez perceptively notes in his reflections on his activist research experience in the Dominican Republic (chapter 7), his activist-intellectual allies were not especially impressed with his academic credentials; they placed much greater importance on efficacy, trust, and long-term commitment. Bringing a geographer's sensibilities to this question, Pulido, in chapter 13, identifies "place" as a critical feature of her own activist research practice, place as socially constructed and peopled, an imagined community of which she forms a part, such that efficacy, trust, and commitment have to do with how she leads her life, quite apart from their role in her research method. This same reverence for place led Jennifer Bickham Mendez (chapter 5) from activist research among *maquila* workers in Nicaragua to similar work on fair-wage campaigns on her own university campus, a move toward "homework" that is essential if activist scholarship is to be held accountable to its own demanding principles.

This accountability, in turn, has to be the most important counterweight to the elitism and hierarchy that pervades conventional forms of knowledge production. Anthropology, for example, has long been constituted around the hallowed principle of telling stories, doing analysis from the "native's point of view." However important this principle, and despite its vaguely populist implications, it carries no inherent impetus to unlearn the privileges associated with the scholar's ultimate control over the research process and sole authority to interpret its results. The same goes for textual reflexivity, which purports to dissipate this authority simply by acknowledging it afterward in an eloquently written anthropological text. When Tang describes her own research priorities, the counterpoint comes especially clearly into focus. Produce some exciting theoretical breakthrough that her colleague-gatekeepers will recognize and reward as such? Perhaps, but this goal will have to wait its turn, patiently, behind two more important ones: capacity building and problem solving, according to the express needs of her place, her communities in struggle. If these priorities are forcefully present in the modest institutional homes for activist scholarship that we create, they will provide a conducive environment—without guarantees, of course—for the egalitarian patterns of knowledge production, and even the alternative ways of wielding power and doing politics, to which activist scholarship aspires.

Yet Tang's resolute statement of priorities, echoed in varying ways by all the authors in this volume, also frames a predicament of individual and collective viability for all those who practice activist scholarship in mainstream university settings. Is there, in fact, a tradeoff between this specific criterion of efficacy and the broader goal of advancing the frontiers of knowledge on a given topic? If so, then the quest to create a home for activist scholarship in institutions where the "frontiers of knowledge" criterion remains intact and dominant is advisable only for those who have job security, who are resigned to willed marginality and to job satisfaction that comes, in the fine tradition of Sisyphus, from constant struggle rather than forward progress. But I fear that even these stalwart few are bound to grow tired and resentful sooner or later. In part the authors gathered here affirm this predicament, and a close reading reveals that nearly everyone is contemplating and exploring, if not actively creating, alternative homes where activist scholarship can be practiced under more hospitable, if less secure and less well-compensated, conditions. Another response to this predicament, very much in the spirit of social struggle that these essays encapsulate, is to change the criteria by which universities evaluate and reward their faculty. There is no reason, as Martínez, Greenwood, and others suggest, why well-documented activist scholarship, evaluated according to its own criteria of efficacy and contribution to social justice struggles, should not enter into the assessment of a given faculty member's value to the university. Yet in part also the authors respond with a direct counterchallenge: making sure first that the "frontiers of knowledge" criterion is sufficiently open and pluralist, and then moving directly to the audacious claim that activist scholarship, quite apart from its other attributes, can also be a privileged source of theoretical innovation. The third and final section of this introduction is devoted to exploring this counterchallenge.

EPISTEMOLOGY AND THEORETICAL INNOVATION

Activist scholarship, as noted earlier, is practiced under many different specific names, which at times connote key methodological, analytical, or political distinctions and at times simply reflect academic product differentiation. Nabudere (chapter 2) provides an intellectual genealogy that also helps to explain one very important political-methodological distinction, between the more institutional "northern" and more empowerment-oriented "southern" variants of our craft. Lykes and Coquillon (2007), Naples (2003), and Bickham Mendez (chapter 5) all reference currents of activist or action research that, despite lofty egalitarian rhetoric, end up reinforcing patriarchal structures, ideology, and practice. Similarly, there is serious reason to question to the extent to which activist scholarship, carried out by predominantly white scholars in Third World settings, or among communities of color in the North, is capable of countering the structured hierarchies of racial privilege. This question highlights another fault line, between variants of this practice that are "race critical" and those that are not. The term *activist research* is not meant to define a clear category beyond all these internal differences; and I sincerely doubt that any author in this collection is interested in devoting energy to defend one self-descriptive term instead of another. Perhaps the only easily and usefully agreed-upon connotation of the term *activist research*, in relation to the others, is an acute awareness of all these fault lines and a commitment to work on them, without any expectation that they will go away. This broad and pluralist approach should then free us up to formulate and explore a general proposition: research that is predicated on alignment with a group of people organized in struggle, and on collaborative relations of knowledge production with members of that group, has the potential to yield privileged insight, analysis, and theoretical innovation that otherwise would be impossible to achieve.

One point of departure for probing this assertion is the notion of "positioned objectivity" discussed earlier. The very conditions of activist research place the scholar in an advantageous position to develop a deep, multifaceted, and complex understanding of the topic under study. The chapters of this volume are filled with examples of this "positionality" advantage. Bickham Mendez (chapter 5) takes part in strategy sessions of workers' rights struggles in both Nicaragua and Williamsburg because she has positioned herself as an ally of, and participant in, those struggles. Nabudere (chapter 2) convincingly argues that the indigenous knowledge systems he seeks to understand would remain hidden or invisible in the absence of simultaneous efforts to strengthen and valorize them. Pierre (chapter 4) adds another facet to this argument by emphasizing how interpellation by societal categories created and produced quite apart from individual intention or volition helps further to constitute this positioned objectivity. When she and the Ghanaians she worked with were all barred from entering a nightclub, and when she, along with them, responded with political outrage rather than aseptic ethnographic curiosity, the event became a critical juncture in her forging of a distinctive analysis of racism and racial formation in Ghana. This example also serves as a caution against celebratory portrayals of the purported positionality advantage: there can be risks and hurtful consequences, there are always difficulties, and as Martínez reminds us (in chapter 7), the desired or ideal relationship of positioned objectivity is often not fully achieved. But every essay in this volume provides affirming examples of the relationship, which cumulatively make for a very powerful argument: that activist research methods regularly yield special insight, insider knowledge, and experience-based understanding.

This argument opens onto another that moves us from positionality to the actual process of knowledge production. Standpoint theory, by making visible the "relations between politics and the scientific production of knowledge" (Harding 2005, 359), has set the stage nicely for activist scholars to pose the analogous self-reflexive question about our own work: How do our political alignments, and the corresponding methodological commitments, shape the forms of knowledge that we produce? Lipsitz's essay (chapter 3) provides a broad answer to this question, arguing that social movements are carriers of unique knowledge of the immediate conditions of their struggles and that scholars aligned with these movements are at times permitted to share in that insight. Crucially, he goes on to provide a series of specific topics—from the prison-industrial complex, to environmental racism, to the intersectional character of global inequality—whose key conceptual advances, recognized as such by mainstream academia, came from activist scholarship. Speed's ethnography (chapter 8) provides another concrete example of this theoretical innovation by showing how participation in an indigenous community's struggle for land rights led her to rethink, at the indigenous activist-intellectuals' resolute insistence, the notions of identity as fluid pastiche and of "strategic essentialism" that have become standard contents in the anthropological tool kit. Joanne Rappaport (2005), conducting activist research with indigenous movements in Colombia, came to a similar conclusion.

Finally, this proposition ultimately raises questions of epistemology. Greenwood (chapter 12) offers the most explicit epistemological explanation for why activist scholarship is well positioned to yield theoretical innovation: it uses a collaborative mode of knowledge production he calls phronesis, a practice that draws out the vast knowledge of the protagonists themselves, to put this in horizontal dialogue with the scholars' distinctive perspective and to keep the resulting creative tension intact as an experience-based challenge to conventional academic wisdom. Others might take issue with some of the specifics of this formulation. Vargas, for example, traces most of his theoretical insight directly back to the wisdom already present in repertoires of the activist-intellectuals with whom he works, and he presents himself more as an apprentice and a scribe than as a full-fledged co-producer of knowledge (chapter 6; see also Vargas 2006). Tang, as mentioned earlier, suggests that even to think of this co-produced knowledge as theoretical innovation within academia may be an unwelcome distraction from the primary objectives of her work. There is no need to seek uniformity in these details to register consensus on the broader point: whatever we contribute, as activist scholars, to struggles with which we are aligned, we are apt to learn much more from these struggles; key elements of what we learn are linked directly and exclusively to activist research methods; these elements are especially apt to challenge existing academic knowledge on the topic.

These contributions materialize not through some idealized fit between activism and scholarship but rather through engagement with their multiple contradictions. In the first place, social struggles themselves are born in contradictions: between the protagonists' aspirations for well-being and the oppressive social conditions they confront; between their own analysis of their surroundings and dominant representations of their oppression as justified or inevitable. Indeed, the challenging alternative forms of theoretical knowledge that these movements' intellectuals carry may even be located in the contradiction between their own understandings of their struggles and various external representations—including academic analysis—of their realities. Examples abound of social struggles of this sort, where the protagonists needed to contest and reformulate dominant representations of themselves and their conditions in order to advance their struggles, and where eventually these new representations became canonized as "theory." Most feminist theorists would acknowledge a primary intellectual debt to women's struggles against patriarchy and sexism. Black militancy has taken the lead for years in efforts to destabilize and discredit "blame-the-victim" explanations for persisting racial hierarchy, debates that subsequently have played out in strictly academic realms. Theories of intersectionality (Combahee River Collective 1983; Collins 2000) emerged first in the context of political struggles against attempts to prioritize one of people's multiple axes of oppression, a practice that inevitably deprives the others of attention and importance. Gramsci developed his theory of hegemony and political subjectivity through efforts to address the bitter contradictions of Italian workers' consciousness and practice under the ascendant influence of fascism. While it is frustrating that the activist origins of theoretical innovation are so often ignored, the basic assertion is hardly controversial: social contradictions and political struggles are generative sources of knowledge.

Yet this same insight is much less frequently applied to the research process itself, a connection that the authors of this volume make repeatedly and systematically. The research process in social sciences and the humanities is an inherently contradictory affair, at least for those who hold out for some connection, in the broadest sense, between this research and the social good. The scholarly endeavor embodies hierarchies and inequalities that we purport to oppose; there is a strong tendency for the knowledge we produce to be irrelevant, if not alienating, to the primary subjects of research; even when this "liberating" knowledge is publicly conveyed, through pedagogy or various public intellectual endeavors, all kinds of institutional patterns end up reinforcing the very inequities that the knowledge ostensibly contests. A large part of the richness of activist research comes precisely from humble, forthright engagement with these ethical-political contradictions of our work. Bickham Mendez and Martínez (chapters 5 and 7) give such engagements a prominent place in their narratives; Pulido's letter to her activist graduate students (chapter 13) conveys an integrity and charisma that comes from naming these problems, grappling with them, admitting mistakes, and trying again, without pat answers or formulas. These essays are not raising these questions for the first time, in some completely original way: poststructuralist scrutiny of social analysis, after all, has been doing this for some time. The distinctive contribution of activist scholarship, rather, is to enact an alternative way of doing research that attempts to contribute to the social good and to modestly advance the frontiers of knowledge, while training a bright light of critical scrutiny on the inequities of university-based knowledge production and attempting to ameliorate these inequities through the research process itself. It is hard to imagine how our universities could not benefit—deeply and extensively—from such efforts.

	Academic audience	*Extra-academic audience*
Instrumental knowledge	Professional (theoretical model building)	Policy (emphasis on means, not ends; applied research)
Reflexive knowledge	Critical (cultural critique, critical theory, etc.)	Public (public intellectual work, activist research?)

FIGURE 1. Dimensions of Disciplinary Knowledge. Adapted from Burawoy 2005, 512.

In this vision, activist scholarship becomes a source of indispensable enrichment of our universities and research institutes, not simply a position from which to launch critiques or a Trojan horse for the displacement of other approaches. Activist scholars, in our training and our ongoing efforts to fulfill our method's promise, can make good use of the distinctive modes of knowledge production that universities encompass. Michael Burawoy (2005) offers a neat four-cell diagram to encapsulate his analysis of the current crisis in U.S. academia. While he would place activist research in the lower right-hand cell, as a variant on his category of "public knowledge" (see Figure 1), the authors in this volume would probably hold out for a reformulation of the diagram that would portray activist research more as a largely suppressed alternative mode of knowledge production all its own (see Figure 2). In any case, Buroway's broader point resonates with the cumulative argument of this volume. Every author has had mainstream academic training, enhanced by political experience and commitments, as well as critical non-academic intellectual traditions. We all have chosen to adopt and adapt certain elements from our university training while adamantly rejecting others. It is now high time for this process to become more mutual: for activist scholarship to offer salutary critiques of mainstream academics that academic institutions can hear and take into account. Kiang (chapter 11) makes this point forcefully in his call for Asian American studies to reconnect with its own revolutionary beginnings: this call expresses his own ethical-political commitments and at the same time launches a methodological challenge. Analytical insights that derive from direct involvement in the political struggles of Asian American communities, quite apart from the potentially important and useful results for these communities themselves, make a crucial contribution to mainstream

	Conditions of intellectual production/reception: academic	Conditions of intellectual production/reception: extra-academic
Instrumental knowledge	Professional/theoretical model building, etc.	Applied/policy
[Suppressed form of knowledge production]	Activist scholarship	
Reflexive knowledge	Critical theory, critique, epistemology	Alignment with subjugated knowledges/politics

FIGURE 2. Dimensions of Disciplinary Knowledge and the Place of Activist Scholarship. Adapted from Burawoy 2005.

Asian American scholarship. Perhaps it is time, then, for administrators to create safe spaces for activist scholarship, out of universities' institutional self-interest, quite apart from their deference to or affirmation of ours.

CONCLUSIONS: PUTTING THIS BOOK TO WORK

We hope this book will both document and contribute to a trend toward greater acceptance of activist scholarship among mainstream research institutions. Basic elements of this practice, of course, have long been a feature of the scholarly landscape, and we all have our particular "ancestors" to acknowledge. But a number of prominent recent publications have pointed to shifting conditions that converge to yield a more favorable environment for this kind of research. In anthropology, Louise Lamphere (2004) has noted how diverse research practices formerly under such headings as *applied, advocacy,* and *public* have converged, yielding increasing receptivity to what we are here calling activist scholarship.[4] Buroway (2005) makes a parallel observation from the discipline of sociology, arguing that "public sociology" is an indispensable part of the solution to problems of parochialism and fragmentation in the social sciences. The Latin American Studies Association is on record in giving high priority to public and collaborative scholarship, and other area studies organizations have similar positions. The specific name or phrase that categorizes this type of research has little importance, as long as key underlying principles are being strengthened and legitimated.

At the same time, we hope this book will provoke debate that springs from our having helped to crystallize key questions, problems, and predicaments that anyone doing this kind of work is bound to confront. Some will say that the notion of activist scholarship put forth here is too restrictive in the type of politics that we support or too limiting in the suggestion that the first step is alignment with an "organized group in struggle." There also are sure to be disagreements with various elements of the strategic approach to activist scholarship presented in this introduction, from the bid to reclaim and resignify key concepts like "methodological rigor," to the challenge to unearned academic privilege, to the insistence on the special role that this research has for mainstream theoretical debate and innovation. These and other objections are welcome, especially if they stimulate further rounds of collective work to create a loosely defined "we," to clarify the work we do, and, in so doing, to contribute to a mapping of the field.

Most important, we hope this book will be used as a resource, for inspiration, and for guidance by those who are carrying out activist research or who aspire to do so. For those inclined to work toward institutional change to create hospitable conditions for activist scholarship, the online appendix, and many particular insights from the essays, should also be welcome. This particular institutional agenda will not be everyone's preferred course of action and cannot be the central focus here. Our primary purpose, rather, is summarized simply and powerfully by Pulido's closing words to her activist graduate student scholars: "Live your truth." You do not have to choose between your deepest ethical-political commitments and your desire to become a scholar. If this combination is your truth, then live it, knowing that the path will be difficult but rewarding, that others already have helped to clear the way, and that we will do everything possible to have your back.

NOTES

1. These affirmations are broad enough to be endorsed by most poststructuralist theory, whether primarily influenced by Foucault, Lacan, Derrida, or combinations thereof. For a recent meditation on "the political" by prominent theorists who take these poststructuralist affirmations as self-evident, see Butler, Laclau, and Zizek (2000).

2. The name varied considerably over the program's fifteen-year history. "International Peace and Security," and "Conflict, Peace and Social Transforma-

tion" are two others that appear in my notes. To my knowledge a comprehensive analysis of this important and fascinating bid to transform "security studies" has never been published.

3. See, for example, the entry "Positivism" in the *International Encyclopedia of the Social Sciences* (Sills 1968, 12:389–95).

4. See also Fox and Field (2007), Lassiter (2005), and Sanford and Ajani (2006).

REFERENCES

Burawoy, Michael. 2005. "Provincializing the Social Sciences." In *The Politics of Method in the Human Sciences,* ed. G. Steinmetz, 508–26. Durham: Duke University Press.

Butler, Judith, Ernesto Laclau, and Slavoj Zizek. 2000. *Contingency, Hegemony, Universality.* London: Zed.

Collins, Patricia Hill. 2000. *Black Feminist Thought: Knowledge, Consciousness, and the Politics of Empowerment.* Boston: Unwin Hyman.

Combahee River Collective. 1983. "The Combahee River Collective Statement." In *Home Girls: A Black Feminist Anthology,* ed. Barbara Smith, 264–74. New York: Kitchen Table Press.

Fine, Michelle, Lois Weis, Linda C. Powell, and L. Mun Wong. 1997. *Off White: Readings on Race, Power, and Society.* New York: Routledge.

Fox, R. G., and L. W. Field, eds. 2007. *Anthropology Put to Work.* Oxford: Berg.

Frankenberg, Ruth. 1994. *White Women, Race Matters: The Social Construction of Whiteness.* Minneapolis: University of Minnesota Press.

Gilmore, Ruth Wilson. 1993. "Public Enemies and Private Intellectuals: Apartheid USA." *Race and Class* 35 (1): 71–78.

Hale, Charles R. 2006. "Activist Research v. Cultural Critique: Indigenous Land Rights and the Contradictions of Politically Engaged Anthropology." *Cultural Anthropology* 21 (1): 96–120.

Haraway, Donna. 1988. "Situated Knowledges: The Science Question in Feminism and the Privilege of Partial Perspective." *Feminist Studies* 14 (3): 575–99.

Harding, Sandra. 2005. "Negotiating with the Positivist Legacy: New Social Justice Movements and a Standpoint Politics of Method." In *The Politics of Method in the Human Sciences,* ed. G. Steinmetz, 346–66. Durham: Duke University Press.

Lamphere, Louise. 2004. "The Convergence of Applied, Practicing and Public Anthropology in the 21st Century." *Human Organization* 63 (4): 431–43.

Lassiter, Luke Eric. 2005. "Collaborative Ethnography and Public Anthropology." *Current Anthropology* 46 (1): 83–106.

Lipsitz, George. 1995. "The Possessive Investment in Whiteness: Racialized Social Democracy and the 'White' Problem in American Studies." *American Quarterly* 47 (3): 369–87.

Lykes, M. B., and M. Coquillon. 2007. "Participatory and Action Research and Feminisms: Towards Transformative Praxis." In *Handbook of Feminist Research: Theory and Praxis*, ed. S. Hesse-Biber, 297–326. Thousand Oaks, CA: Sage Publications.

Naples, Nancy A. 2003. *Feminism and Method: Ethnography, Discourse Analysis, and Activist Research*. New York: Routledge.

Price, David H. 2004. *Threatening Anthropology: McCarthyism and the FBI's Surveillance of Activist Anthropologists*. Durham: Duke University Press.

Rappaport, Joanne. 2005. *Intercultural Utopias: Public Intellectuals, Cultural Experimentation, and Ethnic Pluralism in Colombia*. Durham: Duke University Press.

Ribeiro, Gustavo Lins. 2006. "World Anthropologies: Cosmopolitics for a New Global Scenario in Anthropology." *Critique of Anthropology* 26 (4): 363–86.

Sandoval, Chela. 2000. *Methodology of the Oppressed*. Minneapolis: University of Minnesota Press.

Sanford, Victoria, and Asale Ajani. 2006. *Engaged Observer: Anthropology, Advocacy, and Activism*. New Brunswick: Rutgers University Press.

Sills, David L., ed. 1968. *International Encyclopedia of the Social Sciences*. New York: Macmillan.

Sjoberg, Gideon. 1967. "Project Camelot: Selected Reactions and Personal Reflections." In *Ethics, Politics, and Social Research*, ed. Gideon Sjoberg, 141–61. Cambridge: Schenkman.

Vargas, J. 2006. *Catching Hell in the City of Angels: Life and Meanings of Blackness in South Central Los Angeles*. Minneapolis: University of Minnesota Press.

Weber, Max. 1949. "Objectivity in Social Science and Social Policy." In *The Methodology of the Social Sciences*, ed. E. Shils and H. Finch, 50–112. New York: Free Press.

World Anthropologies Network. 2003. "A Conversation about a World Anthropologies Network." *Social Anthropology* 11(2): 265–69.

PART I

Mapping the Terrain

1. Forgotten Places and the Seeds of Grassroots Planning

Ruth Wilson Gilmore

THE MIX

Forgotten places are not outside history. Rather, they are places that have experienced the abandonment characteristic of contemporary capitalist and neoliberal state reorganization. Given the enormous disorder that "organized abandonment" (Harvey 1989, 303) both creates and exploits, how can people who inhabit forgotten places scale up their activism from intensely localized struggles to something less atomized and therefore possessed of a significant capacity for self-determination? How do they set and fulfill agendas for life-affirming social change—whether by seizing control of the social wage or through other means? In this chapter I will conceptualize the kinds of places where prisoners come from and where prisons are built as a single—though spatially discontinuous—abandoned region. I will then present three exemplary facets of the process I am trying to think through by doing and writing, in order to highlight the potential of certain kinds of research. Here indeed is where scholars can make a difference: not because we have technical expertise (although that matters) but rather because we have the precious opportunity to think in cross-cutting ways and to find both promising continuities and productive breaks in the mix of people, histories, political and economic forces, and landscapes that make up forgotten places (Moten 2003; Robinson 1983; see also Hart 2002a).

Why prisons and prisoners? I didn't turn to the topic because I was driven as a scholar to answer some pressing questions. Rather, the issue hailed me in the early 1990s, when I started to work with some prisoners and their families, and persisted as I pursued a PhD in geography and employment in academia. The entire world of premature death and criminalization was not at all new to me: I've had family members who have done time, some of us have been harmed by others, and one of us has been killed. In short, the problem already, to paraphrase Hall (1980), bit into my existence. But with sometimes surprising intensity during the past decade and a half, my lifelong activism has been mixed into and fixed on the places prisoners come from and the places where prisons are built. In the United States, these people and locations are among the most vulnerable to the "organized abandonment" that accompanies globalization's large-scale movements of capital and labor, and as such they are subject to many other processes that accumulate in and as forgotten places. Here's a chicken-egg conundrum: I don't know whether I think we can find important lessons for making change by studying the margins because I'm a geographer or whether I became a geographer because of how I already thought about contradictions and interfaces. What geography enables is the combination of an innate (if unevenly developed) interdisciplinarity with the field's central mission to examine the interfaces of the earth's multiple natural and social spatial forms (Gilmore 2005a).

Greenberg and Schneider's (1994) "marginal people on marginal lands" suggests the conceptual continuity of forgotten places that I wish both to broaden and specify. People in these locales, exhausted by the daily violence of environmental degradation, racism, underemployment, overwork, shrinking social wages, and the disappearance of whole ways of life *and* those who lived them, nevertheless refuse to give up hope. What capacities might such people animate, and at what scales, to make the future better than the present? What does *better* mean? How do people make broadly contested sensibilities—indeed *feelings*—the basis for political struggle, especially when their social identities are not fixed by characteristics that point toward certain proven patterns (or theories) for action? In terms of prisons and prisoners the goal is double: to find relief for all from the expanding use of cages as all-purpose solutions to social and economic problems and to use the extreme (marginal) case to figure out how social justice activists might reinvigorate an organizational movement after it has spent several decades underground, undertheorized, or under cover of the not-for-profit sector (Incite! 2007).

Forgotten places, then, are both symptomatic of and intimately shaped by crisis. I use *crisis* in the sense summarized by Stuart Hall and Bill Schwarz (1988, 96): it occurs when "the existing social formation can no longer be reproduced on the basis of the pre-existing system of social relations." Crises are territorial and multiscalar; they overlap and sometimes interlock (see Rodney 1972; Fanon 1961; Soja 1989). At the outset of my studies I learned everything I could about what was happening in urban areas because that was where most prisoners came from. But since they were sent away to new rural prisons it seemed necessary to learn about what drove the lockups' location and proliferation.[1] In the early 1990s, Thomas Lyson and William Falk (1993) edited *Forgotten Places*, a volume on uneven development in rural America. Inspired by the editors' framework, I read closely the arguments they and their colleagues—especially Ted Bradshaw (1993)—had made, and I tried to connect their insights with my own and others' research on abandoned urban locales (Gooding-Williams 1993; Pulido 2000; Pastor 2001; Smith 1996; Katz 2004). My goal was to connect rural and urban in a nonschematic way.

Especially at a time when urban and rural appear to be self-evidently and perhaps irreconcilably different (as in the "red state"/"blue state" distinction that has come to stand in for real descriptions *or* explanations of U.S. intranational geopolitics), it seemed important to consider not only how they are connected—an old question for geographers—but also how they are objectively similar. What are the material and ideological linkages that make urban and rural—in some areas of the United States as well as elsewhere—more continuous and less distinct than ordinarily imagined? There are problems with such an approach. One set of them is broadly subjective: What about the self-perception of communities in different kinds of locales, the ways they view other kinds of communities across social and spatial divides, and their understanding of those divides? Another set is material: given that, place by place, past and present pathways and trajectories for capital and labor are often significantly different, can we usefully—even in theory—combine disparate sites into singular objects of scholarly and political action when the decisive motion of productive factors shaping social, political, economic, and physical space might seem necessarily to leave entirely distinctive topographies in their wake (see Katz 2001, 2004)? In short, to make connections raises a number of challenges, which are addressed in the examples given in this chapter.

Urgency and not mere curiosity is involved in scaling up the object of analysis by articulating urban with rural. The urgency has do with the imperative to understand how ordinary people who lack resources but who do not necessarily lack "resourcefulness" (Ganz 2000) develop the capacity to combine themselves into extraordinary forces and form the kinds of organizations that are the foundation of liberatory social movements. Granted the difficulties, where might we find the ground for considering at least some urban and rural forgotten places together—as a single, though spatially discontinuous, abandoned region? There are precedents for such political-theoretical ambitions in many kinds of internationalism, of which Pan-Africanism is a long-standing and by no means outmoded example (see Lemelle and Kelley 1994; Edwards 2003; Robinson 1983). Perhaps the twentieth century's most widely lived and influential example was the meeting of nonaligned states in 1955 in Bandung, Indonesia, where debate and planning, rhetoric and material analysis brought the Third World into self-conscious being.[2]

TOWARD A UNIFIED CONCEPT OF FORGOTTEN PLACE

In previous writing I have used the concept of "gulag" to talk about the places prisoners come from and the places where prisons are built, and I think it works quite well as an indicator and analytical guide. However, it also seems to carry within it a conclusion that is quite the opposite of the actual material and ideological end toward which I have studied prisons so thoroughly: it does not enable description of what else is out there, beyond *its* margins. What concept might get at the kinds of forgotten places that have been absorbed into the gulag yet exceed them?

In the summer of 2002 I had the good fortune to help conceive of and then attend an amazing workshop called "Globalization and Forgotten Places," organized by Yong-Sook Lee and Brenda Yeoh at the National University of Singapore. The group convened to share research and also to look for theoretical and methodological assistance to refine our objects of study, analyze them, and think through what might be done about them. As should be evident from the previous discussion, we looked abroad, not because intranational theories and methods are necessarily threadbare, but rather because it struck us, as it has so many others, that if globalization is indeed *globalization*, we might usefully find convergences at many levels—not solely in the realm of capital concentration or information networks or other typically studied categories. In other words, to take seriously the thinking and actions of generations of internationalists who wish to globalize liberation is in part to take comparison seriously. Comparison is often imagined narrowly to be a statistical or institutional exercise (looking at organizations, practices, outcomes); and while it is indeed a method for discovering crucial distinctions within and between the similar, comparison is also a means for bringing together—or syncretizing—what at first glance seems irreconcilable.

One concept that captured my attention was *desakota*, a Malay word, meaning "town-country," that was brought into economic geography by Terry McGee (1991) to designate and think about places that are *neither* urban *nor* rural. McGee's interest was to characterize regions in Indonesia and other southeast Asian countries where settlement, economic activity, politics, demographics, and culture belie categorization as "either/or"— ambiguous places in the dominant typology of settlement and sector. This kind of thinking derives from the anticolonial and antiracist work of Third Worldist scholars; from Du Bois (1935) to Rodney (1972), from Nkrumah (1964) to Sivanandan (1982, 1991) and Hall (1976, 1994), the goal has been to compare political, economic, territorial, and ideological valences that distinguish and might unite disparate places shaped by external control or located outside particular developmental pathways (for whatever combination of reasons).

So far, so good; but is the concept mobile? I think it works provisionally for California, but not without some adjustment (as any migration requires). A modified concept of *desakota* might give us a way to think the-city-and-the-country (and embrace the "Third World") somewhat freshly without advancing yet another theoretical novelty that stands in for political analysis but is actually only a luxurious evasion of politics (Gilmore 1993; see also Pulido, chapter 13 of this volume). However, freshness is required precisely because inadequate concepts and methods have, as Hart and Sitas (2004) note in their work on and with South African relocation townships, "trapped a large chunk of scholarship into an iron cage of instrumental knowledge and policy recommendations ... sharply at odds with emerging realities" (31).

Desakota indicates a mix that in the California case encompasses the strange combination of sudden settlement changes—urban depopulation along with the establishment of megaprisons on formerly agricultural lands—and the regular circulation of people throughout the entire region without any necessary relation to the formal economy, to the distinct and overlapping political jurisdictions, to the prisons, or even to each other: visitors, prisoners, workers. In addition, *desakota* helps us situate the rural-and-urban forgotten in a relational as well as linked context. It raises for our consideration how dwellers in the more urban areas combine deep rural roots with participation in formal and informal economies (see Flaming 2006) and even subsistence farming,[3] while many of the more rural dwellers work in what are ordinarily thought of as more urban economic sectors and do periodic or annual circular migrations within and beyond the region. The quality of having been forgotten that materially links such places is not merely about absence or lack. Abandoned places are also planned concentrations or sinks—of hazardous materials and destructive practices that are in turn sources of group-differentiated vulnerabilities to premature death (which, whether state-sanctioned or extralegal, is how racism works, regardless of the intent of the harms' producers, who produce along the way racialization and therefore race). Thus California *desakota* is a mix, a region composed of places linked through coordinated as well as apparently uncoordinated (though by no means random) forces of habitation and change. Hart and Sitas's (2004) arguments concerning the formation and possible futures of South African relocation townships help deepen this understanding, in part because voluntary and involuntary movements, layering previous rounds of dispossession, domination, and development, make a particular grounding for politics in relation to capital, the multiple scales of the state, and the rest of society; indeed, the point is that these contradictions at the margin are resolved in and as *desakota* spaces.

In other words, people in forgotten places who lack social or economic mobility, or who simply don't want to move away, act within and against the constraints of capital's changing participation in the landscape and the government's multiscalar and sometimes contradictory struggle to relegitimize state power through the ideology and practices of an antistate state (Gilmore 2007a; Gilmore and Gilmore 2007) in the ambient atmosphere of neoliberalism (Gilmore 2007b). People in forgotten places also act within the institutional and individualized constraints defined by racialization, gender hierarchy, and nationality, and the complex potential mix of these possibilities has produced its own academic specialties old and new: the various branches of the social sciences, area studies, ethnic studies, gender studies, cultural studies—the latter three dedicated to the study of disabling (in the sense of both debilitating and undoing; see Hart 2002b) constraints.

Constraints does not mean "insurmountable barriers." However, it does suggest that people use what is available to make a place in the world. In my research I have found that the constraint of crisis becomes a central element in whole ways of life—that having been forgotten is part of a syncretic culture of "betweenness"—of *desakota* considered not simply as a peculiar spatialization of the economic but also as cultural, social, and political (see Woods 1998, 2002). While the syncretic is no more amenable to change than whatever one can imagine that is not syncretic, the awareness of being "neither/nor," which is to say the awareness of imminent and ineluctable change that comes with abandonment in new ways and at new scales, opens up the possibility for people to organize themselves at novel resolutions.

PRACTICAL SYNCRETISM

Syncretic, which traces its long English-language usage to observations of surprising religious intermixture, is a term that had a lot of academic cachet about twenty-five or thirty years ago—in studies of religion and other aspects of contact culture—but was less used as *hybrid* became popular in the 1980s and 1990s. *Syncretic* appeals more to me than *hybrid* because it avoids suggesting technical intervention (other than perhaps, in the poetical sense, as in Jerome Rothenberg's [1969] *Technicians of the Sacred*). More importantly, it downplays any presumption of prior purity and instead emphasizes a more active and general practice through which people use what they have to craft ad hoc and durable modes for living and for giving meaning to—interpreting, understanding—life. Indeed, Brackette Williams (1989) has long argued that *all* cultures are contact cultures. In any event, *syncretism* denotes qualities key to crafting the kinds of motivated methodologies that enable the continuum of scholarly research as political experimentation.[4]

If we see in a syncretic approach to research and activism provisional resolutions—some more lasting than others—to contradictions and challenges, then we might imagine that the concept is charged at the outset by a particular kind of questioning. Syncretism has a purpose, and asking questions that enable it is part of the challenge of doing research well. This thinking flies in the face of some academic disciplining, even in avowedly interdisciplinary formations. The either/or boundary drawing that secures academic practices and jobs is not inherently useless; it is silly to suggest that the powerful forces of the liberal arts and professions, organized for good, for not-so-good, and for straight-up evil over the last two centuries, could be characterized as thoroughly weak today. But as universities on a global scale struggle through what seem to be endless crises of accumulation of enough students, endowments, and prestige, the retreat into disciplines, no less than the formal (but frequently not real) embrace of "interdisciplinarity," seems to foreshadow if not prove widespread irrelevance, which is exactly (although not exclusively or uniquely) what the activist scholar is *not* about.

The syncretic compels us to think about problems, and the theories and questions adequate to them, in terms of what I have called their stretch, resonance, and resilience. With a focus on questions, let's take each in turn (from Gilmore 2005b):

- *Stretch* enables a question to reach further than the immediate object without bypassing its particularity—rather than merely asking a community, "Why do you want *this* development project?" one asks, "What is development?"

- *Resonance* enables a question to support and model nonhierarchical collective action by producing a hum that, by inviting strong attention, elicits responses that do not necessarily adhere to already existing architectures of sense making. Ornette Coleman's harmolodics exemplify how such a process makes participant and audience a single, but neither static nor closed, category (Rycenga 1992).

- *Resilience* enables a question to be flexible rather than brittle, such that changing circumstances and surprising discoveries keep a project connected with its purpose rather than defeated by the unexpected. For example, the alleged relationship between contemporary prison expansion and slavery falls apart when the question describes slavery in terms of uncompensated labor because very few of the 2.2 million prisoners in the United States work for anybody while locked in cages. But the relationship remains provocatively stable when the question describes slavery in terms of social death and asks how and to what end a category of dehumanized humans is made from peculiar combinations of dishonor, alienation, and violent domination (Patterson 1982; Gordon 2006).

If we assume that identities are changed through action and struggle, what sort of political-economic and cultural projects can draw enthusiastic participation from both rural and urban residents and forge among them a new vision? The term *desakota* highlights the structural and lived relationship between marginal people and marginal lands in both urban and rural contexts and raises the urgent question of how to scale up political activity from the level of hyperlocal, atomized organizations to the level of regional coalitions working for a common purpose, partly because their growing understanding of their sameness trumps their previously developed beliefs in their irreconcilable differences. Insofar as regions are economic as well as cultural and geopolitical units of analysis, this essay will, by depicting a combination of experimental and ethnographic insights, identify ways in which research combines with the actions of everyday people to shift the field of struggle and thus reorganize both their own consciousness and the concentration and uses of social wealth in "forgotten places."

THE PROCESS IN THE TERRITORY

Joining Forces: Stretch

Politically, a solid but supple mix of aims and people is hard to achieve, and very often its categorical contingencies (some will do X but not Y; others will support A but never B) make it far too brittle to withstand the wear and tear of sustained and purposeful practical movement. A tiresomely overdeveloped take on leftist politics argues that the twentieth-century failure of solidarity to endure in the long run should be laid at the door of something the critics call "identity politics." What they seem to mean is antiracist politics, or antisexist politics; and often what they really mean, given the examples they choose, is that Black people or women of all races interrupted and messed up class politics in favor of "militant particularism." That is a pretty silly view for a number of reasons, most of which are well grounded in the evidence of what happened to whom and why. It is also a stupid view, given that capitalism has regularly encountered its "sternest negation" (Robinson 1983) from peoples organized according to a number of principles at once, including antiracism and anticolonialism. A more useful critique of identity complicates its subjective qualities (noting, for example, that class is also an identity rather than an ontology), shows how the complexity operates (as in Hall's [1980b] exquisite "Race is . . . the modality through which class is lived"), and reveals the contradictory ways in which identities fracture and re-form in the crucibles of state and society, public and private, home and work, violence and consent (see, e.g., Alexander 1994; Omi and Winant 1986; Ransby 2006; Kelley 2002).

In other words, if race *is* the modality through which class is lived, but not voluntarily, then the official codes, habits, and institutions, and the military, immigration officers, and other police who maintain order (sometimes through producing a mess to be endlessly fixed up), have a lot to do with the production and reproduction of ways of being in the world (Kim 1999; Brown 1994). It is frightfully unpopular to talk about how top-down identity ascription operates, or even that it is meaningful. A decade ago, during a seminar on the politics of reproduction, the brilliant Nuyorican scholar activist Caridad Souza rolled her eyes and whispered to me, "If one more of these workshop-feminists says 'agency' I'm going to choke her." Within seconds someone uttered the offending word; eschewing nonproductive violence, Souza soon quit academia's ranks. The point here is not that "agency" is an unimportant concept but rather, as I have argued elsewhere, that it is too often used as if it designated an exclusive attribute of oppressed people in their struggle against an opponent called "structure" (Gilmore 2007). Such a dichotomy doesn't stand up to how the world actually works. Structures are both the residue of agency (Glassman 2003) and animated by agential capacities, while the modes in which ordinary people organize to relieve the pressures that kill them and their kin are, or become, structural—especially insofar as they draw from, and operate through, relationships that can only be called structural as well (familial, religious, cultural, etc.; see, e.g., Fernandes 1997). Racialization works—vertically *and* horizontally—through the contradictory processes of structure-agency. Change certainly makes more sense when perceived this way (see Du Bois [1935] for a detailed exposition of structure-agency dialectics in the post–Civil War South). Here, then, we stretch in a couple of directions, both in terms of generalization (to think of key concepts such as structure and agency in relation to each other), and in terms of what we must think about to think at all well.

In February 2001, a group of people trying to figure out how to stop construction of a prison in Delano, California, organized Joining Forces, a conference for environmental justice and antiprison activists. The purpose for the meeting was to develop strategies for mixing issues, understanding, and campaigns throughout the *desakota* of California's prison region. While it did not for them bear the Malay name, the region theorized in this chapter was becoming increasingly visible to the conference organizers, in part because they had taken seriously the scholarship of Mary Pardo (1998), Laura Pulido (1996), myself (Gilmore 1998, 1999), and others; they had learned about the workings of environmental law and environmental justice (Cole and Foster 2001; Bullard 1990); and they were persuaded that the only way to stop the prison would be to build an extensive coalition whose convergence centered on principles other than "Not in My Backyard" (see Braz and Gilmore 2006).

In addition, some of the conference organizers had traveled in the area surrounding the proposed prison in the preceding couple of years, retracing my earlier research path and also following the spatial patterns laid out by United Farm Workers campaigns and emergency relief, by environmental justice cases, and by whoever serendipitously contacted the tiny, all-volunteer California Prison Moratorium Project via its Web site or answering machine. They had learned from grassroots activists in small towns (many of whom thought of themselves, not as activists at all, but rather as concerned citizens, residents, parents, farmers, farmworkers, immigrants, schoolchildren) that attention to what created the continuity of urban and rural—what we might call here its structural betweenness—

was crucial to understanding prison proliferation (California Prison Moratorium Project 2006; see also Gilmore and Gilmore 2004). The organizers had held a miniconference of urban and rural organizers a year earlier and had learned that unlikely organizations and alliances could be created through persuasively appealing to a shifting range of subjectivities differentially located in the wider *desakota's* political, productive, and problem-riddled landscapes.

The conference featured a series of panels in which activists talked about how they had come to encounter, identify, understand, and solve the problems where they lived. To build a coalition, the conference organizers wanted to establish that prisons constitute environmental harms both for the places where prisoners come from and the places where prisons are built: prisons wear out people and places, and that exhaustion has lethal consequences. There were lunchtime breakout sessions organized topically and an open microphone plenary, so that individuals and organizations who had found their way to the conference but hadn't been placed on the formal agenda could speak. The final segment was a planning workshop in which conference participants broke into groups and tried to brainstorm alternative outcomes to life-harming situations (prisons, toxic waste, etc.) that could be realized given what the participants already some idea of how to do or control.

In the first part of the program, each speaker described what their group did and how they had achieved success. A group of immigrant farmworkers, mostly indigenous Mixtec speakers from Oaxaca in south central Mexico, had forced Chevron to clean up the murderous toxic wastes that poisoned their *colonia* outside Fresno. An East Los Angeles group of mostly Mexicana women with green cards had stopped a state prison in their neighborhood and, tracing the roots of school leaving that make children vulnerable to criminalization, had also stopped environmentally harmful industrial production and transport in their community. An East Palo Alto group of people who had been in prison had organized a community-based, non-cop-controlled live-work-treatment facility to help people stay away from prisons and other death-dealing institutions and materials. As these activists spoke, what became increasingly clear was the ways in which they had all encountered, and tried to prevail against, the state-sanctioned and or extralegal production or exploitation of their own group's vulnerability to premature death. A coalition of antiprison and environmental activists brought suit under the California Environmental Quality Act, charging that the proposed prison would harm Delano in a number of ways not dealt with in the official environmental analysis that could, nevertheless, be partly understood in terms of environmental justice. In stretching both the object and the analysis from their parochial struggles to the entire range of struggles represented in the room, conference attendees began to recognize that—*objectively*—they and their places shared a family resemblance that needed further investigation.

The cooperation that came out of the conference might be viewed as multicultural organizing in today's dominant lexicon of cooperation and difference; or it might be viewed as something else. In 1970s and 1980s Britain, in response to the various forces unleashed by Enoch Powell's 1968 "Rivers of Blood" speech, various postcolonials of different generations living in the metropole came together as Black—not African, *Black*—Britain. A bottom-up politics of recognition in the face of threatened annihilation enhanced a syncretic rescaling of identity for these people, even though the novel category directly conflicted with the statistical identities that had officially divided them (see Smith and Katz 1993). In the United States today, *white* people suffering from a concentration of environmental harms in some rural communities have learned to call what is happening "environmental racism" without imagining that they are somehow excluding themselves from the analysis and instead feeling whiteness peel away in the context of their vulnerability. This stretched understanding of racism enables vulnerable people to consider the ways in which harmful forces might be disciplined and harms remedied (rather than areally redistributed—or concentrated out of sight). Race does not disappear; in some instances, reworking race reveals its structural essence to be residue rather than destiny. At least potentially, such a stretch evades (if it cannot quite preclude) any imagined necessity for *desakota* countercoherence to pattern itself according to logics of victim and punishment rather than to tend toward the pleasure of life-affirming political and cultural practice.

Indeed, it was for the future that the conference participants gathered, laboring in triple shifts (work at the job, work at home, work for justice). But lest the reader say, "Ah ha! What you've described is what the workshop feminists mean by 'agency,'" I'd like to take the analysis a bit further. That is, if these participants found a provisionally syncretic identity by comparing their efforts and aims, they also had to re-form the ambitions of their organizations and struggle with mission statements, funding streams, and other boundaries that have enabled many groups working for justice to achieve formal/legal recognition of the legitimacy of their characteristics and objectives. The structures they have come to inhabit in the shadow of the "shadow state" (Gilmore 2007b) enable certain kinds of creativity and achievement but stifle other kinds of association. As a result, organizations become competitive and use comparison to create distances rather than alliances with other organizations. This is a product of many connected practices and the result of specialization and professionalization in oppositional political work (see Gilmore 2007b). That such narrowing occurred *in response to* capital's twentieth-century counter-revolution—which was downright murderous and ultimately resulted in the criminalization of entire generations and communities and practices—goes much farther than the postulation of some prior sentimental or uncritical attachment to an extraeconomic "identity" in explaining the brittleness of political mixes in the present moment. Organizations *became* "legal" under the rules of the Internal Revenue Service to pursue justice, whereas earlier they had *used* "the legal" as a tool to pursue justice.

The people who met at the Delano conference and in similarly ad hoc gathering places (such as prison parking lots and seasonal workplaces) are at once way out on the edge and keenly aware of what they have to lose: they have endured Jim Crow, Japanese American internment, farm fascism,[5] NAFTA. Their marginality is not simply metaphorical but rather a feature of a spatial dilemma. Their consciousness is a product of vulnerability in space coupled with unavoidable and constant movement through space (an inversion, if you will, of gated communities and full-service suburban malls, but based in related conditions and logics). Indeed, the *desakota* region is all about the movement of resources—whether transfers of meager social wealth from public sectors (welfare to domestic warfare) or migration of persons (voluntarily or not) intraregionally or across supraregional spaces to amass remittances that, once sent, counter the apparently unidirectional concentration of wealth. Indeed, all of this movement makes the *desakota* a region of dynamic betweenness—not in dominant development's terms of "catching up" or "falling behind," but rather in the sense that it is the shadow, echo, enabler, and resolution of "globalization." Also, because of their constant motion (which is not the same as "mobility"), people who live in the "between" have a strong sense of it as simultaneously a temporary and a fixed reality. At a general level, they share a sense of possibility based in the necessity for change (which they enact through a-periodic migrations through the region), and their frequent changes of place demand—objectively and subjectively—a respatialization of the social. This, rather than any automatic recognition based in racial or ethnic categories, forms the basis for syncretizing previously separate political movements. They don't transcend, they mix; and it takes a lot of debate, strangely hostile at first because based in narrowly defined ascriptions of difference, for the mixing to happen among such disparate actors as long-distance migrants from indigenous Mexico, African Americans, immigrant women in male-dominated Mexican American households, and so on. All of their learning is based in skepticism as well as reflection, as is the case with all strong scholarly inquiry, and the outcome is as good as its ability to be reproduced throughout the region and to produce the conditions for new and useful outcomes.

The Mismeasure of Man: Resonance

In the mid-1980s, when prison expansion was the latest thing, designed to secure the ideological legitimacy of the advancing neoliberal antistate state by dispersing that state's sturdy presence via the proliferation of cages throughout its expanding gulag (Gilmore 2007a), locations willing to take on these monstrosities in the hope of jobs were awarded significant signing bonuses in the form of "mitigation" funds that could be used to make local infrastructural improvements. At the same time, given the rhetorical urgency with which the claim for endlessly increasing cages was made, federal and state environmental review requirements were sometimes waived—thus further developing the public's perception that "crime" was the paramount harm that any individual or family might encounter. By the early 1990s, however, once the antistate state found itself on firm footing, communities throughout the *desakota* region looking for industries of last resort found themselves back where they had long been—as petitioners of rather than partners in the prison boom. That meant the bonuses evaporated, as did most other demands host towns might make. Representatives of these communities' local development bodies might easily identify with the words of an industry-seeking mayor of Ladysmith, a South African relocation township, who declared to his constituency: "[W]e go kneeling to beg. It is difficult to beg a person and put conditions" (Hart 2002b, 23).

A prison is a city that weighs heavily on the place where it is. The thousands of people who live and work there make environmental and infrastructural demands on the surrounding area that are not offset by the prison's integration into the locality's economic, social, or cultural life. A prison is a political weight that, in a lightly populated jurisdiction, can reconfigure legislative representation by plumping up a district's size because prisoners (who cannot vote) are counted where they are held

(Wagner 2002), and it can tip the electoral balance as well because relatively well-paid prison staff can and do support or oppose local candidates even though they do not live in the district. A prison is also heavy in part because it is a "dead city" (cf. Davis 2003; Mumford 1968, ch. 1), built and staffed for the singularly unproductive purpose of keeping civilly dead women and men in cages for part or all of their lives. James O'Connor (1973) rightly designates spending on prisons and other policing functions as "social expense"—nonproductive outlays that do not, under any mode of accumulation, enhance the present or future capacity of a place to grow and prosper the way "social investment" does. Besides wages, a prison's biggest expenditures are for utilities, which are not locally owned. What do prisons produce besides wave after wave of unhappy involuntary residents? An extremely poor yield of local jobs, mostly because competitive wages enlarge the labor market across space and skill (Hooks et al. 2004); the negative effects of anticipatory investment *and* disinvestment in residential and retail real property; no retail activity; few new residents, lots of traffic as workers come and go; the destruction of both prime agricultural land and endangered-species habitat; and sewage (see California Prison Moratorium Project 2006; Gilmore 2007a). No wonder the bended knee has difficulty straightening out.

Because the residents of prospective prison towns lack political and economic clout (as is true of all localities that turn to industries of last resort), it is not surprising that even as the evidence has accumulated putting the lie to prisons as economic engines, the normalization of prisons as an unending need has caused the urgency-fueled mitigation-dollar largesse to evaporate. Yet prison boosters and prison department public relations personnel have continued to insist that lockups are good for local economies: recession proof and environmentally friendly. Ironically, however, as the urgency of the rhetoric about the need for prisoners has diminished and prisons have been viewed more as being—although public and nonproductive—just like any other industry, it has become easier to criticize the practice of environmental review waiver. From the early 1990s onward, environmental reviews have been produced for state and federal lockups in *desakota* California fairly consistently.[6]

The Federal Bureau of Prisons (FBOP), no less than the California Department of Corrections (CDC), has been on a long-term building binge—famously because of Reagan-era (1980s) and Clinton-endorsed (1990s) drug laws carrying mandatory minimum sentences, but also because starting in the mid-1980s the FBOP began planning to lock up more and more immigrants who the Department of Justice forecast would be convicted of crimes.⁷ The expanded federal capacity is not part of the Immigration and Customs Enforcement (ICE) detention centers; rather, it exemplifies the general trend by the antistate state to use criminalization to "solve" problems, particularly the problem of how the rhetoric of "state-lite" can be coordinated with what is actually happening: the constant evolution of a bigger and more coercive state apparatus run by a strong executive branch (which includes policing and prisons). In 2000 the FBOP published its third Criminal Alien Requirements III (CAR) Request for Proposal for sites in California. A number of towns submitted letters of intent asking to be considered. Some towns withdrew from consideration after they learned from other towns or through their own diligence that the wear and tear of a federal prison would far outweigh any imagined benefit.

One city manager produced his own study (McHenry 2001), which he shared with a group of my undergraduates who had decided to find out why a town would first embrace and then reject the prison solution. His data and analysis made it obvious to him that the meager benefits would accrue elsewhere, where prison employees lived and shopped. In fact, he tried to form a strategic tax alliance with the nearby larger city that would claim most prison employee residence and consumption, but the last thing the larger city was going to do—especially in an age of devolution and boundary tightening—was open the door to other petitioners hoping for a share in the social wage (Gilmore 2007a; see also Cameron 2006).

The FBOP decided to look more closely at two Fresno County towns that stayed in the running—Orange Cove and Mendota. In both towns the elected and appointed leadership were united in their boosterism. The FBOP got to work on the Environmental Impact Statement, which turned out to be a thousand pages of a stylistic hodgepodge of technical description and evaluation that concluded Mendota would be the preferred location. During this time, organizers tried to spread the news that economic benefits would not be forthcoming from a prison, while other harms might ensue. However, constituting audiences to make the argument proved very difficult. The environmental review process provided both topic and method to reach people. Since environmental reviews look at a range of impacts—in theory raising concerns before harms occur—and since they require public comment, they are potentially useful means for publishing findings that would not reach people—vertically or horizontally—by other means.

In the classic analysis of racist science *The Mismeasure of Man*, Stephen Jay Gould (1981) reworked a number of experiments and scrutinized the underlying evidence that supported an array of biological justifications for the political, social, and economic marginalization of certain of the world's people. The book had a second life a few years before the author's untimely death, when Herrnstein and Murray's heinous *Bell Curve* (1994) commanded front-page coverage in newspapers, book reviews, magazines, and other opinion-producing media. Gould put the basic scientific practice of redoing experiments to practical political use. From his exploration of cranial capacity to his later demolition of Herrnstein and Murray's cheap statistics, Gould used the resonance of already produced knowledge—including its origins as well as its circulation—to highlight the intentionally destructive purposes occasioning the original research. He could reach audiences because of his status as a Harvard professor who wrote books (such as *Mismeasure*) for popular consumption. People invited him to speak. He demolished Herrnstein and Murray and others wherever he went.

The environmental review allowed for a modest version of Gould's labor. Taking the environmental review apart piece by piece, a patient researcher could get to the bottom of the data (often with no more technical assistance than a glossary and a calculator) and choose a few high-profile areas to challenge. The next step was to help a number of people speak to the issues in the required public comment periods, both orally at hearings and in writing. The public comment at hearings enabled organizers to meet the few members of the Mendota community who knew about the prison; most supported it and a few were in opposition. At that time it was already possible to present to city officials proof that their claims for the prison would not be realized. Those nonreturns were in, and people from throughout the region could come to testify that a prison would not provide the benefits that the review had enthusiastically insisted it would.

After one of the hearings I approached the city manager, and we had a reasonably cordial conversation in which I told him that he knew very well that the prison could not and would not do what he and other city leaders claimed. He replied that he knew but that he'd been hired, at a generous salary, to bring the town a prison. Unlike that off-the-record exchange, liable to he-said-she-said dismissal, the authors of an environmental review[8] must address the concerns and criticisms of every letter and oral statement. As a result, it became possible to get into the official record written acknowledgment that prisons are not economic engines or otherwise fiscally benevolent. And through publishing—that is, making available—both research and critiques of research in a publicly accessible place, we could persuade the county rural redevelopment agency to deny Mendota money to build water infrastructure for the prison, on the basis of the conclusion that the residents would not get jobs or other benefits. The city was instructed by redevelopment to come back with a development plan that would actually help the town's 95 percent Latino residents, who were a mix of second- and third-generation Chicanos, Mexicans, Salvadorans, and other Central Americans—some with green cards and even more without documents authorizing them to work. The boosters did not reflect the full demographic, only the Anglo and Chicano power elite. The divisions with the community highlight the complex processes of racialization and the fact that mutual political recognition between groups may produce fractures as well as identification.

Both the thousand-page English-language document and the hearings—in which translation was not available and Spanish testimony was not transcribed—became the focus of a sustained campaign because 90 percent of the city's households used Spanish as the primary language. The problem of language resonates in many ways throughout *desakota* California. In a number of other campaigns against locally unwanted land uses (incinerators, toxic dumps) or on behalf of life-enhancing infrastructure (such as wells drilled deeply enough to bypass the pesticide-poisoned upper aquifer), communities have fought against their linguistic exclusion from the decision-making process. In many places (as has been true throughout U.S. history from west to east), English is not the primary language.[9] In addition, certain kinds of technical prose obscure the contents and consequences of land use changes. In South Central Los Angeles, a site that was home to a fourteen-acre urban garden had been slated to be used for toxic waste. Organizers fought against the dump, mobilizing around a number of themes, including the fact that the reports were unreadable. In fact, the reports were barely literate by any measure, perhaps less because of jargon than because of the way these extensive documents merely fulfilled the law in letter but not in spirit. The documents' militant illiteracy suggests that a narrowly technocratic solution (e.g., hiring an ecologist for every community) will not solve the larger problem of civic engagement when the antistate state's purpose is to minimize such engagement. For Mendota, the FBOP eventually drafted a ten-page Spanish-language "executive summary" of the report that focused entirely on the alleged benefits of the prison for the community.

A young organizer from the region canvassed Mendota door to door, eventually meeting several people who agreed to host a house party to discuss the environmental review. They had been organizing among farmworkers and therefore were aware of both risks and opportunities. A surprising number of people came on a weekday evening, and they crowded into a tiny living room with food to share and kids too young to leave at home. The discussion led by two organizers met at first with mild interest as people passed around the short Spanish-language summary. But when one of the organizers pulled the thousand-page document from behind his back, the room's atmosphere changed. Everyone started talking and trading stories about how the same thing had happened in a friend or relative's town. Communication networks in *desakota* California work according to a variety of logics, with constantly shifting workplaces, parishes, supratown union locals, and kin groups all contributing to the richness of exchange. Convinced that a wrong had been perpetrated as it habitually was against people like themselves, they collectively composed a letter of protest. It was written out in Spanish by hand on ruled theme paper signed by dozens of households—all vulnerable to eviction or employment reprisal from prison proponents—and sent to Washington, D.C.

The FBOP refused to honor the demand that the full environmental review be translated, insisting that it could not "be translated because it is *scientific* material." Wouldn't they be surprised in Salamanca! Their refusal was based in what Gould had spent a good deal of his life debunking: racist science that both encourages and justifies the sacrifice of human lives. Such science—which is ahistorical in willfully ignorant as well as methodologically negligent ways—seeks to make both reasonable and inevitable the concentration of locally unwanted land uses where people are most vulnerable to them. The natural and social science practices that underlie the building of the antistate state deliberately ignore the cumulative effects of atmospheric and other toxins, as well as the cumulative impacts of debilitating social policies and economic policies (see Braz and Gilmore 2006), whether these policies and outcomes be pesticide drift, expensive or poisoned water, the hunting down of immigrants, bad schooling, racial profiling, intensive policing, or incinerators spewing dioxin.

One afternoon not long ago, the adults who mobilized against the prison rode buses and vans back from a day in the fields and marched, with their children, from the high school to a park for a rally. Many of these people live lives that circulate throughout *desakota* California and beyond. Most of them are immigrants without documents, but in spite of—or because of—that vulnerability they are willing to participate in the mix and even rally side by side with growers whose opposition to the prison is not yet tempered by an anti-NIMBY consciousness. Indeed, much to everyone's surprise, they have been willing to keep fighting even though construction has begun at the now controversial site. Like the participants in the 2001 conference, these women, men, and young people are simultaneously looking for and creating a guide to action through embodied political experimentation—to theorize or map or plan their way out of the margins.

The Charrette: Resilience

Industries of last resort materially congeal displacement and defer to other places and times real resolutions of economic, social, and technological problems. Such deferral is not respectful but rather exploitative, and those who live in the shadows of such industries, as prisoners or workers or residents, become what a reformed white-supremacist lifer named himself and the white and of-color others who took part in a prison rebellion several years ago: a convict race (Lynd 2004). In today's intransigent rebiologization of difference, race has been again characterized as being in the blood—the genetic determinant of life chances. Yet at the same time the social processes of racialization—carried out through warfare against Third World immigrants, Muslims, African American men, street kids—are apparent. So far we have seen that the deep divisions between vulnerable people are not necessarily an impediment, that people get past certain barriers because they have an already developed sense of the perils and promise of movement, that the practice of circulating within regions underlies potential interpretations of possibility and alliance, and finally that multiply rooted people have a sense of the ways that "elsewhere" is simultaneously "here" (another way of saying that "I is an Other").

When organizers against industries of last resort take to the road, they constantly meet a reasonable question: If not this, then what? In fact, in left-ish discourse in the United States, an insistence that "winnable" solutions be proposed along with problems has become dominant. This dominance is in part an outgrowth of the professionalization of activism of all kinds and its formalization in not-for-profits, which are regularly required to generate "work products" to satisfy funders that the groups are doing what they say they will do. The "what-is-the-solution" imperative is also an outgrowth of the twentieth-century ascendance of the technocrat, specially skilled in breaking problems down into parts and solving them piecemeal. The trouble with technocracy, affecting engaged research and not-for-profit-based political experimentation, is that narrowness often stands in for specificity (and questions lose stretch and resonance along the way). Thus the long struggle to shrink the U.S. prison system through nonreformist reforms has sometimes been undermined by the technocratic imagination stifling work intended to advance the cause. For example, some advocacy research has narrowed the question "How do we shrink prisons?" to "How can we get some women out of prison?" and has ignored the facts—supported by experience—that the women released might wind up in jails or other lockups, or that the arguments advocated on behalf of decarcerating women might deepen and widen the net in which men and boys are captured and kept.

Yet since activist road shows consistently encounter the question, they have to engage it as well as deconstruct it. Otherwise, the culture of human sacrifice kicks in, and what seems as reasonable as demanding a fully formed alternative is embracing the deferral of problems regardless of cost. For example, after I presented remarks on a plenary called "Militarization, the Economics of War, and Cultures of Violence" at the 2003 National Council for Research on Women's "Borders, Babies, and Bombs" conference, an Anglo retired career military woman scolded me that my antimilitarism was bad for young Black women, who develop leadership skills in the armed forces. She turned her back and strode off when I refused to agree that there was no better venue for such development outside the industrialized killing sector or that planning and carrying out the death of other people's children was an appropriate source of self-worth and livelihood for anybody.

Another error is double-edged: that vulnerable communities need mobile specialists who tell them what to do, yet at the same time have a completely thought-through revolutionary sensibility merely waiting to be set free by some visitors. This error recapitulates in two directions the bad thinking that posits structure and agency as opposites in ongoing struggles for self-determination. But if self-determination is a goal, and if *desakota* California, like anywhere else, is made by people but not under conditions of their own choosing, then a real engagement of people's creative thinking mixed with locally or externally available understandings of political and economic possibilities and constraints may be a way of getting at the question "If not this, then what." In other words, the question becomes resilient and depends on people's immediate and longer-range engagement—their own resilience—to realize any outcome.

In the winter of 2002, during a long-term decline in the number of women in California state prisons, the CDC closed one of its three new women's prisons, moving the eight hundred women kept there into bigger lockups. When the department originally sited the facility just east of Stockton in San Joaquin County in the mid-1980s, local boosters could and did "put conditions" to the CDC, which included that the prisoners be women and that the number locked up not exceed eight hundred. One way the county imposed restrictions was through the conditional-use permit—a standard instrument used to divide a territory into districts for different uses and to control the ways in which particular uses might change over time. This, in addition to mitigation funds, allowed the Anglo power elite to approve siting a prison in a former peach orchard.

Shortly after the prison closed, the CDC announced several possible reuses for the site: it could become a men's prison or a training facility for new guards, or it could be traded for some federal real estate and Immigration and Customs Enforcement (ICE) could redevelop the site as an immigrant detention center. Two Valley-based California Prison Moratorium Project organizers set themselves the task of creating a bottom-up movement against all these uses. They relied on research done by my former undergraduates at the University of California at Berkeley that the students decided to share, as well as research done as an academic studio course by graduate students in Berkeley's College of Natural Resources, to get a sense of what had happened in political jurisdictions and at the community level and where organizing might fit in.

The organizers learned that the chamber of commerce had opposed reopening the site as a prison, principally because in the nearly two decades since prison had seemed the only possible economic diversification scheme—to complement declining agriculture—the spread of residential hinterlands from the Bay Area and Sacramento put Stockton into a preferred development path of suburbanization (another in-between phenomenon, not dealt with in this chapter). They also learned that some rising members of the city and county political class wished to use the fate of the site as a method to weaken the long-standing domination of the political elites. These newcomers were not necessarily opposed to prison, but they were opposed to decision making behind closed doors that excluded them. Finally, researchers saw that the demographic mix of Stockton was much like the rest of *desakota* California and that although agriculture was not the area's sole economic engine it still figured prominently in the political economy of the place.

The Latino organizers, one an immigrant whose principal activity had centered on immigrant rights and the other a multigeneration Central Valley Chicana whose work had ranged widely, including to the margins of the Democratic Party, determined that the best way to get a sense of the lay of the land would be to hold a grassroots hearing about the site. They worked closely with a number of immigrants' rights organizers to reach out to farm and other low-wage workers. They also worked their connections in formal political associations to invite representatives of the rising political class to attend the session.

The meeting was announced for 6:00 p.m. At 5:55 the room was fairly empty except for Prison Moratorium Project members, elected officials' representatives, and leadership from a local of the Service Employees International Union (SEIU), some immigrants' rights organizations, and the Stockton League of Women Voters. It looked like a bust. But in the five minutes between the observation of failure and the time the proceedings were to begin, the room filled—mostly with Spanish-speaking workers. It was apparent that people had come to the neighborhood where the meeting was announced and had waited and scouted to see whether it was another of many ICE stings. ICE had been rounding up workers in an intense but random fashion throughout *desakota* California, and this meeting could have easily been such a trap. Once people came they stayed, and although I was there I cannot speak to how they would have secured themselves against an ICE invasion should one have occurred.

The organizers brilliantly invited the elected officials' representatives to sit in the front of the room, facing the audience, arguing that it would be useful for constituents to see them and that they need not speak but could just sit and listen. Good drama. The hearing was well orchestrated, involving a number of people who each spoke for three or four minutes condemning the reuse of the women's prison as a lockup for any purpose. Speakers of course directed their comments to the front of the room. At the end of the hearing, several representatives from Architects and Planners for Social Responsibility, who had been brought in by the Prison Moratorium Project to help set the stage to answer the expected question "If not this, then what?" invited the audience to attend a planning workshop in the same location the following month.

Since that time several community planning workshops, or *charrettes*, have been held in Stockton, in which people consider the prison buildings and site from every angle and propose their renovation for schools, museums, training centers, and other social investment uses. The *charrettes* have enabled people to think about the ways in which social investment works and the political levels at which the purse strings are held, by whom, and how tightly. Where are openings that ordinary people can enter to grasp and redirect a portion of the social wage?

As was seen in the previous section, not all resources that pour into a prison to build it come from a single source. The U.S. state is a jumble of jurisdictions that have been newly federalized in the past twenty-five years. Some of the jurisdictions form a mosaic (as in the counties and states), some overlie others (counties and cities), and some are special-purpose regional governments (e.g., for air quality or water). The unfunded devolution (or respatialization) of certain responsibilities, particularly in the area of social welfare programs, has caused many to think the state is no longer a crucial object of analysis. But if the object of the current analysis is at all correctly conceptualized, it seems more rather than less important to engage with the state at every turn. Certainly, devolution has produced belt tightening and boundary defending by many jurisdictions, and it underlies the widening bifurcation of all of California into richer and poorer (Gilmore and Gilmore 2007).

The *charrette* outcome can be turned to many uses, and planners have developed a volume to show what they are (Lennertz and Lutzenheiser 2006). The resilience of planning, its reworking into the landscape of community action through both workshops and other kinds of political engagement, enables the creative imagination that self-determination requires. Around the United States, communities in other *desakota* regions have developed and implemented plans to revitalize shrunken economies in which revised values of place as the repository and resolution of skills, talents, and preferences enable concentrations of resources that, in the shadow of industries of last resort, seem scarce indeed. For example, in South Georgia a consortium of counties reorganized agriculture, food processing, and transportation to enable farmers to keep farming but not grow tobacco. They cobbled together sufficient collective capital from a wide array of public and other sources, finding in surprising corners of statutes and foundations resources that they could use to buy and build what they needed, transforming the landscape and therefore themselves. In the short run, everyone owns everything needed for processing and product movement, and everyone has also kept individual title to the small farms that they nearly wore out with tobacco. Similar counties that did not scale up or otherwise plan in developmentally imaginative ways have prisons and other industries of last resort. In Louisiana, families and friends of imprisoned young people fought to close down the murderous lockup and send the children home; they then continued fighting to have the site renovated and reopened as a community college. In these and other examples, the details of learning to make the future have animated rather than daunted the resilience of those who ask, "If not this, then what?" By deferring, if not defeating, the proliferation of industries of last resort, they have set a standard and created a context through which the material and ideological margins—*desakota* space—might be syncretically renovated to secure the future.

The purpose of this chapter has been to think through both how to conceptualize a particular mix of socio-spatial relationships and how to operationalize engaged scholarship that matters. Forgotten places are historical geographies animated by real people. As fractured collectivities that are abandoned, yet intensely occupied by the antistate state, these "between" or marginal places might be understandable as a singular region, spatially discontinuous, that is neither urban or rural but in some way a version of *desakota*. How does the practice of engaged scholarship necessarily and ethically change the ideological and material field of struggle? If the fact of observation produces reality (not merely *afterwards*, as a representational artifact, but *during*, as a lived dimension of the field itself), then there are various kinds of work that a scholar might undertake in the mix.

Engaged scholarship and accountable activism share the central goal of constituting audiences both within and as an effect of observation, discovery, analysis, and presentation. Persuasion is crucial at every step. Neither engagement nor accountability has meaning without expanding recognition of how a project can best flourish in the mix. As a result, and to get results, scholar activism always begins with the politics of recognition (Gilmore 1999). Whatever its ultimate purpose, the primary organizing necessary to take a project from concept to accomplishment (and tool) is constrained by people's practices of identification, fluidly laden with the differences and continuities of characteristics, interests, and purpose through which they contingently produce their individual and collective selves (Hall 1994; Gilmore 1999). Such cultural (or ideological) work connects with, reflects, and shapes the material (or political-economic) relations enlivening a locality as a place that both links with and represents (as an example or outpost) other places at a variety of time-space resolutions—global, regional, postcolonial, et cetera (Massey 1984). So here is another conundrum: it is *consistently* true that the engaged scholar of whatever political conviction works in the unavoidable context of dynamics that force her into self-conscious *inconsistency*; she must at times confirm and at times confront barriers, boundaries, and scales (Gilmore 2007a; Katz 2004; Loyd 2005). This is treacherous territory for all who wish to rewrite the world. Plenty of bad research (engaged or not) is produced for all kinds of reasons, and plenty of fruitless organizing is undertaken with the best intentions. Activist scholarship attempts to intervene in a particular historical-geographical moment by changing not only what people do but also how all of us think about ourselves and our time and place, by opening the world we make.

NOTES

I thank Charlie Hale, Ted Gordon, Gill Hart, Laura Pulido, Jack Danger, Yong-Sook Lee, Bae-Gyoon Park, James Siddaway, Denise Ferreira da Silva, and Fred Moten for helping me think through various stages of this project; Mica Smith for research assistance; the California Prison Moratorium Project, and especially Debbie Reyes and Leonel Flores for their astonishing work; the Open Society Institute, the Social Science Research Council, and the National University of Singapore for their generous support; and Craig Gilmore for everything. © 2007 Ruth Wilson Gilmore.

1. I have written an entire book about this (Gilmore 2007a), but the work is far from done.

2. There is plenty of criticism about the Third World as an actual political-economic antidependent formation, and I do not dismiss the critics' learning and insights. However, "Third World" as a condition of existence and category of analysis has been very powerful over half a century, and nonalignment (or perhaps more precisely, *differential* alignment) continues to be acted out as a countertrend to U.S. hegemony on a global scale (e.g., in Brazil and India). I should also like to add that *third* need not indicate a transcendent category (in the sense that fascists deployed the term; Mann 2004), a blurry cosmopolitan space (Soja 1996), or the defeatist-triumphant "third way" of Giddens-Blair Britain. There are threes, and there are threes: in some cases *third* is deployed to suggest completion or resolution (as in bad dialectics), in others *third* opens up the possibility for freshly viewing relationships in the world without succumbing to displacement-as-closure (as in good dialectics; see, e.g., Ferreira da Silva, 2007; Moten 2003).

3. Los Angeles County, which was the premier agricultural county in the United States for more than half of the twentieth century, was until August 2006 home to a fourteen-acre inner-city farm made up of independent gardens—one of the largest in the United States (South Central Farmers 2006).

4. As a result of heinous practices carried out at the expense of people's lives and well-being, researchers rightly hesitate before conducting "human experiments," and U.S. higher education has developed complicated apparatuses to safeguard human subjects from inhumane protocols. That said, all politics are experimental; the question is not whether but how experiments proceed ethically and practically.

5. Paramilitary squads working for wealthy agriculturalists murdered labor organizers to discipline farmworkers in Depression-era Central California (see McWilliams 1939).

6. Environmental reviews are not always done, as was recently the case for a significant expansion to the federal prison in Lompoc. Also, the political model for claiming urgency to evade responsibility is currently being reinvigorated by the state legislature and governor, who have agreed to waive environmental review in

a proposed multi-billion-dollar Sacramento delta flood control project. They are using the New Orleans–Katrina abandonment disaster to weaken state statutes under the guise of responsibly facing up to imminent danger. In the early years of World War II two big cotton growers in the region that is now *desakota* California used a similar set of arguments to get the Army Corps of Engineers to build them a couple of dams that guaranteed both free water and fertile bottomland to their empires (Hundley 1992).

7. The politics of forecasting is an urgent topic for social justice.

8. In this case, a consulting firm with a long-standing FBOP contract that seems to get by with minimal research and maximum Web-based cursory data collection and analysis, as activists in places around the United States have reported at conferences and meetings.

9. Presuming that even people who have developed the psychological habits of the bended knee are not permanently so configured, some scholarship that seeks to intervene does so by combining writing and images. For example, the Real Cost of Prisons Project supplements a series of workshops with three comic books that lay out the dollar and other costs of prisons to prison towns (Pyle and Gilmore 2005), the costs of prisons to women and their children (Willmarth, Miller-Mack, and Ahrens 2005), and the real cost of the war on drugs (Jones, Miller-Mack, and Ahrens 2005). See www.realcostofprisons.org.

REFERENCES

Alexander, M. Jacqui. 1994. "Not Just (Any) *Body* Can be a Citizen: The Politics of Law, Sexuality, and Postcoloniality in Trinidad and Tobago and the Bahamas." *Feminist Review* 48:5–23.

Bradshaw, Ted K. 1993. "In the Shadow of Urban Growth: Bifurcation in Rural California Communities." In *Forgotten Places: Uneven Development in Rural America*, edited by Thomas A. Lyson and William W. Falk, 218–56. Lawrence: University Press of Kansas.

Braz, Rose, and Craig Gilmore. 2006. "Joining Forces: Prisons and Environmental Justice in Recent California Organizing." *Radical History Review* 96:95–111.

Brown, Wendy. 1994. *States of Injury*. Princeton: Princeton University Press.

Bullard, Robert D. 1990. *Dumping in Dixie: Race, Class, and Environmental Quality*. Boulder, CO: Westview Press.

California Prison Moratorium Project. 2006. *How to Stop a Prison in Your Town*. Oakland: California Prison Moratorium Project.

Cameron, Angus. 2006. "Turning Point? The Volatile Geographies of Taxation." *Antipode* 38 (2): 237–58.

Cole, Luke W., and Sheila R. Foster. 2001. *From the Ground Up: Environmental Racism and the Rise of the Environmental Justice Movement*. New York: New York University Press.

Davis, Mike. 2003. *Dead Cities*. New York: New Press.

Du Bois, W. E. B. 1935. *Black Reconstruction in America, 1860–1880*. New York: Free Press.

Edwards, Brent Hayes. 2003. *The Practice of Diaspora: Literature, Translation, and the Rise of Black Internationalism.* Cambridge, MA: Harvard University Press.

Fanon, Frantz. 1961. *The Wretched of the Earth.* New York: Grove Press.

Fernandes, Leela. 1997. *Producing Workers: The Politics of Gender, Class, and Culture in the Calcutta Jute Mills.* Philadelphia: University of Pennsylvania Press.

Ferreira da Silva, Denise. 2007. *Toward a Global Idea of Race.* Minneapolis: University of Minnesota Press.

Flaming, Daniel. 2006. *Poverty, Inequality, and Justice.* Los Angeles: Economic Roundtable, June. www.economicrt.org/. Accessed November 4, 2006.

Ganz, Marshall. 2000. "Resources and Resourcefulness: Strategic Capacity in the Unionization of California Agriculture, 1959–1966." *American Journal of Sociology* 105 (4): 1003–62.

Gilmore, Ruth Wilson. 1993. "Public Enemies and Private Intellectuals." *Race and Class* 35 (1): 65–78.

———. 1998. "Globalisation and U.S. Prison Growth: From Military Keynesianism to Post-Keynesian Militarism." *Race and Class* 40 (2–3): 171–87.

———. 1999. "'You have dislodged a boulder': Mothers and Prisoners in the Post Keynesian California Landscape." *Transforming Anthropology* 8 (1/2): 12–38.

———. 2005a. Interview by Josef Gregory Mahoney with Adam Good, John Bornmann, and Harish Nalinakshan. *Your Black Eye,* February 14. www.yourblackeye.org.

———. 2005b. "Scholar-Activists in the Mix." *Progress in Human Geography* 29 (2): 177–82.

———. 2007a. *Golden Gulag: Prisons, Surplus, Crisis, and Opposition in Globalizing California.* Berkeley: University of California Press.

———. 2007b. "In the Shadow of the Shadow State." In *The Revolution Will Not Be Funded,* edited by Incite! Women of Color against Violence. Cambridge, MA: South End Press.

Gilmore, Ruth Wilson, and Craig Gilmore. 2004. "The Other California." In *Globalize Liberation,* edited by David Solnit, 381–96. San Francisco: City Lights Books.

———. 2007. "Restating the Obvious." In *Indefensible Spaces,* edited by Michael Sorkin. New York: Routledge.

Gilroy, Paul. 2005. *After Empire.* New York: Routledge.

Glassman, Jim. 2003. "Rethinking Overdetermination, Structural Power, and Social Change: A Critique of Gibson-Graham, Resnick, and Wolff." *Antipode* 35 (4): 678–98.

Gooding-Williams, Robert. 1993. *Reading Rodney King/Reading Urban Uprising.* New York: Routledge.

Gordon, Avery F. 2006. "Abu Ghraib: Imprisonment and the War on Terror." *Race and Class* 48:42–59.

Gould, Stephen Jay. 1981. *The Mismeasure of Man.* New York: W. W. Norton.
Greenberg, Michael, and Dona Schneider. 1994. "Violence in American Cities: Young Black Males Is the Answer, But What Was the Question?" *Social Science and Medicine* 39 (2): 179–87.
Hall, Stuart. 1976. "Africa Is Alive and Well and Living in the Diaspora." Unpublished manuscript.
———. 1980a. "Cultural Studies and the Centre: Some Problematics and Problems." In *Culture, Media, Language,* edited by Stuart Hall, Dorothy Hobson, Andrew Lowe, and Paul Willis, 15–47. New York: Routledge.
———. 1980b. "Race, Articulation, and Societies Structured in Dominance." In *Sociological Theories: Race and Colonialism,* edited by UNESCO, 305–40. Paris: UNESCO.
———. 1994. "Cultural Identity and Diaspora." In *Identity: Community, Culture, Difference,* edited by Jonathan Rutherford, 222–37. London: Lawrence and Wishart.
Hall, Stuart, and Bill Schwarz. 1988. "State and Society, 1880–1930." In *The Hard Road to Renewal,* 95–122. London: Verso.
Hart, Gillian. 2002a. *Disabling Globalization: Places of Power in Postapartheid South Africa.* Berkeley: University of California Press.
———. 2002b. *Global Competition, Gender, and Social Wages in South Africa, 1980–2000.* Paper 13. United Nations Research Institute for Social Development, Social Policy and Development Programme.
Hart, Gillian, and Ari Sitas. 2004. "Beyond the Urban-Rural Divide: Linking Land, Labour, and Livelihoods." *Transformation* 56:31–38.
Harvey, David. 1989. *The Limits to Capital.* Chicago: University of Chicago Press/Midway Reprints.
Hernnstein, Richard, and Charles Murray. 1994. *The Bell Curve: Intelligence and Class Structure in American Life.* New York: Free Press.
Hooks, Gregory, Clayton Mosher, Thomas Rotolo, and Linda Lobao. 2004. "The Prison Industry: Carceral Expansion and Employment in U.S. Counties, 1969–1994." *Social Science Quarterly* 85 (1): 37–57.
Hundley, Norris, Jr. 1992. *The Great Thirst: Californians and Water, 1770s–1990s.* Berkeley: University of California Press.
Incite! Women of Color against Violence. 2007. *The Revolution Will Not Be Funded.* Cambridge, MA: South End Press.
Jones, Sabrina, Ellen Miller-Mack, and Lois Ahrens. 2005. *Prisoners of the War on Drugs.* Documentary Comic Book. Northampton, MA: Real Cost of Prisons Project. www.realcostofprisons.org.
Katz, Cindi. 2001. "On the Grounds of Globalization: A Topography for Feminist Political Engagement." *Signs* 26 (4): 1213–34.
———. 2004. *Growing Up Global: Economic Restructuring and Children's Everyday Lives.* Minneapolis: University of Minnesota Press.
Kelley, Robin D. G. 2002. *Freedom Dreams: The Black Radical Imagination.* Boston: Beacon Press.

Kim, Claire Jean. 1999. "The Racial Triangulation of Asian Americans." Politics and Society 27 (1): 105–38.
Lemelle, Sidney, and Robin D. G. Kelley, ed. 1994. *Imagining Home: Class, Culture, and Nationalism in the African Diaspora.* New York: Verso Press.
Lennertz, Bill, and Aarin Lutzenheiser. 2006. *The Charrette Handbook: The Essential Guide for Accelerated, Collaborative Community Planning.* Chicago: APA/Planners Press.
Loyd, Jenna Morven. 2005. "Freedom's Body: Radical Health Activism in Los Angeles, 1963–1978." PhD diss., University of California at Berkeley.
Lynd, Staughton. 2004. *Lucasville: The Untold Story of a Prison Uprising.* Philadelphia: Temple University Press.
Lyson, Thomas A., and William W. Falk, eds. 1993. *Forgotten Places: Uneven Development In Rural America.* Lawrence: University of Kansas Press.
Mann, Michael. 2004. *Fascists.* Cambridge: Cambridge University Press.
Massey, Doreen. 1984. *Spatial Divisions of Labor: Social Structures and the Geography of Production.* London: Macmillan.
McGee, Terry. 1991. "The Emergence of Desakota Regions in Asia: Expanding a Hypothesis." In *The Extended Metropolis: Settlement Transition in Asia,* edited by N. Ginsburg, B. Koppel, and T. G. McGee, 3–25. Honolulu: University of Hawai'i Press.
McHenry, Davin. 2001. "Shafter Abandons Plans for Prison." *Bakersfield Californian,* February 10.
McWilliams, Carey. 1939. *Factories in the Field.* Hamden, CT: Archon Books.
Moten, Fred. 2003. *In the Break: The Aesthetics of the Black Radical Tradition.* Minneapolis: University of Minnesota Press.
Mumford, Lewis. 1968. *The City in History.* New York: Harvest Books.
Nkrumah, Kwame. 1964. *Consciencism.* New York: Monthly Review Press.
O'Connor, James. 1973. *Fiscal Crisis of the State.* New Brunswick, NJ: Transaction.
Omi, Michael, and Howard Winant. 1986. *Racial Formation in the United States.* New York: Routledge.
Pardo, Mary. 1998. *Mexican American Women Activists.* Philadelphia: Temple University Press.
Pastor, Manuel, Jr. 2001. "Common Ground at Ground Zero? The New Economy and the New Organizing in Los Angeles." *Antipode* 33 (2): 260–89.
Patterson, Orlando. 1982. *Slavery and Social Death.* Cambridge, MA: Harvard University Press.
Pulido, Laura. 1996. *Environmentalism and Economic Justice: Two Chicano Struggles in the Southwest.* Tucson: University of Arizona Press.
———. 2000. "Rethinking Environmental Racism: White Privilege and Urban Development in Southern California." *Annals of the Association of American Geographers* 90 (1): 12–40.
Pyle, Kevin, and Craig Gilmore. 2005. *Prison Town.* Documentary Comic Book. Northampton, MA: Real Cost of Prisons Project. www.realcostofprisons.org.

Ransby, Barbara. 2006. *Ella Baker and the Black Freedom Movement: A Radical Democratic Vision.* Chapel Hill: University of North Carolina Press.

Robinson, Cedric. 1983. *Black Marxism: The Making of the Black Radical Tradition.* London: Zed Press.

Rodney, Walter. 1972. *How Europe Underdeveloped Africa.* Washington, DC: Howard University Press.

Rothenberg, Jerome, ed. 1969. *Technicians of the Sacred: A Range of Poetries from Africa, America, Asia, Europe, and Oceania.* New York: Anchor.

Rycenga, Jennifer. 1992. "The Composer as a Religious Person in the Context of Pluralism." PhD diss., Graduate Theological Union, 1992.

Sivanandan, A. 1982. *A Different Hunger: Writings on Black Resistance.* London: Pluto Press.

———. 1991. *Communities of Resistance: Writings on Black Struggles for Socialism.* London: Verso Press.

Smith, Neil. 1992. "Contours of a Spatialized Politics: Homeless Vehicles and the Production of Geographical Scale." *Social Text* 33:54–81.

———. 1996. *The New Urban Frontier: Gentrification and the Revanchist City.* New York: Routledge.

Smith, Neil, and Cindi Katz. 1993. "Grounding Metaphor: Towards a Spatialized Politics." In *Place and the Politics of Identity*, edited by Michael Keith and Steve Pile, 67–83. New York: Routledge.

Soja, Edward. 1989. *Postmodern Geographies.* New York: Verso.

———. 1996. *Thirdspace.* Oxford: Blackwell.

South Central Farmers. 2006. "What We Are About." www.southcentralfarmers.com/. Accessed June 5, 2006.

Wagner, Peter. 2002. "Importing Constituents: Prisoners and Political Clout in New York." www.prisonpolicy.org/importing/. Accessed June 5, 2006.

Williams, Brackette. 1989. "A Class Act: Anthropology and the Race to Nation across Ethnic Terrain." *Annual Review of Anthropology* 18:401–44.

Willmarth, Susan, Ellen Miller-Mack, and Lois Ahrens. 2005. *Prisoners of a Hard Life: Women and Their Children.* Documentary Comic Book. Northampton, MA: Real Cost of Prisons Project. http://realcostofprisons.org.

Woods, Clyde. 1998. *Development Arrested.* New York: Verso.

———. 2002. "Life after Death." *Professional Geographer* 54 (1): 62–66.

2. Research, Activism, and Knowledge Production

Dani Wadada Nabudere

Karl Marx once summed up the contradiction between theory and practice when in his thesis on Feuerbach he argued that philosophers had hitherto interpreted the world but that the real point was to change it. This implied that philosophy should not merely be an arena of scholarly speculation about being; rather, it should concern itself with daily human experience, including action and reflection on that experience. Marx's contribution was to question the then dominant conceptions of the relationship between the state and society in mid-nineteenth-century Europe in a period of political turbulence. His main concern was to create an intellectual atmosphere that could change the old social order to a new revolutionary order (McLellan 1973, 68).

For his part, Gramsci (1971) demonstrated that within the working classes there existed a "spontaneous philosophy" comprising language (as a complex of knowledge and concepts), common sense, and a system of beliefs. He argued that although such philosophies were at times incoherent and dispersed, they were valuable in that they articulated the everyday practice and experience of working-class people. Leftist scholars of the Third World later came to see spontaneous philosophy as the expression and existence of a "common peoples' science existing within their folklore and their practical, vital and empirical knowledge, which has allowed them to survive, to interpret, to create, to produce and to work over centuries" (Fals-Borda 1980, 19–20). It was seen as having a rationality of its own that had to be understood from observations of working-class people's practices.

In this chapter I will examine the continuing polarization of theory and practice as an expression of power relations in the modern world and demonstrate how social science research has been problematized and practiced to confront it. I will recount some of my research experiences in marginalized societies in Africa that demonstrate how the activities of ordinary people have overcome this theory/practice dichotomy through contestation and action.

TOWARD A PEOPLE-CENTERED RESEARCH METHODOLOGY

The tension between the two spheres of human cognition and social activity has continued up to the present day in struggles over the social and political order and its consequences for human existence. Paulo Freire, in *Pedagogy of the Oppressed* (1972), attempted to overcome the theory/practice dichotomy by empowering individuals and communities to engage in productive and reflective activities of learning through action. He argued that modern politics had created a "fear of freedom" among the oppressed, who were politically subjugated in societies where theories about freedom and democracy and their practice did not coincide. Education through what he called "conscientization"—the creation of a critical consciousness through struggle—was therefore the only way that the oppressed could practice freedom and, more importantly, accomplish change.

This was an emancipatory and liberatory pedagogy aimed at eliminating the "fear of freedom" through dialogue and struggle as tools of learning and acting on one's own condition. Freire's work came at a time of intense debate generated by what Talcott Parsons (1978) called the "reflective revolution" of the 1960s, which was characterized by national liberation struggles, the feminist movement, student and workers movements, socialist movements, civil rights struggles, peace movements, and debates about "limits to growth" and its relationship to ecological crisis. The debates about the role of the intellectual in society that had begun in Latin America in the 1960s, and to which Freire was contributing, took place in this context.

In East Africa and specifically in Tanzania beginning in 1973, such academic debates centered on challenges to social science research methodologies with regard to issues of "development" and "social transformation" and the rejection of functionalist anthropology in Africa as an ideological tool of colonial domination and exploitation. The "objectivity" of current social science research methodologies was disputed, and the debates produced a school of thought and a new methodology, combining theory and practice, that came to be called "participatory research."

This methodology had to some extent already been envisioned a few years earlier by leftist activist scholars in Colombia who set out to build a field they called "proletarian science" to counter and neutralize "bourgeois science," which they held responsible for much of Latin American scholars' alienation from the conditions under which most people lived. One of these scholars, Orlando Fals-Borda, later recalled: "We, who participated in these experiences and ideological search, had set to ourselves acceptable goals: we wanted to reduce the gap between labor and intellectual work in order that workers, peasants and Indians ceased to be spiritually subjected to intellectuals; ... stimulate their most developed cadres, so that they could assume some investigative and analytical tasks; and create reference groups constituted by peasants, workers and Indians" (Fals-Borda 1980, 21).

In initiating their own form of "action research" in Colombia in 1972, this group of activist scholars wanted to "fight dogmatism and follow Marx's advice of helping build a social science as the product of the historical movement, and as a science which becomes revolutionary when it ceases to be doctrinaire" (Fals-Borda 1980, 21). Fals-Borda elaborates that this is why they were opposed to the "intellectual leftist colonialism which had castrated so many revolutionary and university student groups." They did not want to appropriate theories and methods of "action research" as these had been formulated in other "latitudes" and countries, in the context of social realities that differed widely from their own. Instead they adopted Marx's historical materialism as the "only guide to devise proletarian science" that could oppose bourgeois science, given what they considered the success of Marxism as an ideology and a science in the Cuban, the Chinese, the Soviet and the Vietnamese revolutions (ibid.). This approach was later found to be inadequate with the rise of neo-Marxism.

Scholars in Tanzania similarly challenged the new "participatory research approach" (PRA) that was then emerging as a qualitative methodology for investigating rural phenomena. They argued that this approach was rooted in the research method of participant observation that was central to the fieldwork of the functionalist school of anthropology and that was used during the colonial period in Africa side by side with neo-positivist survey techniques.

Participant observation emphasized the observations of anthropologists who lived and participated in the societies where they carried out their research. Long-term physical proximity to the people studied and direct communication with them in their own language were regarded as vital to the method. The data collected were from opinions and descriptions articulated by the people being observed, as well as from researchers' own observations of events and social interactions in everyday life.

Researchers recorded their observations in an ethnographic diary and collected and studied folklore and magical formulas as evidence of native mentality and experiences. Despite their immersion in the communities they studied, as well as in the larger context of power relations between their own society and that of their research subjects, participant observers maintained a level of scholarly "detachment" that, in their view, enabled them to secure an "objective" description of what they observed in the society.

In fact, however, the scholars did not study these societies in their historical settings and hence missed deeper meanings that came from the people's cultural-historical background, which the method could not study. They conceived of the societies they studied as harmonious wholes, existing in a timeless present in some kind of state of equilibrium that was not "disturbed" by Western influence, and they drew on the features of these societies to make generalizations about the common features of all "primitive" human societies, with a view to constituting "social laws" that would explain their behavior and actions (Mbilinyi et al. 1982, 34–66).

According to Peter Rigby (1985), another leftist anthropologist working at the University of Dar es Salaam in Tanzania in the 1970s, the very term *participant observer* implied a false standard of objectivity that had been derived from the natural sciences. In the sociological context, it allowed the logical possibilities of being an "observer" without being a "participant" or a "participant" without being an "observer," both of which were "absurd":

> All participants (actors) must be observers in their own right, interpreting and analyzing the situation, or else they would be unable to act or "participate"; similarly, all observers (social scientists?) must, if only by their presence, participate (act?). Unfortunately, some social scientists have either ignored or deliberately denied these fundamental elements in any data collection process.... What presumably is meant by the term "participant observer" as a method of data collection ... is that the "observer" writes down or otherwise records what he has gleaned from his participation in a particular social situation in the light of his "critical" scientific training. This being so, the "observer" is not merely "objectively" scrutinizing what is going on around him, but is involved as a "whole" person, albeit a person with an interpretive equipment which is different from one not trained in his scientific discipline. Any subsequent interpretation of the data resulting from his participation is therefore "an interpretation of an interpretation," not an analysis of self-evident, ontologically objective "facts." (30)

It was no wonder that the new post-Independence scholars who advocated a different approach critiqued this anthropological methodology. Because of these challenges and critiques, international aid agencies eventually dropped their references to the participant observation method and put forth a new approach, called social soundness analysis, that reconceptualized the problems of development in terms of a radical structuralist analysis of underdevelopment and a historical materialist analysis of the implications of capitalist development. According to this new approach, "traditional" societies, far from displaying irrational economic behavior, were after all well adjusted to local conditions and able to make conscious and recurrent decisions about the use of productive assets, the organization of labor, marketing, savings, and investment. But this approach, though in some ways corrective, was still focused on understanding "the other" rather than people determining their own course of action and existence.

In this context PRA emerged as an approach that had its roots in policy-oriented applied research and was aimed at devising strategies to "fight poverty." Tanzanian critics of PRA argued that it was intended to create an "ideological smokescreen, which mystified the nature and underlying contradictions and struggles of the poor" (Rigby 1985, 61). They claimed that donor agencies and foundations had resorted to qualitative methodologies in research for purposes of intervention only because quantitative methodologies had reached a dead end in this field. But the qualitative research approach in its new formulation of PRA merely allowed researchers to "camouflage" themselves as participant observers once again.

Tanzanian critics of PRA advocated instead a methodology they called participatory research, which they referred to as a "pragmatic" approach and distinguished from PRA. They defined it as "research structured by the democratic interaction of the researcher and the oppressed classes of people" that took the form of a "dialectical unification of theory and practice reciprocally between the researcher and the oppressed classes." When this approach was tested in practice, however, it turned out to be incapable of achieving its ideal of unity between the researcher and the oppressed.

The debates surrounding PRA developed into a major movement throughout the Third World and parts of the developed world that called for direct involvement of the people being researched in the research activity so that they would participate in knowledge generation and social transformation (Grossi 1980, 71). By 1977, consensus seems to have been reached within the movement or network about what participatory research was. In the 1980s, a more integrated approach, called participatory action research, began to emerge. Francisco Vio Grossi (1980, 70) reported that "when the network [of researchers from Latin America, Africa, and Asia] met for the first time in Toronto in 1977, participatory research was defined as a research process in which the community participates in the analysis of its own reality in order to promote a social transformation for the benefit of the participants, who are the oppressed. It is therefore a research, educational and action-oriented activity." According to Grossi, this statement, like similar ones published simultaneously, "captured the attention and enthusiasm of social scientists, popular educators, and political activists" because the new consensus was seen as "an approach able to resolve the permanent tension [existing] between the process of knowledge generation and the use of that knowledge, between 'academics' and the real world, between intellectuals and workers, between science and life." But this permanent tension was real and continued to express itself even after the new understanding. This is why Grossi admitted that although the network since then had been in "continuous expansion" and had contributed to "enriching the discussion" and "opening new avenues," the approach had "originated some trends that rely on conceptions [that were], though not absolutely erroneous, at least insufficient" (70).

One of these trends was a "spontaneously naïve" attitude that, according to Grossi, expressed an "idolization" of popular wisdom (73–74). Those who held this attitude believed that participatory research "must start from the representation of the community itself." According to this view, "The people have all the answers because they have the real knowledge." Grossi questioned this, arguing, "If this were the case, then we would not need either adult education, or activists, or even participatory research." The masses had been subjected to centuries of subjugation based on indoctrination; participatory action research would need to initiate a process of deindoctrination that could lead to the liberation and social transformation of the masses.

But then it appeared that the very notion of "social transformation" required more elaboration. According to Grossi, it incorporated the Hegelian concept of "praxis" in that it meant, not just any action, but specifically activity that led to structural social change—that is, change "in the fundamental conditions that engender poverty, dependence and exploitation" (77). Yet the catalyzing of a community to this kind of social transformation was more a political act than a process of participatory research, and it opened up all sorts of possibilities for radical manipulation of the people being studied. But these debates became sterile, and the discussion in East Africa shifted to new areas of contestation.

HISTORY AND THE DAR ES SALAAM SCHOOL

In East Africa, the issue of the relationship between theory and practice took another twist in the humanities, especially in the writing of history and the teaching of law. In history, the Eurocentric challenge was whether Africa had a history and if so what its canons were. The new African historians argued that the history of the people of Africa was "written" in their languages and their traditions and was transmitted orally. Already a rewriting of African history had begun with a group of historians at the University of Dar es Salaam, led by Professors Arnold Temu and Asaria Kimambo, who would later become the chief academic officer of the university. These young Tanzanian scholars had written a history of Tanzania, inspired by the African revolution in general and in Tanzania in particular, that from oral material was able to challenge the view of European historians that Africa had no history because it had no written canons they could consult. It was the beginning of an epistemological revolution concerning Africa, and it challenged the dichotomy between theory and practice because the theory and practice in African history lay with the people who were the custodians of the history and the interpreters of the oral texts.

The scholars who engaged in this rewriting of Tanzanian and African history developed a methodology, based on the use of oral material, that attempted to dynamically interpret African history from an African viewpoint and epistemology rather than from the viewpoint of the colonizers. European peer reviewers of this history regarded it as "nationalistic" and "unscientific" because it did not fit in with the methodological and theoretical approaches of Western historians. They called it "the Dar es Salaam School" to single it out as an approach that was not based on "universal" principles of history writing. Nevertheless, this challenge coming from the African historians eventually began to undermine "mainstream" approaches to the writing of African history and indeed to influence Western writing and understanding of history in general.

Jan Vansina, a Belgian anthropologist and historian who became convinced of the value of the oral tradition earlier than most European historians, recounts in his book *Living with Africa* (1994) how at the School of Oriental and African Studies (SOAS) battles were still being fought in the 1950s about the validity of oral history and the relevance of the then dominant "rules of evidence" paradigms that dominated mainstream Eurocentric scholarship. He says that in 1957 the second conference on African history at SOAS was still caught up in debating the validity of oral tradition. But Vansina's reporting of the results of his own research based on oral materials created a change of attitude on this issue by the end of the conference: "This exposé convinced most of the participants, although they did not necessarily accept the necessity for historians to engage in fieldwork yet. Henceforth the argument that oral tradition could be handled like written sources was the main argument historians of Africa used to convince outsiders that the oral source of 'indigenous African history' were respectable. For many years to come historians would no longer agonize about the overall respectability of oral tradition as a source but would try to locate and use traditions in different types of societies" (54). In this way African history, as told by the people of Africa as producers of their knowledge, was recognized as a distinctive discipline in the European universities and given chairs at various Western universities. This was because it cut across the existing disciplines then dominating the discourse on the humanities and social sciences. The approach also resolved the problem as to whether the history of "Tropical Africa" could be taught as "a subject." From then on, it was.

Indeed, the "methodological problem" had been overcome by the time UNESCO's *General History of Africa* was being written in the 1980s. The research for that book had shown that scholars using oral material collected from ordinary African men and women had to work as a team to interpret it; no single social science discipline or branch of the humanities could make sense of the evidence. Hence interdisciplinary and multidisciplinary approaches became essential, an innovation that in the wide-ranging work of Cheikh Anta Diop (1974) cast new light on African prehistory. The momentous result, as P. D. Curtin (1989) has stated, is that "nowadays, the history of the world is no longer synonymous with the history of Western civilization. In the longer run, the success of these developments will depend on the quality of the work done by African historians and other historians of Africa, and on the broadening of the other social sciences to the point where they take due account of the findings of African researchers before hazarding any generalizations about human society" (24–25).

All in all, the Dar es Salaam debates about "participatory action research" moved the discussion about theory and practice a step further. They brought into the discourse the role of the ordinary African men and women in the production and use of knowledge. They raised issues of representation, and the use of the oral tradition broke down the dichotomy between structure and agency in the production of African history. According to Curtin, the Dar es Salaam school humanized the writing of history, transforming it from a story about kings and dynasties of rulers to a popular history, and this in turn had changed the way Western historians looked at history in general.

The Dar es Salaam school imbued students of African history with national pride and a commitment to the African liberation movements that were active at the time. On a broader scale, it showed the need for an entire university to address the demands for transformation of the African people, and such a university would emerge in time, as we shall see below.

POPULAR ACTIVISM AND POPULAR KNOWLEDGE

In the theorizing about participatory action research, the most significant achievement was pedagogical: the adoption of participatory methods of dialogue developed by the Brazilian adult educator Paulo Freire. These methods were an attempt to bridge the epistemological divide between the researcher and the researched subject by getting rid of the power imbalance that typified their relationship and instead building a horizontal relationship of equality that would promote dialogue between the two actors in order to develop a new, emancipatory knowledge.

Key to both Freire's pedagogy and participatory action research is the sequence of action, reflection, questioning, researching hunches, drawing conclusions, evaluating options, and planning further action based on the learning that has been generated. This spiraling sequence ensures control of the investigatory learning process by all the participants and thus breaks down the anthropological "participant/observer" dichotomy. In this dialogical approach the research activity and the evaluation of the results are on a single continuum. There is no distinction between the researcher and the researched subject; all are involved in the research, dialogue, action, reflection, and further action (McTaggart 1991). In the study to be described below, this methodology for activist research, which aims at linking ordinary people to their world of knowledge, was best achieved by encouraging people to tell their stories orally and making it possible for those stories become part of the historical record.

Traditional and tacit indigenous knowledge from individuals and communities is best discovered and disseminated through the joint endeavors of dedicated scholars working within the rural communities. I felt that my own task as an academic and a progressive lawyer was to combine ideas from Freire's work and that of a Danish adult educator-philosopher, Bishop Frederick S. Grundtvig, with African indigenous knowledge and wisdom drawn from local communities to meet the needs of poor peasants in rural communities. I wanted to try to empower them through the application of their experiences to new forms of activities intended to bring about self-transformation on the basis of their own knowledge as well as that which they considered appropriate from other cultures. This was the beginning of the Yiga Ng'okola (Learn as You Work) Folk Institute in eastern Uganda, an indigenous membership–based nongovernmental organization (NGO) that attempts to empower and position local communities to actively participate in and to favorably influence local governments regarding the issues and policies that affect their lives.

The organization's conceptual and operating values were based on the African cultural values of community work and lifelong learning through activity and human interaction. By way of cross-cultural exchange, the philosophy drew inspiration from the Danish humanistic educational philosophy of learning through dialogue and "education for life."

The activities of the local groups that make up its membership are initiated by cultural animation relevant in their communities. For example, groups are encouraged to begin their projects by carrying out a collective cultural activity such as singing a song, engaging in a dance, telling a story, or retelling a proverb that has a bearing on what the group is trying to achieve. This sets a cultural framework and context to inspire members and creates an environment that is conducive for the activity. It places culture at the forefront of the endeavor, a process that enhances the legitimacy of what the group is trying to achieve. And in accordance with the African belief that, as expressed in a Luganda proverb, *Amagezi ssi gommu* (knowledge is not a monopoly of a single person), all activities end with a similar cultural animation of a congratulatory or critical kind so that the members who have done best are recognized and those who have not done as well are critically encouraged to do better. This cultural approach is intended to be a bottom-up model of transformation instead of the top-down model characteristic of many state-sponsored "development" programs. The Folk Institute has been the starting point for creating other organizations run along similar lines. At the end of ten years six of these organizations have emerged, including the Marcus Garvey Pan-Afrikan Institute, to be discussed below.

Another such organization is the Afrika Study Center. This is a small center aimed at doing research in local communities. More generally, its purpose is to reinforce the research undertaken by community-based organizations in order to create synergies in their work and to bring out the actual experiences gained by the organizations in the course of their activities. Complex cultural and social problems in marginalized pastoralist communities have been further complicated by new globalization pressures that are increasing these communities' marginalization. Some research has contributed to a global understanding of these problems, but much of it has not been accessible to the affected communities. The center's research has been geared toward producing locally usable literature and knowledge that will be more readily accessible to the communities. I have promoted both the Yiga Ng'okola Folk Institute and the Afrika Study Center and worked to link their local activities to the work of international organizations.

FIELD BUILDING AND KNOWLEDGE ACCESS

The activist scholars in the community-based organizations that I have described have understood the importance not only of employing a bottom-up approach but of establishing local-global collaborations to promote the work being conducted in the local communities. As a member of the Global Security and Cooperation (GSC) Committee of the Social Sciences Research Council (SSRC), I embarked on an SSRC-sponsored research activity focusing on local understandings of human security in East African pastoralist communities. This formed part of the larger "field-building" component of the GSC program, described in the Introduction, intended to explore the contributions of "activist scholarship" to "collaborative research" in general. The GSC program's new approach to what had been called "security studies" originated in the realization that the field had changed greatly since the early 1980s as it had become increasingly clear that threats to security of individuals and communities around the world originated from a variety of sources besides the military competition between the Great Powers engaged in the Cold War. Such "small events" as localized wars, small arms proliferation, ethnic conflicts, environmental degradation, international crimes, and human rights abuses were starting to be regarded as central to the understanding of security at local, national, regional, and global levels.

Grassroots work that was already being undertaken in the pastoral communities of East Africa revealed a general sense of extreme insecurity springing from confrontations between the pastoralists and agriculturalists over grazing lands and water for cattle. I therefore considered it important to take advantage of the new global awareness about the importance of localized conflicts by showing how research in these communities might contribute to the GSC program's field-building efforts.

The custodians and practitioners of indigenous knowledge systems were major actors in the production of knowledge about security and cooperation in their communities regarding the issues that affected their lives. But academic researchers, NGOs, and other practically oriented organizations had only minimally analyzed and disseminated the knowledge that indigenous people produced because they had not considered it to be "true knowledge": they had hypothesized that such knowledge was used in limited contexts by few people for immediate purposes and hence had very little replicability and applicability to different conditions.

Therefore I considered it vital to build intellectual capacity that could tap into localized, indigenous forms of knowledge and relate different dimensions of security such as the environment, ethnicity, nationalism, migrations, infectious diseases, food supply, biodiversity, global finance, and crime to each other. It also became necessary to relate these dimensions to the more traditional range of security issues for purposes of continuity and coherence. This meant there was a great need for collaborative (as distinct from merely comparative) research that transcended national boundaries and led to the development of regional and global networks. Such a new approach, I argued, would provide the intellectual tools that could connect the local to the global and move toward a truly global community in which different kinds of knowledge would be integrated and synthesized to promote cross-cultural dialogue and understanding.

Previous field research on security issues in pastoral communities revealed a different framework of perception and understanding of the issues involved that could not be understood by the academic researchers who worked on the field-building project. For this reason, our research team decided to relate this indigenous knowledge to the problems of real communities by engaging in outreach work in East African communities that would test our understanding of the knowledge that previous researchers had obtained and would encourage further participatory research by communities to apply this knowledge to deal with problems of domination and exploitation.

The group assigned by the Afrika Study Center to carry out theoretical reflections on epistemological and methodological implications of field building produced a founding document to guide research in other areas. This paper, which I authored (Nabudere 2003), was soon published by the

African Association of Political Science, although it was still in draft form. It was an attempt to establish a philosophical and theoretical foundation for the possibility that different kinds of knowledge producers can relate to each other through their own ways of understanding. It was also an attempt to generalize and theorize a methodology for fostering dialogue between cultures in which such knowledge is conserved, enriched, and developed further. This reflection was based on the experience gained by the Afrika Study Center through earlier research (in 2000–2001) on conflict and violence in agro-pastoral communities in northeastern Uganda.

During workshop discussions, we realized that scholars needed to understand these different epistemological frameworks if real progress aimed at integrating all forms of knowledge was to take place. We therefore turned our attention to epistemological issues connected with traditional systems of governance, concepts of justice, and conflict resolution and management and how these interface with modern systems of justice and administration. The interface between indigenous knowledge systems and modern systems was considered essential to exploit the strengths of each of the systems. Moreover, our research revealed a conflict between traditional natural resource management and modern resource management. For instance, indigenous knowledge research had revealed that in Uganda there were 261 land races (seed varieties) of superior-quality sorghum that were resistant to drought, disease, and pests, as well as being more nutritious, palatable, and lasting. In contrast, the varieties developed in scientific centers such as Kabana in eastern Uganda were not drought resistant, palatable, or bird resistant. Further, communities had many practices, based on spiritual and cultural ideas, that preserved seeds for planting and prevented them from being consumed in periods of scarcity. These practices included creating taboos about seed consumption, mixing seeds with wine, and storing them in skulls.

Workshop participants cited the activities of the Lutheran World Federation in pastoralist communities as a good example of how an NGO tried to assist the communities in seed multiplication and storage in a way that also allowed communities to draw on their indigenous knowledge systems to supplement modern systems. Modified seed banks were created in accord with traditional practices. Funds were provided to purchase indigenous seeds for distribution by creating community seed banking. Indigenous planting practices of "broadcasting" mixed stands, intercropping, and cultivating in scattered locations to spread risks proved most useful. Scientific investigators and practitioners working in local communities could embrace these ideas instead of imposing "scientific solutions" that were foreign to the indigenous cultural context.

Local communities in the Teso area of Uganda had their own traditional systems of weather forecasting and observation of the phase of the moon and the location of certain stars to decide when to plant crops. Communities accumulated this knowledge over centuries of scientific observation and experimentation. Researchers could investigate such systems to find out their secrets. For instance, research by the National Agricultural Research Organization (NARO) has shown that the traditionally used herb called *ecucuka* is effective in granaries as a repellent against insects that consume millet and sorghum. Government campaigns that encourage the use of high-yield varieties of crops and chemical fertilizers and pesticides tend to undermine indigenous practices, when in fact the latter are more effective.

INDIGENOUS KNOWLEDGE AND HUMAN SECURITY

The field-building research process, in which indigenous knowledge producers and academic researchers educate, inform, and communicate with each other, confronted a central challenge: how could research findings be communicated and made accessible to the communities where the research had been carried out? The researchers who participated in the field-building process noted that the educational system in the relevant communities consisted not only of the formal schooling system, which was based on foreign education theories and philosophies, but also of an informal system of education through which indigenous knowledge was theorized, developed, communicated, and stored.

Feedback between the researchers and the producers of indigenous knowledge was necessary so that this knowledge could be validated. This had pedagogical implications in that the informal education system utilized different techniques of oral communication and communication through art. Such traditional techniques needed to be included in the pedagogy of the mainstream formal schooling system so that education could be linked to the values and norms of the particular community and so that curricula that fit the African cultural context could be developed.

There was therefore a great need to integrate traditional-indigenous education and modern (Western) education in African educational systems. The former was rooted in the cultures and languages of local communities and based on their norms and value systems. The latter was rooted in the ideas of the European Enlightenment and was based on the norms and value systems of those societies. The dominant Western knowledge system's exclusion of African norms and value systems had resulted in the alienation of African people and communities, since the Western ideologues did not understand the indigenous knowledge systems. This meant that Western-educated individuals became hostile to local knowledge systems, which they regarded as "primitive" and "backward." Such alienation and the continued dominance of Western educational systems and paradigms in Africa had contributed to the problems of African development.

The conclusion from this experience was that education was primarily a form of dialogue between different knowledge systems because through dialogue knowledge was created and communicated as information. The more centers of knowledge, the more dialogues and the richer the experience of human existence. Without dialogue communities cannot understand each other and the different kinds of knowledge held by communities around the world cannot be shared. This recognition expresses the African philosophy of "Ubuntu" (humanness)—the belief that without others one cannot exist as a human being. There is therefore a need for what Habermas called "communicative action": communication of information and knowledge between different kinds of communities based on a shared search for answers to problems. For information so communicated to be effective and positively received, it must be relevant to the recipients and expressed in the indigenous languages of the communities concerned. As one participant said: "Communication in people's own languages builds people's self-confidence and in the process empowers them through social transformation. It builds initiatives, and the messages delivered are not obliterated. If messages are given in rough translation, a lot is lost in the process. The result is that the recipients of the knowledge cannot use it, and if they do they are bound to get unsatisfactory results."

This recognition led to the conclusion that education in one's mother tongue is essential to the broadening of global knowledge because it takes into account indigenous knowledge systems. Only through education and research can this process of knowledge creation, retrieval, and communication be sustained and mainstreamed. Carrying out research and educational activities in African languages is therefore key to developing African knowledge, expressing and preserving African values, ethos, norms, and spiritual systems, and bringing about social and economic transformation. Although it is now possible to communicate indigenous African knowledges to a wider public via the Internet, efforts should be made to ensure that it is communicated not only in translations but also in the original language. This is the only way that African communities can learn from other cultures while also promoting their own cultures in a global system of mutually respecting cultures.

In our field-building research exercise we focused on how we could disseminate the knowledge we had obtained through our research. The field-building team felt that much anthropological research was never disseminated back to the communities that had cooperated in producing the knowledge so that they could reflect on it and, if necessary, critique its presentation. This omission amounted to the "colonization" and expropriation of indigenous intellectual property.

One reason researchers had not attempted to communicate their findings back to the communities they had studied was that such communication was not one of the goals of their research in the first place. Another was that the researchers' knowledge production paradigm included only the recognized mainstream systems of dissemination through reporting, article writing, dissertation and thesis writing, and book publication, which turned the knowledge so produced into a new form of "property" owned by the researchers.

We considered this appropriation to be a form of domination, expropriation, and disempowerment of the dispossessed community, who were the true owners, or at least part owners, of the knowledge thus acquired. Most of the research done by scholars was for academic purposes, while the research done by practitioners was for the use of a particular organization and was restricted to that organization's intervention programs. Thus, even without the language barrier, such knowledge was rendered inaccessible to the majority of the population who had helped to produce it. And even if such knowledge were to be translated into local languages, the overwhelming majority of the people would not be able to read it because they were illiterate.

Thus a three-pronged approach to knowledge production within communities was necessary. First, people needed to be involved in the research process, so that the research would become a process of self-definition and self-affirmation for them; and they needed to be involved in designing and determining the issues to be researched, the methods to be used, and the paradigms to organize the data. Second, the results of such research would need to be discussed with the wider community before publication. Third, the most important findings would need to be translated into the local languages and transmitted to the community in a culturally appropriate manner so that the producers of the knowledge could comment, critique, and further develop the "discourse." We called this "research within research."

Finally, the team felt that we needed to do outreach into the communities so that our findings could be communicated to the communities from which the information had been obtained. Our objective would be to get the ideas assimilated and debated through people's own traditional techniques of communication and learning. Techniques such as audio or audiovisual forms of communication in the peoples' languages were considered suitable. In this way, the community could discuss the results in what would be another form of research through dialogue and further action. This implied that we had to pass on the findings to the communities in such a way that the people could appreciate them culturally. The techniques we came up with were drama, dance, poetry, songs, proverbs, and stories.

Africans are very good at relating to situations through such cultural forms as songs and dance. We decided to organize the research results in such a way that they could be put in the form of songs, dances, lamentation, and other forms of drama and performed for audiences, who would then be called upon to discuss and comment on the play or the drama. Local museums could also be built to preserve some of the material cultures of the people. We considered the use of drama in Uganda to sensitize the population about HIV/AIDS as an instructive example.

We conducted our "research within research" through two approaches. The first involved selecting a group of "community facilitators" to investigate communities' understanding of the concept of "security." The second involved feeding back the findings of the research to the community through drama.

In the first research activity, forty "community facilitators" were trained in participatory action research and then deployed to the communities of four countries: Uganda, Kenya, Tanzania, and the New Sudan. They were told to ask about fifty people of both genders and all ages in each community just what the term *security* meant to them.

The answers to the question from all the four countries were similar in that they showed a broader understanding of the concept "security" than that current in mainstream social science. According to one community facilitator working in northern Tanzania in the pastoral communities around the Ngorongoro crater, one elder woman he had asked for her definition of *security* simply answered, "We can say we have enough security if the following are absent: *emuoyian* [diseases that cause death]; *olarraba* [war/conflicts in the community or society]; *olameyu* [drought that may lead to food insufficiency]." And a group of young men and women answered that *security* meant being unintimidated and in harmony, and living in an environment that is physically healthy, produces enough food for human beings and animals such as livestock, and lacks individual and social conflicts. The community facilitator from the Maasai and Kikuyu in the Gilgil division of the Nakuru district of Kenya similarly reported that the Maasai herdsmen had defined security in terms of their ability to engage in nomadic pastoralism, while their Kikuyu neighbors, who lived by crop farming, viewed it in terms of being able to farm without the threat of attacks or eviction by their neighbors. The reports from Uganda and the New Sudan again gave similar answers, and there is no need to repeat them here. What is significant is that all the communities related security to well-being and to the availability of resources to sustain their lives. They perceived insecurity as an inability to meet their physical, economic, social, and psychological needs. The responses also indicated that there was general agreement as to how "insecurity" could be addressed, managed, and controlled. From these responses further programs of action were drawn up that could enable the communities to address some of the obstacles to their security. Further research and action aimed at communities' self-empowerment would be required.

COMMUNITY RESPONSES

The community feedback obtained through the "research within research" was revealing. In some places the communities were not clear on what the exercise was all about. They suspected that the facilitators were trying to benefit from their plight. This reaction was to be expected: it reflected a deep mistrust on the part of people who had developed "research fatigue" from constant harassment by hordes of researchers since colonialism had first knocked on their doors. They had seen researchers come and go while their own conditions had steadily worsened. This suggested to them, with some justification, that the researchers were part of their problem.

To what extent could "activist researchers" be trusted to be different from earlier researchers who had established a relationship of domination over them and had expropriated their knowledge? This was the moment of truth. Some of the participants demanded to be paid for their participation in the discussions, while others argued that the discussions were a government activity intended to weaken them even further. Their interrogation of our research team and their analysis of our explanations became the communities' own process of "research within research."

If indeed, as the researchers and facilitators explained, we were different from earlier researchers, how could a new, qualitatively different relationship be established between them as "objects" of research and ourselves as "activist researchers"? If, as we have argued, control of knowledge is a power relationship between subject and object, could the community participants redefine this power relationship so that both they and the researchers would be subjects of the research? These questions would find an answer in the process of the self-empowerment of the community research subjects. For the time being, with some inducement, some of the community members cooperated and listened to the researchers' presentations.

The discussions generated through workshop discussion were deep and relevant to their conditions. Some in the communities demanded the means to overcome their difficulties such as lack of education for children and lack of food. But they welcomed the use of cultural techniques to address these problems, and some wanted the techniques to become a continuing part of their cultural festivals in order to help raise the community's political awareness about the issues brought up by the research. Some elders commented that the researchers' questions had raised community members' awareness of how pervasive and long-standing the community's problems were. They insisted that the exercise could stimulate the community to seek ways of getting engaged in community development projects.

As part of the attempt to act on the concerns raised by community members' responses to the research questions, one community in Uganda sent a representative across the border to Kenya and discussed with the local Turkana community there the need to increase peaceful contacts between the two settlements. This led to the opening of the Nakiroro road to Kenya, where traffic had been disrupted by raids and counter-raids for cattle.

Different groups articulated the need to become active in addressing the problems facing them, especially the insecurity caused by cattle raids by neighboring communities. This was a step toward what Paulo Freire (1972) called "conscientization," which could be reached only through critical dialogue. The next step was to find how to engage the communities to face up to these challenges and perfect their tools of struggle for self-empowerment through knowledge production and dialogue.

TOWARD A SYNTHETIC KNOWLEDGE PRODUCTION

The above experiences, though limited in scope, have added a new dimension to our understanding of knowledge production, power, cultural identity, and self-empowerment. They have shown that earlier demands that communities "participate" in academic research have been overtaken by more specific demands that communities appropriate the process of knowledge production with the aim of their own empowerment. It has come to be recognized that culture and language are key to the creation of both identity and knowledge and that knowledge production is a right, not a privilege. Further, knowledge production and control are enmeshed in power relations and therefore cannot be neutral.

While "culture matters" (Harrison and Huntington 2000), it cannot be cultivated in isolation to produce desired "development." Development and social transformation are the product of a people's struggle for rights and must be premised on a recognition of their right to education and control over their resources. Culture on its own cannot be a "constraint" to development. Mistaken "development" strategies are what lead to cultural alienation and social fragmentation. Thus, in the struggle for self-empowerment, the people must emphasize their right to produce and share knowledge through education and dialogue. Philosophical and social hermeneutics has added to this understanding.

New philosophical questions have been raised by these developments. Critical theory has postulated a hermeneutic approach in which different propagators of knowledge confront one another through a dialogue in which statements and counterstatements are "validated." As stated earlier, our research method, which draws on the pedagogical participatory approach of dialogue developed by Paulo Freire, has in practice tried to eliminate the power imbalance that typifies the relationship between researcher and research subject and to instead promote a relationship of equality that promotes dialogue between the two actors. The methodology also tries to develop emancipatory knowledge through participatory research. This is the approach we arrived at in our field-building exercise, which attempted to bring different epistemologies and methodologies and their actual representatives into the same "field" of knowledge creation (Nabudere 2002, 26–29).

Our approach centers on researchers' initiation of dialogue between individuals and communities, with a view to creating a common pool of knowledge accessible to all users. Dialogue, unlike monologue, entails the joining of thinking and feeling to create new meanings for everyone involved. New understandings emerge from the interplay of meanings among people. Through this process different contributions can be integrated and synthesized to produce a qualitatively new knowledge in which all the contributions are represented. This is the result of a change in philosophical worldview that goes beyond the "scientific paradigm" and epistemology to recognize that knowledge is not an exclusive preserve of any single individual or community but a human act of all human beings. It is a hermeneutic turn for the better.

The training we undertook later on in our project was aimed at presenting the knowledge produced in the participatory grassroots research to the communities for their intellectual assessment and collective reflection on it. An experienced traditional and modern dramatist trained twenty community facilitators in utilizing all the traditional techniques of African drama-dance, total theater, songs, stories, lamentation, laughter, poetry, dialogue/palaver, proverbs, riddles, and so on to communicate information to the communities and to provoke a response from them.

The idea was to engage people in such a way that the audience would take part in the drama. After the drama, the community facilitators would turn the gathering into an adult learning class in which participants would discuss what they had seen in the drama. In this way, people would be able to comment critically on what was being communicated, and this in turn might lead to further reflection and action, thereby continuing field building within the community.

We used a conference held in Uganda in February 2003 to sum up these experiences. At the end of it, we agreed to continue with field-building activities as a general practice. The scholars associated with the Afrika Study Center now accept field building as something that adds a new dimension to our research and practical work with communities, researchers, NGOs, the private sector, and governments at all levels. Our idea is to strengthen the linkage between modern and traditional knowledge in new ways that recognize the epistemological basis of indigenous knowledge and affirm its validity in this context. We also recognize scientific knowledge as valid in its own cultural context to the extent that it helps indigenous knowledge play a role in forming a global knowledge to which all cultures and knowledge systems contribute.

To this end, we decided to set up five networks, which were to operate separately for the purpose of bringing in new actors. Afrika Study Center was requested to continue to coordinate the networks in their field-building activities. These networks were to enhance the development of indigenous knowledge systems and to define them as "sites of knowledge." A number of sites were indicated, and we planned to build on the experiences in those sites.

The topic of higher education also emerged in our discussions of field building. We decided that a new kind of university was needed that would connect institutions of higher learning to the knowledge generated in communities as part of the process of making education available to all. A first step has been taken in this direction with Afrika Study Center's establishment of the Marcus Garvey Pan-Afrikan Institute in Mbale, Uganda.

The Institute will be an innovative attempt to highlight African indigenous knowledge as a source of valuable human achievement by mainstreaming it through rediscovery, research, and recognition. Registers of the sites and depositories of indigenous knowledge will be created and continually expanded to broaden awareness of these "other" knowledge sources, and the experts, theoreticians, custodians, and carriers of the various forms of knowledge and their practice will be identified.

The Institute will use indigenous sites and knowledge producers, propagators, and practitioners to structure teaching and research. The university that will emerge from this project will at first operate at the postgraduate level. For 20 percent of the time allocated to the program, students will be assigned to these sites according to the knowledge and expertise that they seek. They will be required to establish human relations in the chosen community that will make it possible for the theoreticians, custodians, and practitioners of such knowledge to impart it to them. This will entail entering into cosmological and epistemological encounters with the producers of the knowledge and in that way will open up the avenues of intersubjective communication that facilitate learning.

The institute, and later the university, will develop protocols with the faculties at the sites in which the producers and imparters of such endogenous knowledge will be protected with regard to their intellectual property rights as well as the application and reproduction of their knowledge. It will develop rules for recognizing and acknowledging the knowledge imparted and will reward the producers, practitioners, teachers, and research assistants allocated to the learner. Learners will also be required to use 20 percent of the time they spend at the site to teach some subject in which they are qualified to some individuals in the community. This will ensure a "give and take" relationship with the community at the sites of knowledge and will avoid the one-sided "colonization" and ownership of knowledge characteristic of the present elite-oriented system of education.

The university will include in its planning the creation of some infrastructure for learners as well as for teachers at the sites of knowledge. Where possible, this will include capacity building and the creation of information and communications technology facilities in the form of broadband Internet to which the community and students can have access. It will also include building huts to accommodate students while they are at the site and developing a library facility where the downloaded knowledge and other learning materials from the community will be deposited in the community's language. This procedure will not only enable the recording of such knowledge but also create archives for its preservation.

The community teachers and research assistants who will take part in teaching the students will be given a certificate as recognition of their contribution by the university. The holder of the certificate will use it for accreditation in the form of "recognition of prior learning" (RPL) in the process of admission to higher institutions of learning. Since the Fifth International Conference on Education (CONFITEA V), UNESCO has officially recognized such accreditation as a channel through which adult learners can have access to higher education. Since the Mumbai Statement, issued by the University of Mumbai (Bombay) after the UNESCO 1997 world conference, implementation of this "prior learning" accreditation principle has begun. RPL certification will lead to the diminution and eventual elimination of the knowledge-based divide between African elites and the wider African population.

On return to the university site, students will be guided by their supervisor in analyzing and better understanding the material they have obtained from these new sources by using and at the same time going beyond existing multidisciplinary and comparative analytical methods and techniques. Initially the use of these methods and techniques will reveal their limitations in giving students a full understanding of the "other" knowledge that they have just accessed.

Students will attempt to develop an open-ended hermeneutic approach that will eliminate these conceptual limitations by bringing forth the meanings of the "other" knowledge understood in their cultural contexts. To fully develop a holistic, all-inclusive epistemology and paradigm, students will need to explore new approaches to research that can enable a continuous accessing, integration, and synthesis of knowledge that includes all forms of knowledge from all cultural sources, including African sources.

Information and communication technologies will be promoted to establish e-learning and e-health/telemedicine in rural communities and to set up broadband Internet links through satellite to educational, health, governmental, and other centers of knowledge. This will open up opportunities for lifelong learning and distance education in collaboration with the Global University System based in Finland and the Uganda National Council of Science and Technology and will facilitate institutional collaboration around the world in advocacy to encourage field building in all areas of knowledge.

The struggle for self-determination and participation in knowledge production and practice has at a cultural level produced a new understanding of the need to develop new forms of knowledge through self-empowerment of all actors. The replacement of vertical power relations between the researcher and the researched with horizontal relations that promote communities' involvement in learning and research ensures that all knowledge producers can, through dialogue and collaborative effort, contribute to building fields of knowledge accessible to all. A hermeneutic approach ensures that all knowledge sources are recognized, and welcomed, and integrated and that all human experiences are taken into account.

The field-building project that was embarked on in Uganda as a result of the research activities that had been under way in the pastoral communities has added a new dimension to these collaborative efforts. A new sense of direction and identity has emerged among scholars, practitioners, and indigenous knowledge experts and custodians (Nabudere, Wambette, and Mukuma 2003). New programs in which the communities play a direct role as active producers of knowledge have enriched the work of the three types of actors in the field.

The activity has also created an awareness of the need to set up a pan-African university that is rooted in local communities. In such a university, students would both learn directly from experts in the communities and impart some knowledge to the communities so that everyone would share in the production of knowledge. Learners would be credited with their prior acquired knowledge, upon which they could build and advance to higher learning. In this process, no distinction would be made between "modern scientific" knowledge and "traditional" or "indigenous" knowledge. Both would contribute to a new global knowledge located in different cultural and civilizational sites.

Our research project shows that in people's struggles for self-empowerment much can be achieved by building bridges between the different kinds of skills and expertise that are to be found in different knowledge locations. The institutionalization of the idea of a cultural and civilizational dialogue between peoples of the world is the only way we can make the twenty-first century a century of peace.

REFERENCES

Curtin, P. D. 1989. "Recent Trends in African Historiography and Their Contribution to History in General." In *General History of Africa*, vol. 1, *Methodology and African Prehistory*, edited by J. Ki-Zerbo. Berkeley: University of California Press.

Diop, Cheikh Anta. 1974. *The African Origin of Civilization: Myth or Reality*. Chicago: Lawrence Hill.

Dubell, Folke, ed. 1980. *Research for the People, Research by the People: Selected Papers from the International Forum on Participatory Research, Ljubljana, Yugoslavia, 1980*. Sweden: Linköping University Department of Education.

Fals-Borda, Orlando. 1980. "Science and the Common People." In *Research for the People: Research by the People, Selected Papers from the International Forum on Participatory Research, Ljubljana, Yugoslavia, 1980*, edited by Folke Dubell. Sweden: Linköping University Department of Education.

Freire, Paulo. 1972. *Pedagogy of the Oppressed*. London: Penguin.

Gramsci, A. 1971. *Selections from the Prison Notebooks*. London: Lawrence and Wishart.

Grossi, Francisco Vio. 1980. "The Socio-Political Implications of Participatory Research." In *Research for the People: Research by the People, Selected Papers from the International Forum on Participatory Research, Ljubljana, Yugoslavia, 1980*, edited by Folke Dubell. Sweden: Linköping University Department of Education.

Harrison, L. E., and S. P. Huntington. 2000. *Culture Matters: How Values Shape Human Progress*. New York: Basic Books.

Mbilinyi, M., U. Vuerela, Yusuf Kassam, and Y. Masisis. 1982. "The Politics of Research Methodology in the Social Sciences." In *Participatory Research: An Emerging Alternative Methodology in Social Science Research*, edited by Yusuf Kassam and Kamal Mustafa. New Delhi: Society for Participatory Research in Asia.

McLellan, David. 1973. *Karl Marx: His Life and Thought*. London: Paladin.

McTaggart, R. 1991. "Principles for Participatory Action Research." *Adult Education Quarterly* 41 (3): 168–87.

Nabudere, D. W. 2002. "Field Building Program of Activities 2002." Working paper, Afrika Study Center, Mbale, Uganda.

———. 2003. "The Epistemological and Methodological Foundations for an All-Inclusive Research Paradigm in the Search for Global Knowledge." *African Association of Political Science Occasional Papers* 6 (1).

Nabudere, D. W., J. Wambette, and B. Mukuma. 2003. "Field Building through Institutional Collaboration in Research and Community Outreach Activities." Paper presented at the Field Building Conference, Makerere University, Kampala, February 15.

Parsons, Talcott. 1978. *Action Theory and the Human Condition*. New York: Free Press.

Rigby, Peter. 1985. *The Persistent Pastoralists: The Nomadic Societies in Transition*. London: Zed Press.

Vansina, Jan. 1994. *Living with Africa*. Madison: University of Wisconsin Press.

3. Breaking the Chains and Steering the Ship

How Activism Can Help Change Teaching and Scholarship

George Lipsitz

> I learned so much at *Fuerza Unida*. This is the best school you could have, working with people, listening, chairing meetings—all the things you have to understand to carry out the struggle. Here we are not just individuals. We go to support and participate in all struggles in the movement.
>
> PETRA MATA, quoted in Miriam Ching Yoon Louie, *Sweatshop Warriors*

> Certain scholars will be among the first to raise the new and meaningful issues because of their connection with the most dynamic groups in society. Thus when African peoples were mounting a struggle for political independence . . . they automatically became interested in recalling previous resistance. Initially only a scholar committed to . . . the present emancipation drive would find it possible to seek out and unearth the experience of earlier struggles.
>
> WALTER RODNEY, "The African Revolution"

On my way to participate in an oral history workshop inside the stately Butler Library at Columbia University, I noticed a classic revival frieze high above the building's front steps. Above the tall limestone columns framing the library entrance, stonemasons had inscribed the names of some of the great writers and thinkers of the Western tradition—Homer, Herodotus, Sophocles, Plato, Aristotle, Demosthenes, Cicero, and Virgil.

I began my presentation at the workshop by noting how the building in which we were holding our meeting made me feel at home. I joked that I too live in a place where young men put their *placas* and tags in highly visible public spaces. I promised to inform my friends Frame, Chaka, Chuca, and Lefty about the writing of their East Coast counterparts.

Pretending to misrecognize philosophers' names as graffiti tags did not stem from any disrespect on my part for the classics from the age of antiquity. The problems we face as scholars and citizens are daunting. We need all the help we can get. All knowledge should be respected, and the great intellectual traditions of the West still have much to teach us. I could not help but think, however, that the writing on the wall above the entrance to the Butler Library marked that building as a particular kind of a space, as a place where those who enter are invited to think of themselves as the heirs to only one lineage. The frieze proclaims that Homer, Herodotus, Sophocles, Plato, Aristotle, Demosthenes, Cicero, Virgil, and their literal or figurative descendants are welcomed here. But what about everyone else?

What honor is done to the great thinkers of the past by inscribing their names permanently in stone? This conveys the impression that all the important things have already been thought and said. Wouldn't it be better instead to inscribe the philosophers' actual curiosity and creativity into our intellectual work, to use their ideas to help discover the kinds of thinking and action that are most appropriate to our own time?

Throughout our lives most of us have encountered serious people in all walks of life who lack the dignity of being taken seriously. Their acts of reflection, contemplation, and creation generally take place without any recognition or reward, in spaces quite unlike the Butler Library. They work with the tools available to them in the arenas to which they have access. Their names will never appear in newspapers, much less be chiseled into friezes on classic revival buildings. Yet they leave their mark on the world in other ways. They often mine unexpected and nontraditional archives. They generate fundamentally new imaginaries, fashioning ways of knowing and ways of being that are as important to our understanding of the world in which we live as the great works of famous philosophers.

Michael Eric Dyson draws on a story from the classical literature of antiquity to metaphorically illustrate the chasm that divides people who have official roles in society as intellectuals from the far greater number of people who think and do important work with their minds without institutional validation. Dyson reminds us of the Trojan Horse in Homer's *Odyssey*. He encourages us to make ourselves like the gift that the Trojans received from their enemies. We enter universities, libraries, and lecture halls where others cannot go. Dyson suggests that we keep hidden inside ourselves the knowledge that we have gleaned from all those people we have met in life who had important things to say but no opportunity to say them in public. When we gain access to the printed page, the speaker's podium, the performance stage, the camera, the computer, or the painter's canvas, we can be like the Trojan Horse: at the appropriate moment we can open ourselves up and let all those other people out.

Scholar activists have been disseminating the situated knowledge of communities in struggle for many years. Information gleaned initially by activist fair-housing groups as a result of the 1984 Community Reinvestment Act created the databases necessary for pathbreaking scholarship on housing segregation and wealth inequalities in the 1990s by Melvin Oliver, Thomas Shapiro, Douglass Massey, and Nancy Denton.[1] Robert Bullard and Laura Pulido, scholarly advocates for environmental justice, have derived ideas, evidence, and arguments from activist groups like the Commission for Racial Justice of the United Church of Christ and the Labor Community Strategy Center.[2] Julie Sze's direct participation in the environmental justice movement informs her analysis of pollution and neighborhood race effects in New York, while the political perspectives and educational activities of the Coalition Against Police Abuse shape the contours of João Costa Vargas's brilliant ethnographic work on the many meanings of "blackness" in contemporary Los Angeles.[3]

Queer theorists Roderick Ferguson, Juana Rodriguez, and David Roman have fashioned important tools for understanding the intersectional nature of social identities out of the rhetorics, tactics, and organizing strategies of activist groups Contrasida por la Vida, Aids/US, and the Audre Lorde Project.[4] Martha Matsuoka and Yoko Fukumura have raised fundamental challenges to academic analyses of globalization and definitions of security by drawing on the epistemological brilliance of the Okinawan Women Act Against Military Violence.[5] Ruth Wilson Gilmore has formulated the first fully theorized explanation of the dramatic expansion of prison building in California by drawing on her long history as a scholar activist in support groups organized by families of incarcerated inmates.[6]

In an era when most political scientists have treated neoliberal structural adjustment policies as natural, necessary, and inevitable, Walden Bello has drawn on the experiences and understandings of activist groups from the Philippines and around the world to produce a ringing critique of neoliberalism that has proven itself correct in every respect.[7] The generative analysis of states, politics, and vanguard parties articulated in the writings of John Holloway, Elofna Palaez, and Eloina Palaez flows directly from their engagements with the political strategies of the EZLN insurgents in Mexico.[8] Many innovative activist groups raising original and generative arguments have only recently begun to attract academic interpreters. Al Gedicks and Zoltan Grossman have called attention to the important ideas of the Wolf River Watershed Education Project and the Midwest Treaty Network in Wisconsin. Stephanie Tai has delineated the challenges posed to legal paradigms by the young organizers affiliated with the Laotian Organizing Project in California. Amy Kastely has identified the tactical brilliance and epistemological sophistication of the Esperanza Peace and Justice Center in Texas.[9]

It should not be surprising that activism helps generate excellent scholarship. The practice of social mobilization often requires intellectual contestation. Advocates for environmental justice, fair housing, and augmented funding for AIDS research, and opponents of massive prison-building projects, urban redevelopment schemes, and neoliberal economic policies, need to challenge the expert knowledge of scientists, judges, physicians, criminologists, bankers, urban planners, and economists. In their struggles, it has rarely been enough to add new evidence to existing paradigms. Instead, it has been necessary to expose and challenge the epistemological and ideological underpinnings of contemporary science, law, medicine, urban planning, and business. In the process of struggle, activists develop new ways of knowing as well as new ways of being. They discover nontraditional archives and generate nontraditional imaginaries as constitutive parts of mobilizations for resources, rights, and recognition.

Of course, anything worth doing can be done badly. Combining scholarship and activism offers no automatic guarantee of either better scholarship or better activism. Scholar activists have to grapple with serious challenges. The two realms in which they work can seem incommensurable. Evaluation, recognition, and reward in academic life usually proceed through relentlessly individual and individualizing processes. Activism on the other hand, encourages collective, collaborative, and social thinking. Prevailing professional practices encourage scholars to seek distinction for themselves by distinguishing their work from the research conducted by others. They are encouraged to present themselves as atomized individuals rather than as participants in a collective and collaborative conversation. Scholars secure professional recognition and reward for single-authored books or articles in professional journals that might be less useful, at least immediately, to social movement activists than descriptive empirical research about the nature, extent, and history of pressing present problems. Similarly, the skills that academic practice hones and refines might be more useful to activist groups when channeled into the production of pamphlets and press releases delineating the results of research conducted by others than in the form of original research projects.

Moreover, establishing working relationships between scholars and activists can entail serious practical and ethical problems. There is always the danger that scholars might seek to appropriate the dynamism and egalitarian imagination of activist groups merely to gain personal advantages for themselves or to secure psychic reparations for the ways in which professional obligations impoverish their own inner lives. The insights, analyses, and epistemologies of activists can have monetary value in this society. Scholars sometimes profit personally from passing off perspectives gleaned from activists as their own ideas, neither acknowledging nor compensating the sources of their insights. They take without giving back, lulling themselves into believing that if scholarship on social movements succeeds, then the social movements themselves are succeeding. Even worse, as Hazel Carby has long argued, the worthy goals of desegregating the college curriculum and the college classroom do not necessarily do much to desegregate the myriad other structures, institutions, and practices that skew opportunities and life chances in this society along racial lines.[10]

On the other hand, the pressing practical needs of social movement struggle can lead activists to abdicate their responsibilities to learn everything they can about the problems they face. They can come to believe that asking and answering abstract historical and theoretical questions constitutes an unacceptable diversion from the struggle. Activists often feel too busy, too pressured, too embroiled in activity to think much about their philosophy, ideology, or structure. Yet not thinking about problems does not make them go away. Movements pay a price for unsolved intellectual problems. In the heat of battle, activist groups tend to borrow wholesale from the few models available to them, to appropriate ideas, slogans, and organizational forms from elsewhere, whether these serve their actual purposes or not.[11] The very solidarity on which activist groups depend can make them narrow, insular, and isolated from criticism, from new approaches and ideas. The harrowing nature of collective struggle can shape individual and collective identities so much so that they become threatened when new information indicates a need for changes in strategies and tactics.[12]

Scholars and social movement activists have much in common, however. In both activism and the academy, we suffer when we do not know enough, when critical reflection becomes too far removed from practical activity, and when the imperatives of our daily work leave too little opportunity for analysis, reflection, and critique. Schools and social movements are both important institutions in U.S. society. The outcomes of their activities influence what reporters report, what teachers teach, what writers write, and what decision makers decide. When scholars and activists work together, they gain access to a broader array of analyses, practices, and tools than they would have otherwise.

Powerful forces fuel the rise of contemporary scholar activism. The combination of the perpetual profitability crisis within capitalism and the ideological opposition among elites to the very existence of public institutions that are not guided primarily by the profit motive makes some of the most powerful people and some of the most powerful institutions in our society promote the privatization of education. These efforts constrict and constrain intellectual work in debilitating ways. They pressure teachers to privilege technical expertise over critical, contemplative, and creative thinking. High-stakes testing, school-to-work programs, and efforts to transform universities into the research and development arms of transnational corporations exacerbate inequalities and undermine the ability of higher education to serve as a vehicle for equal opportunity and social justice. At the same time, economic concentration and corporate synergy within for-profit conglomerates in the news, publishing, and entertainment industries deprive citizens and communities of necessary knowledge while inundating them with marketing campaigns and public relations initiatives intended to place the pursuit of commodities at the center of the social world. These processes produce dissatisfied educators and disaffected citizens who have much to say to each other when they meet.

The execrable social, spiritual, and moral conditions of everyday life in this society compel us to pay attention to the potential for change in any of its institutions, practices, and processes. All the institutions that produce exploitation and alienation have the potential to become sites for social change. Particularly promising are what James Lee calls "the provisional spaces that institutions tolerate but do not fully sanction, the conversations that compel us to read different kinds of books and nudge us, at times, to put our books down."[13]

Inside K–16 schooling, sincere, dedicated, and principled individuals often hope that education can be connected to ways of living more freely, decently, and honorably than our society seems now willing to allow. The kind of classroom knowledge they champion can have important and positive uses. It can help people solve certain kinds of problems, and it offers information and skills that are necessary for survival in the contemporary world. But under current conditions, K–16 education too often focuses on *what* students learn rather than on *how* students learn. Instead of creating critical thinkers and interactive and collaborative lifelong learners capable of solving problems on their own, K–16 schooling increasingly resembles a glorified scavenger hunt where knowledge is presumed to rest solely in the textbook, in the lecture presentation, or in the carefully supervised steps taken by researchers in the laboratory. Within this system, the job of the dutiful student is simply to retrieve information and deposit it in the appropriate place. Students trained by these methods come to see education as a series of unrelated and purposeless tasks that end up in a credential. Teachers trapped within this curriculum and pedagogy become treated as tutors obligated to train students but unable to show them how to think and work by themselves and for themselves. While private firms secure huge profits by selling school systems tests and test-taking strategies, education for democratic citizenship suffers. Teachers pretend to teach and students pretend to learn, but literally as well as figuratively no one is the wiser.[14]

Like other privatization schemes ranging from lucrative contracts secured by multinational firms to carry out military and police missions in Iraq to the emergence of private investment accounts as a rival to social security, the privatization of education is part of a broader pattern of looting public resources for private gain. It exacerbates the existing educational crisis, not only by producing inferior education, but by provoking more fiscal crises that lead to more austerity, retrenchment, and budget cuts in the short run and the adoption of "one size fits all" standardization masquerading as standards in the long run.

Under these conditions, we need to acknowledge the shortcomings of the practices, processes, and procedures that dominate the educational system and create alternatives to them. Scholar activism is one of those alternatives. Scholarly work with social movements does more than provide new research objects for professors and students. The deliberative talk and face-to-face decision making that permeates the practices of most activist organizations offers models of interactive and collaborative learning with great relevance for classroom pedagogy. Challenging credentialed experts requires activists to develop new definitions of competence, qualifications, and knowledge and to counter the privileges of power with creative and credible arguments.

Whereas in the classroom social roles and social relations can often be static and difficult to change, activist organizations constantly need to renegotiate relations between individuals and the group, between humans and the environment, and among different constituencies. They need to produce new leaders from their own ranks and to attract allies and advocates from the outside. This forces them to think about people as flexible, fluid, and in process, to imagine the identities and identifications people might create in the future as well as the ones they already have. These are essential approaches for good teaching as well.

Robin D. G. Kelley offers a formula that encapsulates the radical potential of combining scholarship and social activism. "Revolutionary dreams erupt out of political engagement," he writes, adding, "Collective social movements are incubators of new knowledge."[15] The history of social movements is replete with illustrative examples of the kinds of organizational learning that activism envisions and enacts. Research by Kelley, Barbara Ransby, Charles Payne, and Francesca Polletta shows how both labor movement organizers in Alabama in the 1930s and civil rights organizers in Mississippi during the 1960s made educational work the center of their efforts.[16] In the historical and social contexts in which they worked, study groups and freedom schools gave their constituents access to forms of education that had been denied them by the dominant society. Organizing by educating for them revealed previously occluded dynamics of power, how the dominant society routinely imposed impediments to black education and upward mobility.

These movements also succeeded in part because they enabled students to develop a new sense of themselves by participating in discussions about the world and their places in it.[17] According to the civil rights activist Mike Miller, teachers in the 1960s freedom movement functioned as particularly effective organizers because they encouraged people to see their problems both from close up and from far away, to blend immediate questions like "What is the problem?" "How many other people feel the same way?" and "What precisely do we want?" with analyses of prevailing power structures, alternative political visions, and people's personal goals.[18] Miller explains, moreover, that civil rights activities required the teachers to develop new and better techniques and perspectives once they brought their professional skills outside the classroom.

Perhaps the most important problem to be solved by both scholars and activists concerns moving beyond simple resistance and working to bring about truly transformative change. Rebellious practices can produce oppositional identities and ideas, but these are never enough. Indeed, in this society they run the risk of replicating and reinforcing the ways of thinking responsible for alienation, inequality, and injustice in the first place. Social justice amounts to something more than a more equitable distribution of resources and power; it requires the reconstitution of social relations on a new basis.

Scholar activist Vincent Harding helps us see how resistance can lead to transformative change in his magnificent study of slave resistance and rebellion, *There Is a River*, where he discusses the difference between "breaking the chains" and "steering the ship."[19] Harding explains that enslaved Africans on ships during the Middle Passage understandably longed for freedom. Captivity forced them to imagine and execute ways of breaking the chains that held them in bondage. They soon learned, however, that this was not enough. On board sailing vessels, in the middle of the ocean, they could not secure freedom simply by breaking the chains. They had to learn to master the ship as well, to take command of the vessel and steer it toward Africa or to some Caribbean island or South American shore to secure freedom.

Emancipation from centuries of slavery compelled African Americans to learn this lesson anew. Their successful struggle for freedom during the Civil War left them with the problem of how to enter into participation in the political life of a republic premised on their exclusion and subordination. It was not enough for them to be nominally free in a society dependent on exploitation, hierarchy, and racism. The end of slavery as a formal institution did not terminate the kinds of forced servitude produced by poverty, racism, and organized state or vigilante violence. Freed people had to change the society they wished to enter.

Through relentless, widespread, and decentralized grassroots activism, freed people organized political conventions where they debated their visions for the nation. They formed and joined more than three thousand local chapters of the Union and Loyalty League, an institution set up to promote unity, to secure land, to mobilize for self defense, and to secure political power. People who had been slaves a few years before built sophisticated coalitions in electoral politics, joining with poor whites to expand access to the ballot and to expend state funds on infrastructure improvements and universal free education.

What W. E. B. Du Bois named abolition democracy emerged out of these communities of struggle.[20] Most enslaved Africans in America had been denied literacy, could not travel freely, and lived in isolation on small plantations. Free blacks confronted overwhelming obstacles, such as the state of Missouri's constitutional prohibition against educating African Americans. Yet collective struggle turned out to be a great equalizer. In captivity, blacks spread information about escape routes and often hid runaways in plain sight of slave owners who could not distinguish one African from another. During the Civil War, they disseminated news about the approach of Union troops, about Lincoln's Emancipation Proclamation, and about defeats inflicted on Confederate forces. After emancipation, freed people embraced literacy classes and championed universal free education. Their extraordinary unity in the postwar era stemmed from a stance that saw social activism and education as parts of the same project.

This exuberant activism on the part of freed slaves led to the creation of abolition democracy, the first real democracy ever in the United States. Fusing the freedom dreams of a formerly enslaved people with the egalitarian ideas and practices generated in the course of abolitionist struggle, their efforts ultimately culminated in the Fourteenth Amendment. More than a constitutional provision guaranteeing equal protection of the law to all, the Fourteenth Amendment functioned as a broader social warrant that undermined the previous hegemony of white male propertied power and legitimated new forms of collective responsibility for equal protection and equal rights. It was the Civil War that ended slavery, but it took abolition democracy to make the freed people unavailable for servitude.[21]

It would have been understandable if former slaves had simply tried to emulate their oppressors, to secure inclusion for themselves by policing the boundaries of exclusion against others. Whites certainly feared that abolition would turn the tables, replacing the white racial dictatorship they knew and condoned with a black racial dictatorship that they feared. Many whites could imagine no other outcome from abolition. Freed people interested only in breaking their chains might indeed have resorted to that kind of behavior.

Yet abolition democracy did something else. Blacks entered into alliances with poor whites, working with them to produce programs designed to help people across racial lines. Their success in providing universal education and in funding public works projects helped their white allies even more than these endeavors helped blacks, but in the process they created the preconditions for democracy in the United States for the first time. The abolition democracy authored by African Americans aided other groups as well. The Fourteenth Amendment established that children born to Asian immigrants ineligible for naturalized citizenship would be citizens, while black elected officials like Mississippi Senator Blanche K. Bruce led the fight against the 1882 Chinese Exclusion Act. Abolition democracy tried to open up opportunity for all, rather than merely changing the identity of the oppressed. It was an intellectual and epistemological breakthrough as well as an activist achievement.

The legacy of activism forged during slavery and freedom generated both intellectual and political resources. It fell to African Americans and their allies to author the Fourteenth Amendment and establish abolition democracy because the struggle compelled them to think more comprehensively and clearly about the nature of U.S. society than anyone else. Precisely because they could not solve their problems by hoping to live slightly more comfortably in the nation that already existed, they had to educate themselves about the complexity of social relations and devise ways of transforming them. Struggle helped produce better ideas and analyses, while those ideas and analyses led to more effective and more transformative actions. The success of abolition democracy depended in no small measure on its intellectual ambition, but that ambition emerged incrementally from the organizational learning enabled by shared social struggle. As Du Bois noted, it was not the ideology of egalitarianism that made the revolution of abolition democracy but rather the revolution that made the ideology.[22]

Harding's history helps us see how activism and scholarship might be mutually constitutive in our time. Ashamed of the injustices and inequalities that pervade our society, oppressed by its calculated cruelty and mediated mendacity and meanness, we long for social movements that might break our chains. Yet this very longing can make us mirror images of the enemies we fight.

This is the way hegemony works. Those who rule choose not only *their* leaders but *our* leaders. They not only articulate their own politics but circumscribe the range of allowable responses to those politics. They make us think that we need to be like them: that if *they* have heroic leaders, *we* need heroic leaders, that if *they* succeed by promoting hate, hurt, and fear, *we* need to promote counterhate, counterhurt, and counterfear. But what works for them does not work for us. We cannot resort to hate: we have to educate—and agitate, and litigate, and demonstrate. It will not be sufficient for us to simply break the chains. We have to learn how to master the ship.

Gaining political power or controlling existing institutions will not be enough. We need to change ourselves and others to become the kinds of people who can create institutions, practices, beliefs, and social relations capable of generating a more just world. Steering the ship means understanding how schooling, literacy, and intellectual work function as nodes inside a larger network of domination and control. It means creating activist organizations that do more than desegregate the ranks of the pain inflictors of this world and instead set in motion processes that might make us fit to found society anew.[23] Steering the ship means educating ourselves so that we can see clearly how we are actually governed.

It can be depressing to think that we are still fighting for abolition democracy some 140 years after its founding. Willie Nelson's song "Three Days" captures the problem perfectly. There are only three days in our lives filled with tears and sorrow, Nelson's lyrics assure us. But these days are "yesterday, today, and tomorrow." Today's problems did not begin yesterday, and they will not be solved tomorrow. The problems we face today look very much like those confronting the builders of abolition democracy a century and a half ago. The relentless commodification of every human relationship and every human activity in this society elevates the avarice and calculation of the consumer over the conscience and responsibility of the citizen. It calls into question the relationships between people and property. The evisceration of the social wage and the fragmentation of the polity into antagonists competing for services, amenities, and advantages breed anxiety, envy, and disrespect. Contempt for other people permeates our political discourse and our cultural life.

These policies, processes, and practices only exacerbate inequality, increase social tensions, and make defensive localism and hostile privatism the affective core of our culture. As each group seeks to maximize rewards and minimize obligations at the expense of others, we defund the economic and social infrastructure required to produce prosperity, stability, and security. Every subunit of government seeks to pass on obligations to every other subunit. This zero-sum game leads inevitably to disappointment, and disappointment promotes resentment. Resentment grows into rage and righteous indignation, which then function as the modal structures of feeling among homeowners' associations, tax limitation groups, and callers to right-wing talk radio.[24] We live in a society that contains surely the most embittered, disgruntled, and angry agglomeration of "haves" in the history of the world.

The "free-market" fundamentalism at the core of transnational corporate capitalist culture is demoralizing in both senses of the word. It destroys morale by fragmenting communities, eliminating meaningful work, and stoking the fires of personal envy, avarice, and aggression. It destroys morality as well, making commodities more valuable than people, reducing all encounters among humans to a common denominator of calculated acquisitiveness. Yet while it undermines both morale and morality, this system produces enormous amounts of moralizing and many moral panics. When its promises of personal prosperity lead to collective austerity, when new freedoms for capital require increased constraints on people, the culture of transnational corporate capitalism turns to the language of moralism, blaming individuals for what has been created systemically.

In *The Twilight of Equality*, Lisa Duggan demonstrates how the public political projects of labor exploitation, income inequality, and gender and racial subordination that have dominated public policies since the 1970s have depended on the mystification and glorification of an imaginary private sphere, a utopian site where properly gendered marriage produces families capable of managing social crises by imbuing their members with morality, restraint, and civility.[25] Bad social conditions are blamed on bad families, while selfishness and greed are lauded and legitimated as efforts to protect and promote the interest of one's own family in competition with others. Duggan shows how in our time the public deployment of discourses about private behavior serves to represent inequality and injustice as natural, necessary, and inevitable, while making collective caretaking and interpersonal empathy seem impractical, inefficient, and even immoral. These discourses make social movements more important than ever, because social movements produce one of the few sites in U.S. society where people create and maintain intimate relations outside the contexts of property and family, where alternatives exist to what Jurgen Habermas termed "civil-familial vocational-privatism."[26]

Under these circumstances, we need new kinds of scholars and new kinds of social activists. Scholars have to concern themselves with more than merely adding on new research objects to existing methods of study. Social activists have to be concerned with more than the identification of novel strategies and tactics. Scholars and activists alike need to change ourselves as we change the institutions in which we work. We need to create new identities, affinities, affiliations, and identifications. We need to change the culture of learning as well as its conditions and contents. We need to initiate open-ended processes of exploration and experimentation designed to traverse old boundaries and bring new polities into being. We still need to learn how to break the chains, to be sure, but we must also learn how to steer the ship.

The Okinawan Women Act Against Military Violence (OWAAMV) activist group offers a powerful example of how activist struggles for social justice can produce new ways of knowing and being. The organizational learning emanating from the OWAAMV offers an exemplary model of how the urgent imperatives of struggles over power can enable people to produce new social relationships and new ways of knowing and being.[27] Living far from some of the metropolitan centers of power where decisions are made that shape their lives in serious ways, the Okinawan

Women have been impelled to create new cognitive mappings, to challenge prevailing assumptions and ideas, to rethink nearly every core category that scholars take for granted. Their activism has led them to fashion radically new understandings of the nation, gender, and geography, to develop fundamentally new forms of political struggle, and to challenge the most powerful people and institutions in the world. They draw on U.S. scholar Betty Reardon's efforts to rethink the meaning of the word *security* and the chain of practices that flow inexorably from its prevailing definition.[28]

Coming from a country that has been serially colonized since the seventeenth century and that has been occupied militarily by both the United States and Japan, OWAAMV activists cannot solve their problems within a single national context. Disadvantaged by colonialism, racism, and sexism, they cannot afford to embrace national liberation, antiracism, or feminism as their sole axis of identity and struggle. Coming from a small island with a limited population in a corner of the world far removed from metropolitan centers of power, they must forge alliances with outsiders based on political affinities and identifications, rather than counting on the solidarities of sameness that sustain most social movements.

Perhaps most important, the members of the OWAAMV draw upon their situated knowledge and historical experiences as Okinawan women to challenge the world to face up to the grim realities of warfare, to its collective, cumulative, and continuing costs. As eyewitnesses and heirs to brutal combat on their island in 1945 that killed more than 130,000 civilians (one-third of the local population) and tens of thousands of Japanese and U.S. military personnel, the OWAAMV find it impossible to celebrate organized violence and masculinist militarism.[29] They see military bases in their country as sources of environmental pollution, as land stolen from local farmers that could have been put to other uses, and as the driving force behind the presence of commercial sex establishments, sex tourism, and rapes of civilian women and girls by military personnel in the lives of Okinawan women.

The OWAAMV have produced new ways of being and new ways of knowing that contain enormous generative power. They do not seek to make their nation militarily superior to others. Instead, they argue that massive preparation for war increases rather than decreases the likelihood of violence. Moreover, they argue that the military spending that purports to create security for states and financial institutions creates only insecurity for people, especially for women, children, and the elderly.

They charge that expenditures on war serve to contain and control people like themselves who oppose the global economic system and who challenge neoliberal policies designed to privatize state assets, lower barriers to trade, and limit the power of local entities to regulate the environment.

Perhaps most important, they call for a new definition of *security*, one that places the security of people and the environment ahead of the security of the state and financial institutions. They "queer" the nation—not because they take an explicit position on the rights of gays and lesbians, but because they interrupt and contest the narrative of patriarchal protection upon which the nation-state so often rests.

The OWAAMV argues that real security would mean protection of the environment so that it can sustain natural and human life. They call for meeting the survival needs of humans by guaranteeing food, clothing, shelter, health care, and education to the people of the world. They insist that human dignity and cultural differences be respected and honored. They articulate a clear set of specific and particular local demands—calling for full investigation of crimes against women in Okinawa, for the reduction, realignment, and removal of U.S. military bases from their island, and for full disclosure of toxic contamination caused by the presence of the military and mandatory cleanup of toxic hazards. Yet the group also advances broader general demands in their call to transcend national barriers and create a peaceful global society free of military violence.

The uniquely generative vision of the OWAAMV emerged from concrete conditions and from lessons learned during social struggle. Women activists from Okinawa had long participated in local, national, and global feminist organizations. At home, they fought for the establishment of rape intervention crisis centers and for training programs to teach work skills and set up cooperative businesses to draw women away from sex work in Okinawa.[30] At the national level, they sought to elect women as representatives in the Japanese parliament and to secure more resources for the Okinawan prefecture from the federal government. On a global scale, Okinawan women sent representatives to the World Women's Conference in Nairobi, Kenya, in 1985 and in Beijing, China, in 1995 to present their ideas about military violence as a feminist issue before the worldwide women's movement.[31]

Operating on the local, global, and national levels inhibits recourse to atomized, discrete, and homogenous identities. Different battlefronts require diverse tactical responses. Male leaders from Okinawa routinely pressure the OWAAMV to subordinate their gender-specific concerns about women in favor of nationalist (and patriarchal) politics built on a simple binary opposition between Okinawa and Japan. At the national level, many Japanese expect the Okinawans to subordinate their particular grievances to a broader (and presumably unified) nationalist project of advancing the interests of Japan against the interests of other nations. On a global level, leaders and citizens from the "G8" (financially powerful, industrialized) nations expect the OWAAMV to favor the kinds of "security" framed by neoliberalism and the war on terror. Even among their fellow feminists at global meetings, the OWAAMV find that not all feminists recognize the disproportionate funds expended on military matters to be a distinctly feminist issue. These uneven and contradictory pressures compel the OWAAMV to reject singular identities and narrow nationalisms and instead to create dynamic, fluid, and ever-changing alliances, affinities, and identifications.

On September 4, 1995, a day when feminists from Okinawa were attending the World Conference on Women in Beijing, China, a twelve-year-old Okinawan girl was abducted and raped by three men serving in the U.S. military—Marcus Gill, Rodrico Harp, and Kendrick Ledet.[32] Although merely one of a long list of brutal crimes and sexual assaults against Okinawan women, this case provoked mass mobilizations and protests for three main reasons. First, the twelve-year-old girl who had been raped had the courage to reveal what had happened to her and to demand that her assailants be prosecuted. In the past, many rape victims felt so shamed by the crime that they did not have the emotional and psychic resources necessary for bringing charges. Second, U.S. military officials responded to the assault in callous and contemptuous ways, doing more to protect the rapists than to seek justice for their victim. Okinawan police officers identified the suspects on September 8, for example, but the military did not turn the three men over to local authorities until September 29. Admiral Richard C. Macke wondered in public why the soldiers had rented a car in order to carry out the abduction, noting that "for the price they paid to rent the car, they could have had a girl."[33] Third, the OWAAMV formulated an analysis of the event that placed it in a credible broader context for large numbers of Okinawans, while at the same time developing strategies and tactics that linked education and agitation about a matter of immediate anger to more abstract, complicated, and complex structural issues.

Less than three weeks after the rape occurred, the OWAAMV organized a mass speak-out that featured one-minute testimonies by individual women about their experiences with sexual violence on the island. The "one minute on the mike" format departs from the practices of most social movement rallies that promote eloquent oratory by inspirational leaders. Eloquence in this setting comes from accumulation of individual voices that transforms private and personal horrors into public issues. Several speakers revealed for the first time in public that they too had been raped by military personnel. The opening provided for their testimony by the "one minute on the mike" format helped demonstrate how women collectively share much of the burden imposed on Okinawa by military occupation.[34] One month later, more than eighty thousand Okinawans congregated to voice their opposition to the continued presence of U.S. military bases.

The OWAAMV insisted on placing one publicized rape in a broader context. They refused to be drawn into arguments designed to isolate the crime from the conditions that enabled it to take place. The commander of U.S. forces in Japan, Air Force General Richard Myers, dismissed the rape as an isolated incident, insisting that it was not representative of the character of "99.99 percent of U.S. forces."[35] This would be the same position Myers would subsequently take in 2004 as chairman of the U.S. military's joint chiefs of staff in response to reports of systematic abuse of prisoners by U.S. soldiers and privately hired mercenaries in Iraq.[36] Yet a study published in the conservative Japanese newspaper *Nihon Keizai Shimbun* revealed that the Okinawan prefectural police had implicated U.S. service personnel in 4,716 crimes between 1972 and 1999, an average close to one per day. At U.S. military bases in Okinawa the incidence of reported rapes is eighty-two per every one hundred thousand persons, exactly double the rate in U.S civilian life, where it stands at forty-one per every hundred thousand people.[37]

The three convicted rapists received sentences of seven years in prison for the main perpetrator and six and a half years for the two judged to have been in more subordinate roles. The OWAAMV insisted, however, that the incarceration of the perpetrators of this particular rape did not address the systemic causes and consequences of military violence. When reporters asked OWAAMV spokespersons if they were satisfied with the severity of the sentences, the group issued "An Appeal for the Recognition of Women's Rights," which outlined how broader cultural and social structures create the conditions through which rape becomes routine.[38]

The mother of one the defendants refused to believe that her son had committed the crime because she knew him as a good boy who attended church every Sunday. Okinawan peace activist Fumiko Nakamura commented, "I believe the woman when she says her son was a decent boy; I think it was the military that changed him, though. How could he *not* be affected by the drills they perform? They actually learn to kill and hurt people. That's what I'm opposed to."³⁹

The OWAAMV range widely in search of allies. The group's Suzuyo Takazato reaches out to U.S. women, noting that "when the military personnel return home to the U.S., their training in violence returns with them; thus, the targets of violence now become their American wives and girlfriends. For these reasons, I believe that we must work together to achieve not only an Okinawa free of military bases and military forces. We must also transcend national barriers and create a global society that is free of military violence."⁴⁰ Takazato's words proved to be eerily prescient. In August 2006, twenty-two year-old college student Lauren Cooper was found dead in her apartment in Kennesaw, Georgia, next to the body of Kendrick Ledet, one of the three marines convicted of the 1995 rape in Okinawa. Police officers concluded that Ledet committed suicide after raping Cooper and killing her by striking her on the head with a blunt instrument.⁴¹

Ties between women in Okinawa and the United States make strengths out of potential weaknesses. As Japanese citizens, Okinawan women can do little to influence legislators in the United States, whose decisions determine a great deal that happens to them. U.S. women, however, can mobilize as citizens on behalf of understandings of peace and security that would benefit women in Okinawa. Women with U.S. and British passports generally find it easier to obtain travel visas and raise money than women from nations in Asia, Africa, and Latin America. These relative privileges could be sources of conflict, but the network struggles to connect privilege to responsibility, to recognize that differences open up productive possibilities for differentiated contributions to a common struggle.⁴²

The organizational learning that emerges within groups engaged in collective struggle has shaped the kinds of alliances, affiliations, and identifications linking the OWAAMV and other Okinawan peace groups to similar organizations around the world. The significant number of Filipina women working as dancers in Okinawan bars catering to U.S. service personnel made it logical for members of the group and the supporters to see resemblances between their work and the activities to stop the sexual degradation of women by the Gabriela network headquartered in the Philippines.⁴³ Memories of military occupation by the Japanese Empire and the conditions created by the contemporary presence of U.S. troops in the region encourage pan-Pacific feminism based on recognition of "families of resemblance" linking women in Okinawa to women in Korea, the People's Republic of China, and Taiwan.[44]

Initially, the OWAAMV raised a demand for the removal of U.S. troops from Okinawa. Their contacts in the East Asia-U.S.-Women's Network Against Militarism, however, helped them see that removing military installations from Okinawa would only increase military presence elsewhere—in the Philippines, Puerto Rico, or Hawai'i. Gradually, the OWAAMV and their network came up with a new cognitive map, one that envisioned Puerto Rico as part of a greater "pacific" region, a "place" defined by history rather than by mere geography, as part of what literary scholar Allan Isaac terms "the U.S. tropics." This cognitive remapping transcends the juridical and geographic boundaries of nations. It focuses on affinities among aggrieved groups as the basis for a new cultural morphology. It configures physical places as intersections and crossroads rather than atomized entities divided by binary oppositions between "us" and "them."

The OWAAMV specializes in tactics that enact the world they envision. In rallies at the Kadena Air Force Base and outside meetings of a G-8 Summit held in Okinawa, they deployed human chains—thousands of demonstrators linking arms to surround a site of presumed power. The potential strength of the masses becomes visible and tangible as participants encircle and contain the sites that purport to police and control them.

The particularities of place—and the effects they have on politics, culture, and social struggle—do not disappear under these circumstances. On the contrary, they can become stronger. The U.S. military presence in Okinawa brings to the fore key aspects of the history of both the United States and Okinawa. Okinawans may not know all the details about the betrayal of abolition democracy and the start of overseas imperialism in the nineteenth-century United States. They inherit the legacy of those events in highly visible ways, however, through the presence of U.S. troops sent overseas to protect the acquisition of markets, raw materials, investment opportunities, and cheap labor for U.S. capitalists, as well as in the racial tensions among U.S. soldiers that the island inherits along with the troops. Okinawan feminist Nobuko Karimata remembers how increases in the military population on Okinawan bases during the Vietnam War led to racial incidents and hate crimes. "Most of the trouble occurred in Koza," she recalls. "The streets up there were segregated; one area for whites, and another for blacks. If a white guy went over to the black area, he was beaten up. And likewise, if a black guy entered white territory, he was beaten up. Seemed like we were always hearing about bar fights and robberies, rapes and traffic violations in that area."[45]

On some occasions, representatives of the tradition of abolition democracy have been important allies to the Okinawan people. In 1970, black U.S. soldiers sympathetic to the Black Panther Party supported popular Okinawan demands that a U.S. serviceman be prosecuted for a hit and run accident that had killed a local Okinawan.[46] In 1998, U.S. feminists and peace activists supported the OWAAMV peace caravan by introducing them to U.S. audiences and elected officials.[47] Yet the beneficiaries of abolition democracy in the United States have also profited directly from the oppression and suppression of Okinawan women over the years in many ways. U.S. citizens are largely unaware of the consequences of their support for military spending and the deployment of U.S. troops overseas. Okinawans, however, live with the presence of thirty-eight military bases in their prefecture. Okinawans have lost land, foregone development opportunities, been exposed to environmental hazards, and surrendered political sovereignty as a consequence of military occupation.[48] Despite the best efforts of dedicated activists, however, militarism in the United States rarely faces sustained or substantive critiques. To be sure, Americans hold debates about whether women or gays should be included in the military, or about whether violence should be unleashed in any particular situation, but the larger issues of how security gets defined and who suffers as a result remain largely unaddressed. The OWAAMV and their allies attempt to stimulate that discussion.

Groups like the OWAAMV have much to teach us. They build on the situated knowledge and the privileged viewpoint on power made possible and necessary by their local history. They work simultaneously at local, national, and global levels, within and across national boundaries, identity groups, and movements. Consistent with Chela Sandoval's concept of "differential consciousness," they can be feminists, environmentalists, pacifists, national citizens, anticolonial nationalists, anticorporate activists, and anti-imperialists at different times and at different moments. Sandoval explains, "Differential consciousness requires grace, flexibility, and strength: enough strength to confidently commit to a well-defined structure of identity for one hour, day, week, month, year, enough flexibility to self-consciously transform that identity according to the requisites of another oppositional ideological tactic if readings of power's formation require it; enough grace to recognize alliance with others committed to egalitarian social relations and race, gender, sex, class, and social justice, when these other readings of power call for alternative oppositional stands."[49]

Connection to activist groups enables scholars to ask and answer research questions in novel and generative ways. Just as the activism of the OWAAMV led them to unexpected affinities and affiliations with environmental and women's groups in Puerto Rico, Hawai'i, and the Philippines, scholars transformed by their involvement in social movements often transcend traditional research boundaries. Kosuzu Abe combines her primary research about Puerto Rican rent strikes and squatters' movements in New York City with activism in support of social movements in Okinawa. She sees commonalities as well as differences with Okinawa in her interpretations of African American struggles for reparations, rent strikers and squatters, and diasporic Puerto Ricans in New York City. Abe participates in an informal network named Project Disagree that promotes imaginative and imaginable projects for social transformation by bringing musicians and artists into dialogue with activists and academics.[50]

Yoko Fukumura and Martha Matsuoka combine scholarship about the OWAAMV with activism within the movement. When making scholarly presentations, they answer questions carefully and precisely. They do not foreground their own observations or opinions but instead present the politics, aspirations, and epistemology of the organization as accurately as possible. Although well aware of the generative nature of the ideas emanating from the struggle in Okinawa and proud to deploy them in their own work, Fukumura and Matsuoka regret that scholars have sometimes misrepresented the group's perspectives, undermined their projects, and been unwilling to help the group's work even while using evidence about it for their own professional advancement.[51] Fukumura and Matsuoka have become members of the OWAAMV network, and as a result they view others in the network not as subjects but as "allies and partners in shared and mutually defined work."[52]

Robin D. G. Kelley describes social movement activism as a kind of poetry. "Progressive social movements do not simply produce statistics and narratives of oppression," he argues. "The best ones do what great poetry always does: transport us to another place, compel us to imagine a new society."[53] Scholars and activists alike need to create that kind of poetry, to carry out sophisticated intellectual tasks. They both have a stake in the creation of new institutions, practices, and identities. Scholars need activism to change the spaces in which we work, to alter power relations in the communities our students come from and to which they return. Activists need the perspectives, connections, and critiques that scholars can supply.

Kelley warns us that oppositional social movements are often contained, marginalized, and repressed because they are more articulate about what they are against than about what they are for and because they spend too much time raging against the status quo and too little time building the seeds of a new society in the shell of the old. He urges us to look to the poetics of struggle and lived experience, to the utterances of ordinary folk, to the cultural products of social movements, and to the reflections of activists to "discover the many different cognitive maps of the future of the world not yet born."[54]

Social movements and socially minded scholars have their work cut out for them in this day and age. They may not look or sound like the people presented as experts on our condition by the political system or the media. But serious people who believe that they have important work to do can get a lot done. Like the authors of abolition democracy in the United States or the advocates of global justice in the OWAAMV, they have the potential both to break the chains and to steer the ship.

NOTES

Chapter epigraphs are taken from Miriam Ching Yoon Louie, *Sweatshop Warriors* (Boston: South End Press, 2001), 95, and Walter Rodney, "The African Revolution," in *C. L. R. James, His Life and Work*, ed. Paul Buhle (New York: Allison and Busby, 1986), 34.

1. Melvin Oliver and Thomas Shapiro, *Black Wealth: White Wealth* (New York: Routledge, 1995); Thomas Shapiro, *The Hidden Costs of Being African American* (New York: Oxford Univ. Press, 2004); Douglas Massey and Nancy Denton, *American Apartheid* (Cambridge, MA: Harvard Univ. Press, 1993).

2. Charles Lee, "Beyond Toxic Wastes and Race," in *Confronting Environmental Racism: Voices from the Grass Roots*, ed. Robert Bullard (Boston: South End, 1993); Laura Pulido, *Environmentalism and Economic Justice: Two Chicano Struggles in the Southwest* (Tucson: University of Arizona Press, 1996); Julie Sze, "Expanding Environmental Justice: Asian American Feminists' Contribution," in *Dragon Ladies: Asian American Feminists Breathe Fire*, ed. Sonia Shah (Boston: South End Press, 1997).

3. Julie Sze, *Noxious New York* (Cambridge, MA: MIT Press, forthcoming); João Costa Vargas, *Catching Hell in the City of Angels* (Minneapolis: University of Minnesota Press, 2006).

4. Roderick Ferguson, *Aberrations in Black* (Minneapolis: University of Minnesota Press, 2004); Juana Rodriguez, *Queer Latinidad* (New York: NYU Press, 2003); David Roman, *Acts of Intervention* (Bloomington: Indiana University Press, 1998).

5. Yoko Fukumura and Martha Matsuoka, "Redefining Security: Okinawa Women's Resistance to U.S. Militarism," in *Women's Activism and Globalization:*

Linking Local Struggles and Transnational Politics, ed. Nancy A. Naples and Manisha Desai (New York: Routledge, 2002).

6. Ruth Wilson Gilmore, *Sunshine Gulag* (Berkeley: University of California Press, 2007).

7. Walden Bello, *Dark Victory: The United States and Global Poverty* (London: Pluto Press, 1999).

8. John Holloway, Elofna Palaez, and Eloina Palaez, *Zapatista: Reinventing Revolution in Mexico* (London: Pluto Press, 1998); John Holloway, *Changing the World without Taking Power* (London: Pluto Press, 2005).

9. Al Gedicks, "Racism and Resource Colonization," in *The Struggle of Ecological Democracy*, ed. Daniel Faber (New York: Guilford Press, 1998), 272–92, and "Resource Wars against Native Peoples," in *The Quest for Environmental Justice: Human Rights and the Politics of Pollution*, ed. Robert D. Bullard (San Francisco: Sierra Club Books, 2005), 168–87; Zoltan Grossman, "Let's Not Create Evilness for This River: Interethnic Environmental Alliances of Native Americans and Rural Whites in Northern Wisconsin," in *Forging Radical Alliances across Difference*, ed. Jill Bystydzienski and Steven P. Schacht (Boulder, CO: Rowman and Littlefield, 2001), 32–51; Stephanie Tai, "Recent Development," *Asian Law Journal* 6 (May 1999): 190–91; Amy Kastely, "Esperanza v. City of San Antonio: Politics, Power, and Culture," *Frontiers: A Journal of Women's Studies* 24 (2003): 185–99.

10. Hazel V. Carby, "The Multicultural Wars," *Radical History Review* 54 (1992): 7–18.

11. Grace Lee Boggs, *Living for Change* (Minneapolis: University of Minnesota Press, 1998), 145–46.

12. Francesca Polletta, *Freedom Is an Endless Meeting: Democracy in American Social Movements* (Chicago: University of Chicago Press, 2002), 22.

13. James Kyung-Jin Lee, *Urban Triage: Race and the Fictions of Multiculturalism* (Minneapolis: University of Minnesota Press, 2004), xxx.

14. Alfie Kohn, *The Schools Our Children Deserve* (New York: Houghton Mifflin, 2000).

15. Robin D. G. Kelley, *Freedom Dreams* (Boston: Beacon, 2002), 8.

16. Robin D. G. Kelley, *Hammer and Hoe* (Chapel Hill: University of North Carolina Press, 1991); Barbara Ransby, *Ella Baker and the Black Freedom Movement: A Radical Democratic Vision* (Chapel Hill: University of North Carolina Press, 2003); Charles Payne, *I've Got the Light of Freedom* (Berkeley: University of California Press, 1995); Polletta, *Freedom*.

17. Kelley, *Hammer and Hoe*; Ransby, *Ella Baker*; Payne, *I've Got the Light*; Polletta, *Freedom*.

18. Quoted in Polletta, *Freedom*, 187.

19. Vincent Harding, *There Is a River: The Black Struggle for Freedom in America* (San Diego: Harvest/HBJ, 1993), 10.

20. W. E. B. Du Bois, *Black Reconstruction in America, 1860–1880* (New York: Touchstone, 1995).

21. Avery Gordon, "Something More Powerful Than Skepticism," in *Keeping Good Time* (Boulder, CO: Paradigm Press, 2004), 193.

22. Cedric Robinson, *Black Marxism* (Chapel Hill: University of North Carolina Press, 1983), 238.

23. Karl Marx, "The German Ideology," in *The Marx-Engels Reader*, ed. Robert C. Tucker (New York: W. W. Norton, 1972), 193.

24. George Jackson, *Blood in My Eye* (Baltimore: Black Classic Press, 1990), 182.

25. Lisa Duggan, *The Twilight of Equality: Neoliberalism, Cultural Politics, and the Attack on Democracy* (Boston: Beacon Press, 1993).
26. Jurgen Habermas, *Legitimation Crisis* (Boston: Beacon Press, 1975), 71.
27. Yoko Fukumura and Martha Matsuoka, "Okinawan Resistance to U.S. Militarism," in Naples and Desai, *Women's Activism*, 239–66.
28. Martha Matsuoka, pers. comm., September 8, 2006; Betty A. Reardon, "Human Rights as Education for Peace," in *Human Rights Education for the Twenty-first Century*, ed. George J. Andreopoulos and Richard Pierre Claude (Philadelphia: University of Pennsylvania Press, 1997), 21–34.
29. Laura Hein and Mark Selden, "Culture, Power, and Identity in Contemporary Okinawa," in *Islands of Discontent: Okinawan Responses to Japanese and American Power*, ed. Laura Hein and Mark Selden (Lanham, MD: Rowman and Littlefield, 2003), 13.
30. Linda Isako Angst, "The Rape of a Schoolgirl: Discourses of Power and Gendered National Identity in Okinawa," in Hein and Selden, *Islands of Discontent*, 151.
31. Carolyn Bowen Francis, "Women and Military Violence," in *Okinawa: Cold War Island*, ed. Chalmers Johnson (Carlsbad, CA: Japan Policy Research Institute, 1999)190.
32. Chalmers Johnson, "The 1995 Rape Incident and the Rekindling of Okinawan Protest against the American Bases," in Johnson, *Okinawa*, 116.
33. Ruth Ann Keyso, *Women of Okinawa: New Voices from a Garrison Island* (Ithaca London: Cornell University Press, 2000), 139.
34. Francis, "Women and Military Violence," 191.
35. Johnson, "1995 Rape Incident," 114.
36. Brian Knowlton, "Top General Blames 'a Handful' for Abuse in Iraq," *International Herald Tribune*, May 3, 2004.
37. Johnson, "1995 Rape Incident," 114–15.
38. Francis, "Women and Military Violence," 193.
39. Keyso, *Women of Okinawa*, 52.
40. Francis, "Women and Military Violence," 199.
41. Yolanda Rodriguez and Aixa Pascual, "Police ID Ex-Marine as KSU Student's Killer," *Atlanta Constitution*, August 22, 2006, Metro Section, 1.
42. Martha Matsuoka, pers. comm., September 8, 2006.
43. Fukumura and Matsuoka, "Redefining Security"; Keyso, *Women of Okinawa*, 120.
44. Hein and Selden, "Culture, Power," 15.
45. Keyso, *Women of Okinawa*, 87.
46. Yuichiro Onishi, "The Making of the Freedom Struggle in U.S. Occupied Okinawa: A Study in Anti-imperialist Coalition Building in Koza, 1969–1972," unpublished paper, 2005.
47. Fukumura and Matsuoka, "Okinawan Resistance."
48. Hein and Selden, "Culture, Power," 5.
49. Chela Sandoval, *Methodology of the Oppressed* (Minneapolis: University of Minnesota Press, 2000), 60.
50. Kosuzu Abe, pers. comm., July 31, 2006. See "Project Disagree," http://disagree.okinawaforum.org, and "Peace Music," www.peace-music.org (both accessed July 8, 2007).
51. Yoko Fukumura, pers. comm., August 18, 2006.
52. Martha Matsuoka, pers. comm., September 8, 2006.
53. Kelley, *Freedom Dreams*, 9.
54. Ibid., 10.

PART II

Troubling the Terms

4. Activist Groundings or Groundings for Activism?

The Study of Racialization as a Site of Political Engagement

Jemima Pierre

> In response to [those] who have argued against both liberatory and global theoretical descriptions of and prescriptions for the times, we will see that the present age is global, and indeed all-too-global, in a tragic way.
>
> LEWIS GORDON, *Her Majesty's Other Children: Sketches of Racism from a Neocolonial Age*

It is the middle of a hot afternoon in Accra, Ghana, and I am in the cool, quiet office of a university administrator at the University of Ghana, Legon. He is an old friend. We had first met when I was an undergraduate exchange student years earlier. I was in his office attempting to establish formal university affiliation, one that would allow me access to resources such as the library while I was in Accra conducting ethnographic research. For most of the conversation, we had focused on the logistics of my request. Once we had covered the necessary details, we settled down into a more informal conversation about life in Africa compared to the United States, his time as a student in California, my time in Ghana in the early 1990s, and, of course, my intellectual trajectory that had brought me back to the country. He was especially curious about my research project, which, throughout the discussion, I had avoided talking directly about. Finally, he asked me directly: "What is it exactly that you are researching here?" "I'm here to study race in Ghana," I replied. "Race in Ghana?" he asked. He chuckled, shook his head, and said: "Race. That's a U.S. problem."

I could certainly understand his comment. Indeed, my own reluctance to disclose my "research project" in Ghana anticipated his reaction. I was often in this awkward position—made to reveal and discuss a topic that, at best, was seemingly a nontopic for most people in a country like Ghana. This certainly was not South Africa, the United States, or even Brazil, where issues of race, race relations, and, more importantly, racial discrimination were often beneath the surface in any discussion of society. My research topic—as well as my ambivalence and apprehension about its significance—posed a specific kind of challenge to ethnographic fieldwork. After years of traveling to Ghana as a student, as a year- and months-long resident, and finally as a researcher, I was convinced that race was deeply implicated in structuring daily life and individual identities in Ghana. But few Ghanaians I encountered believed this to be the case—at least few felt compelled to name certain processes and interactions as "racial." And on a broader level, race was rarely, if ever, discussed as a major *national* problem. Instead, individual acts of racial discrimination—more often than not implicating the large and established Asian and Lebanese communities—would only occasionally be discussed on morning radio shows or in local "dailies."[1] It became clear early on in my research that I was not going to find an organized movement against racial discrimination in Ghana. Indeed, I often wondered if there was truly a need for such a movement. This was Ghana, after all; the first Black nation to gain independence on the African continent, the home of Pan-Africanism, and a country governed by Black people. Who was I to suggest that there could exist a subtle (though sometimes not so subtle), but nevertheless insidious, racial hierarchy that informed local realities—and worked in conjunction with broader, indeed global processes—as much as it did in other places in the African diaspora? Furthermore, if the racializing and racially explicit experiences and practices that I research in Ghana are often not conceptualized as "racial," then are the people whose experiences I describe *racially* oppressed? Further, if there is no specific, articulated notion of racial disparity—and there are no direct organized group struggles around matters involving "race" in which I can actively participate—then how can I claim, as I often do, that my work about race in Ghana is "activist"?

Not only are these questions central to my ethnographic work in Ghana, but I hope they reflect my hesitant approach to the discussion of the relationship between "research" and "activism" in academia. There is a wide spectrum of what is considered activist research, and consensus within this spectrum is hardly forthcoming. Recently, for example, George Marcus (2005) has asserted that "activism" has become "a condition or circumstance of most fieldwork projects" and has suggested that contemporary younger ethnographers present a "challenge to the classic dispassionate scholar" (677). This view makes the relationship between research and activism quite amorphous. Does a researcher need only to be passionate about a topic of research for the research project to be "activist"? Is it enough to just critique a system (or political process or sets of relationships)? At the same time, Marcus seems to also promote a more conventional notion of activist research with his discussion of the role of the "public" anthropologist, suggesting that many contemporary scholars are engaged with organized movements. Thus activist research and scholarship seemingly occur only when the researcher is involved in organized struggle with the specific marginalized group under study. The researcher may actively lobby local or national governments on behalf of this group or conduct necessary research and other related activities to help legitimate the group's claims for redress from their oppressors. This type of activism rests on the assumption that the "researcher" and the "community" in active struggle can have a mutually beneficial, mutually transformative, egalitarian relationship. There is also a sense that the marginalized group represented in this type of research, or collaborating with the researcher, is organized and self-consciously working against a particular system or hierarchy of oppressions. Furthermore, in some cases, it is understood that the marginalized group itself determines the direction of the activist project and, in the process, structures the academic's research agenda. When such requirements are not met, the researcher may not be considered politically engaged enough or, worse, her research will not be considered activist. In many conversations about research and activism, I have often felt this uncomfortable tension, that my research is somehow less legitimately "activist" because I do not engage or take explicit research cues directly from an organized marginalized local group already involved in its own program for liberation.

I focus on this tension here as I attempt to discuss the nature of activism and political engagement in academic research. My ethnographic study of the discourses and practices of race and racialization in urban Ghana will frame this exploration. First, I examine how the study of racialization—and the attendant project of naming and delineating racial practices in Ghana—can be considered a site of political engagement with a community, and, in many senses, activist. At the same time, I challenge certain conventions of activist research, offering an alternative to thinking about research, activism, and politics in academia. Here I draw and expand upon Lewis Gordon's notion of "academic activism" and his model of "instrumental politics" to delineate the ways that academics, Black academics in particular, are potentially engaged in the ideological and embodied struggle to define identity and construct community. Furthermore, convinced that anti-Black oppression is global, and inspired by Black feminist analyses of the politics of knowledge production, I will suggest that what is most powerful and crucial—and therefore "activist"—for our research is our conscious deployment of our unique individual and collective positionality toward truly liberatory politics (Collins 2000; Lorde 1984). I devote the second part of the essay to demonstrating the inescapable connection between positionality—individual and collective—and global relations of power, and I interrogate the implications for activist research. I discuss how my site of research developed from my active and conscious contestation of knowledge production on contemporary Africa, as well as my relationship, as a Black woman, to structures of race, class, gender, and power across a number of geopolitical and sociohistorical spaces—Haiti/the Caribbean, the United States, and Ghana/West Africa. My research project, therefore, emerged out of my activist response to my particular positionality through time, space, and place, necessarily establishing my "activist groundings" with marginalized Black peoples against global and interlocking systems of oppression.

These two aspects of my discussion are inextricably linked, as they clearly both reveal the relationship between the personal and the political and show how the personal and political are also academic. My research topic and my ability to engage it reflect a conscious politics, one that is shaped by (and in turn shapes) my personal structural location within a global racial hierarchy in which patriarchal whiteness holds the power position. Yet, as Black and Third World feminist theorists often remind us, such "personal" relations to structures of power are hardly ever completely personal or individual. Both in my unlikely position within the U.S. academy as Africanist anthropologist and in my work on race—and its various hierarchies and contestations—in postcolonial Africa, I situate my research within a broader Black radical tradition (Robinson 1999; see also Mupotsa 2006) that has, as its goal, global Black emancipation. This essay thus offers a way to rethink activist research, arguing not only that our individual projects in the "field" are intimately connected to our individual/collective experiences as positioned researchers but, more importantly, that it is possible to consciously and constructively deploy such experiences in ways that are potentially liberatory.

It was a late summer Saturday evening in Accra, and I was with two male Ghanaian friends on our way to visit a new entertainment facility in the city. This new facility had been advertised extensively in the weeks prior to its opening and had promised a number of exciting activities for its opening night. Located in the near-exclusive (and foreign-populated) section of the Osu neighborhood in Accra, the entertainment club already commanded a privileged status—and assumed clientele—among the area's numerous social spots. My friends and myself were aware of this and had expected to encounter a group of club-goers who were mostly white expatriates or members of local elite groups, which included Ghanaians as well as Lebanese and Indians. We were nevertheless surprised at the blatant and, initially, unapologetic way we were turned away from the club.

We pulled up into the parking lot of the club, parked, got out, and headed for the entrance. As we were approaching, three partygoers (whom we assumed to be expatriates)[2] walked out the front door, apparently leaving for the evening. When we reached the front door, the Ghanaian guard quickly and menacingly blocked our way, indicating that we were not allowed in. As he did so, he told us the entry fee. Jack, one of my companions, responded by asking the guard why he felt compelled to quote us the entry fee without prompting. When the guard did not respond, Jack announced that we had enough money to pay the cover charge, and we all continued to head toward the front door. The guard then told us that we were not allowed in, stammering that the club was too full to allow anyone else in. Jack repeated that we had enough money to pay, but the guard continued to refuse us admission. My friends and I looked at one another in disbelief. Peter, our other companion, said in an incredulous, but nevertheless agitated, tone: "We just saw three people leave, and we are only three, so why isn't there space for us?" Sensing our increasing suspicion and hostility, and hoping to control the situation, the guard quickly called over the club manager. The Ghanaian manager came, looked us over, and echoed the guard, adding that, since the club was to close in less than an hour, it was imprudent to let us in. Peter quickly rebuffed, "You won't let us in because we are Black and Ghanaian!" The manager, obviously uncomfortable with the developing situation and how such public disagreement in the doorway might affect the image of the club on opening night, began to soften his look and shift his stance. By this time, however, Peter's anger was brimming. He admonished the Ghanaian guard and manager against "covering for the foreigners" and doing "the white man's dirty work," adding that "you turn against your own people for them." Jack then began walking away from the front door and motioned for us all to leave. As we headed toward the parking lot, Peter exclaimed out loud, "I can't believe our people! These [expatriates and foreigners]—they come over here, disrespect us, [sleep with] our women, and [then] treat us like animals!"

Much like Jack and myself, Peter was quite aware that our exclusion from the club had to do with much more than its being "full." We all quickly recognized how our collective treatment that evening resonated with a set of race- and class-inflected practices that structure local relationships in urban Accra, even the most mundane. Indeed, the significance of our being turned away from the club that summer evening had (at least for me) less to do with how the Ghanaian guard and manager acted, as Peter would say, on behalf of the foreign or "white" owners of the club to exclude us; I felt, instead, that this experience of exclusion and white privilege, while unique, was not exceptional in Ghana or many other places in postcolonial Africa. Many other experiences I have had in Ghana (and in other parts of western, eastern, and southern Africa), as well as many discussions with friends, colleagues, and informants, confirm this. It is not unusual, as I have found out, for the average white man behind me in the queue at the bank in downtown Accra, or at the Internet café in certain neighborhoods, at times to be served before me. My friend Ama once recollected a time when she had accompanied her husband to the airport, only to be turned away at the front door because she was not the one traveling. The guard at the door insisted that she present a plane ticket as well as passport in order to accompany her husband to the airline ticket counter inside the airport. As she was arguing with the guard, she remembered, a white man walked right passed them and into the airport without being stopped and asked for documentation. When she pointed out this discrepancy to the guard, he sheepishly allowed her into the airport without comment. "He was embarrassed," Ama told me, especially after she forcefully admonished him for behaving in a way that allowed whites privileges not available to Ghanaians in "our own country."

Of course, my work does not characterize white racial positionality as unrestrained privilege. To be sure, negotiations of identity in this contemporary urban and postcolonial space rest on a complicated set of historical realities, assumptions, and relationships that work, often, to structure a hierarchy of positions that is by no means completely rigid. White positionality in Ghana often does not go unchallenged. It is challenged in the most mundane of instances, from local stereotypes of whiteness ("The white man is selfish," or "The white man is greedy"), to assumptions about unrestricted white wealth as well as white gullibility in Ghana, to blatant and active denunciations of white privilege by various individuals and groups. Nevertheless, what makes this discussion significant is the fact of the discussion itself. In other words, the enjoyment of rights, advantages, and special treatment by a relatively small group as a result of wealth or social status derived seemingly from membership in a particular minority "race" is significant inasmuch as it occurs in modern-day Ghana. Ghana is considered an African country with no clear-cut history of de jure apartheid or white settler politics, and ultimately no overt anti-Black racism. At the same time, the country is well known and admired for its extensive history of Pan-Africanist politics and activism. The assumption, then, is that issues of white privileged positionality—indeed, issues of race—cannot, and should not, be considered issues at all. As a researcher committed to global racial and social justice, how do I negotiate my many experiences of discourses and practices that ensure the continued privileging of whiteness in this society?

To speak of white racial privilege in Ghana is not to deny the complexities of ethnic, gender, nation, class, and religious differences and hierarchies. Nor is it to disregard Ghanaian agency and counternarratives against what can be considered "white" norms. Indeed, what has always struck me as I have lived in and worked in Ghana is the contradictory nature of perceptions of and relationships with white Europeans and North Americans (including honorary "white" others, such as the Chinese and South Asians), as well as with those from the "Diaspora." I remember well a discussion that emerged as I sat in a barbershop in Osu (a tourist-filled area in Accra) chatting with friends. We had been curiously watching the stream of "foreigners," mostly young white visitors, and commenting on their characteristic backpacks, Birkenstocks, and ever-present water bottles, when the discussion suddenly turned to "Black Americans." After a group of obviously non-African Blacks passed by,[3] Eddie, one of the barbers in the shop, turned to me and said: "I hate these Black Americans. They don't try like the whites do. They don't eat our food; they don't learn our language. The whites ride the 'tro-tros'[4] and are very friendly. [The Black Americans] are not like the whites!" As a couple of the other barbers nodded in agreement, I searched for a response. Indeed, Eddie felt comfortable speaking this way to me about the "Black Americans" because I was not considered one of "them." Most of my friends and acquaintances knew of my Haitian background, a fact, as I will show below, that determined my specific insertion and positionality, and indeed structured my research, within urban Ghana. As Eddie spoke, I quickly thought of both the many whites I knew who did not engage Ghanaian life and culture in the way he described and the many Blacks ("Black Americans") who did. Specifically, I thought about the group that I often call "development whites," whose members are sheltered from directly interacting with Ghanaian life and society by their air-conditioned SUVs, heavily guarded houses, and patronage of near-segregated coffeehouses and bars (Pierre 2003). I also tried to reconcile Eddie's obvious disdain toward African Americans with Ghanaians' continued fascination with that same group, particularly in terms of popular culture. In fact, even as Eddie spoke, I could not help but notice the hip-hop music video (featuring African American artists) playing on the television screen above his head. My response to Eddie and my other acquaintances in the barbershop was measured: "Well, I know a lot of Black Americans who do try, and I know a lot of whites that don't." That, too, also yielded a few nods from the other barbers. Yet the sting of Eddie's comments remained with me, even though this was certainly not the first—or last—time I would hear such views about African Americans articulated. Elsewhere, I have suggested that Ghanaian perception of and interaction with African Americans is at once specific, complex, and under continuous negotiation (Pierre 2002). On one level, it speaks to the ambivalence with which African Americans are perceived, as well as the transnational race-inflected stereotypes through which this ambivalence is revealed and experienced. Ironically, there seems to be a very specific familiarity with African Americans—or at least with an *image* of that group—that points to an intricate and entrenched racial discourse. This complicated relationship, I suggest, results from a combination of Ghanaian sentiments of identification with, resentment of, respect for, but indignation toward, all at once facilitating a certain fascination with, "Black Americans."

These discussions about "Black Americans" and "whites," as well as discussions about Lebanese and Indian racism toward the local population, affirmed for me the existence of a complex system of identity formation and politics of race in Ghana. Such discourses also demonstrate how the constant negotiation of race, space, and place occurs on multiple levels. To be sure, my analysis of racialization processes does not begin— or end—with simple comparisons of Ghanaian perception of and interaction with foreign whites or Blacks. Nor does it naively map (or "impose") a U.S. racial model onto postcolonial Africa. Instead, I take as a point of departure Charles Mills's (1998) observation that so-called Third World nations are part of a global racialized economy "dominated by white capital and white lending institutions . . . [and] by the cultural products of the white West" (102). My research seeks to uncover the not-so-hidden transcripts of "race" and processes of racialization that color daily life in this urban, postcolonial setting and that are all the while indexed to a broader transnational template about difference, power, and status. Along the road of racial discovery in urban Ghana, I have encountered a number of competing racial projects that both challenge and reaffirm the global racial hierarchy in which whiteness holds the power position. These racial projects, though always contradictory, point to a concrete set of practices and lived experiences. My focus remains on how Ghanaian engagement with whiteness (and whites) and with discourses of race, racial difference, and privilege occurs within a broader set of processes whereby local relationships continue to be structured by current global configurations of identity, economics, and politics. These current relationships, I maintain, are continuing the legacy of a very recent history of colonial/imperial domination. As "whiteness" is being more firmly entrenched into global economic and cultural order and is seemingly inseparable from power, "race"—understood in both its broad and its specific sense—matters, in Ghana and elsewhere.

Charles Mills (1998, 99–100), echoing Walter Rodney (1981), argues that we need to understand the racial dimension of historical and contemporary European domination, which has as its basis a white power system that is international in character and reaches across the globe. He suggests that we conceptualize "global white supremacy as a political system . . . a particular kind of polity, so structured as to advantage whites." Mills points out, however, that the system of white supremacy most often works with other systems of domination and that it is not "synchronically uniform or diachronically static" (100). Rather, global white supremacy is a "family of forms"; it has different articulations, in different parts of the world, and evolves over time, arranging different racial projects—of labor, cultural representations, legal standings, and so on. The key element in this global system, however, is the privileging of whites/whiteness. This privileging "is compatible with a wide variety of political and institutional structures . . . [while] the status of nonwhites within the system can vary tremendously . . . without threatening the crucial premise of nonwhite inferiority" (101).

Mills's characterization of the contemporary world order as something thoroughly structured by and through notions of racial difference is convincing and radical. In this climate of "postracial" theories of identity and politics, where notions of race and racism—particularly in Africa—are safely archived in the annals of a distant colonial (or apartheid) past, it is quite unfashionable to speak of race in the postcolonial era. After all, did not the anticolonial movements, and ultimately independence, ensure the demise of white racial power in Africa? We could also say, as some scholars are quick to suggest, that the notion of white racial privilege in Africa is not accurate, since individual whites were as much victims as Africans of international capitalism (Ranger 1979, 1998). Furthermore, aren't contemporary problems in Africa attributable to "ethnic conflicts," the neoliberal economic reforms taken on by Africa's corrupt and bourgeois leaders, or class differences? And what of the sensational, anthropological favorite, the "occult," which is characterized as one of the most important sources of identity, culture, and politics for local African communities? Given the dearth of research and analysis on what can easily be called de facto racial subordination and white privilege in most postcolonial spaces, one would have to think that these issues were both unimportant and unnecessary. Thus, as Faye Harrison (2002, 52) reminds us, those who study "international relations still need to be urged to include race and racism in their analysis of global politics and political economy." Scholarship and research on contemporary Africa are explicitly implicated in this process of conceptual and epistemological "deracialization."

Within my own academic discipline of anthropology, there seems to be an exclusionary theoretical and methodological dynamic that affords no "conceptual entrée" (Mills 1998) for issues of race. This lacuna is particularly glaring in Africanist anthropology and ethnographic research. Race and processes of racialization are not considered relevant research topics for contemporary African societies (outside southern Africa). Indeed, in my intellectual and personal engagement with many U.S. Africanists, my research topic in urban Ghana is often met with blank stares or agitated questioning of either my use and definitions of "race" (as opposed to "ethnicity" or "culture") or my research methodology. And as I constantly struggle against the defensive posture I am forced to take because of this research topic, I often marvel at how most ethnographic representations of contemporary Africa fail to fully appreciate and incorporate the continent's continued racially inflected local practices and their relationships to global relations. This is despite acknowledgment of Africa's long historical engagement with racial slavery and colonialism, as well as its ongoing dialogue with communities in the African diaspora.[5] Thus, within this (white-washed?) intellectual and political context, the very act of naming and mapping out these processes—of persistent, postcolonial African articulation with local and global politics of race and racialization—is expressly radical and importantly activist.

This too is the context in which I—as a racially marked, gendered individual—live and conduct research in Ghana. When I was working in Ghana, the challenge was to highlight processes of racialization in a way that explicitly linked me, my Ghanaian counterparts, and people of African descent more generally to a powerful and all-encompassing, and globally significant, conversation about race. To be sure, this is a world where continental Black African communities continue to have to justify their existence and prove their humanity against Western-constructed discourses of pathological cultural/political practices and unfair socioeconomic policies. This is a world where Africa's contemporary economic marginalization—a marginalization that breeds despair and makes daily survival an achievement—is directly linked to its historical subjugation to global racial colonial exploitation. This is a world where race—and its articulations with gender, sexuality, nation, and class—matters. My research project is informed by this reality and my overwhelming and paralyzing sense of anger and frustration at such glaring examples of the racisms of Western global hegemonies. It is a perspective about which I make no apologies. But it is also a perspective that obligates me to engage my intellectual endeavors concretely and politically—to begin, at the very least, naming the multiple inequalities that continue to structure our contemporary world.

I first went to Ghana in the fall of 1993 as an undergraduate exchange student from Tulane University. In our group of ten from Tulane University, I was one of two students of African descent. During the six months of my stay, daily confrontations with what I saw to be the privileging of the white students in our group and their attainment, without effort, of the respect and admiration of the local population deeply saddened and frustrated me. At the same time, I felt intimately connected to Ghanaian students on the University of Ghana campus and to Ghanaian society in ways that the whites in our group could only imagine. My Haitian background, and my early experiences of living in a so-called Third World country, no doubt contributed to the ease of my transition in a postcolonial urban African space. My new Ghanaian friends were fascinated by this peculiar background, a fact that helped to structure my relationship to Ghana in particular and to Africa in general. In later trips, after I began studying anthropology, I became much more aware of the complexities of local notions of race, culture, and identity in Ghana. I was particularly struck by the ways in which local discourses and practices of race—the high status of whiteness, light-skin color valorization, and notions of "Black" consciousness—resonated, and were in dialogue, with transnational/diasporic identity politics and formations. But I was also cognizant of the continued fascination with all things "African American." The mid-1990s were particularly significant as rap music and hip-hop culture exploded on Ghanaian radio frequencies and television stations. I often vacillated between frustration and intimation as I struggled to cope with both the continued privilege of white expatriates in Ghana and young Ghanaians' identification with Blacks from the Diaspora, myself included.

Yet my positionality in Ghana remained both complex and contradictory. I was often seen as a "Black American," primarily due to my U.S.-accented English, my dress, and, of course, my status as a former college student from "America." But I was also Haitian. And often, especially in my younger years, I felt the need to foreground this identity as I sought to escape the criticism and condemnation directed toward "those Black Americans." Nevertheless, I did not fully escape a particular type of gendered racialization. Though undoubtedly privileged by all that my permanent residence status in the United States represented, I could not help but feel frustration at what I saw as my own negative racial marginalization as a dark-skinned woman of African descent in Ghana. My dark skin color and the company of my friends often hid my "foreignness" from many Ghanaians and left me open to being mistaken for, and therefore treated like, a Ghanaian in a number of contexts. This allowed me acute glimpses into practices and assumptions that fostered racio-cultural inequality, as well as the differential treatment meted out to some locals in certain contexts. The moments in which I felt as explicitly marginalized because of my "race" or skin color were few and far between. But the psychological effects of continually being structured within (and against) practices and discourses that perpetuated global notions of white privilege, even in Ghana, were enough to force me to recognize that sites of racialization extend beyond the country's borders, across the Atlantic through to the Caribbean and the United States.

My varied experiences in Ghana were filtered through my complex positionality as a Black immigrant permanently residing in the United States. My insertion within the U.S. racial hierarchy as a Haitian Black woman also positions me against practices and discourses of white domination and privilege. Whereas my immigrant status in the United States, when revealed, sometimes offers me a certain amount of distinction in the face of a homogenizing racialization,[6] it also marks me as "Black" and Other, contributing to my marginalization. Thus racialization positions me within damaging U.S. discourses of Blackness that establish my membership in a community of the racially stigmatized and marginalized. And as my racially marked body travels through communities and across borders, it encounters and engages the changing sameness of race, a sameness that reveals the power and consistency of global white supremacy across time and space. The positioning of Haiti and continental and diasporic Africa as racialized "Black" spaces within a global hierarchy of races, cultures, and nations (Trouillot 1994) structures my relationship both with U.S. society and with other racialized Black peoples. My complex positionality as a Haitian person of African descent living in the United States and conducting research in Ghana therefore led to my particular insertion in discourses and practices of race and racialization on *both* sides of the Atlantic. In this context, the "activist" part of my research was both my acceptance and deployment of this positioning toward a project of global Black emancipation. As such, my experiences and structural positioning (across local and global spaces) effectively delineated my "sites" of research and, ultimately, my ethnographic "site" of political engagement.

The uniqueness of my presence in Ghana—in Africa—as a Black academic researcher speaks volumes to a history that places knowledge production squarely within the *longue durée* of European empire making that saw the racialized sociopolitical and intellectual construction of Africa and peoples of African descent. In this history, anthropology's own disciplinary development as both the "handmaiden of colonialism" (Gough 1968) and the "science of races" through its specific engagement with Africans and African realities places me in dubious company (Pierre 2006). In addition, the "racial division of labor" (Armory 1997) that continues to plague U.S.-based African studies ensures that most research in Africa, on Black Africans, will be done by foreign whites. This curious situation is rarely openly acknowledged, much less engaged (see, however, the critiques by such African scholars as Mafeje 1998; Mabokela and Magubane 2004; Mamdani 1990; Zeleza 1997). Nevertheless, this type of race-inflected knowledge production works with and through broader, indeed global, sociopolitical and economic processes that continue to marginalize Africa and peoples of African descent. It explains, for example, the inability of many (white) Africanist researchers to interrogate the myriad processes that implicate global white supremacy in Africa. My unexpected academic presence in Ghana, my research topics and ethnographic methods, my political engagement—all work, however inadvertently, to challenge these structures of power. My entrée, then, within this world of knowledge production is, in and of itself, subversive. Accordingly, I expected my research project to yield strong and effective critiques of, and concerted efforts against, global white supremacy. The study of racialization quickly became for me an active site of political engagement and contestation. Soon I realized how specific political proclivities, coupled with ethnographic research practice, allowed for direct critique and advocacy.

In this, my research work follows theorization by Black and Third World feminists that challenges masculinist and racially hierarchical knowledge production by recognizing the value of affirming different ways of knowing (Guy-Sheftall 1995; Collins 2000; James 1997; King 1988; Mabokela and Magubane 2004; Ransby 2001). The affirmation of personal narrative and experiences as legitimate sources of knowledge and the recognition that positionality (i.e., "standpoint") is an important aspect of all knowledge production have endowed us with key theoretical and methodological insights. Further, the possibilities available for the insertion of the racialized female at the center of both research and analysis have opened up a space for nuanced critiques and innovative praxis. As a Black woman researcher and Africanist anthropologist, I have found myself occupying a space that was never intended for me. Given this reality, I have realized that consciously positioned, politically engaged ethnographic practice has the potential to provoke uncommon conversations, the exploration of unpopular sociocultural issues, the discussion of seemingly "nonsubjects," disagreements, debates, and active participation in local constructions of identity. When I am engaged in ethnographic research in Ghana, my theoretical and political orientation is clear from the kinds of questions I ask, the conversations I have with friends, colleagues, and interviewees, the debates I have about the prevalence of white racial privilege and Black subordination, and my advocacy of organized (local and global) movements against racial injustice. I recognize that research is always already informed by one's presuppositions and political commitment. But I privilege the kind of situated knowledge (Haraway 1988) that enables the contestation of global white supremacy.

Claiming this specific space of privilege has directly informed my ethnographic research on racialization in Ghana, as well as my understanding of activism. In Ghana, the framing and content of my interview questions have opened up a space for extremely uncommon yet productive discussions. This was clear to me after I conducted a series of focus-group interviews with University of Ghana students on race, whiteness, and Blackness. Throughout the discussion and after, student participants remarked how they appreciated the conversation. Most said that the discussion had helped them articulate views on a topic that they had not realized, until the interviews, was an important issue to them. A number of students admitted that that topics of difference, like ethnic and national difference, and of the economic and cultural privilege of "foreigners," were all actively, though informally and haphazardly, discussed among their friends but that they were not discussed in the language of "racialization" or racial privilege or understood within the context of a global economy of race. Though I recognize how novel these conversations could have been for many of the students, I maintain that there is an already established racial vocabulary in urban Ghana that is variously deployed—from direct references to a racially distinct group of "whites" to the specific identification of "Black Americans" as distinct from other expatriate populations.

My daily interactions with friends and colleagues also allowed for much debate and discussion on uncommon or unpopular topics. For example, during my stays in Ghana, I variously and continuously express anger, frustration, and indignation about certain practices and discourses that I believe affirm particular gender and racial hierarchies. My experiences often ensure that I will subject my Ghanaian friends to numerous conversations about the repeatedly obvious relevance of "race" as well as the perpetuation of "gender" disparity and discrimination. For example, Ama's tale of white racial privilege (recounted above) emerged during a heated debate among a group of my Ghanaian friends about the nature of white positionality and the seeming desire for lighter skin in the country. The discussion opened up when one of them, John, recounted an encounter with a "bleacher" at the outdoor Makola market in downtown Accra and remarked on the problematic nature of skin bleaching in Africa. As they and I sat around at a party on Sunday afternoon, a debate erupted about the reasons behind the recent proliferation of skin bleaching and the government's attempt to stem the practice. John insisted that bleaching was only a matter of aesthetic preference, while Fred charged that it was a form of internalized racism. Ama dismissed the problem as of one of "poor street women" who were too uneducated to know better. Afua, a married graduate student, offered instead that, though bleaching was primarily a "lower-class" phenomenon, many middle- and upper-class women bleached, not only "to gain more favor from their husbands," but also, they believed, to secure better promotions in their places of employment. Joseph insisted that "they do it because they hate Black. They want to be white." The debate continued, leading to a more broad-ranging discussion about light skin color privilege, gender, class, and, of course, race.

My point here so far has not been to make any claims about my ability to singlehandedly open up discussions about race in Ghana. I am highlighting a well-known anthropological conversation about the need to acknowledge and take seriously the idea of "situated" nature of research and knowledge production. Donna Haraway (1988, 590) stressed the importance of recognizing an "epistemology and politics of engaged, accountable positioning," paradigmatically reframing our understanding of social scientific research and knowledge production as partial and limited, as situated. "Situated knowledges," in this sense, are those "ruled by partial sight and limited voice"; they are knowledges for "the sake of connections and unexpected openings"; they are community formation—about "accountability and responsibility for translations and solidarities" that link partial views, partial voices, into a collective vision (590). I am also highlighting the important Black feminist contribution to the conversation about such situated knowledges that argues that racially marked gendered bodies yield differential structured positions. While it is the generally accepted truism that positionality—of both the researcher and the researched—always informs the research process, I believe this ideal has not thoroughly been appreciated or, more importantly, fully exploited in ways that are truly liberatory. I make no apologies about my positionality; instead, I engage its complications and contradictions while consciously deploying it in ways that allow for the mutual transformation of the research, the researcher, and the researched. My particular insertion among communities in urban Ghana, and within various sets of discourses, has also directly informed my approach to research, the kinds of questions I ask, the language I use to ask them, the mutual identification of me and those in my research community, and my well-known political goal for worldwide Black emancipation. However inconsequential this approach may seem, it allows for my active participation in cultivating the grounds of activism that holds promise for active collective contestation of the growing global hegemony of racial and economic privilege.

I want to bring together the various strands of this essay by exploring in greater detail the relationship between research and activism and the relationship of activist research to politics, positionality, and my study of racialization in urban Ghana. Lewis Gordon (1997, 199) points to the tendency, in discussions of activism in academia, to construct a caricature of "inactive thinkers in opposition to people of action." For some, even the notion of "activist research" implies a particular form of action, one that is diametrically opposed to the idea of intellectual work. Given that many view critical theory and general liberal-humanist rhetoric to be the limits of legitimate engagement or activism on the part of scholars, the call for direct action and community involvement has merit (see Hale 2006). I wonder, however, whether this dichotomous confrontation might constrain the discussion and close off other possibilities for exploring the relationship between scholarship/research and activism. For example, the idea that real activism can occur only through collaboration with organized (and presumably marginalized) local groups is based on a set of assumptions—that marginalized group politics are inherently progressive, or that social transformation can occur only through such politics—that do not *necessarily* hold true for all organized movements. This view of activism has a disciplinary function, where participation in organized group politics serves as the only authenticating source of political commitment (Weigman 2002). My experiences in urban Ghana, as well as in other national and cultural contexts, should demonstrate that our activist visions cannot be so constrained.

Gordon (1997) provides a unique perspective on research and activism that complements my suggestion that progressive activist research is also about experience, particularly the conscious deployment of one's positionality for liberatory politics. He argues that the Black academic is activist by virtue of his or her gendered racialized positionality not only within the university setting but also within the broader, indeed global, context of "anti-Blackness." Thus the political struggles for "Black academic activists" are complex, multiple, and overlapping, and they span various communities. Gordon suggests that an important site of struggle for the Black academic activist is ideology. The Black academic's activism is importantly ideological because of participation in what he calls a *geist*, a "spirit war": "In that war, there is a struggle for no less than self-identity from the local level straight up to the global level. In that task, the black academic activist's task is to help forge an identity . . . that facilitates all of the other levels of activism" (202–3).

My work advocates this reinterpretation of academic activism. I see my research in Ghana as part of a set of struggles that span geographical areas, ideological transformations, gendered/racial positionalities, and time periods. In fact, it is the anti-Blackness that I continue to experience as my racially marked and gendered body travels across time and space that affirms and strengthens my ongoing commitment to global Black emancipation.

Yet while I endorse Gordon's argument about the special position of the Black academic, I also question the subtext of "inevitability" that undergirds his formulation of (progressive) Black academic activism.[7] It is true that, as racialized/gendered subjects in a white supremacist world, Black academics often have the opportunity to respond critically and through progressive politics. Such a response, of course, has the potential to inform research practices and knowledge production. However, this response should not be assumed because it is not necessarily inevitable. Rather, it is contingent and only one of many different possibilities. For example, in Ghana (as well as other places), I could have responded to my racial and gendered marking with dismissal, denial, or oblivion. I did not have to directly challenge white privilege through my work; I could have easily ignored or deemphasized the workings of a global racial hierarchy in Ghana. I could have not drawn on my experience and positionality to conduct research on racialization. Similarly, a researcher could very well be working on behalf of, or in collaboration with, a marginalized group and still reinforce certain hierarchies, especially if the researcher does not actively and consciously interrogate his or her own identity, positionality, and experience within structures of power. Thus it is not inevitable that the Black academic will respond in "activist" (i.e., antistructure, antihierarchy) ways. To me, what seems important for exploring the relationship between activism and research is that we recognize activism as an integrated process, as a combination of positionality/experience and politics. For the contextually marginalized Black academic, the acceptance and politically progressive deployment of our experiences during research can be potentially transformative. At the very least, it is activist—and patently so.

Reflecting upon his positionality as an academic engaged in political activism, W. E. B. Du Bois described the impossibility of being a detached "and calm seeker for truth." He reported how his work was instead informed by "an inner emotional reaction at the things taking place about [him]" (quoted in Gordon 1997, 203). A similar "inner emotional reaction" fuels my research work and hence my activism. I am quite aware that such reaction is the result of a certain set of experiences linked with particular sympathies and progressive politics. In this way, my research work in Ghana is never just about "research," nor is it confined only to Ghana; it is part of an integrated process of activism that is as much informed by global race and gender relations and class and political hierarchies as it is by my movement through the myriad spaces that construct and affirm such relations and hierarchies.

NOTES

I would like to thank João H. Costa-Vargas for introducing me to this forum, and Charlie Hale for his support and encouragement throughout the project.

1. The local name for the many newspapers that are published daily throughout Ghana.

2. It is not difficult to distinguish between local members of the population and "expatriates" in Accra. Given that Ghana is a relatively racially homogeneous Black nation, given the reality that the majority of expatriates are (and are seen as) racially distinct from the local population, and given the known locations where foreigners congregate, it becomes easier still to quickly determine expatriate identities.

3. African Americans are easily detectable in Accra by their physical appearance—dress, usually lighter skin color, and U.S.-English accent.

4. "Tro-tros" are minivans that are used as vehicles for public transportation. They are the cheapest way to travel throughout the country and are mostly used by the working poor.

5. Within the disciplines of anthropology and history, there is a burgeoning literature on race and colonialism, especially historical ethnographies (see especially Comaroff and Comaroff 1991; Cooper and Stoler 1997; Stoler 2002). Yet with few exceptions (particularly Mamdani 1996, 2001), race drops out of analyses of postcolonial societies, implying—incorrectly, I think—the complete demise of racially structured relationships in this historical moment.

6. I am referring here to the literature on Black immigrants in the United States that often points to the potential of such immigrants to escape brutalities of U.S. racism/racialization by stressing individual "ethnic" and "cultural" distinctions. Elsewhere, I have argued that this position both lacks critical analysis of how processes of racialization work in the United States and is itself a racializing move that uses racist stereotypes of African Americans to make a case for advocating Black immigrant cultural distinction (Pierre 2004).

7. I thank Charlie Hale for his insights in this section.

REFERENCES

Armory, Deborah. 1997. "African Studies as American Institution." In *Anthropological Locations: Boundaries and Grounds of a Field Science*, edited by Akhil Gupta and James Ferguson. Berkeley: University of California Press.

Collins, Patricia Hill. 2000. *Black Feminist Thought*. 2nd ed. New York: Routledge.

Comaroff, Jean, and John Comaroff. 1991. *Of Revelation and Revolution: Christianity, Colonialism, and Consciousness in South Africa*. Vol. 1. Chicago: University of Chicago Press.

Cooper, Frederick, and Ann Stoler, eds. 1997. *Tensions of Empire: Colonial Cultures in a Bourgeois World*. Berkeley: University of California Press.

Gordon, Lewis. 1997. *Her Majesty's Other Children: Sketches of Racism from a Neocolonial Age*. New York: Rowman and Littlefield.

Gough, Kathleen. 1968. "New Proposals for Anthropologists." *Current Anthropology* 9 (5): 403–35.

Guy-Sheftall, Beverly. 1995. *Words of Fire: An Anthology of African-American Feminist Thought*. New York: New Press.

Hale, Charles R. 2006. "Activist Research v. Cultural Critique: Indigenous Land Rights and the Contradictions of Politically Engaged Anthropology." *Cultural Anthropology* 21 (1): 96–120.

Haraway, Donna. 1988. "Situated Knowledges: The Science Question in Feminism and the Privilege of Partial Perspective." *Feminist Studies* 14 (3): 575–99.

Harrison, Faye. 2002. "Global Apartheid, Foreign Policy, and Human Rights." *Souls* 4 (3): 48–68.

James, Joy. 1997. *Transcending the Talented Tenth*. New York: Routledge.

King, Deborah. 1988. "Multiple Jeopardy, Multiple Consciousness: The Context of Black Feminist Ideology." *Signs* 14 (1): 42–72.

Lorde, Audre. 1984. *Sister Outsider: Essays and Speeches*. New York: Crossing Press.

Mabokela, Reitumetse, and Zine Magubane. 2004. *Hear Our Voices: Race, Gender and the Status of Black South African Women in the Academy*. Pretoria: University of South Africa Press.

Mafeje, Archie. 1998. "Anthropology in Post-Independence Africa: End of an Era and the Problem of Self-Definition." *African Sociological Review* 2 (1): 1–43.

Mamdani, Mahmood. 1990. "A Glimpse at African Studies, Made in the USA." *CODESRIA Bulletin*, no. 2, pp. 7–11.

———. 1996. *Citizen and Subject: Contemporary Africa and the Legacy of Late Colonialism*. Princeton: Princeton University Press.

———. 2001. *When Victims Become Killers: Colonialism, Nativism, and the Genocide in Rwanda*. Princeton: Princeton University Press.

Marcus, George. 2005. "The Passion of Anthropology, circa 2004." *Anthropological Quarterly* 78 (3): 673–95.

Mills, Charles. 1998. *Blackness Visible: Essays on Philosophy and Race*. Ithaca: Cornell University Press.

Mupotsa, Danai. 2006. "A Radical Black Feminist Standpoint? A Very Preliminary Discussion of Methods and Methodology." *Postamble* 2 (2): i–viii.

Pierre, Jemima. 2002. "Race across the Atlantic: Mapping Racialization in Africa and the African Diaspora." PhD diss., University of Texas at Austin.

———. 2003. "Race, Migration, and the Re-imagining of Contemporary African Diasporas." *Wadabagei: A Journal of the Caribbean and Its Diaspora* 6 (3): 37–78.

———. 2004. "Black Immigrants and the 'Cultural Narratives' of Ethnicity." *Identities: Global Studies in Culture and Power* 11 (2): 141–70.

———. 2006. "Anthropology and the Race of/for Africa." In *The Study of Africa*, edited by Paul T. Zeleza, vol. 1. Dakar: CODESRIA.

Ranger, Terence. 1979. "White Presence and Power in Africa." *Journal of African History* 20:463–69.

———. 1998. "Europeans in Black Africa." *Journal of World History* 9 (2): 255–68.

Ransby, Barbara. 2001. "Black Feminism at Twenty-One: Reflections on the Evolution of a National Community." *Signs* 25 (41): 1215–21.

Robinson, Cedric. 1999. *Black Marxism: The Making of the Black Radical Tradition*. Chapel Hill: University of North Carolina Press.

Rodney, Walter. 1981. *How Europe Underdeveloped Africa*. Washington, DC: Howard University Press.

Stoler, Ann L. 2002. *Carnal Knowledge and Imperial Power: Race and the Intimate in Colonial Rule*. Berkeley: University of California Press.

Trouillot, Michel-Rolph. 1994. "Culture, Color, and Politics in Haiti." In *Race*, edited by Steven Gregory and Roger Sanjek. New Brunswick: Rutgers University Press.

Weigman, Robyn. 2002. "Academic Feminism against Itself." *National Women's Studies Association Journal* 14 (2): 18–37.

Zeleza, Paul T. 1997. Manufacturing African Studies and Crises. Dakar: CODESRIA.

5. Globalizing Scholar Activism

Opportunities and Dilemmas through a Feminist Lens

Jennifer Bickham Mendez

Today's world is rife with contradictions—globalization is said to cause the world simultaneously to come together and fall apart (Barber 2001). Cultural, economic, and political integration occur alongside increasing disparities between the rich and the poor. An oft-overlooked contradiction of globalization is the serious challenge posed to knowledge production—particularly within the social sciences. Globalization disrupts underlying assumptions of what constitutes a society, traditionally defined as the confines of the nation-state, and destabilizes embedded notions of "place" and "community." Thus globalization calls into question social science's primary object of scholarly inquiry, and in so doing challenges researchers to reconfigure their units of analysis and rethink methodologies (Gille and Ó Riain 2002; Albrow 1997; Marcus 1995).

Another source of critique of social science methods is activist research—an area that has garnered increased recognition in recent years. Debates about the blending of political commitments with scholarly research agendas raise epistemological questions about the nature and value of research as well as political questions about how scholarship might act in conjunction with struggles for social justice. The convergence of both critiques at this juncture calls out for critical analysis.

This chapter will explore the new roles and shifting challenges that globalization has brought to politically engaged research and will examine the possibilities and limitations of this kind of research practice in globalized contexts. First, I provide background regarding political and economic globalization and its implications for social science methodological and analytical strategies. Next, I turn to a discussion of the many variants of "activist research," also known under a myriad of other labels—"participatory," "action," or "community-based" research to name a few. Unfortunately, the debates about activist research have often failed to engage with the important work on feminist methods, and I attempt to bridge this gap by highlighting the contributions of feminism(s).

The next sections of the chapter discuss the collaborative, coalitional politics that has emerged among social justice struggles under globalization in which information has gained new predominance as a form of power. To explore possible sites of intervention for the scholar activist, I draw from a diverse set of research experiences that I argue shed light on the implications and contradictions of "doing" research activism in globalized contexts. The forays into politically engaged research that I discuss include collaboration with a woman's labor organization in Nicaragua (see Bickham Mendez 2005); my active participation in the coalition that spearheaded a living wage campaign (LWC) and a resulting unionization of housekeeping staff at my home institution, the College of William and Mary (Bickham Mendez and Spady, forthcoming); and my more sporadic involvement with the global justice and antisweatshop movements in various capacities.

These experiences, though characterized by different levels of participation and combinations of activist and research activities, all involve collaboration with fragile coalitions of organizations and individuals struggling in opposition to the effects of economic globalization. Such movements connect the global and the local in meaningful ways, and for this reason I refer to their occurring in "globalized contexts." Finally, collaborations with these movements reveal the internal power dynamics based on race, class, gender, and sometimes nationality that have flavored and shaped their strategies, practices, and coalitions. I argue that scholars committed to incorporating social justice goals into their research must identify and grapple with the dilemmas associated with collaborative roles, but without the illusion that these spaces will ever be contradiction-free.

Although this chapter analyzes the many dilemmas and complexities associated with globalizing scholar activism, my aim is to move beyond critique. I seek to write in the space between the practical and the theoretical—the space of strategy. The chapter concludes with a discussion of how researchers might meet the challenges of undertaking activist research projects in globalized contexts. I argue that insights from feminist debates on research methodologies and epistemologies offer both highly relevant critiques and important tools for confronting these challenges.

Given current configurations of global and institutional relations of power, a difficult but worthwhile position for the scholar activist is that of "strategic duality," in which the researcher uses her position within the academy to contribute to social justice struggles, while at the same time working to place at the center alternative voices and ways of knowing (see Charles Hale's introduction to this volume). I contend that elements of feminist thought such as a process-oriented view of social change and transformation, a redefinition of "the political," a reconceptualization of power as multidimensional and intersectional, and a feminist critique of conventional academic epistemologies represent key resources for striking the delicate balance necessary for this strategic positioning.

GLOBALIZATION AND THE SOCIAL SCIENCES

The past two decades have witnessed impressive shifts within the international political economy. The worldwide expansion and intensification of post-Fordist capitalism, characterized by flexible accumulation strategies and the dramatically increased mobility of capital and labor, which create and maintain a global system of production, is just one aspect of the phenomenon known as "globalization" (Jameson 1998; Sklair 1995; Castells 1993; Sassen 1988). For the sake of conceptual clarity (the term's abstractness has rendered it almost meaningless), I use globalization to refer to the historical, economic, social, and cultural processes through which individuals, groups, and institutions are increasingly interconnected on a worldwide scale (Glick Schiller 1999). Other social, cultural, and political processes that this term encompasses—to name a few—include the global dominance of neoliberal political orientations that emphasize free-market forces and divest the state of social welfare responsibilities, the increased power and autonomy of supranational institutions (e.g., the World Trade Organization, International Monetary Fund, and World Bank), the development of the corporate media and telecommunications technologies and the resulting global flows of information and cultural forms, and the internationally recognized political framework of human rights. Defined in this way, global processes reach worldwide, although certainly not completely or evenly, and occur largely as disembedded from specific national territories or localities. Thus under globalization geography becomes disassociated from community "belonging." For example, economic globalization has resulted in a process of "Third-Worlding" of urban and even rural and suburban areas in the United States. Corporations can outsource jobs to "Third World" locations to reduce labor costs, or, in the case

of industries such as meatpacking, poultry production, and the hotel industry, they can "import" Third World workers and wo95
rk conditions.

Globalization challenges the long-standing social science assumption that "nation-states" are the appropriate locus for examining social relations and the idea that "community" is rooted in geographical location. It calls into question how the "social" should be defined, so as to capture and make understandable how social relations occur across local settings and in deterritorialized space (Gille and Ó Riain 2002; Albrow 1995; Giddens 1991). Theorists have developed different analytical techniques for studying the contradictory processes associated with globalization, which both homogenize and foster connections across space and time but also play themselves out in locally situated and historically specific ways. Some have focused attention on the interconnections and interplay between the global, local, and national (Guidry, Kennedy, and Zald 2000; Sassen 2001). Transnational studies ground the abstract and general notion of globalization by centering analysis on the ways in which everyday people react to, engage with, and even re-create and influence global processes (Glick Schiller 1999; Smith and Guarnizo 1998; Basch, Glick Schiller, and Blanc 1994).

The challenge of globalization has particularly significant implications for ethnography, since it destabilizes the very notion of "thereness" that is so crucial to participant observation. Ethnographers have responded by shifting their units of analysis to flows of cultural products, people, discourses, and commodities across national borders and space; social relations and fields of activities that transcend borders; and politically produced and contested "places" or place-making projects (Gille and Ó Riain 2002, 274–77; see also Alvarez 2006; Burawoy et al. 2000; Freeman 2000).

ACTIVIST RESEARCH

Although the label *activist research* implies the existence of an agreed-upon, neat, and clearly demarcated category, in reality this general rubric encompasses a broad and messy array of disciplinary approaches, schools of thought, and methodological practices. The common thread, however, is that the goal of activist research is to reconfigure knowledge production so as to shift power and control into the hands of the oppressed or marginalized, privileging "subjugated knowledges" (P. Collins 2000) and transforming oppressive social structures (Stoecker 1999; Hall 1993; Fals-Borda and Rahman 1991).

The aim of politically engaged research is to form an admittedly fragile and difficult coalition between "grassroots," "local," or "experiential" knowledge and "theoretical," "data-driven," or "scholarly" knowledge. Brought together by a shared commitment to social transformation, academic and popular knowledge would collaborate to reject "the asymmetry implicit in the subject/object relationship that characterizes traditional academic research" and would achieve "authentic participation" in the research process (Fals-Borda 1991, 5). Proponents of activist research explicitly reject the role of the disinterested researcher and actively seek ways to be politically *relevant* in the "real world" (Stoecker 1999).

Like advocates for activist or participatory research models, feminists have raised questions about what the purpose of research is and whose voices are privileged in the production of scholarship. Feminists, particularly "Third World" feminists and feminists of color, have been some of the most vocal critics of the ways in which research reproduces hierarchies of power and have waged powerful critiques of positivism, calling into serious question the role of the detached, objective (read: male) observer (Cancian 1992; Haraway 1988; Mohanty 1991; P. Collins 2000). In endeavoring to construct projects "by, for and about women," they have sought to develop research methods that transcend the dichotomies of "theory" and "praxis," researcher and researched, and subject and object (Hesse-Biber and Leckenby 2004, 209–10; Naples 2003, 4–5). Similarly, feminists have called attention to unexamined political dimensions of research methodologies and have endeavored to engage in methods that reflect a commitment to the transformation of gendered power structures (Wolf 1996; Visweswaran 1994; Sprague and Zimmerman 1993).

Unfortunately, the literatures on and practices of activist research have not always included women, focused on gender issues, or engaged with feminist debates about research methods (Maguire 1996, 2001). As Maguire so astutely points out, feminist perspectives are, in fact, integral to politically engaged research. A feminist conceptualization of power not as a zero-sum game but as multisited and "situated and contextualized within particular intersubjective relationships" (Bloom 1998, 35) sheds light on the complex ways in which power is embedded in research relationships. Feminism(s) have called attention not only to whose voices are missing or marginalized from knowledge production but also to how categories like "community," "the oppressed," or "the poor" might obfuscate differences of power and perspective. Feminist advocates for activist research argue for incorporating (multiple) feminist perspectives—including the second-wave feminist principle that the personal is political—into research models to interrogate who exactly is empowered (and who is not) by activist scholarship (Maguire 1996, 111; Naples 2003).

There are many other critiques of politically engaged research. For example, some have worried that "community-based" research will become a patronizing endeavor through which the privileged—out of charitable goodwill—will "help" the powerless, further blurring structural inequalities (Bowes 1996; Nyoni 1991, 112). Yet increasingly scholars have devoted efforts to politically engaged research (broadly defined). The promise of activist research is the possibility that one can contribute to counterhegemonic projects and that intellectual activity can become social justice work. Furthermore, the promotion of activist research could be a step toward democratizing knowledge production and developing a blueprint for a vastly different society (Gaventa 1993, 40). This is no small payoff. If we are committed to pursuing research aimed at social justice goals, then what are the possibilities and limitations that we confront in today's globally interconnected world? And how do we critically assess the very real contradictions of engaging in collaborative, coalitional initiatives as they occur within the spaces that emerge under globalization?

COALITIONAL POLITICS AND OPPOSITION TO THE EFFECTS OF GLOBALIZATION

One of the many paradoxes of globalization has been its intensification and spread from "above" *and* "below."[1] The spread of electoral democracies of recent years,[2] although uneven and perhaps better categorized as involving "market-based" democracies (Robinson 2003), combined with the transnationalization of public spheres, has resulted in the emergence of an increasingly "global" civil society. Transnational social movements and local and international nongovernmental organizations (NGOs) have exploded onto the international political stage as new actors that challenge the tenets of neoliberal and corporate globalization (Brecher, Costello, and Smith 2000).

Political movements that struggle against the effects of globalization have occurred at the national, regional, and often transnational levels and have taken the form of coalitional initiatives, bolstered, and in some cases made possible, by the advancement of information technologies (Starr 2001). The development of these technologies and the "time-space compression" (Harvey 1990) that has resulted from them have allowed for the diffusion and exchange of information, resources, strategies of contention, and discourses of resistance (Guidry, Kennedy, and Zald 2000).

Examples of transnational, coalitional movements of this kind are numerous and include the struggles of the EZLN in Chiapas, Mexico, the global justice movement and subsequent World Social Forums; the antisweatshop movement, and transnational networks that comprise human rights, women's, workers', and pan-indigenous movements.

Labor has also experienced a resurgence of internationalism with cross-border networks and partnerships forged among workers' organizations. For example, the 1997 UPS strike waged by the Teamsters received support and assistance from unions in the United Kingdom, India, and the Philippines, contributing to a dramatic victory around the issue of part-time workers' benefits, pay, and promotion (Clawson 2003, 155–56). In Central America and Mexico union drives in the garment industry in *maquiladora* factories have been supported through transnational campaigns waged by the Campaign for Labor Rights, the National Labor Committee, and UNITE and other U.S. unions. Women workers' organizations have also formed regional and transnational coalitions to organize and lobby around the particular issues facing this largely female workforce (Bandy and Bickham Mendez 2003).

National-level labor movements have also grown increasingly coalitional. In response to the decline of manufacturing in the United States and accompanying processes of deunionization, bolstered by decades of antilabor legislation and policies, renewed labor activity has emerged among workers in traditionally nonunionized service sector occupations and among immigrants and workers of color. This resurgence of labor activity, often termed *social movement unionism,* has involved a reorientation toward grassroots organizing along with working collaborations with community organizations, religious groups, workers' centers, and other social justice organizations (see Clawson 2003, 103–4). The LWCs, launched by coalitions of academics, students, and community activists, that have emerged on college campuses and in municipalities across the country to pressure for just wages are an identifiable case in point.[3]

A notable characteristic of oppositional politics under globalization has been a heavy reliance on the strategic use of information (Keck and Sikkink 1998). Social movements and NGOs use diffuse, transnational links with organizations in other national contexts (often via e-mail and the Internet) to transmit information and reach other national or transnational public spheres and "foreign reference publics" (Keck and Sikkink 1998). Through these linkages movements exert international pressure directed at state or supranational institutions (such as the World Bank), or even corporations, to accomplish their goals. The practices involved in such politics include negotiation, lobbying, and media campaigns. Even when combined with direct action, such as the mobilization strategies implemented by the global justice movement, the role of information has achieved heightened importance as movements seek to exert impact by changing perceptions and values and challenging the meaning of democracy under global capitalism (Schild 1998). Thus there is an increasing need for NGOs and social justice organizations to know how to compile and effectively "package" information in order to access national and transnational public spheres, and the "NGOization" of social movements[4] has been accompanied by an increase in the importance placed on research (Harper 2001; Gaventa 1993, 31–32). Likewise, information plays a major role in the coalitions that have mobilized around economic justice issues. For example, in the case of LWCs, data about the number of working families below the poverty line as well as other information about the impact that living-wage statutes could have on the local economy are important tools for campaigns' success.

Through information politics, movements and NGOs gain influence by serving as alternative sources of information, but for transnational advocacy campaigns to be effective the information must be conveyed as "rigorously argued cases" based on "objective" data in order to convince powerful national and international decision makers that change is warranted (Harper 2001, 248; Keck and Sikkink 1998, 16). In policy arenas the forms of knowledge that communities and small organizations possess (testimonials, *vivencias,* popular knowledge) may not be considered "hard" enough evidence. For coalitions of NGOs and social movement organizations, moral economy strategies (what Keck and Sikkink [1998] call "moral leverage") may be the only available method for gaining access to different public spheres (including transnational ones) to pressure state and international decision makers. Yet this very strategy can be dismissed by decision makers as political bullying or shaming tactics that fail to address the evidence or properly engage the issues.

STRATEGIES AND SITES OF INTERVENTION FOR GLOBALIZED SCHOLAR ACTIVISM

Doing Research as Information Politics

The increased need for research for use in local, national, and transnational campaigns suggests a possible role for academics, who could put their cultural capital to work for social movements as translators who "package" oppositional narratives or lived realities so that they resonate with policy makers. Decision makers might assume research presented by academics to be more rigorous and reliable than that put forth by campaigning NGOs, lending a level of legitimacy and credibility to social justice struggles (Harper 2001, 258).

For example, in the case of the LWC at the College of William and Mary, research and the compilation of information came into play at important junctures. The college is located in Virginia, a "right-to-work" state, and one of the arguments that workers encountered was that it was "illegal" for state workers to form a union. In response, a faculty member developed a flyer and fact sheet entitled "Yes, Virginia, you CAN join a union," and campaign members distributed it widely. The flyer explained the misconception about right-to-work laws and showed that it was a constitutional right to join a union. Other flyers and fact sheets were important lobbying tools. For example, the campaign's petition drive generated some 2,600 signatures (on a campus of 7,000 students), and the cover sheet of the petition used data drawn from various sources, including human resources data obtained through the Freedom of Information Act, to document that starting salaries for housekeeping and trades-utility jobs were well below the national poverty level. Workers and leaders of the union local that formed on campus as a result of the campaign also used this tactic and began the practice of making Freedom of Information Act requests of the public university part of their campaign against a wave of privatization of university services.

Accessing Public Spheres through Social Capital

Though the existence of transnational public spheres has enabled transnational political organizing to have a certain level of effectiveness, public spheres are always constituted by systematic exclusions based on structures of class, gender, and race (Guidry, Kennedy, and Zald 2000, 10). Academics' privileges grant them greater access to transnational and national public spheres. They are familiar with how to write newspaper editorials; they may have knowledge about e-mail listservs or know how to create a Web site. Their personal or professional networks might include influential actors such as board members of funding organizations, journalists, contacts in embassies, or policy makers. These forms of social and cultural capital take on a transnational dimension in the case of scholar activists from the North working with groups from the South. The following examples from my work as a *cooperante*/researcher with a Nicaraguan women's labor organization highlight how the possession of "transnational" social capital can shape the abilities of political movements to access public spheres.[5]

Between 1994, the year that the Working and Unemployed Women's Movement, Maria Elena Cuadra (MEC), formed as an autonomous organization after splitting from the Sandinista Workers' Central (CST), and 1997, I collaborated with MEC as a *cooperante*, basing my dissertation and subsequent book on the ethnographic research that I conducted with them. MEC's formation as an autonomous women-only space was prompted by gender-based conflicts within the CST after former members of the trade union confederation's Women's Secretariat were prevented access to positions of decision-making power and kept from managing the funds that they had acquired to run their programs and projects for women workers.

A few years after emerging as an independent organization, MEC organizers were actively pursuing their own strategies to raise national and international awareness about issues facing women in *maquila* factories. They sought to establish working collaborations with labor and solidarity organizations in the North in order to pressure state officials to take measures to improve factory conditions. Organizers sent faxed inquiries to UNITE and the National Labor Committee, but their requests to collaborate with these U.S.-based labor organizations went unanswered.

In 1997, however, the CST-affiliated textile and apparel workers' federation with its outspoken male leadership, which had largely ignored women in the Free Trade Zone, began turning its attention to unionizing *maquila* assembly workers. The CST was able to reactivate previously established linkages with activists and organizations from the solidarity movement of the 1980s in the United States. In 1999 and 2000, in collaboration with this federation, the Campaign for Labor Rights and the National Labor Committee launched a major campaign and, using e-mail action alerts, coordinated leafleting actions and fax campaigns to protest union-busting activities in the factories of the Free Trade Zone. In addition to the e-mail alerts and Web sites, the campaigns received coverage by the *New York Times* (Gonzalez 2000), National Public Radio (2000), and even *Rolling Stone* (Marsh 2000). Despite their long history of organizing and providing services for *maquiladora* workers and the much larger numbers of workers involved in their programs and activities, the voices of the women of MEC and their gender perspective were absent from this international news coverage. In other words, despite a closer tie to a social base of women workers and a clearly more substantial presence in the *maquila* factories, MEC's lack of transnational social capital prevented the organization from being able to transmit their gender perspective and vision into a transnational advocacy campaign. MEC organizers were unable to reach a transnational public sphere, and gender was one factor underlying this exclusion (see Bickham Mendez 2005).

The digital divide is another manifestation of how public spheres exclude. Though the global justice movement has relied heavily on the Internet to plan and organize mass mobilizations around the world, and though transnational coalitions among organizations in the North and South are formed and fostered through information technology, access to these technologies is shaped by global gender, class, and race inequalities.[6] And this disparity does not merely correspond with a simple North/South divide, as illustrated by the LWC at William and Mary.

Access to e-mail was an important issue for the fragile coalition of faculty, students, and staff that formed the LWC. College policy provides all personnel with access to a free e-mail account. And important campuswide announcements—such as college closing due to inclement weather conditions and information about changes in health insurance—are circulated by voicemail and e-mail. For example, after the Virginia General Assembly voted to grant state workers a bonus instead of a pay increase, the office of human resources sent an e-mail message to all personnel that they were required to submit a form in order to receive this benefit. In my building individual faculty and concerned office staff tracked down custodial workers to make sure that they knew about the form. Most had no idea. Lack of e-mail access made custodial workers and housekeeping staff, in effect, second-class community members, excluding them from important knowledge about their jobs. It was also a liability for the campaign. Although the coalition could mobilize students and faculty to attend a meeting or event using e-mail, housekeepers and maintenance workers could not be reached, and movement organizers had to devise an elaborate phone tree for getting the word out about LWC activities. Though e-mail had become a global tool for political mobilization, for this LWC the digital divide manifested itself locally.

The campaign began to pressure administrators to comply with college policy and create e-mail accounts for all workers. A campaigner who was a tenured member of the faculty was particularly instrumental in suggesting which administrators should be contacted, and she made phone calls and e-mailed inquiries herself to push along the process when it stalled several times. Eventually, when the campaign was successful in achieving this goal, it was clear that this faculty member's persistence and influence had played a major role. William and Mary campaigners discussed strategies and plans of action at animated meetings, which became key organizational spaces for students, faculty, and staff to come together and dialogue about the goals and possible actions in the campaign. And the coalition found it to be a useful strategic role for this particular faculty member, who had no reason to fear for her job, to speak out about issues such as e-mail access. Nonetheless, it is important to point out that housekeeping staff were the overwhelming majority of those who walked the picket lines for the duration of the campaign.

Making Global-Local Connections to Foster Cultures of Solidarity

Knowledge about the many faces of globalization presents another interesting possibility for activist research. Globalization produces problems that manifest themselves in intensely local forms but have broader implications that are not always readily observable to people on the ground. On the other hand, the intricate ways in which people experience global processes have not always made it into scholarly texts. During my fieldwork with MEC, organizers would repeatedly mention their desire to develop their understandings of geopolitics, trade policy, and economics in order to better understand the growth of the *maquila* industry in their country and hence strategize for improving work conditions in the factories. I remember clearly the words of one organizer, "We all have to be political economists now."

Groups like the Coalition for Justice in the Maquilas (CJM) are broad networks of organizations that launch transnational campaigns to improve work conditions within *maquila* factories. By integrating local workplace grievances into a global framework of resistance, these networks can function "like a transnational counter-public with cosmopolitan citizens and trans-cultural values" (Bandy 2004, 34). Such efforts to create a "culture of solidarity" (Fantasia 1988) also serve a counterhegemonic purpose of creating alternatives for resisting the dominant "neoliberal paradigm" (Rosen 2003). Coalitions like the CJM and the Network of Central American Women in Solidarity with Maquila Workers illustrate how linking local issues, grievances, and even identities to an understanding of global processes can promote the development of counterhegemonies, creating a space for solidarity and exchange that makes possible difficult coalitions across barriers of national origin, race, gender, and class (Bandy and Bickham Mendez 2003).

Thus an important contribution of scholar activism could be to engage in transformative educational projects about global-local connections.

Networks such as those mentioned above as well as organizations that make up the global justice movement, such as the Institute for Policy Studies and Global Exchange, already engage in such educational endeavors. Collaborations with such organizations to shed light on the global aspects of resistance struggles such as local LWCs—revealing the existence of "right-to-work" areas all over the world—could perhaps help marginalized people put knowledge about the global political economy to use in struggles against the adverse effects of globalization.

LIMITATIONS AND PITFALLS OF GLOBALIZING SCHOLAR ACTIVISM

The Contradictions of Transnational, National, and Local Public Spheres

The potential opportunities for scholar activism that I have discussed up to this point are far from free of dilemmas or contradictions. Many of them involve the scholar activist as a source of cultural or social capital for oppositional initiatives, and one of the most important dilemmas that emerges in this regard emanates from privilege under globalization. That is, as much as scholar activists may wish to contribute to struggles for global justice, they are strongly linked to and definitely benefit from global capitalism. It is easy to imagine a transnational corporate jet-setter, off to broker the latest privatization deal or international corporate merger, sharing an airplane armrest with a "transnational" scholar en route to the latest international conference in a five-star hotel in which his or her sheets will be changed by Third World immigrant workers (most likely brown or black women).

Questions also arise with regard to scholar activists' efforts to frame information in order to make it more palatable to decision makers. Though alternative narratives may not carry sufficient authority in policy arenas, local communities and organizations are precisely where counterhegemonic projects are born. If we turned all endeavors toward translating or packaging local "truths" in language that policy makers or state actors responded to, we would be giving up on the counterhegemonic potential of subjugated ways of knowing. To contribute to counterhegemonies, the vision and objectives of economic justice initiatives, like LWCs, must be founded on experiential ways of knowing and doing grounded in the lived realities of those facing injustice—even if the use of other forms of knowledge becomes a strategic political method.

Proponents of participatory research (Fals-Borda 1991, 9) maintain that projects must return knowledge to the community, whose members are the rightful owners. But once information reaches a transnational public sphere, questions emerge about who controls that information, how texts are interpreted, and how information gets used politically by various political and social actors. For example, in the antisweatshop movement, there have been several cases in which transnational campaigns like the one leveled against Kathy Lee Gifford and J. C. Penney and Wal-Mart, which called for implementing independent monitoring of shop floor conditions, resulted in factory closures, leaving workers with no jobs (J. Collins 2003; Köpke 2000). Thus, in their collaborative efforts, scholar activists must carefully consider the consequences of particular kinds of information reaching a transnational public sphere.

Scholars who practice politically engaged research as part of "information politics" will also confront the ways in which intersecting forms of power shape the ability of political movements to access public spheres and disseminate information. For example, during my collaboration with MEC in Nicaragua, the organization's coordinator suggested that we coauthor an article on gender and discrimination within the state-owned Free Trade Zone for *Envio,* the news magazine published by the University of Central America. Included in our analysis would be a gender critique of unionization efforts in the zone. At this time the issue of work conditions and human rights violations within the Nicaraguan Free Trade Zone had only recently begun to receive public attention and had yet to be subjected to international scrutiny.

An early draft of my section of the piece began with a political economic analysis, situating the Nicaraguan *maquila* industry within the context of the global factory. Although my coauthor cut my long introduction—"People don't want to read long-winded analyses about political economy"—*Envio's* editor still rejected the piece, maintaining that the article's style was too academic and that *Envio* aimed its publication at a popular audience. My reaction to this news differed dramatically from that of the *compañeras.* When I good-naturedly returned to MEC to report that the editor had suggested revisions before the article could be published—my interpretation of the interaction—MEC organizers expressed outrage. In their view this was yet another example of the FSLN and its supporters' militant rejection of critiques and their continued refusal to engage with gender issues. Though I was surprised by the vehemence of their reaction, the editor's reasoning did seem questionable considering *Envio's* usual highly analytical fare. When I suggested that we revise the piece, my coauthor and the other members of the MEC team dismissed my suggestion as a waste of time, since politics were to blame for the piece's rejection. Parts of the analysis were later published in a feminist magazine, though neither I, nor the MEC coordinator, nor the MEC were listed as the authors.

The reason given for the article's rejection was particularly ironic. I believe that MEC's coordinator was attempting to deploy the research-activist strategy that I have discussed above. That is, she sought to harness the legitimacy and weight that my position as a *gringa* and an academic perhaps lent the piece in order to enable the issue of gender inequities in the labor movement to reach a national, public sphere. In this particular case gender politics prevented this strategy from being successful.

Transnational Accountability Chains

"Globalization from below" has been much celebrated, but underlying transnational social movement networks are relations of power and dependency. For under the "neoliberal paradigm," local organizations in the South have become dependent upon funding from international or northern-based NGOs. Establishing and maintaining relations with NGOs in the North or with international funding institutions, then, becomes crucial to the survival and continued work of NGOs or social movement organizations in the South. Despite the best intentions of donors from the North, the dependency of groups in the South on external funding limits the range of activities that they can engage in and shapes their practices (Chigudu 1997; Stewart and Taylor 1997). Programs must be designed to fit funding agency requirements and must coincide with the principles and goals of international donors (Sethi 1993, 234). Organizers, then, constantly walk a tightrope between accountability to their constituents, to their political principles, and to international donors (Bickham Mendez 2002).

Organizations are faced with an additional balancing act and become skilled in the use of the language of funding agencies, underlying which is a "politics of virtue" that impels funding recipients to demonstrate that they are deserving of help and that their projects are worthwhile (Mindry 2001, 1193). Often a "deserving" organization is one that can show close ties to local communities and can represent itself as an agent for "grassroots" transformation.

In a context of globalization the word *grassroots* hardly seems to carry meaning. Yet global funders continue to be galvanized by an image of an ideal "grassroots enough" version of the local that lends legitimacy and authenticity to projects—in large part because of accountability of foundations to individual donors or of NGOs to foundations and so on. A transnational chain of accountability, then, links global and local actors up and down, with local organizers' political goals making them accountable (downwards) to their base but upwards to NGO funders, who are in turn accountable to foundations and donors or to governments who provide their funding.

Organizations in the South are caught in an interesting bind. On the one hand, their dependency on funds from international NGOs means that they must strive to represent themselves as worthy recipients of funding and "authentically" local representatives of grassroots communities. On the other hand, to represent themselves effectively in this way, they must have professional skills such as grant-writing abilities. Thus organizers must both appear "local enough" (that is, connected to the grassroots) and be "global enough" by developing and maintaining professional skills and keeping up to date regarding the latest trends in international funding.

An example from my work with MEC illustrates how a researcher activist can become involved in the "local enough" assessment of an organization. Shortly upon my return from Nicaragua, a small NGO from San Francisco that works in partnership with local organizations to support community development contacted me for help in locating women's organizations in Nicaragua that were involved in development issues. I immediately suggested MEC. Some members of the board were reluctant to establish a partnership with MEC, since its work with *maquiladora* workers and unemployed women—job training in nontraditional skills; education about labor, reproductive, and civil rights; legal services for support in filing complaints with labor courts; and gender awareness training—would not be considered a traditional urban development project. Most organizers were not workers themselves, and MEC's office was not located in the main communities where workers reside. Was MEC an "authentic" actor for grassroots development?

The partnership was eventually established, and MEC was funded by the NGO. However, it took a concerted effort on the part of a committed director of the NGO to educate the board and challenge members to think critically about their definitions of "community development." The NGO had to come to terms with and interrogate presuppositions about the relationship between locality and community in the contemporary moment. It also became apparent that if the NGO's goal was to form partnerships with a women's organization, it had to move beyond a model of traditional urban community development projects that often privileges male voices (Staudt, Rai, and Parpart 2001).

Parpart is rightfully critical of the transnational chain of accountability and evaluation. She sees global funding agencies as "disciplining" small-scale projects with their requirements for outcomes (Staudt, Rai, and Parpart 2001, 1255). Also, with accountability comes a system of evaluation that redirects important time and energy away from social justice pursuits and toward satisfying agencies and donors that local organizations are sufficiently accountable to their social base as well as other requirements that are imposed by "global agents."

Yet as Thayer (2001) notes, organizations' social base and connection to grassroots communities also can represent a kind of symbolic capital or "local power" within the politics of NGOs' work. And NGOs' influence in policy making can come from the very same claim to authenticity that they must constantly strive to prove to international funders. Thus the global/local dichotomy is problematic in that it is the basis for North/South power differentials within transnational coalitions, but it is also a categorization with hegemonic resonance that *can* be used to the advantage of social movements seeking to affect change or improve conditions for poor, disenfranchised communities.

Those who have written about activist research also note that engaging in this kind of research involves a heightened level of accountability of the researcher to the community with whom she is working. Stoecker (1999) describes an intense process in which the researcher obtains community input at multiple stages of the project. In this way scholar activists who are undertaking collaborative projects could contribute to a shift in the direction of South-to-North accountability, making the "global power" of the scholar activist accountable to the "local power" of the community or organization.

Difference within "Local" Communities

One of the many problems with representing organizations as authentically "local" is the underlying assumption of homogeneity. As Rai notes in her discussion of gender and development, use of the concept of "the local" as a hallowed space of freedom, grounded in "authentic" cultures, hides its splintered nature—divisions of class, ethnicity, language, and caste that divide and fracture the local (Staudt, Rai, and Parpart 2001, 1253). Confronting and negotiating difference within local communities and organizations would seem to be a major issue for scholar activists seeking to engage in collaborative activist projects.

Scholar activists should be careful not to presuppose a Pollyanna view of poor, guileless, local organizations incapable of "using" the scholar activist or research projects to further particular individual, political, or small-group agendas. We should not assume some kind of rosy, romantic relationship between scholar activists and "local" organizations. In an age of globalization we should also be wary of romanticizing local communities as the repositories of "authentic, local truths." Communities and organizations are not homogenous, nor are they free from internal conflict, power struggles, and contradictions. I would submit that it is virtually impossible for the scholar activist to assume the position of neutral observer when it comes to these internal conflicts. Simply stated, sooner or later one has to choose sides or risk taking on the role of the disinterested expert who cannot stoop to the level of taking a stand on issues.

Ostensibly, activist research moves beyond the objective, scientific observer, but then where does it end? Must the scholar activist become embroiled in every internal battle? On the other hand, if the researcher tries to remain neutral, he or she could be in the position of contributing to a contradiction and perhaps compromising the social justice orientation of the project.

Such dilemmas also raise the question of differing transformative visions. Can we assume that the scholar activist and all members of local communities or organizations have a common vision? For example, people on the ground who directly face conditions stemming from globalization might have much more invested in concrete, short-term goals than in more lofty goals of changing society. Such a position can be the case in coalitions with workers' movements. In LWCs, workers tend to be focused on achieving a raise and the respect that it symbolizes, while students and faculty who obviously do not risk losing their jobs or who do not face the same constraints as workers may be more interested in discussions of human rights and global economic justice.

Another issue raised by differences within local communities relates to how the intersections of global relations of power have an impact on scholars' engagement in activist research. Not surprisingly, in my collaborations with MEC my whiteness and national origin as a *gringa* set me apart in important ways from the other *compañeras* and contributed to my outsiderness. As a *chela* (white person) and a foreigner, even though I did not work for a funding institution, to the women of MEC I represented the "eyes of the North." This, of course, was highly compounded by the affiliation with the U.S. embassy that my Fulbright Fellowship granted me. MEC organizers did not like airing the movement's "dirty laundry" in front of the *chelas*. Indeed, on a number of occasions I was invited to attend certain internal meetings precisely because my presence would temper the outbreak of open conflict.

In some instances my presence at internal meetings was resented, and at one point it became a source of conflict among the women of the collective. At this meeting one of the organizers asked me to leave. Although I had repeatedly requested that MEC organizers alert me if my presence was not desired, I left the meeting somewhat puzzled. For MEC's coordinator herself had asked me to organize the meeting—probably for very strategic reasons. Later, two of the *compañeras* confided to me that the coordinator had sharply admonished the organizer for requesting that I leave, as the former perceived this as inappropriate treatment of a *compañera* who has been *solidaria* (in solidarity) with the movement. The organizer in question complained that I was a *gringa metiche* (North American who is nosy or meddlesome). And indeed, at the time I thought that she had a point.

The coordinator's defense of my presence at this particular meeting highlights some of the relations of power that underlay my relationship with MEC participants. My connection to the North symbolized by my whiteness contributed to MEC organizers' feeling compelled to put up with the *joderera* (messing or screwing around) of this *gringa metiche*. There is no question that my involvement with MEC and the role that I played as I conducted my research and collaborated with them would have been very different had I been Nicaraguan or shared other aspects of social location with MEC members. And as my German colleague who also collaborated with MEC constantly reminded me, it would have been strikingly different (he would contend impossible) had I been a man—and I think equally so had I been directly associated with a northern NGO or funder.

What is clear is that I brought privilege based on my race, class, and nationality with me as a researcher activist, and this privilege opened some doors to me and to MEC as an organization, but it also constrained MEC organizers in several ways and placed some added burdens on them and on me. Power imbalances affected how they could or could not enforce boundaries with regard to my involvement within the organization. I do not mean to say that organizers had no power over this—I saw MEC's coordinator send a *cooperante* packing when she did not feel that the northern collaborator was sufficiently committed to the organization.

But I do know that my status as a *gringa* and an academic greatly influenced both the kind of involvement that MEC organizers wanted me to have as well as the nature of involvement I was able to achieve.

Finally, my whiteness and national origin became a symbol of legitimacy and transnational social capital for MEC, especially at meetings and events that occurred in the larger public. At outside events it was clear to me in not-so-subtle ways with whom I should sit. Frequently I would overhear MEC organizers point me out to members of other organizations and say, "She's with us." I was mentioned in funding proposals as well as reports to funding organizations, and I frequently appeared in MEC's photos to document its activities. The line between imposition and collaboration—between being a privileged, unwanted outsider and being a *compañera* —was always, ever so painfully thin.

Where does all this leave the scholar activist? Certainly the dilemmas facing him or her are daunting. But it seems to me that we should not let them paralyze our attempts to leave the comfortably familiar ivory tower. How do we go about "engaging the contradictions" as we formulate and evaluate practices of globalized scholar activism?

I believe that the examples that I have presented in this chapter demonstrate that feminism(s) offer important insights and conceptual tools for the development of politically engaged research strategies. One of the most significant contributions of feminist thought is the reconceptualization of power as intersectional, multisited, and existing in multiple forms. Feminist approaches help us recognize power not just as an "external" force present in broad economic or institutional structures but also as constituted in microlevel dynamics occurring within communities, organizations, and even social movements. This conceptualization of the varied dimensions of power can serve scholar activists in evaluating the impact of transnational political strategies and collaborating in the development of more inclusive forms of transnational mobilization.

As I have discussed in the preceding sections, a recognition of the intersections of global relations of power is useful for understanding how the social location of the activist researcher affects and shapes his or her engagement in research practices and collaborative relationships—that is, how our (personal) lived experiences as socially positioned individuals and researchers are inextricably connected to the (public) practice of this kind of scholarship (see Pierre, chapter 4 of this volume). A view of power as intersectional helps us reflect on scholar activists' institutional and social position within the academy, a site of global privilege that reproduces international race, class, and gender inequalities. Thus in designing activist research projects it is crucial for collaborators to reflect on the ways in which they both benefit from and are oppressed by global capitalism. The very power/knowledge that scholar activists use as a tool for social justice emerges in part from the global processes that create the inequalities addressed in the research project. And though it is uncomfortable to acknowledge, using research as part of an overall political strategy must entail an awareness of this contradiction.

A processual view of social change is another conceptual tool offered by feminism(s). Rather than viewing social transformation in absolutist terms, variants of feminism present an alternative approach that conceptualizes social change potential, not as a preexisting condition, but rather as constructed through political practice (Eschle 2001, 96). Feminism(s)' emphasis that the means of struggle are as important as, and are inextricably related to, outcomes also represents a significant insight for confronting the contradictions inherent in politically engaged research.

In today's world in which global capitalism has achieved such a stranglehold, we cannot dismiss those who seek to put the "Master's tools" (Lorde 1984) to work for social justice—nor can we rely solely on the Master's tools for the creation of alternatives to the dominant neoliberal paradigm. Rather, the practices and products of activist research projects should be treated as part of a larger political strategy, and collaborators must reflect on the dilemmas and contradictions embedded in projects as they construct them.

Another contribution that feminism(s) makes to the construction of politically engaged research strategies is the second-wave principle of the personal as political. Ultimately the development of strategic practices of activist research must emerge out of relationships and dialogue (what Latin American organizers often call "exchange of experiences") between the scholar activist and collaborators. As other feminists have noted (Richards 2006), this kind of research practice requires collaborative social relationships that must be rethought from outside conventional approaches to research.

Feminist debates about epistemologies have challenged the ways that certain forms of knowledge (objective and scientific) are valued while others are marginalized and subjugated (Haraway 1988; P. Collins 2000). This insight leads us to shift our attention to institutional changes that must occur within the academy to sustain activist research. Academics must push the boundaries of what is deemed "legitimate scholarship," and the currency of peer-reviewed publications may need to be broadened or changed. To create new public spheres scholars and activists must work to establish forums for the presentation of research that will be accessible and of interest to other publics beyond the academic community.

Other changes need to address the content and form of research products, making texts less and less a conversation among a few academics within particular subfields of study, and instead a discussion among a wider group of people committed to social change. These kinds of changes would also involve community members and organization participants' gaining more control over knowledge about globalization. The implications of this process might be giving up some of our discipline-specific jargon, concepts, and phrases, or at least creating spaces in which alternative language and knowledges are valued—that is, we could create alternative academic public spheres.

Restructuring the reward systems of our universities and transforming academic public spheres would do much to generate a context in which activist research could thrive. And as Hale points out in his introduction to this volume, we cannot look to the conventional academic reward system to know if we are "getting activist research right"; rather, we must look to the people with whom we collaborate. Can we imagine our work's being "peer" reviewed, not only by academic experts in the field, but also by members of local communities in which the study took place?

In conclusion, although insights drawn from bodies of knowledge such as feminist thought provide some clues, we may not be able to expect always to know how to engage in scholar activism as disconnected from grounded situations. But we can be open to dialogue and future imaginings that might allow us to unlock the counterhegemonic potential of academic pursuits. Such changes would involve rethinking the mission, purpose, and politics of the academy. These are lofty goals, but they correspond with valuable principles. Even if we are never able to achieve such transformations, it is in strategizing to reach such objectives that scholar activism can perhaps make its greatest contribution to social justice.

NOTES

This analysis has greatly benefited from the comments and insights of several colleagues and friends. I wish to thank Charles Hale, Gül Ozyegin, and Angela Stuesse, as well as two anonymous reviewers, for their useful suggestions. In addition, I am grateful to the participants and organizers of the 2003 conference entitled "Engaging the Contradictions," held in Los Angeles and organized by the Social Science Research Council, for giving me the opportunity to think more systematically about these issues and to dialogue with others committed to carving out a space for social justice work within the academy. I dedicate this chapter to my students at William and Mary—Camielle Compton, Lauren Jones, Lilli Mann, and Catherine Schwenkler—who have taught me so much and who never let me forget what really matters.

1. Elsewhere, I have been critical of the dichotomous notion of globalization from "above" and "below," as this binary tends to gloss power differentials among individuals and organizations that seek to resist and engage with the effects of neoliberalism and economic globalization (Mendez 2005). Notwithstanding, the distinction does have value as a heuristic device for understanding some of the varied forms of globalization.

2. According to the United Nations Development Programme (UNDP 2002, 15), between the years of 1980 and 2000 the number of democratic regimes doubled (from forty-one to eighty-two), while the number of authoritarian regimes fell from almost seventy to fewer than thirty.

3. Another example of labor activity that has involved such coalitional politics and has occurred outside the traditional framework of unionization is the current broad-based campaign challenging Wal-Mart's labor policies, involving collaborations among labor lawyers, unions (the United Food and Commercial Workers' Union), NGOs, and Wal-Mart workers themselves (Seligman 2006).

4. *NGOization* refers to the process through which increasingly social justice organizations operate with a bureaucratic and formalized structure that usually includes a professional, paid staff, and dependence on funding from other NGOs, foundations, or governments. In addition, NGOs tend to devote more efforts to the provision of services than to direct action or grassroots organizing.

5. Peggy Levitt (2001) in her analysis of Dominican transmigrants in the Boston area notes that social capital can have a transnational dimension through her development of a concept of "social remittances." But I wish to borrow from this and apply it to the ways in which transnational politics can or cannot work.

6. According to the UNDP (1999, 63), in 1999 19 percent of the world's population accounted for 91 percent of Internet users.

REFERENCES

Albrow, M. 1995. *The Global Age: State and Society beyond Modernity.* Cambridge: Polity Press.

———. 1997. "Traveling beyond Local Cultures: Socioscapes in a Global City." In *Living the Global City: Globalization as Local Process*, edited by J. Eade, 20–36. New York: Routledge.

Alvarez, Robert R. 2006. "The Transnational State and Empire: US Certification in the Mexican Mango and Persian Lime Industries." *Human Organization* 65 (1): 35–46.

Bandy, Joe. 2004. "Paradoxes of Transnational Civil Society: The Coalition for Justice in the Maquiladoras and the Challenges of Coalition." *Social Problems* 51 (3): 410–31.

Bandy, Joe, and Jennifer Bickham Mendez. 2003. "A Place of Their Own? Women Organizers Negotiating the Local and Transnational in the Maquilas of Nicaragua and Northern Mexico." *Mobilization* 8 (2): 173–88.

Barber, Benjamin R. 2001. *Jihad vs. McWorld*. New York: Ballantine Books.

Basch, Linda, Nina Glick Schiller, and Cristina Szanton Blanc, eds. 1994. *Nations Unbound: Transnational Projects, Postcolonial Predicaments and Deterritorialized Nation-States*. Langhorne, PA: Gordon and Breach.

Bickham Mendez, Jennifer. 2002. "Organizing a Space of Their Own? Global/Local Processes in a Nicaraguan Women's Organization." *Journal of Developing Societies* 18 (2–3): 196–227.

———. 2005. *From the Revolution to the Maquiladoras: Gender, Labor and Globalization in Nicaragua*. Durham: Duke University Press.

Bickham Mendez, Jennifer, and James Spady. Forthcoming. "Organizing across Difference and across Campus: Cross-Class Coalition and Worker Mobilization in a Living Wage Campaign." *Labor Studies Journal*.

Bloom, L. R. 1998. *Under the Sign of Hope: Feminist Methodology and Narrative Interpretation*. Albany: State University of New York Press.

Bowes, A. 1996. "Evaluating an Empowering Research Strategy: Reflections on Action-Research with South Asian Women." *Sociological Research Online* 1. http://kennedy.soc.surrey.ac.uk/socresonline/1/1/contents.html.

Brecher, Jeremy, Tim Costello, and Brendan Smith. 2000. *Globalization from Below: The Power of Solidarity*. Cambridge, MA: South End Press.

Burawoy, Michael, Joseph A. Blum, Sheba George, Zsuzsa Gille, Teresa Gowan, Lynne Haney, Maren Klawiter, Steven H. Lopez, Seán Ó Riain, and Millie Thayer. 2000. *Global Ethnography: Forces, Connections, and Imaginations in a Postmodern World*. Berkeley: University of California Press.

Cancian, Francesca. 1992. "Feminist Science: Methodologies That Challenge Inequality." *Gender and Society* 6:623–42.

Castells, Manuel. 1993. "The Informational Economy and the New International Division of Labor." In *The New Global Economy in the Information Age*, edited by Martin Carnoy, Manuel Castells, Stephen S. Cohen, and Fernando Henrique Carodoso, 15–43. University Park: Pennsylvania State University Press.

Chigudu, Hope. 1997. "Establishing a Feminist Culture: The Experience of Zimbabwe Women Resource Centre and Network." *Gender and Development* 5 (1): 35–42.

Clawson, Dan. 2003. *The Next Upsurge: Labor and the New Social Movements*. Ithaca, NY: ILR Press.

Collins, Jane. 2003. *Threads: Gender, Labor and Power in the Global Apparel Industry*. Chicago: University of Chicago Press.

Collins, Patricia Hill. 2000. *Black Feminist Thought*. London: HarperCollins Academic.

Eschle, Catherine. 2001. *Global Democracy, Social Movements, and Feminism*. Boulder, CO: Westview Press.

Fals-Borda, Orlando. 1991. "Some Basic Ingredients." In *Action and Knowledge: Breaking the Monopoly with Participatory Action-Research*, edited by Orlando Fals-Borda and Mohammad Anisur Rahman, 3–12. New York: Apex Press.

Fals-Borda, Orlando, and Mohammad Anisur Rahman, eds. 1991. *Action and Knowledge: Breaking the Monopoly with Participatory Action-Research*. New York: Apex Press.

Fantasia, Rick. 1988. *Cultures of Solidarity: Consciousness, Action, and Contemporary Workers*. Berkeley: University of California Press.

Freeman, Carla. 2000. *High Tech and High Heels in the Global Economy: Women, Work and Pink-Collar Identities in the Caribbean*. Durham: Duke University Press.

Gaventa, John. 1993. "The Powerful, the Powerless, and the Experts: Knowledge Struggles in an Information Age." In *Voices of Change: Participatory Research in the United States and Canada*, edited by Peter Park, Mary Brydon-Miller, Budd Hall, and Ted Jackson, 21–40. Westport, CT: Bergin and Garvey.

Giddens, Anthony. 1991. *The Consequences of Modernity*. Cambridge: Cambridge University Press.

Gille, Zsuzsa, and Seán Ó Riain. 2002. "Global Ethnography." *Annual Review of Sociology* 28: 271–95.

Glick Schiller, Nina. 1999. "Transmigrants and Nation-States: Something Old and Something New in the U.S. Immigrant Experience." In *The Handbook of International Migration: The American Experience*, edited by Charles Hirschman, Philip Kasinitz, and Josh Dewind, 94–119. New York: Russell Sage Foundation.

Gonzalez, David. 2000. "Nicaragua's Trade Zone: Battleground for Unions." *New York Times*, September 16, 3A.

Guidry, John A., Michael D. Kennedy, and Mayer N. Zald. 2000. "Globalizations and Social Movements." In *Globalizations and Social Movements: Culture, Power, and the Transnational Public Sphere*, edited by John A. Guidry, Michael D. Kennedy, and Mayer N. Zald, 1–32. Ann Arbor: University of Michigan Press.

Hall, Budd. 1993. Introduction to *Voices of Change: Participatory Research in the United States and Canada*, edited by Peter Park, Mary Brydon-Miller, Budd Hall, and Ted Jackson, xiii–xxii. Westport, CT: Bergin and Garvey.

Haraway, Donna. 1988. "Situated Knowledges: The Science Question in Feminism and the Privilege of Partial Perspective." *Feminist Studies* 14 (3): 575–99.

Harper, Caroline. 2001. "Do the Facts Matter? NGOs, Research and International Advocacy." In *Global Citizen Action*, edited by Michael Edward and John Gaventa, 247–58. Boulder, CO: Lynne Rienner Press.

Harvey, David. 1990. *The Condition of Postmodernity: An Enquiry into the Origins of Cultural Change*. Cambridge, MA: Blackwell.

Hesse-Biber, Sharlene Nagy, and Denise Leckenby. 2004. "How Feminists Practice Social Research." In *Feminist Perspectives on Social Research*, edited by Sharlene Nagy Hesse-Biber and Michelle L. Yaiser, 209–26. New York: Oxford University Press.

Jameson, Frederic. 1998. *The Cultural Turn*. New York: Verso.

Keck, Margaret, and Kathryn Sikkink. 1998. *Activists beyond Borders: Transnational Advocacy Networks in International Politics*. Ithaca: Cornell University Press.

Köpke, Ronald. 2000. "Las experiencias del equipo de monitoreo independiente de Honduras." In *Códigos de conducta y monitoreo en la industria de confección: Experiences internacionales y regionales*, edited by Ronald Köpke, Norma Molina, and Carolina Quinteros, 100–119. San Salvador: Fundación Böll.

Levitt, Peggy. 2001. *The Transnational Villagers*. Berkeley: University of California Press.

Lorde, Audre. 1984. *Sister Outsider: Essays and Speeches by Audre Lorde*. Freedom, CA: Crossing Press.

Maguire, Patricia. 1996. "Considering More Feminist Participatory Research: What's Congruency Got to Do with It?" *Qualitative Inquiry* 2 (1): 106–18.

———. 2001. "Uneven Ground: Feminisms and Action Research." In *Handbook of Action Research*, edited by Peter Reason and H. Bradbury, 59–69. Thousand Oaks, CA: Sage Publications.

Marcus, George E. 1995. "Ethnography in/of the World System: The Emergence of Multi-sited Ethnography." *Annual Review of Anthropology* 24:95–117.

Marsh, Katherine. 2000. "Spring Break in Managua." *Rolling Stone*, October 26, 85–88.

Mindry, Deborah. 2001. "Nongovernmental Organizations, 'Grassroots,' and the Politics of Virtue." *Signs: Journal of Women and Culture in Society* 26:1187–1211.

Mohanty, Chandra Talpade. 1991. "Under Western Eyes: Feminist Scholarship and Colonial Discourses." In *Third World Women and the Politics of Feminism*, edited by Chandra Talpade Mohanty, Ann Russo, and Lourdes Torres, 51–80. Bloomington: Indiana University Press.

Naples, Nancy. 2003. *Feminism and Method: Ethnography, Discourse Analysis, and Activist Research*. New York: Routledge Press.

National Public Radio. 2000. "Unions in Nicaragua." *All Things Considered*, August 18.

Nyoni, Sithembiso. 1991. "People's Power in Zimbabwe." In *Action and Knowledge: Breaking the Monopoly with Participatory Action-Research*, edited by Orlando Fals-Borda and Mohammad Anisur Rahman, 109–20. New York: Apex Press.

Park, Peter, Mary Brydon-Miller, Budd Hall, and Ted Jackson, eds. 1993. *Voices of Change: Participatory Research in the United States and Canada.* Westport, CT: Bergin and Garvey.

Richards, Patricia. 2006. "A Feminist Sociologist's Reflections on Collaborative Research." *LASA Forum* 37 (4): 16–18.

Robinson, William I. 2003. *Transnational Conflicts: Central America, Social Change and Globalization.* New York: Verso Press.

Rosen, Ruth Israel. 2003. *Making Sweatshops: The Globalization of the U.S. Apparel Industry.* Berkeley: University of California Press.

Sassen, Saskia. 1988. *The Mobility of Capital and Labor: A Study in International Investment and Labor Flow.* Cambridge, MA: Harvard University Press.

———. 2001. "Spatialities and Temporalities of the Global: Elements for a Theorization." In *Globalization,* edited by Arjun Appadurai, 260–78. Durham: Duke University Press.

Schild, Veronica. 1998. "New Subjects of Rights? Women's Movements and the Construction of Citizenship in the 'New Democracies.'" In *Culture of Politics, Politics of Culture: Re-visioning Latin American Social Movements,* edited by Sonia Alvarez, Evelina Dagnino, and Arturo Escobar, 93–117. Boulder, CO: Westview Press.

Seligman, Brad. 2006. "The Class Action Suit against Wal-Mart." Paper presented at the Gender and Labor: What's Working Conference, Austin, TX, October.

Sethi, Harsh. 1993. "Action Groups in the New Politics." In *New Social Movements in the South: Empowering the People,* edited by Ponna Wignaraja, 230–55. Atlantic Highlands, NJ: Zed Books.

Sklair, Leslie. 1995. *Sociology of the Global System.* Baltimore: Johns Hopkins University Press.

Smith, Michael Peter, and Luis Eduardo Guarnizo, eds. 1998. *Transnationalism from Below.* New Brunswick, NJ: Transaction Publishers.

Sprague, Joey, and Mary K. Zimmerman. 1993. "Overcoming Dualisms: A Feminist Agenda for Sociological Methodology." In *Theory and Gender/Feminism on Theory,* edited by Paula England, 255–89. New York: Aldine de Gruyter.

Starr, Amory. 2001. *Naming the Enemy: Anti-corporate Social Movements Confront Globalization.* London: Zed Books.

Staudt, Kathleen, Shirin M. Rai, and Jane L. Parpart. 2001. "Protesting World Trade Rules: Can We Talk about Empowerment?" *Signs* 26 (4): 1251–63.

Stewart, Sheelagh, and Jill Taylor. 1997. "Women Organizing Women: 'Doing It Backwards and in High Heels.'" In *Getting Institutions Right for Women and Development,* edited by A. M. Goetz, 212–22. New York: Zed Books.

Stoecker, Randy. 1999. "Are Academics Irrelevant? Roles for Scholars in Participatory Research." *American Behavioral Scientist* 42 (5): 840–54.

Thayer, Millie. 2001. "Joan Scott in the Sertão: Rural Brazilian Women and Transnational Feminism." Paper presented at the annual meetings of the Latin American Studies Association, Washington, DC.

United Nations Development Programme. 1999. *Human Development Report, 1999.* New York: UNDP.

———. 2002. *Human Development Report, 2002.* New York: UNDP.

Visweswaran, Kamala. 1994. *Fictions of Feminist Ethnography.* Minneapolis: University of Minnesota Press.

Wolf, Diane L. 1996. "Situating Feminist Dilemmas in Fieldwork." In *Feminist Dilemmas in Fieldwork,* edited by Diane L. Wolf, 1–54. Boulder, CO: Westview Press.

6. Activist Scholarship

Limits and Possibilities in Times of Black Genocide

João H. Costa Vargas

Between 1996 until 2006 I collaborated with two Los Angeles–based grassroots organizations, the Coalition Against Police Abuse (CAPA), and the Community in Support of the Gang Truce (CSGT). The beginning of that period was also when I started fieldwork as part of my academic training toward a degree in anthropology at the University of California, San Diego.

In this essay, I explore how my training in anthropology and my involvement with organizations working against anti-Black racism and for social justice have generated a blueprint for ethnography that does not shy away from projecting explicit political involvement. How do the knowledge and methods of social inquiry already present in grassroots organizations inflect our academic perspectives, enhancing their depth and uncovering previously silent assumptions about "subjects" and "objects" of "scientific inquiry"? On the basis of the description and analysis of my fieldwork in South Central Los Angeles, especially between 1996 and 1998, when I worked daily at CAPA and CSGT, I argue that the dialectic between academic training and on-the-ground everyday community work provides valuable insights into the possibilities of political activism, generating knowledge that interrogates the self-proclaimed neutral strands of academic research. This interrogation projects the visions of liberatory social organization so necessary in times of continuing Black genocide. I make the case for an often unrecognized aspect of fieldwork with advocacy groups, in particular when that work is conducted by someone who, like me, had relatively few applicable skills to the everyday grind of assisting victims of police brutality, unfair evictions, and gang warfare: that scholars, especially those in the beginning of their career, benefit from their involvement with grassroots organizations in ways glaringly disproportionate to what we can offer them.

The essay is organized in three parts. In the first part, I present a brief overview of the history and activities of CAPA and CSGT. I then describe my insertion in these organizations: how I became involved, the activities that I helped develop, and the knowledge of community organizing that I was fortunate to learn from Los Angeles activists. The final section is about some of the lessons—practical and theoretical—that can be drawn from what I call observant participation in such organizations vis-à-vis both academic training and necessary political interventions.

HISTORY AND ACTIVITIES OF CAPA AND CSGT

The Coalition Against Police Abuse

Founded by Black Panther Party members who survived the FBI's Counter Intelligence Programs (COINTELPROs), CAPA has been in South Central Los Angeles since 1976. It was formed primarily in response to the historically persistent waves of police shooting, beatings, and harassment that define predominantly Black neighborhoods. Michael Zinzun, a nationally known community activist and former Black Panther Party member, who coordinated CAPA until his untimely death in 2006.[1] The institution embraces a variety of causes that are the result of both CAPA's historical antecedents of community-related political activity and its analysis of and intervention in emerging events such as the 1980s great wave of immigration from Latin and Central America, the Reaganomics-generated unemployment crisis, gang activity, and large-scale, high-tech, militarized, publicly sanctioned police repression.

While CAPA's original and main purpose is to legally assist victims of police brutality, CAPA considers police abuse part of a wider context of oppression. Its members see their struggle against police brutality as necessarily connected to broader structural and historical inequalities. The struggle against police brutality, in this way, is nothing but the struggle toward social justice.

> CAPA sees not only the necessity of organizing against police abuse, but also the need to link increases in police abuse to the rising economic crisis presently taking place in the United States. In other words, if workers strike for higher wages, who is called? The police. If you can't pay your rent and refuse to move into the streets, who is called? The police. And if you organize demonstrations against a corrupt and unjust system, who is called? The police, whether with force or as un-

dercover spies. CAPA believes the police are a necessary element in the maintenance of a system controlled by a few millionaires and politicians who put profit before people.[2]

CAPA defines itself as a direct product of the Panthers. It is a place where several ex-Black Panthers gather, reminisce, and discuss present issues. CAPA's logo is a black panther encircled by "All Power to the People," the emblematic Black Panther phrase that condensed much of the party's goals.

The theoretical and practical guidelines adopted by the coalition are based on the writings of Carmichael and Hamilton, Frantz Fanon, and Malcolm X, among others. CAPA activists usually explain such guidelines as derivations of Black Power. Among those guidelines is the recognition that Black Americans ought to consider themselves part of a wider, international community. As colonized people in the United States, Black Americans should link their struggles with those of people in similar conditions. "Black Power means that Black people see themselves as part of a new force, sometimes called the 'Third World'; that we see our struggle as closely related to liberation struggles around the world. There is only one place for Black Americans in these struggles, and that is on the side of the Third World" (Carmichael and Hamilton 1967, xi). Blacks in this country, the argument goes, endure hardships common to several colonies throughout the globe. By transcending the physical and ideological horizons of the mainstream United States—by questioning values of consumption and individualism, recognizing the intrinsic racist nature of American institutions, and embracing the radical traditions of the African diaspora—Blacks gain an alternative perspective for their collective struggles. Inspired by Frantz Fanon's rejection of European epistemological and political models, Black Power suggests an expanded notion of community as an antidote to the illusions of full integration and racial equality in U.S. society.

An international community, if only virtual, is thus established. This is a significant theoretical and practical step toward liberation. It permits visualizing realities beyond the confines of Black inner cities and relativizing taken-for-granted modes of thought. It enables a new language and praxis. The utopia of an international community of struggles becomes palpable for Black Americans as it rescues a tradition of Black U.S. and diasporic radical tradition, links this tradition to present predicaments—at home and elsewhere—and in the process attempts to revitalize and expand local communitarian bonds.

The coalition has been successful in expanding its geographical horizons with frequent interchange visits to organizations of various cities in the United States and abroad. In recent years, CAPA members have visited England, France, Ghana, Namibia, Jamaica, Haiti, and Brazil. Persons from these countries and various American cities are constantly coming to Los Angeles and spending time at the coalition, exchanging information and techniques of community organization. Although most of these persons are Blacks of the African diaspora, since the early 1990s there has been a substantial increase in the number of non-Black persons of color participating in the coalition's programs, especially Latina/os.

This international praxis, together with the many years of effective community organizing, has made the coalition's politicization of the unlawfulness of law enforcement rather successful.³ CAPA activists are frequently contacted by local and national media to speak about their activities—especially in the wake of the common cases of police misconduct. CAPA has established itself as an important, widely recognized voice of the inner city. Accumulating knowledge and public exposure of its causes, the coalition serves as a fundamental base upon which emerging social movements in the inner city build their momentum. When the gang truce between Bloods and Crips was signed in 1992, for example, CAPA served as one of the main intermediaries for the elaboration and maintenance of the peace terms. The coalition's historical genealogy and its contemporary practices have prepared the terrain for the incorporation of ex- and current gang members willing to establish and expand the Watts Gang Truce.⁴

I now turn to CSGT, which shares the same building CAPA occupies.

The Community in Support of the Gang Truce

Photographs of the Million Man March in Washington, D.C., on October 16, 1995, show former enemy gang members from Los Angeles shaking hands and pledging to continue and expand the Watts truce formalized in 1992. The pictures are part of CAPA's permanent exposition, arranged in panels distributed in the main room of its building, and are obvious counterpoints to the pictures of police brutality and racism that occupy nearby space. At the office, one not familiar with the meanings of the photographs may hear from an old-timer or member of CSGT the explanation that one of the key events that made possible the Million Man March was the establishment of the gang truce. There would not have been so many people listening to Louis Farrakhan and other Black public figures were it not for the cessation of hostilities between gangs of all parts of the United States that started in Los Angeles.

On March 27, 1992, representatives of the four housing projects of Watts (Nickerson Gardens, Jordan Downs, Imperial Courts, and Hacienda Village) signed the truce. The negotiations had been going on since at least the late 1980s (Jah and Shah'Keyah 1995). The results were almost immediate. On June 17, 1992, the *Los Angeles Times* reported that "gang-related homicides in South Los Angeles have dropped markedly—to 2 last month, compared with 16 in May 1991—leading police to give new credit to the truce declared between Black gangs." Meanwhile, various community organizations willing to support and expand the Watts cease-fire were being formed.

Founded in March of 1991—a year before the Watts cease-fire was formalized—CSGT's main goal is to support the gang peace treaty by "addressing the totality of issues affecting that truce."[5] To understand this claim, it is necessary to consider that CSGT is closely linked to CAPA. Both organizations share a building on Western Avenue, on the northern fringe of South Central. Many of CSGT's members work closely with CAPA activists. This means that, in practice, the lines that separate and define CAPA and CSGT are tenuous—even though each organization has its own independent nonprofit legal status.

Not surprisingly, the 1960s Black Power theses, as CAPA's old-timers perceive them, play a considerable role in CSGT's outlook. CSGT defends a concept of economic development, for example, that is "different than the market-driven or corporate dominated approaches that are often promoted by big business and government."[6] Furthermore, CSGT believes that economic development, rather than pitting one person against the other, or one group against the other, should advance the individual *and* the community. So instead of enterprise zones, CSGT calls for cooperative zones, which, they claim, "promote social and economic justice, and are free of racism, sexism, and other forms of oppression."[7]

In this spirit, CSGT offers video classes, silk-screen training, the "off the roach" program, and computer classes and lately has been developing plastic domes for the homeless. There is also training and encouragement to participate in a speakers' bureau, a media bureau, and a rumor resolution hotline.

While CSGT's programs and their scale may not be the most suitable for the full economic recovery of the inner city, they nevertheless provide an alternative project of community by politicizing aspects of inner-city life that top-down sweeping plans are incapable of addressing. In politicizing the conditions and lives of poor youth, CSGT also establishes a public voice that, in itself, breaks the silence to which inner-city grassroots movements are usually condemned. Inspired by CAPA's long history of activism, CSGT calls for community control of the police and a Civilian Police Review Board.[8] CAPA's influence is also evident in the legal advice that CSGT provides for juveniles involved with the criminal justice system. CAPA members, following a tradition that can be traced back to the Panthers, are meticulous students of the law. Much of the legal knowledge gathered over thirty years of community activism was transferred to the efforts in maintaining and expanding the gang truce.[9]

MY RESEARCH APPROACH

I contacted CAPA as soon as I moved to South Central, in January 1996. I wanted to work for the organization, and I also wanted to learn about the lives of those who participated in it. So I called Michael Zinzun, a well-known organizer whom I had heard about from activists working against anti-Black racism and police abuse in San Diego. During our phone conversation, I was asked a series of questions aimed at revealing my political convictions. The fact that I supported and had campaigned for the Workers' Party in Brazil (Partido dos Trabalhadores)—a grassroots, democratic socialist organization that eventually reached the presidency with Lula in 2003—certainly helped Zinzun's decision to invite me to the office so that we could extend our conversation and see in which ways, if any, I could work at CAPA. Zinzun had been in Brazil for the first time in 1993, less than two months before our first conversation, with a group of thirteen students, professors, ex-gang members, persons who had been incarcerated, and community organizers. The purpose of this trip had been to "both learn and offer help with the growing consciousness-building that is taking place there among the poor, the disenfranchised and people of color."[10]

An important part of our telephone conversation was devoted to a discussion of Brazil's racial composition. According to Zinzun, Brazil was the second-largest Black nation on earth, with almost seventy million Black people. Only Nigeria, with a population of one hundred million, had more inhabitants of African descent than Brazil. As we extended our discussion, I realized he was as much interested in *my* racial identity. I told him I considered myself Black, even though, coming out of a mixed-race family, my phenotype is ambiguous. He then proceeded to talk about Malcolm X—how conscious he was of the contradictions of his light skin and how this aspect of his identity was an important component of his critique of white supremacy and the need to embrace Blackness. Zinzun himself, he confided, was the product of several distinct ancestries, including his Apache father. Still, what mattered for Zinzun was that people of color understand their history, recognize their differences (and the privileges and disadvantages that derive from them), and above all not become entangled in self-deceptions and competition with other people of color. The political aspect of Blackness was crucial to how he understood identity.

At the office, I was given a series of questionnaires, leaflets, brochures, and papers on CAPA and CSGT. While I completed a questionnaire (about my willingness to participate in the organization's events, receive its newsletter, and contribute to its finances), Zinzun explained some of the organizations' programs, which, of course, I only came to understand through everyday participation in its activities. What I present in this essay, therefore, is the product of an initial two-year study in which I supplemented what I learned from this participation with various documents and ethnographic material that I collected about the coalition, as well as with historical and sociological research on L.A.'s residential segregation patterns, labor market, everyday violence, and institutionalized forms of discrimination such as that operated by the police. My account, furthermore, is informed by my ongoing collaborations with CAPA and CSGT activists. All of this is to say that, even though there is a tendency, in academia, to separate lived experiences—and the knowledge that is an integral part of them—from theoretical and descriptive efforts informed by disciplines, I was able to articulate these seemingly disparate fields into a political and research agenda that was both a valuable tool in the struggle against police brutality and a contribution to the academic debate on race, segregation, social movements, and justice.

The projects I became involved with at CAPA and CSGT were not part of academic agendas. While I later learned about graduate programs that encourage involvement with and work about community organizations seeking social justice, such orientation is far from common in anthropology, much less in the social sciences, in the United States. Anthropology, its theories and methods, did not make much sense in South Central L.A.'s context of massive marginalization, brutality, and premature death. There was an urgent need to intervene, and my training in the discipline was not of great help. It should not have been a surprise. Cedric Robinson (1983/2000), Patricia Hill Collins (1998), Kimberlé Crenshaw (1995), and Gayatri Spivak (1999), among many others, have written on the close connection between Western academic disciplines and their White-centric, excluding, and dehumanizing assumptions. Robin Kelley (1997), more specifically, reflecting on the relationship between anthropology and U.S. Black neighborhoods, analyzed the ways in which authors such as Ulf Hannerz (1969) have perpetuated stereotypes about African Americans by drawing broad generalizations based on limited contact. An essentialist notion of Black culture (Kelley 1997, 35) is one among many blind spots preventing not only a complex appreciation of Black social life in segregated communities but also an understanding of and need to engage with transformative local collective efforts. The fact remains that the social sciences in the Western world, and their practitioners, willingly or not, further hegemonic common sense about Blacks, albeit—or should I say, especially—by ignoring their plights and the works they produce. We do not even have to dwell on the specific texts to reach such conclusions—and by this I am certainly not diminishing the importance of *principled* deconstructions of hegemonic narratives. Just consider how many graduate and undergraduate students in the United States and other countries of the African diaspora read and seriously engage with the works of Black scholars such as W. E. B. Du Bois, C. L. R. James, Frantz Fanon, James Baldwin, Audre Lorde, Barbara Smith, and Angela Davis? Not many, and when these works are read they are often not taken as seriously as the so-called white classics. This fact alone is a good indication of the white bias of disciplines such as sociology, political science, and anthropology, just to remain within the "social sciences." In such disciplines, while Blacks figure prominently in what are considered classic studies of Africa (and inner-city neighborhoods in the United States), they are not as commonly rendered the subject of social-scientific inquiry in the United States. When they are, stereotypical and therefore dehumanizing renditions abound (Wilson 1996; Anderson 1990; Waters 1999).[11]

Despite what is still taught in anthropological methods classes, no detached, fly-on-the wall is approach possible. Such an approach in anthropology, considered an antidote to the influences of one's subjectivity on the research process, only obscures the fact that even those who try to be invisible are, at the very least, already influencing the social environment in which they choose to do their fieldwork and, more importantly, are already committing themselves to a very clear moral and political position—that of letting things remain as they are, of leaving the status quo untouched.

Given CAPA's explicit political orientation, I would not have been accepted as a collaborator if my political and racial allegiances were not clear. It is very telling that, while I was job hunting and going to academic conferences, I was often asked about the objectivity of my research. The implication, of course, was that my work was not as valuable as that conducted by a dispassionate observer, since my political inclinations tinted, so to speak, my "data." I was frequently asked by academics: "How would your research change if it were conducted by someone else?" The question, of course, suggested a "someone else" without explicit political commitment. Guided *somewhat* by the scientific premise of experimental repeatability that requires controlled environments and methods that should consistently produce the same results, such inquiries also interrogate the disciplinary integrity of engaged research and researchers. It should go without saying that when both the site of research and the researchers are not white, the alleged scientific discourse becomes aligned with a well-known history of delegitimization that casts a deep suspicion on nonwhite practitioners of academic disciplines (Collins 1991).

That a feeble connection exists between the social sciences and the natural sciences (hence my emphasis on the *somewhat*) underscores the circular dynamics connecting hypotheses, methods, and results that accompany the overwhelming majority of scientific research (e.g., Feyerabend 1988). The answer to my respected (sometimes even idolized) white interrogators was straightforward: there would be no research if there was no involvement. I would not have become a CAPA collaborator if their members had not found my political commitment compatible with their program of social emancipation. Objectivity, if understood as detachment, was simply impossible, for a mere observer would not have been welcome into the building on Western Avenue more than a few times.

Adding to the impossibility of taking a "detached" stance vis-à-vis the organization I chose to work with was that CAPA had a long history of infiltration by agents provocateurs and undercover police officers. Thus a "fly-on-the-wall approach" to obtaining information about CAPA, while certainly adopted by the police and FBI, would have never worked for me—not as a research strategy (for that would clearly align me with those trying to undermine the work that the coalition was producing) and even less from an ethical standpoint, since choosing the "neutral" route would mean nothing short of choosing the side of those in power for whom the oppression of Black people is a source of privilege (Lipsitz 1998).

Spying has always been a concern for those working at the coalition. During the Black Panther years, agents provocateurs played crucial roles in the wars carried on by the FBI and its Counter-Intelligence Programs—COINTELPROs (Churchill and Vander Wall 1990; Cleaver and Katsiaficas 2001). Such strategies continued when the survivors of those wars formed new organizations in the late 1970s and early 1980s, precisely when the New Right, with Reagan as its prominent symbol, gave (at the very least tacit) carte blanche to repressive tactics against progressive movements in the United States and abroad (Chomsky 2003; Gordon 1998; Sinavandan 2003).

For example, in 1979, after discovering that CAPA had been infiltrated by police agents, its members, together with those of other progressive organizations that had also detected and documented the presence of spies in their headquarters, sued the Los Angeles Police Commission for violation of their constitutional rights to assembly, privacy, and association. Juridically assisted by American Civil Liberties Union (ACLU) attorneys and staff persons, in 1983 the 131 plaintiffs agreed to a $1.8 million settlement. The plaintiffs also imposed a list of nine resolutions upon the city bureaucracy and the Los Angeles Police Department. It was agreed that the California Supreme Court would have jurisdiction over the settlement agreement and would thus regulate and be a guarantee against future spying.[12]

The facts that started the case happened unexpectedly. CAPA and other progressive civil society organizations were pressuring the Los Angeles Police Department to, among other matters, incorporate more persons of color into its staff. In response to these demands, the LAPD issued a press release with a list of persons who were already part of its staff and who had nonwhite backgrounds. To the surprise of many CAPA members, the list contained thirteen names of persons who either had worked or were still working at the coalition. Zinzun's then personal secretary was one of the LAPD staff. The thirteen infiltrators had worked with several progressive organizations, and, as Zinzun showed me, they appear in several photographs of manifestations and rallies against police brutality. It would almost be humorous if it weren't tragic.

I was confronted with the persisting *effects* of this history of spying, infiltration, and intimidation during the whole period I worked at the office, first as a person suspected of being an infiltrator, then as the object of routine threats originating (so attest coalition members) from the police. In the first few months working at CAPA, I was never left alone in the office; I had no access to documents or to certain rooms and drawers, and I was never permitted to be the last one to leave. Old-timers informed me that such precautions were necessary routine. That was when I first heard about the spy cases—they were the rationale offered for the suspicion shown toward new members. I was to be given keys to the office only when the staff agreed that my allegiance was beyond doubt. Because I was at the office every day and developed close rapport to a number of activists there, the process of acquiring keys took over three months. Before that happened, however, as I engaged in daily work at the office—mainly writing flyers, answering the phone, participating in meetings on strategies of community organization, acquiring and rearranging the furniture in the office—I was given several CAPA videos to watch during weekends. The videos were about the LAPD's racism and violence and about the Black Panther's community programs; some were videos of Zinzun's monthly television program *Message to the Grassroots*. I was asked about them later, and it was evident that I was being carefully observed and that my political allegiances were being evaluated.

So much for anthropology's agenda of participant observation—I, the anthropologist, was the object of close scrutiny. Since anthropology is a white-dominated discipline, and therefore one that has historically been associated with spheres of institutionalized power—anthropologists, after all, arrived in unexplored lands as part of the colonization apparatus, together with the army and clergy (see, e.g., Césaire 2000)—it is obvious that its practitioners neither learn how to nor are comfortable with being the ones subjected to observation. The uneasiness with which my work was received in many traditional and conservative academic milieus derives in great part from this reversal of roles. Such reversal becomes even more problematic when Black persons are the subjects of the scrutiny, thus directly questioning not only anthropology but Western thought in general and its deep-seated reliance on the transparency and ultimate imposed (if only imagined) transparency and therefore objectification of the "native informant" (Spivak 1999).

It quickly became clear, however, that activists at the office were not the only ones observing my activities. My "fieldwork" was given yet another twist when, as soon as I was given the keys to the office, I started receiving threatening phone calls. The distorted, metallic low voice told me to "get out of the 'hood'" and made several other threats, the less radical of which promised to kick my ass "real bad." I asked Zinzun about the intimidating phone calls; he responded, matter-of-factly, that they were common. He was certain they were from the police. They were recorded messages sent to everyone working at the coalition and other community organizations.

Threatening phone calls were not the only signs of activity clearly aimed at destabilizing the coalition. The office had been broken into several times since its foundation. One break-in occurred in mid-March of 1996, less than three months after I started working there. Another occurred in August of that same year. As usual, the actions were carried out to resemble robberies: a VCR and some inexpensive objects were taken away and all the drawers and files were searched.[13] But office members knew better. According to Zinzun, the object of the "robberies" was documents that CAPA has been gathering about police brutality over the last twenty years. Psychological intimidation was also an obvious purpose of such break-ins. Yet even though these "burglaries" always caused worry and anger, old-timers downplayed their effectiveness: after all, they had been happening for such a long time that, if they generated some frustration, they caused no more surprise.

These facts only underscore the constant presence of surreptitious surveillance and intimidation focused on those working at the coalition. In 1996, however, this presence was only a pale reminder of the full-scale spying operation that had taken place at CAPA until it was discovered and made the object of a lawsuit in the early 1980s. If the most obvious COINTELPRO operations had ceased with the dismemberment of the Black Panther Party, it was nevertheless evident that their form, content, and inspiration had continued, not only during the years of systematic spying at CAPA, but also in recent events. Zinzun often says the office has been infiltrated from its very first days of existence. In the late 1970s, before the coalition moved to its present Western Avenue office, members of the coalition daily ate and held conversations in the small storefront restaurant next door. The amiable woman who owned and managed the place, and who seemed particularly fond of the young activists, would years later be identified as a police undercover agent.

All of this is to say that—and going back to the frequent question fellow anthropologists and academics asked me—unless your allegiance was beyond doubt, you would neither gain the trust of CAPA activists nor be able to circulate unencumbered in the building. So forget being a graduate student in anthropology trying to do participant observation. You were an activist first and, circumstances permitting, an observer second. Hence the expression I use to characterize my experience at the coalition as it pertains to ethnographic methods: *observant participation*, rather than the traditional *participant observation*. While *participant observation* traditionally puts the emphasis on the observation, *observant participation* refers to active participation in the organized group, such that observation becomes an appendage of the main activity. Indeed, that is how my days were spent: after hours of numerous activities in the office, at night I would write down notes about the day's events and reflect on how they affected and were inflected by the strategies that we were utilizing to combat Black people's oppression. The field notes had at least a double function. Whereas they obviously served to record details about office routine (e.g., interactions between different persons; cases of police brutality we were working on; personal stories offered in the midst of conversations), they were also a means to reflect on the effectiveness, transformation, reformulation, and application of everyday interventions to reverse Black oppression. In other words, what on the surface may appear self-reflexive note taking—the stuff from, about, and in which the self-reflexive moment in anthropology was launched in the mid-1980s (e.g., Marcus and Fischer 1986; Clifford and Marcus 1986; Crapanzano 1980)—in reality constituted the process of self-critique and eventual reformulation that we all underwent as members of the coalition.

DEVELOPING A DIALOGICAL ARGUMENT AND EXPLORING WIDER HORIZONS

As much as activists value self-critique and reformulation of theories and practices associated with the mechanics of community organization, self-critique and reformulation are not enough for the deep and broad comprehension of the phenomena affecting Black people in South Central. As the activists frequently recognized, the critical edge of the discourse and praxis of community organizing necessitated linking the present to the past, the innumerable everyday occurrences to systematic policies affecting the criminal justice system, human geography, employment, and health, among others. An intersectional analysis informed much of the critical consciousness valued at the coalition. Thus, emulating the various seminars that CAPA held on capitalism, Pan-Africanism, racism, and the criminal justice system, I searched for structures of meaning in narratives provided by academic disciplines, archives, and of course the coalition's own documents and hidden transcripts of social intervention. By contextualizing the events of everyday life within a greater framework of historical-genealogical information about the production and maintenance of racialized inequalities, and by juxtaposing this larger framework with the microphysics of everyday life, I attempted to formulate a critical discourse whose form and content, rather than being those of a Cartesian *demonstration*, suggest an *argument*.

An argument is more easily permeable to debate than a demonstration (Perelman 1970). The open-ended character of arguments reflects their necessarily partial, localized, historically determined, and dialogical nature. All the phases involved in critical ethnographies—especially the never-ending feedback that is established between those who are part of the study and what the study presents—are necessarily dialogical. Complicating the process are the inevitable critique and reformulation of the provisional results that one reaches after undertaking research and engaging in dialogue with both oneself and those persons involved in the realities being studied. At CAPA, there was no shortage of incentive to carry out such vital critiques.

In the midst of such radical deconstructions, however, there were palpable and, I would like to think, useful results. I did systematize CAPA's history, from the Panthers to its inauguration in 1976, leading to its present-day perspectives, activities, and dilemmas. The layers and layers of scattered documents that reported on decades of struggles against racist police brutality I was able to put in a narrative that placed local efforts in the context of greater struggles in the United States and the African diaspora. This historical narrative made it possible not only to better understand the theory and praxis of contemporary struggles but also to place those struggles in a transnational perspective. Although present in many of the activists' consciousness, such a historical narrative was not easily transmitted to newcomers, much less to other community activists who could draw from this knowledge important insights into strategies of locating and averting processes of anti-Black marginalization.

The pressing need to explore wider horizons of understanding and action is a fundamental message offered by these organizations. The exploration of wider horizons is manifest in several ways: in the establishment of dialogue according to basic principles of communicative rationality; in the attempts to understand, draw on, and at the same time expand given racial classifications; and in the formation of effective, locally and globally based social movements. Widening horizons means searching for deep historical roots and broad social structures and connecting these to personal and collective action aimed at building alternative modes of sociability at home and abroad. CSGT is not only increasingly Latina/o but fast becoming more international. As well, CAPA and CSGT recognize their problematic reliance on patriarchal modes of organizing. Men and women often talk about the specific forms of male-centered behavior that impede the full blossoming of the movement's emancipatory potential. Widening horizons implies not only questioning the common subordination of politics to essentialized identities—interrogating and learning and building from so-called identity politics—but also, and most importantly, defining identities in accordance with an inclusive and radical political praxis, a praxis that searches, persistently, for greater equality and justice beyond the physical and ideological limitations defined by rigid hierarchies based on race, gender, and sexuality. Widening horizons, finally, means questioning and moving beyond local and national borders.[14]

It can be argued that translating scattered information into a linear narrative, besides unnecessarily changing the nature of the anarchic and improvisational methods of community organizing, also makes such methods more easily domesticated and appropriated by individuals and institutions who may not have the same political liberatory goals. Such an argument presents another critical problem for activist research: In which ways, if any, does it advance the agenda of those who are featured in academic media (papers, books, talks) but are not a part of these media? Although activists at the coalition and CSGT often reminded me that I was contributing, I am more skeptical.

That the liberation-oriented knowledge is more clearly articulated and practiced in activist settings such as CAPA and CSGT underscores the many ways in which activist research is often based on a disproportionate exchange of skills and information. What did I bring to the coalition? What benefits accrued from my presence? Other than my time and willingness to perform banal office work and sometimes engage in projects that could have been conceptualized and carried out by almost anyone—such as the computer classes Zinzun and I started in 1996—there was not much in my set of skills that was of vital importance. The personal, intellectual, and political lessons that I learned were far greater and more vital than anything that I could have ever offered to the activists in Los Angeles. When he heard my opinion on these matters, Zinzun did not disagree. Yet he always insisted that I keep doing what I did: that is, occupy the space in academia, teach, conduct research, and as importantly continue to bring people like him and other freedom fighters to the closely policed spaces of the university. In this wisdom was the recognition that we academics can play a role, but one that is always marginal and necessarily informed by long his/herstories of freedom dreams.

NOTES

1. For further description and analysis of CAPA, CSGT, and the Los Angeles context within which these organizations operate, see Vargas (1999).

2. CAPA, "CAPA Report: 1989 through 1993," n.d., unpaginated.

3. In 1979, after discovering that CAPA had been infiltrated by police agents, its members, together with those of other progressive organizations that had also detected and documented the presence of spies in their headquarters, sued the Los Angeles Police Commission for violation of their constitutional rights to assembly, privacy, and association. Juridically assisted by American Civil Liberties Union (ACLU) attorneys and staff persons, in 1983 the 131 plaintiffs agreed with a $1.8 million settlement. The plaintiffs also imposed a list of nine resolutions upon the city bureaucracy and the Los Angeles Police Department. It was agreed that the California Supreme Court would have jurisdiction over the settlement agreement and thus regulate and be a guarantee against future spying. In 1986, after being beaten by Pasadena police officers and losing his sight in one eye, Zinzun won a $1.2 million suit against the city. In July 1994, Zinzun was awarded $512,500 after a dispute with the LAPD's second-in-command, Assistant Chief Robert L. Vernon. While Zinzun was campaigning for the Pasadena Board of City Directors in 1989, Vernon accused Zinzun of terrorist acts. For an analysis of various lawsuits waged by CAPA members against the Los Angeles Police Department, see Vargas (1999, ch. 6).

4. It is important to note that the connection between gang members and progressive political organizations was a common occurrence in Los Angeles during the years of the Black Panther Party. Two of the BPP's most well-known members, Bunchy Carter and Jon Huggins, had been members of local street gangs. U.S. members killed Carter and Huggins (Churchill and Vander Wall 1990; Churchill 2001).

5. CSGT, "Fund for a New L.A." proposal, December 1994, 1.
6. CSGT, "Statement of Economic Development," n.d., 3.
7. Ibid. This proposal is an obvious alternative to Rebuild Los Angeles (RLA), a nonprofit corporation headed by Peter Ueberroth that embodied the revitalization program launched in May of 1992 by Mayor Tom Bradley following that year's rebellion in South Central. Even though RLA spoke the language of a public-private partnership, the initiative was clearly corporate minded, dominated by representatives of major companies and closed to public participation. In the end, the market-driven model that structured RLA failed to provide enough or adequate jobs. For an insightful analysis of the limits of RLA, see Labor/Community Strategy Center (1996).

8. As stated in "Our Demands: What Our Community Needs"(n.d.):

Stop the criminalization of our youth!
   1. Eliminate the national gang database which currently gives youth a permanent record for simply being detained for *"suspicion of being a gang member,"* even if the youth is later released for lack of evidence. What must happen is changing state legislation to erase the records of any individual unjustly detained or arrested and permanently recorded. This record often prevents them from being employed.
   2. Eliminate federal programs such as "Weed and Seed" that target whole communities as being non-rehabilitable, subject them to repressive law enforcement programs and place social service monies under the jurisdiction of law enforcement agencies.
   3. Eliminate illegal searches and gang sweeps.
   4. Stop police abuse and their "Us Against Them" attitude. (8)

These demands stand against an array of law enforcement measures that are specific to the 1980s and whose main results were to further criminalize, arrest, and stigmatize brown and Black youth. For an analysis of 1980s law enforcement policies and practices in Los Angeles, see Davis (1992, ch. 5).

The urgency of such demands became even clearer when the Rampart scandal erupted. The scandal began when LAPD officer Rafael A. Perez was arrested on August 25, 1998, on suspicion of stealing cocaine from the LAPD headquarters. In September 1999, Perez pleaded guilty of stealing eight pounds of cocaine. He accepted a confidential plea agreement according to which he is expected to receive a reduced sentence on the drug charges in exchange for identifying other police officers involved in crimes and misconduct. Subsequently twenty officers were relieved of duty, were suspended without pay, were fired, or resigned. See Cannon (2000).

9. Of great concern among inner-city Black and brown youth is the "three-strikes law," which gives persons with three felony convictions a mandatory sentence of twenty-five years to life in prison. Juveniles sixteen years and older can face adjudications that can be counted as "strikes." These strikes become a permanent part of one's police record. "*Do not plead guilty* to any felony without first understanding that the *plea will result in an automatic strike* on your record," advises CSGT. "It is unethical for your attorney to not clearly explain the danger of life imprisonment with a guilty plea to felony charges in the '3 Strikes' environment ... Juveniles 16 years or older who face adjudications that can be counted as 'strikes' should demand *an adult trial with legal representation and all constitutional protection, including a jury trial*" ("Statement of Economic Development," 11). For a pertinent analysis of the official justifications and effects of the "three-strikes law," see, for example, Donziger (1996, chs. 1 and 4). For an account of the impact of the criminal justice system on young Black men, see Miller (1996).

10. As was reported in the *Pelican Bay Prison Express*, April 1996, 25. CAPA has been successful in expanding its geographical horizons, maintaining contacts and frequent interchange visits with organizations of various cities in the United States and abroad. In recent years, coalition members have visited England, France, several African countries, and Brazil. Persons from these countries and American cities are constantly coming to Los Angeles and spending time at the coalition, exchanging information and techniques of community organization. Zinzun's national and international visibility—and that of other coalition and CSGT members—has projected their cause well beyond the City of Angels' core neighborhoods.

11. Exceptions: MacLeod (1995); Gregory (1998); etc.

12. These facts are also narrated in Escobar (1993).

13. In 1992, for example, following the uprisings, a more radical "robbery" was conducted. VCRs, televisions, tapes, and other valuables were taken. Yet even though several offices were housed in the same building, only CAPA drawers were searched—a clear sign that the "robbers" knew exactly where and what to look for.

14. These political stances, it should be noted, do not constitute outright negations of identity politics. Contrary to critics of race-based identity politics on the right and left of the political spectrum, organizations such as CAPA and CSGT clearly operate under the concept that identity politics is necessary. These organizations, however, are constantly engaged in reinventing their identities and, for that matter, revisiting their notions of race as these are inflected by the international experience. Thus they recognize that identity politics, while necessary, are not fixed and not sufficient. Various authors, according to my interpretation of

their texts, have localized similar tensions in progressive grassroots organizations; see Kelley (1997); Collins (1998); Sudbury (1998).

REFERENCES

Anderson, Elijah. 1990. *Streetwise: Race, Class, and Change in an Urban Community.* Chicago: University of Chicago Press.
Cannon, Lou. 2000. "One Bad Cop." *New York Times Magazine*, October 1, 32.
Carmichael, Stokely, and Charles Hamilton. 1967. *Black Power: The Politics of Liberation in America.* New York: Random House.
Césaire, Aimé. 2000. *Discourse on Colonialism.* New York: Monthly Review Press.
Chomsky, Noam. 2003. *Hegemony or Survival: America's Quest for Global Dominance.* New York: Metropolitan Books.
Churchill, Ward. 2001. "'To Disrupt, Discredit and Destroy': The FBI's Secret War against the Black Panther Party." In *Liberation, Imagination, and the Black Panther Party*, edited by Kathleen Cleaver and George Katsiaficas. New York: Routledge.
Churchill, Ward, and Jim Vander Wall. 1990. *Agents of Repression: The FBI's Secret Wars against the Black Panther Party and the American Indian Movement.* Boston: South End Press.
Clifford, James, and George Marcus, eds. 1986. *Writing Culture: The Poetics and Politics of Ethnography.* Berkeley: University of California Press.
Collins, Patricia Hill. 1991. *Black Feminist Thought: Knowledge, Consciousness, and the Politics of Empowerment.* New York: Routledge, 1991.
———. 1998. *Fighting Words: Black Women and the Search for Justice.* Minneapolis: University of Minnesota Press.
Crapanzano, Vincent. 1980. *Tuhami: Portrait of a Moroccan.* Chicago: University of Chicago Press.
Crenshaw, Kimberlé, et al., eds. 1995. *Critical Race Theory: The Key Writings That formed the Movement.* New York: New Press.
Davis, Mike. 1992. *City of Quartz.* New York: Vintage Books.
Donziger, Steven, ed. 1996. *The Real War on Crime.* New York: HarperPerennial.
Escobar, Edward J. 1993. "The Dialectics of Repression: The Los Angeles Police Department and the Chicano Movement, 1968–1971." *Journal of American History* 79 (March): 1483–1514.
Feyerabend, Paul. 1988. *Against Method.* London: Verso.
Gordon, Edmund. 1998. *Disparate Diasporas: Identity and Politics in an African-Nicaraguan Community.* Austin: University of Texas Press.
Gregory, Steven. 1998. *Black Corona: Race and the Politics of Place in an Urban Community.* Princeton: Princeton University Press.
Hannerz, Ulf. 1969. *Soulside: Inquiries into Ghetto Culture and Community.* New York: Columbia University Press, 1969.

Jah, Yusuf, and Sister Shah'Keyah. 1995. *Uprising: Crips and Bloods Tell the Story of America's Youth in the Crossfire.* New York: Scribner.

Kelley, Robin. 1997. *Yo' Mama's Disfunktional! Fighting the Culture Wars in Urban America.* Boston: Beacon Press.

Labor/Community Strategy Center. 1996. *Reconstructing Los Angeles—and U.S. Cities—from the Bottom Up.* Los Angeles: Labor/Community Strategy Center.

Lipsitz, George. 1998. *The Possessive Investment in Whiteness: How White People Profit from Identity Politics.* Philadelphia: Temple University Press.

MacLeod, Jay. 1995. *Ain't No Makin' It: Aspirations and Attainment in a Low-Income Neighborhood.* Boulder, CO: Westview Press.

Marcus, George, and Michael M. J. Fischer. 1986. *Anthropology as Cultural Critique: An Experimental Moment in the Human Sciences.* Chicago: University of Chicago Press.

Miller, Jerome G. 1996. *Search and Destroy: African-American Males in the Criminal Justice System.* New York: Cambridge University Press.

Perelman, Chaim. 1970. *Le Champ de l'argumentation.* Brussels: Presses Universitaires de Bruxelles.

Robinson, Cedric. 1983/2000. *Black Marxism: The Making of the Black Radical Tradition.* Chapel Hill: University of North Carolina Press.

Sinavandan, A. 2003. "Racism and the Market-State." *Race and Class* 44 (4): 71–76.

Spivak, Gayatri. 1999. *A Critique of Postcolonial Reason: Toward a History of the Vanishing Present.* Cambridge, MA: Harvard University Press.

Sudbury, Julia. 1998. *"Other Kinds of Dreams": Black Women's Organizations and the Politics of Transformation.* London: Routledge.

Vargas, João H. Costa. 1999. "Blacks in the City of Angels' Dust." PhD diss., University of California, San Diego.

Waters, Mary C. 1999. *Black Identities: West Indian Immigrant Dreams and American Realities.* New York: Russell Sage Foundation.

Wilson, William Julius. 1996. *When Work Disappears: The World of the New Urban Poor.* New York: Knopf.

7. Making Violence Visible

An Activist Anthropological Approach to Women's Rights Investigation

Samuel Martínez

Anthropologists live among the humans whose ways of life they study, but rarely do they treat these people as research collaborators rather than as research subjects. Why should this be so? Why should the people whose lives anthropologists study be left only reactive channels of influence (the answers they give to the scientists' questions) over how their own ways of life will be represented to the rest of the world? The "science hawks," who consider it a basic principle of scientific validity that research scientists alone should decide what questions are asked (Gross and Plattner 2002), are a minority within anthropology. Yet many more anthropologists, I suspect, simply do not think of questioning conventional limits to community members' research participation, even as these anthropologists strive to open up information and insights not attainable through interviews or casual interaction by participating as fully as they can in their host societies. The contradiction is clear: the anthropologist's participation in community life is valued even as the community's participation in ethnography is devalued. Considering also how much critical scrutiny has turned toward the production of knowledge in our discipline, it seems doubly odd that anthropologists so rarely ask why methodological authority remains concentrated in their hands. After all, cultural anthropologists should be particularly well situated, when compared to researchers in other disciplines, to activate the interested participation in the research process of the people we live among as we study their lives. Why, then, is "subject participation," participant observation's opposite and complement, not more often a salient approach to ethnography?

To my eyes, it is hard to explain anthropology's methodological exclusionism only if one views ethnography in the power vacuum of abstract knowledge. A starting premise of my essay is, to the contrary, that power cannot be excluded from any full discussion of social research methods. I expand upon Merrill Singer's (1994) argument that ethnography is a "dominative" method of study when guided solely by the researcher's priorities and carried out through methods that make no sense to the people being studied. While anthropologists might not seem to be powerful people, it is a form of power to have the authority and ability to say what is important to study (and even more crucially, what is not important), dictate how it shall be studied, and decide to whom and in what forms the results of the research will be distributed. Self-limiting though it is to confine our power chiefly to the halls of academe, power even in small doses brings comfort. Conversely, risking your power, by sharing it with the people among whom you do your fieldwork, is apt to provoke anxiety, even if the risk brings opportunities to generate another kind of power: wider attention and respect for our research and writing outside academia. Power of another, institutional, kind inheres in the formulation and use of tallies of knowledge production, in deciding pay, privileges, promotion, and prestige. I will say more about those institutional constraints on activist scholarship below (see also Pulido, chapter 13 of this volume).

But I want first to hold onto the point that anthropologists can do much more than they generally have done to activate people's interested collaboration by involving them in designing the research to yield benefit to both parties. Charles Hale articulates a methodological justification for this kind of research in a recent issue of the Social Science Research Council's (SSRC's) *Items and Issues* (see also Speed, chapter 8 of this volume):

> A sweeping claim to "better" results from activist research will no doubt prove difficult to substantiate. But it surely can be defended on at least two more particular grounds: a) people, who ultimately are the sources of social science "data," tend to provide much more, and much higher quality, information when they feel they have an active stake in the research process. Often, especially when the topic is charged or sensitive, they only provide information under these conditions; b) collective participation of these "subjects" in data collection and its interpretation inevitably enriches what we end up learning from the research. (Hale 2001, 15)

In what follows, I offer limited confirmation of Hale's points by relating some of my experiences in pursuing collaborative research on a highly "charged and sensitive" topic, the subordination and sexual exploitation of Haitian immigrant women in the Caribbean nation of the Dominican

Republic. From July through September of 2002, the middle months of a six-month field research trip to the Dominican Republic, I sought to forge a partnership with a leading advocacy and development group, the Movimiento de Mujeres Domínico-Haitianas (Movement of Haitian-Dominican Women, MUDHA). This collaboration was but one part of a larger study, comparing the agenda and action strategies of Haitian-Dominican rights organizations, including MUDHA, with those of international human rights monitor groups that have worked on behalf of Haitian-Dominicans' rights. From the standpoint of my larger aims, the research was a qualified success in that I gained greatly from the time I spent with MUDHA staff. However, the collaborative dimension of the research was not in the end realized in the form that I had envisioned. My relationship with MUDHA continues. Since my field research, I have provided support for litigation they successfully pressed against the Dominican state in the Inter-American Court of Human Rights. I plan to do more field research on advocacy for Haitians' rights, and I look forward to collaborating more closely with MUDHA and other Haitian-Dominican nongovernmental organizations (NGOs) in future years. Yet I think it is not premature to attempt a sober assessment of our collaboration to date. My aim is not to question the desirability, validity, or even feasibility of activist scholarship but to evoke how complex Hale's proposed research agenda is and to ponder what obstacles may block its wider implementation in the anthropological discipline.

CONTRADICTIONS ALL AROUND

I was driven to craft a proposal for collaborative research with MUDHA partly by the personal motive of paying back part of my debt to the people among whom I had done my earlier fieldwork, Haitian immigrants working in the lowermost echelons of the Dominican Republic's sugar industry. Like many another anthropologist, I have on my conscience the asymmetry between what I and my research subjects in Haiti and the Dominican Republic have gained from the ethnographic relationship. In large part on the basis of my research among them, I have gained the highest academic degree, publications, and job security. They mostly remain in poverty, some even still living in the same ramshackle barracks in which I found them when I made my first of many fieldwork visits to the Dominican Republic in 1985. But in seeking this research partnership, I mainly sought practical help in getting at what lay underneath an odd silence, the inattention to the lives of the women of that community that has characterized the reports of dozens of humanitarian, academic, and journalistic observers over three decades. The magnitude of the rights violations against women, involving human trafficking, sexual exploitation, sexual violence, and domestic violence, has gone almost totally unrecognized in what has been published about the situation of Haitians in the Dominican Republic. In earlier ethnographic research I had found that, as early as the 1940s up to the suppression of forced labor recruitment practices by the government of President Leonel Fernández in 1997, tens of thousands of women entered the Dominican Republic from Haiti, many of these women being relocated involuntarily to the sugar estates along with the men who cut the sugarcane. Though the women did not do much work in the sugarcane fields, they shared living quarters with the men and struggled for survival alongside them. During and after their detention and relocation, many of these women suffered sexual violence and exploitation. And, even now that the most flagrant abuses involving the forced relocation of Haitian entrants have been suppressed, these women's daughters of the second and third generation may continue to be preyed upon by men in power on the sugar estates. The evidence that the women's rights abuses affecting Haitians in the Dominican Republic were highly prevalent and serious led me to propose research collaboration with MUDHA, an advocacy organization with unsurpassed ties among Haitian immigrant women. Once I embarked upon this research, I would find that advocates for Haitians' rights in the Dominican Republic could provide detailed accounts of such abuses, amply confirming my suspicions about the seriousness of the wrongs. While I knew that finding women to provide their own, first-person testimony would be difficult, I was surprised that even organizing a research team to do these interviews was challenging.

Prior to this experience I had stuck pretty closely to the academic pole on the continuum from academic reflection to activist praxis. When Charles Hale first invited me to make a presentation to the L.A. workshop on activist scholarship, I harbored doubts about my qualifications to speak to the issue. I now think that my primarily academic pedigree is one good reason why my experience may hold lessons about the worth and challenge of doing activist anthropology. To the degree to which my experience highlights challenges likely to be faced by "wannabe" activist scholars, cautionary conclusions may be tentatively drawn from it regarding the likelihood of activist anthropology gaining converts among academicians like me. As someone whose practice had not previously involved either professional advocacy or collaborative research, was it enough for me simply to feel dissatisfied with the lack of influence of my work outside academe and to have identified what seemed like an ideal case to break out of the box of ethnographic convention? My answer to this question can be instructive to others to the degree that it reflects challenges that other well-meaning, highly informed but advocacy-inexperienced anthropologists would be likely to confront in attempting to forge similar activist research collaborations. I am unsure how much can be generalized from the successes and failures of my fieldwork. Nevertheless, I feel certain that I raise a concern of wider applicability to activist anthropology: How easily can the research practice of primarily academic anthropologists be "retrofitted" to an activist mold? If the answer is "Not very easily," then what are the implications for activist anthropologists of the future?

Before taking up the case study, I will briefly compare activist anthropology with earlier broad programs of "real-world-relevant" anthropological research, giving particular attention to the hidden power imbalances behind conventional research models and how activist anthropology may redress these.

ACTIVIST ANTHROPOLOGY VERSUS APPLIED ANTHROPOLOGY

Dating back to the middle of the twentieth century but with increasing rapidity since the 1960s, a succession of proposals have been made to render the findings of anthropology more comprehensible, accessible, and useful to government, business, humanitarian outreach, and the philanthropic sector. Clearly the most influential—even hegemonic—has been "applied anthropology." From a mainstream anthropological standpoint, the question will inevitably be asked: What sets activist anthropology apart from applied anthropology and other prior approaches that claim to contribute to the solution of social problems?

Beyond the obvious features of activist scholarship (taking an explicit political stand, most often critical of harmful business practices or government policies, in alignment with the agenda of a group with which you have done research), I think that activist anthropology's distinctive characteristics are methodological and, even more importantly, institutional. For activist anthropologists, the methods and institutional contexts of research are as much political issues as the aims toward which the knowledge is applied.[1] Activist anthropology takes as its starting point an institutionally focused and globally contextualized critique of anthropol-

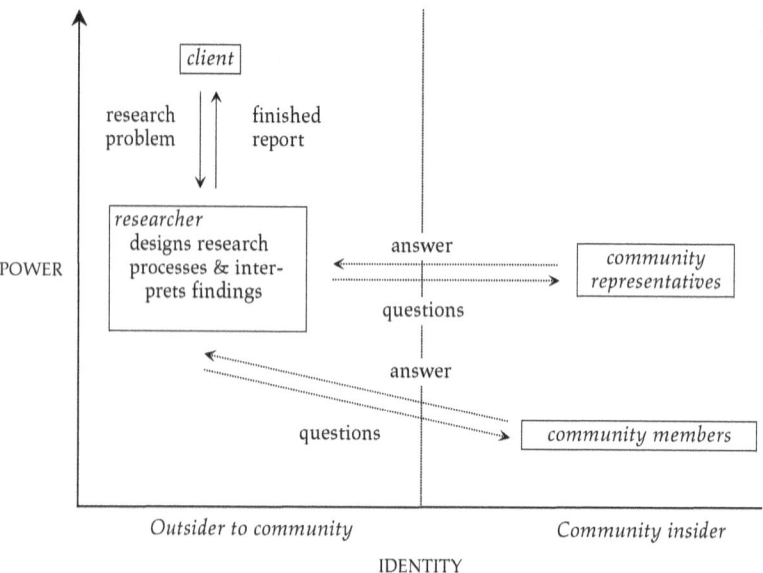

FIGURE 3. Structure of Knowledge Production in Applied Anthropology

ogy (building and amplifying upon the critical turn in the anthropological discipline of recent decades) and follows through on this critique of knowledge, not with a postmodernist shrug of futility, but with a novel and politically engaged program of study.[2] The latter program is defined not by a global theory or set of methods but by the resituating of the ethnographer as a political ally of the people among whom she is doing fieldwork rather than as a live-in inquisitor.

This contrast can be made clearer by briefly considering the institutional structure of applied research in anthropology. It is crucial to note that "applied anthropology" involves a vast and varied group of anthropologists, ranging from "practicing anthropologists," who hold nonacademic jobs, all the way to anthropologists with academic appointments who do "applied research" only in the sense that they study important problems—for example, in agricultural development or public health—but whose research and publication practices may be otherwise indistinguishable from the academic mainstream and whose findings may never end up being applied at all.[3] While there is a continuum with shades of gray between the academic and practicing profiles, the far reaches of the continuum are clearly distinct, with contract research at one end and research carried out under academic auspices at the other. For clarity's sake and with the caveat that I simplify greatly, I here consider the practice of the former—contract researchers and anthropologists who work full time for business corporations, government, and international finance and development institutions—as the distinctive institutional model for applied anthropology.

At this nonacademic pole of the applied anthropology continuum, a common institutional condition of contract and practicing anthropology is that both are client driven. Whether the client is his permanent employer or a contracting agency, in government, business, or an international financial, health, or development agency, the contract or practicing anthropologist does research to provide answers to the questions his client is asking. Dependence on clients imposes a strictly vertical structure of knowledge production and dissemination (see Figure 3). The contract/practicing anthropology model differs from the academic model less in the structure of knowledge acquisition than in the way in which knowledge is finally disseminated.[4] Research subjects provide the raw material of information, which is passed through a value-adding process of refinement, processing, and packaging by the contract or practicing anthropologist. He, in turn, passes his findings, in the form of finished reports, upward to the firm or agency that is paying for the research, rather than "contributing" these, in the less obviously mercenary style and parlance of academia, to an amorphous "body of knowledge." The agency that commissioned the work decides whether, when, how much, and through what channels the information gathered by the applied anthropologist will ever be released to the public or shared with partner organizations.[5] For the most part, the anthropologist conducts this contract research without forming partnerships with organizations based in the host communities, though that may be changing at least superficially as a result of the increased influence and prestige of NGOs in development, health, and humanitarian outreach.

None of this precludes the applied anthropologist's creation of horizontal links on his own. Practicing anthropologists doubtless get a lot of their best insights by talking with local practitioners and community representatives "on the side." Often, when the research setting is unfamiliar to them, the only way applied anthropologists can "get up to speed" on local affairs is to crib notes from the professionals who have on-the-ground experience. At times, sincere and lasting ties of friendship and collegiality are formed. Yet these horizontal ties remain optional and for the most part weak. Local advocates are not often given a say about what is to

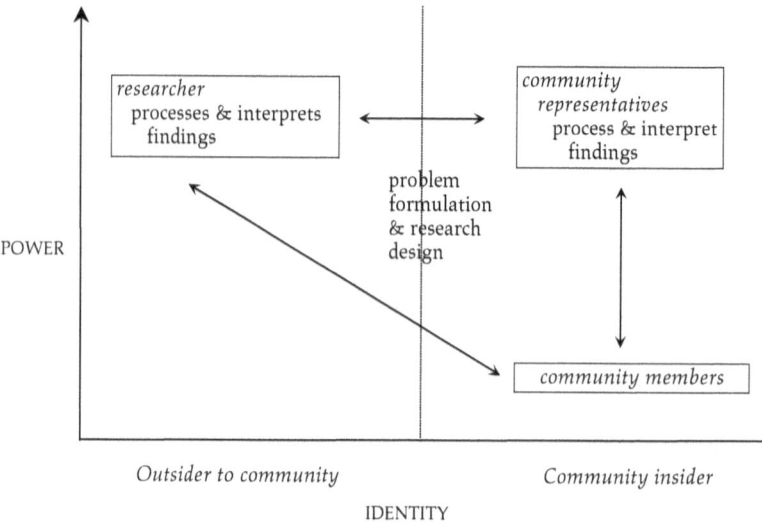

FIGURE 4. Structure of Knowledge Production in Activist Anthropology

be researched or how, a source of considerable frustration among the staffs of NGOs in the global South. These people often regard the visiting anthropologist, whether academic or applied, as a parasite that lands in their offices, sucks out valuable insights and information, and then takes flight, never to be heard from again (see also Pulido, chapter 13 of this volume on the importance of "accountability" and "reciprocity" within activist scholarship).

The activist model of knowledge production departs from the applied anthropology model first by lopping off the top of this vertical structure. Without a sponsoring client to set the research agenda, the activist researcher enjoys greater freedom to engage local practitioners and advocates, marginalized in the applied model, in a reiterative dialogue about the goals and methods of the research (see Figure 4). Realistically, it must be recognized that our erstwhile research subjects in low-income communities remain below us on the research power gradient. It is perhaps also unavoidable that, even when communicating through the medium of "base community organizations," community members do not always speak with a single voice and may be more reticent than hoped for, tending too readily to defer to their own leaders and to researchers and practitioners of higher socioeconomic status. Even in the activist research model, therefore, responsibility for knowledge formulation and dissemination may thus often rest unequally in the hands of the primary research partners. Yet one already noted goal of activist research is to bring members of the population targeted for action into the research-design dialogue. For what the activist anthropologist seeks at the outset is not answers to predefined questions but clues about what the research questions should be, vis-à-vis priorities for action that can be identified only through dialogue with community members and community organizers. Rather than a vertical chain, which assigns the actors at each level of power highly distinct and discrete functions and unequal power to set the research agenda, the activist research process ideally generates a dialogic triangle. In this triangle, even the most humble participant can provide information, insights, or objections that set in motion an agenda-modifying discussion among the research team.

Activist anthropology is also predicated on full information sharing between the researcher and her partner organization(s). Rather than a contract, the social relations of knowledge production of activist anthropology might be appropriately compared to a *convite*, the festive, collective agricultural work days still commonly practiced by peasants in the Dominican Republic and their neighbors in Haiti (who call this custom *konbit*). The *Almanaque folklórico dominicano* describes the *convite* as follows:

> When a peasant is going to roof his house, plant his crops, or collect his harvest, etc., and does not have the means to pay, he invites his neighbors and friends to carry out the task in question between them all without receiving any monetary remuneration for this.
>
> The organizer of the *convite* or *junta* is responsible for [providing] food and drink for the participants. Beautiful work songs are sung there, and at mealtime instruments are also played. (Domínguez, Castillo, and Tejeda 1978, 118, my translation)

Like the *convite*, activist anthropology puts people to work alongside each other, each side maintaining a distinct project, the anthropologist hoping to harvest academic publications even as he helps activists cultivate political or organizational gains. As in peasant agriculture, the goal of activist anthropology is not generating maximum output but generating sustainable and equitably shared gain. And, as in the *convite*, reciprocity guides the activist anthropological partnership—at every stage of the research cycle, from problem formulation to dissemination of findings—rather than giving either contracting agencies or the researchers control over what questions matter and how to study them.

THE IMMIGRANTS AND THEIR ADVOCATES

Among the many imaginable venues for activist anthropology, few engage the special skills of anthropologists better than collaborating with not-for-profit organizations dedicated to formulating effective responses to social, health, and economic development problems. Anthropologists' knowledge and ways of learning are highly adaptable to these organizations, their work settings, and their goals. Our linguistic fluency, knowledge of local communities, and flexible field research methods prepare us well to collaborate with local partners in producing information that is reliable and relevant to household and community-level problems. We are used to spending large amounts of unstructured time in our research, listening to and learning from people of all social strata and walks of life. Our experience writing grants and reports is, by contrast, underutilized while we are in "the field," but this resource could also be put to good use in working with an NGO. These were the kinds of possible roles I envisioned developing in my Dominican Republic research in 2002. My immediate aim was to learn about the social organization and guiding concepts of two Haitian-Dominican NGOs by accompanying their staff in their everyday activities. It was understood by all that a further aim was to be the formulation of a viable participatory project for gathering information about the underexposed human rights abuses experienced by Haitian immigrant women.

It is significant that this way of doing anthropological research only crystallized in my mind in response to the challenge of competing for a grant that explicitly required such horizontal academic-practitioner collaborations. The seed of an activist research approach may have lain in my mind for years, but to grow into a proposal it needed the fertile ground of a reward comprehensible to an academician: grant money for fieldwork and research leave. The SSRC's Global Security and Cooperation (GSC) program, foreseeing the need to build bridges between scholars and practitioners in the broad field of international security, ran a two-year experiment with funding from the John D. and Catherine T. McArthur Foundation. They invited proposals by scholars to learn by participating in the activities of governmental, multilateral, or nongovernmental organizations. The idea was that, by contributing to ongoing projects, academicians could learn from the inside how such organizations work. It was anticipated that through these situated learning experiences trust would be built, communication across the academic-practitioner divide would flow more clearly, and new ideas for collaborative research would emerge through discussion. As I wrote the proposal, I felt that my research aims fell easily and naturally into the program's situated learning frame. Perhaps latent in my mind for some time, the idea needed only an appropriate institutional stimulus to hatch.

With support from the GSC program, I carried out six months of field research in the Dominican Republic. I focused on the human rights agenda and modes of activism of two small NGOs, founded and staffed by second-generation immigrants from neighboring Haiti (Haitian-Dominicans), MUDHA and the Centro Cultural Domínico-Haitiano (Haitian-Dominican Cultural Center, CCDH). The CCDH was the first Haitian-Dominican rights organization, founded in July 1982 in the southeastern sugar port city of San Pedro de Macorís. Its main goals are (1) to promote recognition, in law and in fact, of the Dominican nationality and citizenship of all Haitian-Dominicans and (2) to affirm and valorize the Haitian origin of Haitian-Dominicans. MUDHA spun off from CCDH in 1983 but was not officially incorporated as an organization until 1992. Its coordinator, Solange Pierre, has always been a dominant presence in the organization and has emerged in recent years as the leading voice in international forums for her community's rights. MUDHA's main mission is to defend and promote the rights of female Haitian immigrants and to attain rights of full citizenship for their Dominican-born children. MUDHA's mission statement defines these rights in the widest terms: "civil, political, economic, social, cultural, and human." Both groups place primary emphasis on grassroots organization and capacity building among their constituent community groups. To gain further understanding of the organizations' goals, a few words of background are necessary about the history and political economy of immigration from Haiti to the Dominican Republic.

On the Dominican side of the border, the main sources of demand for Haitian immigrant labor fall into two broad categories. The first is the sugar industry, which since the early decades of the twentieth century has recruited men from rural Haiti as cane cutters (braceros). The second major source of demand has been industries other than sugar, which have pulled in Haitian immigrants both from the sugar estates and directly from Haiti. Historically, the two main nonsugar employers have been coffee and construction, but many Haitians, particularly women, have also found work in domestic service and petty commerce (Silié, Segura, and Dore Cabral 2002). As late as the 1970s, a combination of police vigilance, social isolation, and widespread discrimination restricted the employment of Haitian labor mainly to a few trades. Now Haitians are employed not just in the sugar and coffee industries but in agricultural sectors where they were previously rarely found (Lozano 1993). Also, it seems that a variety of informal income-generating opportunities, including petty commerce and domestic service, are attracting Haitians to the city in growing numbers (Facultad Latinoamericana de Ciencias Sociales [FLACSO] 2004, 32). Evidence of the continued expansion of Haitian labor into new urban employment niches is observable in many parts of the Dominican capital, Santo Domingo. Also, sugar is no longer as central as it once was to the Dominican economy, and this industry's demand for cheap harvest labor has declined significantly.

The plight of the Haitian braceros became a topic of international scrutiny in the late 1970s and has gone in and out of the human rights spotlight repeatedly in the quarter-century since. Monitors from at least seven multilateral and NGOs, along with independent journalists and human rights advocates, have repeatedly brought the situation of the immigrants to international attention, often alleging that the constraints placed on the braceros' freedoms were so severe as to constitute de facto slavery. These reports have presented firsthand testimony of men, and even boys as young as seven, being recruited in Haiti by sugar-company touts with false promises of easy, well-paid employment in the Dominican Republic. They have reported undocumented Haitian entrants being captured by Dominican police and military agents, then forcibly relocated to state-owned sugar estates. And they have evoked images of these recruits being forced at gunpoint to cut sugarcane, for below-minimum wages, under dangerous and unsanitary conditions.[6]

The accuracy and completeness of these reports are questionable at a number of levels. Costly gaffes resulted from the errors in the approaches and analyses of the international NGOs. In 1991, the clumsy use of pressure tactics without adequate coordination with local Haitian rights advocates was undoubtedly the major proximate trigger for an official backlash in the form of the largest-ever deportation of undocumented immigrants to Haiti (Martínez 1995, 164–67). Until the mid-1990s, it could safely be said that international pressure had achieved little other than pushing the Santo Domingo government to enact cosmetic reforms in migrant labor recruitment and employment practices.

Perhaps most problematic among the omissions and simplifications that have characterized the international human rights reportage on this case has been the all-too-frequent silence of journalists, monitors, and academicians about the situation of both second-generation Haitians and female Haitian immigrants generally, attention having focused almost exclusively on the slaverylike conditions of recruitment and employment of male sugarcane workers from Haiti. What led highly experienced international monitors, with relatively free access to the affected communities, to overlook whole categories of victims and types of abuses? Why did observers focus so narrowly, for more than two decades, on the civil and political rights abuses that constituted the alleged enslavement of male sugarcane workers, to the exclusion of other abuses and other segments of the Haitian immigrant population?

Brighter prospects for effective international solidarity have emerged more recently. A major turning point came in 1996 with the election of opposition candidate Leonel Fernández to the Dominican presidency. Under Fernández, reforms were instituted in the procedures by which Haitian immigrants were recruited as cane workers. Most importantly, his government ended the practice of forcibly relocating undocumented Haitians to the state-owned sugar estates. On the negative side, the Fernández government instituted routine deportations of tens of thousands of Haitian nationals each year, a practice continued by subsequent administrations.

In the late 1990s, the struggle for Haitians' rights assumed a major new dimension with the presentation of claims before the Inter-American Court of Human Rights (IACHR) by the Berkeley and Columbia University human rights law clinics and the Washington-based Center for Justice and International Law (CEJIL), in collaboration with MUDHA. The plaintiffs in these cases have sought remedies from the Dominican state on behalf of Haitian nationals who were repatriated without due process and for Haitian-Dominicans who were deported in spite of carrying valid legal identity documents identifying them as Dominican citizens. Partial victories have been won in the IACHR, and the Dominican government has been forced to facilitate the readmission of certain plaintiffs into the country (Pierre 2001). In March 2005 an important new case was brought before the Inter-American Court by MUDHA, with help from the Berkeley and CEJIL legal team. This case was filed on behalf of two Dominican-born girls of Haitian parentage who had been denied Dominican citizenship in spite of their mothers' having presented all the legal documents generally considered necessary for granting citizenship by Dominican civil registries. Like these girls, tens of thousands of other Haitian-Dominicans born in recent decades have been rendered de facto stateless persons and consequently denied basic rights of education, identity, and internal and international mobility. Important as this litigation has been, it is of comparable significance, in my opinion, that now at last international advocates are working as partners with Haitian-Dominican advocates who are active on the ground. The days when priorities and strategies of advocacy were defined entirely by international NGOs, with minimal consultation with local activists, are fortunately now past.

Recent reports sponsored by the National Coalition for Haitian Rights (Gavigan 1996), the Inter-American Commission for Human Rights (IACHR 1999), and Human Rights Watch (2002) have laudably broadened the scope of the human rights reporting to at last include the second generation and immigrants living outside the sugar estates. Yet past and present sexual violence and exploitation still remain largely unexamined. To my knowledge, I am the only outside observer to have recorded firsthand testimony concerning the forced relocation of Haitian women to the sugar estates (Martínez 1995, 122–23), even though Haitian-Dominican activists will readily speak in detail about this practice and a gamut of other human rights abuses against women.[7] While the very presence of Haitian immigrant women in the Dominican Republic is no longer overlooked, their stories of adversity and survival remain largely unrecorded.

MY RESEARCH

All this helps explain why the main collaborative research activity I put forward in my GSC proposal was a project to collect the life histories of Haitian immigrant women and their daughters born in the Dominican Republic. MUDHA's director, Solange Pierre, on repeated occasions expressed enthusiasm for this project. In an interview that I did with her in 1999 she eloquently characterized the immigrant women's stories as an as-yet-unwritten chapter in the history of relations between Haiti and the Dominican Republic. Rather than participating directly in the interviews, I envisioned organizing a team of female interviewers for this purpose, in the expectation that the women interviewees would sooner speak to women than to men of sexual abuse and exploitation and other wrongs of an intimate and psychologically traumatic nature.

Seeking to fill remaining gaps and uncertainties in my knowledge, I spent the first two months of my field research gathering background information from a variety of sources. Staff at both organizations also permitted me to accompany them to community workshops and meetings held on site in *bateyes* (company compounds for agricultural workers) in present and former sugar-producing zones, where the population of Haitian nationality and ancestry is most heavily concentrated. These site visits opened up insights into the relationship between NGO staff and base community groups, as well as shedding light on *batey* communities' priorities for activism. More generally, my background research strongly confirmed my main hypothesis that the Haitian-Dominican NGOs pursue a much broader agenda of activism than the international NGOs have done. Both CCDH and MUDHA view cultural revitalization, citizenship rights, women's empowerment, and community social and economic development as inextricably linked goals that must be pursued simultaneously rather than giving priority either to civil-political or social, economic, and cultural rights.

I also found it useful to spend as much time as I could in the offices of CCDH and MUDHA even if I had no meetings to attend, documents to read, or any other particular reason to be there. My most frequent and in-depth contacts were with MUDHA staff, both because and in spite of an acute financial crisis in that organization after its funding was discontinued by two foreign governments' aid agencies. Recognizing that there was an opportunity to make myself useful in this crisis, even if it meant departing somewhat from my proposed research agenda, I volunteered to help in any way I could. I researched possible sources of funding and passed this information along to MUDHA, and I participated in exchanges of information via e-mail among overseas "friends of MUDHA" concerning avenues of outside solidarity at this difficult juncture.

While MUDHA's financial crisis presented an unexpected opportunity for me to render assistance, it also created limits. Their ordinary grassroots organizational work went on but at a diminished pace, due to sharply reduced staffing. The search for potential funding sources and preparation of applications put extraordinary demands on the time and energy of the remaining staff. The sheer lack of time and the almost palpable stress and fatigue in the MUDHA office made it at times difficult for me even to find opportunities to meet with particular staff, let alone find ways of involving myself usefully. The circumstances of our collaboration were complicated further by political concerns. MUDHA was the target of harsh criticism in the press and Pierre even received anonymous death threats following their presentation of a document at the 2001 Durban World Conference on Racism, identifying anti-Black racism as a basic element behind the hostile reception accorded Haitian immigrants in the Dominican Republic.[8] MUDHA staffers normally interpret intimidation tactics positively, as a sign that their message is reaching its target. Yet the suspension of their outside funding so soon after the "Durban controversy" led some in MUDHA to wonder openly if they were being quietly punished for being too outspoken in international forums.

I opened discussions aimed at recruiting a research team during the second week of July, two full months into my stay. I needed this time to get adequate confirmation from MUDHA and other knowledgeable practitioners and scholars that there were in fact no existing sources of testimony from immigrant women that might take the place of these interviews and thus obviate asking the women to recount psychologically traumatic events. CCDH director Antonio Pol Emil and others there agreed that MUDHA was better prepared than they were to act as partners in research on sexual violence and on women's rights generally. Meetings and conversations with MUDHA staff over the subsequent three weeks confirmed the need for creating such a corpus of testimony.

These discussions also broadened the scope of the project considerably beyond what I had initially proposed. The MUDHA staffers were emphatic that many more interviews and a broader geographical sample than I had envisioned would be needed for the interviews to be useful to them. They pointed out, correctly, that Haitian women in the more openly racist and anti-Haitian northern half of the Dominican Republic would not have the same experiences as their sisters in the south. I resisted the pressure to expand the study, citing the inadequacy of my funding and the large amount of time it would take to analyze each in-depth interview. Feeling that it would be too time consuming to try to obtain a representative sample of interviews, I wished simply to obtain corroboration and more in-depth testimony concerning the abuses I had uncovered in the mid-1980s and had later heard described in greater detail by Haitian-Dominican rights advocates. In the end, we agreed on a compromise that at least four interviews would be done in each of three regions: the southwest (near the Haitian border), the north, and the south.

Reaching agreement that the interviews would have mainly educational and advocacy aims, rather than evidentiary value, was easier, it being understood that few Haitian immigrant women would talk if they thought they or their abusers might later be identifiable. Besides, I lacked the legal training to judge what kinds of statements could be admitted as evidence by an international court. It was foreseen that the interviews, beyond possibly being published as an edited volume of testimony and contributing to my mainly scholarly publications, might yield material that MUDHA could use in community-level workshops with Haitian-Dominican women on the topics of gender relations, reproductive health, and self-esteem. They would gain knowledge as I gained knowledge, and a major gap in the human rights record concerning Haitians in the Dominican Republic would be addressed for the first time. We got as far as discussing the logistics of identifying interviewers among the Haitian-Dominican women who had worked with MUDHA as community organizers and planning dates and procedures for bringing them to Santo Domingo for training and other interview preliminaries.

It is important to note that MUDHA's lead coordinator, Pierre, was out of the country for the greater part of May, June, and July. I was frequently reminded by the MUDHA staffers with whom I had been negotiating in Pierre's absence that MUDHA worked on a democratic basis of consensus building. Yet it did not immediately sink in that, without Pierre, a needed piece of the consensus was missing. I was therefore surprised that, during an evening meeting late in July with Pierre and the others, all the issues that I thought had been resolved were again set forth for discussion as problems. Geography, sampling size, and the fact that anonymous interviews could not be used as legal evidence ended up being the main focus of a discussion that I had hoped would bring us close to final agreement about the interview procedures and personnel.

In the end, agreement could not be reached with MUDHA, and I opted to assemble an all-female interview team without the hoped-for participation of experienced advocates. The interviews did not yield the anticipated testimony about abuses suffered at the hands of soldiers, police, and sugar company bosses, for reasons that I can only guess at. While the kind of first-person testimony I wanted was not produced, I did learn a great deal about these abuses from secondhand sources, through interviews with Haitian women's rights advocates. These interviews focused specifically on the human rights situation of Haitian women in the Dominican Republic and covered a wide range of topics, including forced relocation to sugar camps, sexual exploitation, and the denial of rights of citizenship to their Dominican-born children. These interviews lack the immediacy and impact of the kind of first-person accounts that I had hoped to bring back. Yet they do constitute a significant resource when seen against the dearth of information and analysis concerning Haitian women's lives in the Dominican Republic.

IMPLICATIONS FOR WOMEN'S RIGHTS INVESTIGATION

A few years after publication of Amnesty International's (1991) report *Women on the Frontline*, storms of controversy erupted concerning the length of time it took for international observers to report the phenomenon of mass rape in the Bosnia and Rwanda conflicts (Human Rights Watch 1996; Stiglmayer 1994). Since that time, students of human rights have been more than ever concerned with why sexual violence in wartime and other flagrant mass infringements of women's rights so often escape expert detection and public notice. In dozens of articles, feminist critical legal theorists have challenged the gender neutrality of international human rights instruments and bodies of national law.[9] Far fewer works have given comparable attention to gender bias in the monitoring and enforcement of women's rights. Lacunae regarding violence against women have been much more often remarked upon in passing from a human rights perspective or dealt with as if these were purely matters of investigative techniques rather than interrogated and explained in depth as products either of patriarchy or of global race/class inequality.[10] Important gains have been made at the level of the international community's consciousness of sexual violence as a human rights challenge. And, in a landmark ruling in 2001, the International Criminal Tribunal for the Former Yugoslavia convicted three former Bosnian Serb Army commanders for rape, torture, and enslavement, defining these wrongs as crimes against humanity (Human Rights Watch 2001). But what are we to make of reports since 2001 that international human rights investigators were again slow to denounce mass rape in wartime, in settings as diverse as the conflicts in Sierra Leone, Congo, Sudan, Iraq, and Colombia (Human Rights Watch 2006; Amnesty International 2004)? Ten years on from the conflicts in Rwanda and the former Yugoslavia, the walls of silence around gender violence sadly seem to be resisting demolition by well-intentioned and hardworking human rights experts.

Though my own research did not take place during an armed conflict, the powerlessness of the survivors vis-à-vis the perpetrators, many of whom have been men in power, and the institutional barriers that have isolated the sugar company compounds from outside legal scrutiny and intervention are no doubt powerful disincentives for the survivors of sexual violence to reveal their truths to any human rights investigator. Considering that my interviews with NGO staffers yielded ample independent confirmation that Haitian women in the Dominican Republic were still experiencing a broad gamut of rights violations, I can only suspect that some of the immigrant women who were interviewed by my research team had experienced or seen bona fide human rights abuses but felt hesitant to divulge such sensitive information to interviewers with whom they had no prior acquaintance and rapport. One irony is that the

Haitian and Haitian-Dominican women whom I interviewed during my dissertation fieldwork were more forthcoming with accounts of human rights abuses than the women interviewed by female researchers fifteen years later. Trust and linguistic fluency, such as I built up over months of community fieldwork in 1985–86 (the lead interviewer on the research team did not know Haitian Creole), carry an undetermined weight. I think it is fair to point out also that women played lead roles in nearly all the human rights fact-finding missions that failed to uncover either the trafficking of Haitian women or their rape and sexual exploitation while on route to and in residence on the Dominican sugar estates. Though my interviews with members of these fact-finding teams are only at a beginning stage, what I have gathered thus far suggests, not that these monitors tried to gather information on women's rights abuses and failed, but that it simply was not brought to their awareness that the women were experiencing infringements of their rights any different from the men's. These observations suggest that the gender of the interviewer, though doubtless important, may matter less than I had assumed. It is not that the balance of sexes in fact-finding investigation teams does not matter (Gardam and Charlesworth 2000) but that still further changes in human rights investigation may be needed to bring testimony of sexual violence to light in a timely manner. Consultation with local human rights advocates might yield less in the chaos of wartime, but, in the case of Haitian immigrant women's rights, the silence of human rights reportage on gross and systematic infringements seems attributable in large part to international monitors' failure to consult earlier and more widely with organizers among the Haitian-Dominican community itself.

I sense a trend toward more partnerships being sought by academic anthropologists with local and international development and human rights organizations. I anticipate that this path will be followed especially often by our graduate students, more of whom than ever before, it seems, are coming back to academia to pursue advanced degrees in cultural anthropology after working for some time in the not-for-profit sector. For many, a commitment to one or more progressive political causes will be a primordial motivation for going into anthropology. For them, working alongside practitioners seeking positive change will simply expand their earlier political engagement into a scholarly program. Others—especially midcareer scholars like me, who are coming back to the field after completing their dissertations—will be motivated more by feelings of obligation to do some service to the people who have given them so much.

While my pursuit of this research partnership had a solid scholarly justification, I see now more clearly that my interest in applying for the GSC grant grew also from the realization that I was and would continue to be an extractive researcher until I surrendered some of the power to define the agenda of my research and its methodology to the people with whom I work.

Activist anthropology is no panacea for the practical and ethical dilemmas that stem from anthropology's identity as an intellectual project of the global North. The prevailing institutional structure of social science inquiry poses such great obstacles to implementing activist research projects that the growth of activist anthropology will continue to be impeded if incentives for globally equitable social scientific research are not developed, such as those offered by the GSC from 2001 to 2003. No research panel, from the university department level on up, could seriously consider funding a proposal that basically asks for money to go find out what the people in some far-off place would like an anthropologist to study. For the research to gain needed funding, it must be justified first and foremost on theoretical and methodological grounds deemed valid by the anthropological community. Once researchers receive funding, they must go out and get results that address the hypotheses set forth in their proposal, taking up time and energy that could be devoted to cultivating relationships with local advocates. Doctoral candidates and junior faculty in many departments of anthropology might also feel discouraged from admitting even the slightest influence on their research agenda from nonscientists, out of fear that this would diminish the importance of their findings in the eyes of their professors or colleagues. Funding, approval of the doctoral dissertation, publications, and ultimately tenure depend on our research being perceived as having scientific rigor. There are no corresponding institutional incentives for anthropologists to produce findings that are useful to the people who aid us in doing our fieldwork.

It is less fully appreciated that the world of advocacy and community activism also has its institutional structures of knowledge and professionalism, into which the free-floating academician may not always easily fit. Access, as my experience shows, presents a first set of potential pitfalls. Given the politically sensitive nature of the topic that I was studying, it is understandable that the collaborative dimension of the research proved more challenging than I expected. With organizations, such as MUDHA, caught in highly politicized struggles for rights or resources, I think it is to be anticipated that even highly informed and experienced researchers who have no previous work history with the host organization(s) may encounter difficulty establishing an internal role and a relationship of trust. In some instances, the activist researcher will assiduously attempt for weeks or months to cultivate a working relationship with an organization, only to meet with rejection from the would-be partner. If setbacks of this kind occur frequently as more anthropologists seek research collaborations with activist organizations, greater uncertainty of meeting predefined research goals may emerge as one important limitation to the wider adoption of an activist research approach. Senior scholars who are secure in their jobs and reputations may shrug off the potential loss of time and effort more easily than our graduate students and junior colleagues can.

Once admittance is gained, my experience shows that it is not always easy for affiliated scholars to insert themselves into the host organization's set routines, or for underfunded and understaffed organizations to make time for scholars' needs. Also, community organizers who are used to collaborating with people in other organizations may find it hard to understand right away how to work with a lone academician. Unease may flow from ambiguity about the independent scholar's position in a field of power. Where external collaborations are generally either "vertical"—with international sponsors—or "horizontal"—in the form of networks or partnerships with like organizations—where is the anthropologist coming from, vertically or horizontally? We may propose an equalitarian exchange, but that does not necessarily diminish the tendency of our would-be institutional partners in the global South to see us as powerful outsiders.

The perceived power imbalance, as Joanne Rappaport (2002) points out, may be more real than most anthropologists would like to admit. For Rappaport, while North-South intellectual *exchange* is always possible, it is a dangerous illusion to think that horizontal *collaboration* may be achieved. Even when ethnographers think we are proposing an open and horizontal collaboration with indigenous or citizen intellectuals of the global South, our own research generally ends up taking priority, in effect converting our "collaborators" into "research assistants." Hierarchy will thus reassert itself in collaborations between northern academicians and southern research partners, submerging their concerns and approaches once more under our theories and methods. Rappaport's own preferred model of activist research, developed over years of work with indigenous historians of the Colombian Andes, is not melding the two parties' research aims but working in parallel with citizen intellectuals of the global South.[11] I harbor some skepticism about how often we may find the opportunity to work alongside the people with whom we do our fieldwork as intellectual peers, in the way she has. Her model has the limitation of assuming that our partners have the inclination and time to pursue their own independent research projects as we do ours. Certainly, at the time of my fieldwork my MUDHA partners sorely lacked the time to do extensive investigation. Yet I think activist researchers would generally do well to take into consideration her larger point that it may not often be possible to join our research goals seamlessly with those of the groups with whom we work as ethnographers. The effort to do so can even undermine our larger politically progressive aims if the agendas of northern researchers insidiously subsume the aims of southern activists.

The general significance of these observations is not that activist research is not doable or worth doing. I sooner think the following conclusions flow from my experiences in retooling myself as an activist scholar:

- Activist research, to a greater degree than other research models, depends upon the establishment of a relationship of trust between the researcher and the activists.
- His relationship of trust often cannot develop quickly but only over months or years.
- Trust will probably grow more surely if the visitor volunteers to work for a time purely as an activist rather than a researcher.
- The relationship of trust is all the more essential and time consuming to establish if the study takes on a highly politically sensitive topic or brings a researcher with a politically dominant national, racial/ethnic, or gender identity into collaboration with members of a subordinated community.

In the context of activist scholarship, the "situatedness" that Donna Haraway (1988) is responsible for popularizing in the academic lexicon is as much or more a matter of where you are coming from than a matter of where you elect to stand. Even as I approve of Jennie Smith's (2001) cogent prescription for "un-doing ourselves," as a first step toward reshaping anthropology into an instrument of social justice, I wonder how straight the path is toward this aim. We anthropologists always bring a lifetime of experiences with us into the field and confront an uncontrollable set of associations in the eyes of our erstwhile research subjects and would-be political allies, relating to nationality, race, gender, age, institutional affiliations, and more. It would be too pessimistic to say, "You are what you are," for you can always adjust and adapt your research practice to new circumstances. Yet you cannot remake yourself into someone you are not, much less control how others will perceive you.

One crucial corollary is that more anthropologists must take up activist scholarship earlier in their careers. New generations of graduate students who enter anthropology with established practitioner allegiances and qualifications will mostly find the path to developing activist scholarship projects easier to negotiate than those who lack solid prior activist contacts and credentials. Academia will likely never reshape itself into an activist mold; to be so transformed, it must instead be colonized by activists from without. A major obstacle to realizing this goal of broadening the anthropological profession's profile to include more activist scholars lies in our professional gatekeeping criteria. The professional profile of the people who are most likely to succeed at activist research differs from what graduate school admissions committees and grant-giving foundations normally include among their criteria of merit. Clearly, we in the academy must give greater value than we currently do to professional advocacy experience, as well as to personal affiliations with subordinated minority groups, if more students and junior faculty are to be moved into activist scholarship early in their careers. All of our students should be directed where appropriate to seek out community activists at the earliest possible stage and to negotiate the incorporation of their concerns into graduate research. To the degree that non–North American or European, nonwhite, and nonheterosexual male researchers, depending on the social and cultural context, are more likely to find acceptance among would-be activist research partners, the intellectual justification for all measures to expand diversity among anthropologists is strengthened.

NOTES

I carried out field research in the Dominican Republic under the auspices of a MacArthur Foundation–funded grant from the Social Science Research Council's Global Security and Cooperation (GSC) program. The assistance in the Dominican Republic of staffers from the Haitian-Dominican rights organizations Movimiento de Mujeres Domínico-Haitianas and Centro Cultural Domínico-Haitiano is gratefully recognized. A preliminary version of this paper was presented at a GSC-sponsored workshop on activist scholarship, organized by Charles Hale, April 2003. I also thank Hale and two anonymous reviewers for their suggestions for revision; all errors of commission and omission are solely my responsibility.

1. It must immediately be added that the participatory approach to which I give emphasis is neither unique to activist anthropology nor alien to applied anthropology. Any number of applied anthropologists have solicited community participation and attempted to tap into public opinion or knowledge as they define

their research goals. Methodologically, then, activist anthropology might easily be understood to overlap with another active and varied area of applied research, reaching well beyond anthropology: "action research" or "participatory action research" (Greenwood and Levin 1998).

2. Considering how deeply anthropology's academic critics are rooted in what they are criticizing, it should perhaps come as no surprise that they are generally more timid than anthropology's nonacademic critics. Charles Hale (in the introduction to this volume) focuses laser-sharp criticism on anthropological postmodernists' pretensions to do "politically engaged scholarship." Rather than focus on the macro-social power imbalances that have given the discipline its characteristic form and content, anthropology's academic critics usually have focused on the micropolitics of fieldwork or have critically analyzed the radically "Othering" effects of anthropology's dominant scientific realist writing conventions (Speed, chapter 8 of this volume). As Michel-Rolph Trouillot (1991, 18–19) observes, "current calls for reflexivity" within American anthropology are neither "products of chance" nor "a passing fad": "Rather, they are timid, spontaneous—and in that sense genuinely American—responses to major changes in the relations between anthropology and the wider world, provincial expressions of wider concerns, allusions to opportunities yet to be seized." For Trouillot, the critique of anthropology remains political only at the level of the discipline's "electoral politics," relating to who gains what rewards from academic institutions and professional associations. Few academic critics have followed Trouillot in suggesting that our writing conventions are not the root of the problem so much as the narrowness of the constituencies we address, the ineffectual, scholastic aims of our publications, and the exclusion from the circuit of knowledge production of the people with whom we do our fieldwork. Worse, anthropology's postmodernist critics fall into the trap of bootless cynicism by defining the discipline's narrowness and exclusivity not as shortcomings that can be redressed in practice but as unavoidable features of the ethnographic enterprise (Clifford and Marcus 1986).

3. The line between applied and practicing anthropology is important enough to have been recognized institutionally, within the American Anthropological Association, through the establishment of a practicing anthropology interest section, distinct from the larger and considerably older Society for Applied Anthropology.

4. We academic anthropologists, too, receive the "raw ore" of data handed to us by thousands of impoverished producers from the global South, take this home with us to the North, and there refine it and package it into finished scholarly products for sale in northern intellectual markets. At no point need we in academia stop to consider what information will "sell" in the largely low-income communities where we do field research. The people among whom we do our research are not the ones who hand out the rewards.

5. Not coincidentally, contract and practicing anthropologists tend strongly to take "clinical" rather than "critical" methodological/theoretical approaches. They frame their research questions around the needs of client organizations that seek to intervene constructively on behalf of individuals enmeshed in "social problems." The larger circumstances in which these problems are rooted matter less, to contract/practicing research, than do recommending better ways for providers of social services to provide outreach to individuals and communities "in trouble." The activist anthropologist generally tends, by contrast, to highlight perceived ultimate causes.

6. These reports include Americas Watch (1989, 1990, 1992); Human Rights Watch (2002); Inter-American Commission on Human Rights (1999); Lawyers Committee (1991); Gavigan (1996).

7. In an interview that I recorded in 1999 with Pierre, she recalled the following kind of scene played out each year in her childhood on a sugar plantation in the Dominican Republic's Cibao Valley when truckloads of new migrants would arrive from Haiti:

> For example, in the *batey* where I was born and raised, a head *batey* on the old Ingenio Catarey, ... in the corral ... they would unload seven or eight trucks—the famous "Catareys," old flatbed Mercedes Benzes, that was the mode of transport!—there, four, six, even eight trucks would unload an enormous quantity [of people]. And then, after the boss and the authorities of the place picked their women, then ... the *viejos* would come by to pick among the ones who were left there to live with them. Many of those women, besides serving the guy, [he] automatically became their pimp.

8. An English translation of selections from this document was published in the *GSC Quarterly*, no. 5 (Summer 2002), www.ssrc.org/programs/gsc/gsc_quarterly/Archive/.

9. Cook and Oosterveld (1995) is a recent bibliography; basic works include Charlesworth, Chinkin, and Wright (1991), Cook (1995), and Gardam and Charlesworth (2000), as well as essays in Cook (1994) and Peters and Wolper (1995).

10. MacKinnon (1993) and Stephen (1995) are important exceptions.

11. Rappaport's research partners have gathered legally admissible evidence via oral history and have studied the landscape for information regarding past land use and land tenure at the same time as she has studied the forms in which indigenous knowledge of the past is formulated and preserved. Their approaches have been braided together over the years through innumerable meetings at which each has brought forward information and ideas of interest to the other. Yet their aims, methods, and audiences remain distinct. Rappaport uses the same kind of metaphor for this approach that I introduced earlier as an alternative to the contract model of applied anthropology when she refers to her exchanges with local historians as "intellectual *mink'as*," the *mink'a* being an indigenous Andean form of festive labor exchange similar to the Dominican *convite*.

REFERENCES

Americas Watch. 1989. *Haitian Sugar-Cane Cutters in the Dominican Republic*. New York: Americas Watch, National Coalition for Haitian Refugees, and Caribbean Rights.

———. 1990. *Harvesting Oppression: Forced Labor in the Dominican Sugar Industry*. New York: Americas Watch, National Coalition for Haitian Refugees, and Caribbean Rights.

———. 1992. *A Troubled Year: Haitians in the Dominican Republic*. New York: Americas Watch and National Coalition for Haitian Refugees.

Amnesty International. 1991. *Women on the Frontline: Human Rights Violations against Women*. New York: Amnesty International.

———. 2004. "Colombia: 'Scarred Bodies, Hidden Crimes': Sexual Violence against Women in the Armed Conflict." October 13. http://web.amnesty.org/library/Index/ENGAMR230402004?open&of=ENG-COL. Accessed May 15, 2007.

Charlesworth, Hilary, Christine Chinkin, and Shelley Wright. 1991. "Feminist Approaches to International Law." *American Journal of International Law* 85: 613–45.

Clifford, James, and George E. Marcus, eds. 1986. *Writing Culture: The Poetics and Politics of Ethnography.* Berkeley: University of California Press.

Cook, Rebecca J., ed. 1994. *Human Rights of Women: National and International Perspectives.* Philadelphia: University of Pennsylvania Press.

———. 1995. "Women." In *United Nations Legal Order,* vol. 1, edited by Oscar Schachter and Christopher C. Joyner, 433–71. Cambridge: Grotius Publications and Cambridge University Press.

Cook, Rebecca J., and Valerie L. Oosterveld. 1995. "Religious and Cultural Rights: A Select Bibliography of Women's Human Rights." *American University Law Review* 44:1429–71.

Domínguez, Iván, José Castillo, and Dagoberto Tejeda. 1978. *Almanaque folklórico dominicano.* Santo Domingo: Editora "Alfa y Omega."

Facultad Latinoamericana de Ciencias Sociales. 2004. *Encuesta sobre inmigrantes haitianos en la República Dominicana.* Santo Domingo: Facultad Latinoamericana de Ciencias Sociales, Programa República Dominicana.

Gardam, Judith, and Hilary Charlesworth. 2000. "Protection of Women in Armed Conflict." *Human Rights Quarterly* 22 (1): 148–66.

Gavigan, Patrick. 1996. *Beyond the Bateyes: Haitian Immigrants in the Dominican Republic.* New York: National Coalition for Haitian Rights.

Greenwood, Davydd J., and Morton Levin. 1998. *Introduction to Action Research: Social Research for Social Change.* Thousand Oaks, CA: Sage Publications.

Gross, Daniel, and Stuart Plattner. 2002. "Anthropology as Social Work: Collaborative Models of Anthropological Research." *Anthropology News* 43 (8): 4.

Hale, Charles R. 2001. "What Is Activist Research?" *Items and Issues* 2 (1–2): 13–15.

Haraway, Donna. 1988. "Situated Knowledges: The Science Questions in Feminism and the Privilege of Partial Perspective." *Feminist Studies* 14 (3): 575–99.

Human Rights Watch. 1996. *Shattered Lives: Sexual Violence during the Rwandan Genocide and Its Aftermath.* New York: Human Rights Watch.

———. 2001. "Bosnia: Landmark Verdicts for Rape, Torture, and Sexual Enslavement." February 2. http://hrw.org/english/docs/2001/02/22/bosher256.htm. Accessed May 15, 2007.

———. 2002. *"Illegal People": Haitians and Dominico-Haitians in the Dominican Republic.* New York: Human Rights Watch. www.hrw.org/reports/2002/domrep/.

———. 2006. "Women and Armed Conflict; International Justice." www.hrw.org/women/conflict.html. Accessed May 15, 2007.

Inter-American Commission on Human Rights. 1999. *Report on the Situation of Human Rights in the Dominican Republic.* Washington, DC: Inter-American Commission on Human Rights, Organization of American States.

Lawyers Committee for Human Rights. 1991. *A Childhood Abducted: Children Cutting Sugar Cane in the Dominican Republic.* New York: Lawyers Committee for Human Rights.

Lozano, Wilfredo. 1993. "Agricultura e inmigración: La mano de obra haitiana en el mercado de trabajo rural dominicano." In *La cuestión haitiana en Santo Domingo: Migración internacional, desarrollo y relaciones interestatales entre Haití y República Dominicana,* edited by Wilfredo Lozano, 79–105. Santo Domingo: Facultad Latinoamericana de Ciencias Sociales, Programa República Dominicana.

MacKinnon, Catherine A. 1993. "Crimes of War, Crimes of Peace." In *On Human Rights: The Oxford Amnesty Lectures 1993,* edited by Stephen Shute and Susan Hurley, 83–109. Oxford: Oxford University Press.

Martínez, Samuel. 1995. *Peripheral Migrants: Haitians and Dominican Republic Sugar Plantations.* Knoxville: University of Tennessee Press.

Peters, Julie, and Andrea Wolper, eds. 1995. *Women's Rights, Human Rights: International Feminist Perspectives.* New York: Routledge.

Pierre, Solange. 2001. "Court Victory for Expelled Haitians." *Outsider* 56. www.minorityrights.org/Outsiders/outsider_issue.asp?ID=5.

Rappaport, Joanne. 2002. "Research and Ethnic Pluralism: Doing Collaborative Research in Colombia." Society for Latin American Anthropology Presidential Lecture, presented at the annual meeting of the American Anthropological Association, New Orleans, LA, November 20–24.

Silié, Rubén, Carlos Segura, and Carlos Dore Cabral. 2002. *La nueva inmigración haitiana.* Santo Domingo: Facultad Latinoamericana de Ciencias Sociales.

Singer, Merrill. 1994. "Community-Centered Praxis: Toward an Alternative Non-dominative Applied Anthropology." *Human Organization* 53 (4): 336–44.

Smith, Jennie Marcelle. 2001. *When the Hands Are Many: Community Organization and Social Change in Rural Haiti.* Ithaca: Cornell University Press.

Stephen, Lynn. 1995. "Women's Rights Are Human Rights: The Merging of Feminine and Feminist Interests among El Salvador's Mothers of the Disappeared (CO-MADRES)." *American Ethnologist* 22 (4): 807–27.

Stiglmayer, Alexandra, ed. 1994. *Mass Rape: The War against Women in Bosnia.* Lincoln: University of Nebraska Press.

Trouillot, Michel-Rolph. 1991. "Anthropology and the Savage Slot: The Poetics and Politics of Otherness." In *Recapturing Anthropology: Working in the Present,* edited by Richard G. Fox, 17–44. Santa Fe: School of American Research Press

PART III

Putting Activist Scholarship to Work

8. Forged in Dialogue

Toward a Critically Engaged Activist Research

Shannon Speed

ANTHROPOLOGY: CONFRONTING CONTRADICTIONS,
TRANSFORMING THE DISCIPLINE

In the wake of decolonization struggles throughout the world, the discipline of anthropology itself was challenged to decolonize. Beginning in the 1970s, serious internal and external critiques motivated the discipline to question and redefine some of its most basic precepts. These critiques came not only from our postcolonial research "subjects" but also from feminist, postmodern, postcolonial, and critical race theorists.[1] All of these scholars challenged anthropological representations of "others" and pointed to the discipline's history of collusion with colonial power in producing representations that supported colonialist logics and rationalities. Scientific epistemology came under fire: the definition of anthropology as a social science was questioned, and the validity of claims to a knowable truth regarding human cultures was disputed. Following feminist theorists, anthropologists grappled with the understanding that our representations of others were products of our own social positioning and our own "situatedness" in relation to the people and cultural dynamics we chose to represent. Further, these subjective representations had concrete and at times powerful effects on those we represented in our work (Clifford 1988; Haraway 1988; Lyotard 1984; Marcus and Fischer 1986; Spivak 1988; Said 1978). Attention was drawn to the ways that the myth of scientific objectivity had served to conceal both indirect, unintended effects of anthropological research and work with obvious political ends, such as spying for government agencies under the guise of fieldwork (Price 2000). Thus scientific objectivity was not only an impossible goal but also potentially something more insidious: a cover for the harmful political effects of our work on those whom we researched and wrote about.

Thus anthropology's history, as well as the relations of power between anthropologists and their research subjects, had to be reckoned with. The "crisis of representation" meant that anthropologists had "no choice but to seriously examine how we conduct our business in the everyday world" (Denzin 2002, 482). For some, it led to a retrenchment in the realm of the theoretical and the textual (Clifford 1988; Clifford and Marcus 1986; Marcus and Fischer 1986) that allowed cultural critique to stand alone as anthropology's contribution and avoided the messier engagement with increasingly vocal and critical research subjects. Others took a different tack, endeavoring to address the politics of anthropological knowledge production and to decolonize the relationship between researcher and research subject through the research process itself (Harrison 1991; Tuhiwai Smith 1999; Mutua and Swadener 2004; Hale 2004) and engaging in a form of anthropology that was committed to human liberation (Gordon 1991; Scheper-Hughes 1995). Certainly, there have been many kinds of responses to the crisis in representation, and a comprehensive review of them is beyond the scope of this chapter. What I want to highlight here is a divergence in approach, on the one hand emphasizing the anthropological product (ethnographic text as literary genre, or cultural theory writing that comes close to purging ethnographic matter altogether) and on the other highlighting the research process as a privileged site for frontally addressing the critiques and creating mutually defined projects with research "subjects." Joanne Rappaport (n.d.) has recently written about this dichotomy and notes that the vast majority of anthropological work today falls into the former category, emphasizing text over research as the fundamental form of ethnographic work.

This uneasy dichotomy was reflected in a recent volume edited by Wendy Brown and Janet Halley (2002) that problematizes academic activism in the legal realm and advocates for cultural critique. Brown and Halley are not anthropologists, and their critique is directed to leftist academics and intellectuals more generally, though many anthropologists certain fall into this category. They rightly note that in the current era, "so saturated by legalism is contemporary political life, that it is often difficult to imagine alternative ways of deliberating about and pursuing justice" (19). They further argue that "legalism . . . incessantly translates wide-ranging political questions into more narrowly framed legal questions" (19). Thus the concern of Brown and Halley is that activist scholars who are engaged in legal struggles too often focus on short-term legal goals and fail to reflect critically about the manner in which their scholarly production, geared to these legal goals, may actually reinforce structures and discourses of inequality—in part by "fixing" identities and delimiting culture in the law, subjugating them to "a stable set of regulatory norms" (24; see also Merry 1997). I agree with Brown and Halley, up to this point. However, these authors call for a privileging of cultural critique *over* direct engagement as the form of activism intellectuals should undertake. I disagree with this conclusion. In fact, I disagree with the premise that direct political engagement and critical analysis are necessarily distinct and separate undertakings.

In this paper, through the lens of my own experience of research collaboration in a legal struggle waged by a community in Chiapas, Mexico, before the International Labor Organization (ILO), I consider the potential for critically engaged activist research. By *critically engaged*, I acknowledge the fundamental enterprise of anthropology: critical cultural analysis. This is what our specialized training prepares us to do, and it can make a contribution not just to our theoretical understanding of social dynamics but also to concrete political objectives on the ground. By *activist research*, I mean the overt commitment to an engagement with our research subjects that is directed toward some form of shared political goals. What I want to argue—and the reason I use the term—is that the two can be productively practiced together as one undertaking.

This kind of research is necessarily collaborative and foregrounds the dialogue between anthropologists and those we work with through *the research process*. I suggest that a retreat into the textual or "pure" critique disengages from the "subjects" of research and thus sidestep ethical issues that should be met directly through a critically engaged dialogue with our research subjects. By ceding collaboration, that potentially difficult but also potentially productive and fruitful dialogue is lost and cannot inform the analysis.

This does not mean that the multiple tensions and contradictions that exist between anthropologists and those we work with cease to exist; instead, it means that these are productive tensions that we might strive to benefit from analytically rather than seek to avoid. My proposal is that this kind of research contributes to the transformation of the discipline of anthropology by addressing the politics of knowledge production and working to decolonize our studies without a retreat into the text as the site for change. While I focus here on the relationship of anthropologists with indigenous peoples in Latin America, many of the conclusions may have broader relevance.

NICOLÁS RUIZ AND THE INTERNATIONAL LABOR ORGANIZATION: A CRITICALLY ENGAGED ACTIVIST RESEARCH EXPERIENCE

A Community in Conflict

Nicolás Ruiz is a community and municipality in the Central Zone of the state of Chiapas, Mexico. With a population of less than five thousand, it is one of the smallest municipalities in the state. Founded by Tzeltal Indians, it has not been defined as an indigenous community by the state or by residents for several decades. However, the community has recently reasserted its indigenous identity. For more than a century, Nicolás Ruiz has been engaged in an ongoing land struggle, waged alternately against large landholders and against the state. In recent years, Nicolás Ruiz was one of the municipalities most often mentioned in news articles and reports on the Chiapas conflict. This notoriety was caused not only by the land conflict but also by the serious and often violent intracommunity political conflict that Nicolás Ruiz has suffered since 1996, a conflict that is tied to the larger one affecting the state, engendered by the Zapatista uprising and the counterinsurgency practices of the Mexican government.[2]

The community was formed in 1734, when Tzeltal Indians from the nearby area of Teopisca purchased a large tract of land from a Spanish landholding family.[3] Over the course of the nineteenth century, the community lost significant portions of it to regional landowners and political bosses, mostly through deception or fraud.[4] Further lands were lost during the years of the agrarian reform in Chiapas, when parcels of land claimed by Nicolás Ruiz were granted to other groups as *ejidos* (communal land grants). Residents of Nicolás Ruiz have fought continuously to regain these lands by petitioning the government, invading lands, and using any other means at their disposal. Much of the community's history and identity into and through the twentieth century has been forged in the struggle to regain its lost lands.

Markers of indigenous identity were disappearing in Nicolás Ruiz by the mid–twentieth century. According to inhabitants, by 1960, men and women no longer wore traditional dress and few Tzeltal speakers remained.[5] Residents whose parents or grandparents had been Tzeltal speakers told me that their parents purposefully did not teach their children the language because they felt it would "keep them from getting ahead."[6] It is important to note that in Mexico the primary identifier of an indigenous person is language. This association is made in official designation of indigenous status: in the census, for example, language is the identifier of an indigenous person. But the linkage is made much more widely: most of the people that I interviewed throughout the course of several years' research, including activists and indigenous people, asserted that someone who did not speak an Indian language was not indigenous. I have been told or have heard on several occasions that a person from an indigenous community who has stopped speaking the language after relocating to a city "used to be indigenous." In 1999, then–Secretario de Gobierno (State Interior Minister) Rodolfo Soto Monzón told representatives of Nicolás Ruiz that if they wanted to be considered indigenous they would have to provide proof that they still spoke Tzeltal.[7] In current census statistics, the indigenous population of the municipality is listed as less than 1 percent.

The historical record clearly demonstrates that the people who founded Nicolás Ruiz were Tzeltales. The only significant influx of outsiders took place when the indentured servants of nearby ranches concentrated in the town during the violent years of the Mexican Revolution. Undoubtedly, the current residents of Nicolás Ruiz are descended primarily from Tzeltal Mayans. Their institutions, like those of virtually all indigenous peoples, are not pristine duplications of pre-Conquest forms; they are inevitably shaped by centuries of influence by the state and other outside actors. Nevertheless, they are arguably distinctive from those of the dominant culture.

Since the community's formation, land has been held communally in Nicolás Ruiz. Today, 90 percent of the land is still held communally and is distributed in parcels to individuals. Men become *comuneros*, which means that they are entitled to work a parcel of land and have a corresponding responsibility to participate in the community assembly. Decisions about virtually every aspect of community political life are made in the community assembly by consensus (of the adult men), in which all *comuneros* participate.[8] Maintaining consensus is critical to the functioning of the system; for people in Nicolás Ruiz, consensus is the heart of their form of local governance.

In political decisions, the consensus for several decades was that the community should adhere to the ruling party, the Revolutionary Institutional Party (PRI), and benefit from this political alliance, hopefully by recovering their lands.⁹ The consensus model worked sufficiently well for the community to be able to select the candidates for municipal president in the community assembly, then simply ratify this decision at the ballot box. Until 1996, voting statistics in Nicolás Ruiz reflected 100 percent of votes as for the ruling party. This changed, however, with the Zapatista uprising of 1994, which challenged the PRI party's hegemonic power and presented alternatives for political organization and struggle. In 1995, the *comuneros* of Nicolás Ruiz shifted their loyalty to the PRD party by consensus decision in the community assembly and in 1996 elected the first PRD municipal president. That same year, Nicolás Ruiz declared itself a "community in resistance" and became a Zapatista base community.

This move marked the entry of Nicolás Ruiz into the Chiapas conflict. Only a short time later, local conflict surged when, in 1998, twenty-three families officially returned to the PRI party. This division and the ensuing conflicts have kept Nicolás Ruiz in the newspapers for the last four years. The majority felt that the dissent was an intolerable violation of the norms of the community, which had been long based on consensus decision making. As one resident expressed it, "We were in agreement for 264 years [since the founding of the community in 1734], and this changed everything."¹⁰ Although this comment probably masks significant past incidents of internal disagreement, the fact remains that open conflict of this kind had never existed in Nicolás Ruiz.

In their March 1998 assembly, the *comuneros* decided to revoke the land use rights of the dissenting community members because they were no longer fulfilling their corresponding responsibility of participating in the assembly. This revocation resulted in a massive raid by the army, state and federal police, and immigration officials on June 3, 1998. The raid was a clear sign that the state government was going to back the small PRI minority by force.¹¹ PRI community members, wearing masks on their faces, accompanied the police through the town, pointing out houses of community leaders. They entered the private home where the important documents of Bienes Comunales (Communal Properties, the body charged with administering communal goods including land) were kept, and they removed the original land titles, among other vital records. The community has never recovered these documents. One hundred and seventy-seven people were arrested; sixteen were charged with *despojo* (despoilment). The judge in the case ultimately found them innocent, and they were released after having spent half a year in prison. The conflict has never been resolved, and the violence that characterizes it led one journalist to characterize Nicolás Ruiz as the "Tierra sin Ley" ("Lawless

Land"; Gurguha 2000). Such "lawlessness" was not something inherent to Nicolás Ruiz or its inhabitants; in fact, community fractionalization and internal violence were prevalent throughout the zones of Zapatista support and were also understood by many to be part of a government "divide and conquer" strategy characteristic of low-intensity warfare. That this raid was one of several carried out by government forces in 1998, all against autonomous or pro-Zapatista municipal seats, tied both the local conflict and the government's role in it to the larger conflict—particularly to state counterinsurgency tactics.

The history of Nicolás Ruiz has involved, in large part, residents' struggle to recover their lands. These struggles, and the enemies and allies in them, have defined their identity over time. Identity in Nicolás Ruiz is historically and continuously constructed in relation to other social groups and through the ongoing struggles over its land and territory. During the period in which land struggles were waged via the state through agrarian reform and agrarian policies, Nicolás Ruiz's community identity became *campesino* (peasant). That is, indigenous identity gave way to campesino identity as state discourse and state policies engaged land struggles through agrarian reform and agrarian assistance to the campesino population. As the state made reforms designed to facilitate its entry into the neoliberal world order, its discourse shifted. In 1992, constitutional reform recognized the existence of indigenous people as part of a "pluriethnic" population. After 1994, the Zapatista uprising and Chiapas conflict brought Nicolás Ruiz into dialogue with new interlocutors, including the Zapatistas, organized groups of civil society, NGOs, and human rights groups. Community members had increased engagement with the discourse of human and indigenous rights, and as the discourses of the state shifted away from the agrarian and toward the indigenous as a basis for rights, people in Nicolás Ruiz began to rethink and redefine their understanding of themselves. By the year 2000, this redefinition had led them to reassert their identity as an indigenous community. Because of the indigenous conflict in the state, however, the government was reluctant to class them as "indigenous," preferring to deal with the conflict in the community as an agrarian conflict.

Enter the Activist Anthropologist

Thus, in 2000, Nicolás Ruiz was facing three problems: its historic land struggle, the internal conflict with the local *priistas* (PRI party militants), and the related problem of the government's refusal to accept their self-identification and negotiate with them as an indigenous community.

I confronted these issues through my own lens. The questions had a personal aspect for me as a "mixed-blood" Native American who was raised in Los Angeles, does not speak an indigenous language, and is not readily identified phenotypically as Native American. My own sense of Chickasaw identity is bound up with questions of descent, self-identification, and the recognition and acceptance of the Chickasaw Nation. As criteria for establishing who is Indian, they are vastly distinct from the criteria of language and dress. In fact, these criteria have been established in international law partly in recognition of the multiple historical processes that worked to eliminate Indian language and dress as a form of cultural domination. Thus challenging the Mexican state's use of these criteria had a larger meaning for me than the Nicolás Ruiz case alone.

My own insertion in Chiapas, while tied to local projects, emerges from my commitment to a larger struggle for social justice for indigenous and other marginalized peoples. Since 1996, I have worked in Chiapas as an activist anthropologist on issues of human rights and indigenous rights. This work has included, since 1998, serving as an advisor to the Red de Defensores Comunitarios por los Derechos Humanos (Community Human Rights Defenders' Network). This organization trains young indigenous people from conflict zones of the state to conduct their own human rights defense work, reducing the communities' reliance on NGOs and attorneys and thus contributing to local autonomous processes.

The Defenders' Network and I had relationships with the community through several channels. The founder of the network, my husband, had been the attorney for the community since the government forces had carried out the raid and jailed residents. Two of the network's members (called "defenders") were from the community of Nicolás Ruiz. I had begun conducting doctoral research in the community in 1999. We had important political and ethical reasons for working with the *comuneros*, as opposed to the dissenting *priistas*. First, the *comuneros*, in allying with the Zapatista struggle, were part of a larger struggle that we (I as an individual and the Defenders' Network as an organization) also allied with. The *priistas*, on the other hand, struggled for a return to a form of political power (PRI party rule) that from our perspective had maintained power relations that had oppressed indigenous people for decades. Although the *priistas* were a minority in Nicolás Ruiz, they were backed by the full force of state power, as the raid demonstrated, whereas the *comuneros* formed part of an opposition political party and an oppositional movement being strongly repressed by the state. In short, we, and I, had a particular insertion into the community and the conflict that was based on multiple overlapping factors: political, personal, and organizational.

The Representation(s) of Nicolás Ruiz to the ILO

At the Defenders' Network, we saw possibilities for the *comuneros* of Nicolás Ruiz in ILO Convention 169. In 2000, the Defenders' Network initiated Project ILO 169.[12] Mexico has signed and ratified the convention, and thus, like all ratified international agreements, it is considered law at the level of the Mexican Constitution. ILO Convention 169 provides the broadest international agreement to date on the rights of indigenous peoples, establishing respect for "the full measure of human rights and fundamental freedoms" (Art. 3.1) as well as "the full realization of the social, economic and cultural rights of these peoples with respect for their social and cultural identity, their customs and traditions and their institutions" (Art. 2.2.b). Three aspects of the ILO Convention 169 were of particular importance for Nicolás Ruiz. First was the establishment of self-identification as the criterion for defining indigenous groups (Art. 1.2). Second was indigenous groups' right to "retain their own customs and institutions" (Art. 8.2) and their right to respect for "the methods customarily practiced by the peoples concerned for dealing with offences committed by their members" (Art. 9.1). And third was the issue of land rights (Arts. 13–16). ILO Convention 169 establishes that indigenous peoples have a right to "the lands or territories, or both as applicable, which they occupy or otherwise use," and it emphasizes in particular "the collective aspects of this relationship [to the land]" (Art. 13.1).

In June of 2001, we approached the authorities of Nicolás Ruiz regarding the possibility of jointly preparing a representation before the ILO.[13] We explained our view that the community had a claim to recover lands, that they deserved restitution for unrecoverable lands, and that the Mexican government had been complicit in reducing their land titles through the discriminate use of land censuses and agrarian reform, a violation of ILO Convention 169 Land Articles 13, 14, and 16.[14] We pointed out that in defense of their position in revoking the land rights of the dissenting minority members of the community, they themselves had invoked their *usos y costumbres* (traditional customs and practices), a position that would be supported by ILO Convention 169's Articles 8 and 9. We also discussed the possibility of arguing that the government was violating Article 1.2 on self-identification by defining Nicolás Ruiz as "nonindigenous" because they had lost the use of their language.

For the representation, it was fundamental that Nicolás Ruiz as a community establish its right to define itself as indigenous. As a *pueblo indígena* (indigenous people), the community could fight for its land claims as territory rather than private property. Further, the community authorities would have the right to make internal decisions about punishment of its members (such as revoking land rights) based on its internal customs. The state's right to intervene on behalf of the dissenting members it favored would be limited: as an indigenous community, Nicolás Ruiz would have the right to autonomy in local decision-making. The ILO case presented a new strategy for pursuing their goals and their self-defense, one that was dependent on this reemergent indigenous identity.

The response from the community authorities, and later the full assembly, was positive. They were clearly interested in making a claim for lands they had lost over the years as well as in defending themselves against further violent invasions by state forces. Notably, they were particularly interested in the potential for asserting their identity as an indigenous community and establishing their right to define themselves in this way. In the words of one, "I think this is very important to be able to say to the government, 'We are not *Zona Centro* [a region defined as nonindigenous]; we are Tzeltales, we feel that we are part of the *pueblos indígenas.*'"[15] Another said, "This is what is most important [about participating in the ILO representation], that they recognize who we are. We are Tzeltales."[16] Two weeks later in the community assembly, more than six hundred *comuneros* voted unanimously to "declare themselves as indigenous people" as part of the ILO representation.

To document their claims, they needed anthropological information and analysis. This would be fundamental to the case; without it, they would have nothing on which to base their claims. I was asked by the attorneys working on the representation,[17] in collaboration with the Defenders' Network and the community, to supply the ethnohistorical information and analysis necessary to substantiate the community's claims to indigenous identification and to territorial rights. Ellen Messer (1993) suggests that one important potential form of activism has emerged "as anthropologists respond to indigenous demands for historical cultural documentation on human rights claims" (237). The integration of my ethnohistorical work into the ILO case fell within this field of engagement. I was eager to participate, understanding it as an opportunity to work collaboratively with the *comuneros* on a jointly defined activist research project. Our goals were not identical; rather, they overlapped in a way that allowed us to work together in a collaborative fashion.

FORGED IN DIALOGUE: CONSIDERING THE ACTIVIST RESEARCH ENGAGEMENT

Starting from the Ethical and Practical: On Addressing the Politics of Knowledge Production

Few people would debate that it is ethically tenuous for anthropologists to go into a field site and extract information from people struggling from a disadvantaged position for their most basic rights—to their lives, to their self-determination, and to their culture. It is even more so when we acknowledge the unequal relations of power between the researcher and the research subjects. Although the balance of power between the researcher and the researched varies in different contexts, in many cases researchers have a good deal more to say in how the research is defined, what would be important to know, and what should be done with the knowledge produced. This power imbalance can increase the potential for harmful effects of one's knowledge production on the people in question.

An activist engagement with research subjects, at a minimum, demonstrates a shared desire to see their rights respected, a promise to involve them in decisions about the research, and a commitment to contribute something to their struggle through one's research and analysis. I believe most anthropologists studying human rights have some basic commitment to them, whether in universal or culturally particular forms. Those doing research with indigenous peoples often share a broad overlap of goals with their research populations—whether cultural survival, development rights, or indigenous liberation. An activist engagement provides a way for those mutual goals to be made explicit and defined in dialogue between researcher and research subject. This does not mean that it will be an equal dialogue; relations defined in larger fields of power still determine this relationship. However, it necessitates acknowledgment of and dialogue about those power relations in the definition of a shared project.

The question of whether a researcher should have a commitment to, or accountability to, his or her research subjects, especially when they are marginalized and disadvantaged, is not just one of anthropological ethics; in many cases it is practical. Today, the research subjects themselves are likely to expect and demand such a commitment. Cognizant of the potential for exploitation by researchers and the potentialities for research products that undermine rather than support their struggles, indigenous people and others are increasingly demanding a voice in what is researched, how the research is conducted, and what is done with the knowledge produced. They frequently require evidence of political solidarities and a clear commitment to producing knowledge that is of some benefit to them.

This stance on the part of indigenous communities and organizations was (and remains) marked in Chiapas, where political conflict simmered and the situation was highly polarized. Suspicion abounded; an air of "If you aren't with us, you are against us" prevailed. People living in tension-ridden environments that regularly broke into open conflict, as in Nicolás Ruiz, could not afford to have anyone present—particularly someone engaged in information gathering—who was not "on their side." I was able to approach the community only because of my work as an activist, in particular my affiliation with the Defenders' Network. By approaching them as an activist researcher, I was able to make explicit my solidarity, and we could establish what the extent and the limits of that solidarity would be.

Contentious Encounters? Tensions and Contradictions in the Activist Engagement

Although the dialogic construction of the research process in activist research contributes to addressing the practical and ethical issues inherent in knowledge production, it is by no means free of tensions and contradictions. In my work with Nicolás Ruiz on the ILO representation, several complexities and challenges in our interaction merited acknowledgment and careful attention.

The Anthropologist as "Culture Expert": Respecting Indigenous Knowledge. One contradiction in this case lay in the manner in which the casting of the anthropologist as "culture expert" in the legal arena reinforces hierarchies of power. When the anthropologist is brought in as the expert witness in legal cases to provide evidence that indigenous culture is present—which was my role in the ILO representation of Nicolás Ruiz—such hierarchies of knowledge are reinforced. Members of "cultures" are not often granted the authority to speak for themselves or define their own cultures and identities; only anthropological specialists are granted the authority to do so. In fulfilling the role of "culture expert" in the

Nicolás Ruiz case, I reinforced those valorizations even as I sought to challenge them in my research process.

The decolonization of anthropological research entails more than finding overlapping goals with our research populations around which to organize investigation and confirm alliances. It also involves interrogating the discursive processes that invest anthropological analysis with authority and designate it as "expert" while relegating indigenous knowledge to the realm of "experience" (to be related to the anthropologist for subsequent analysis). It involves the recognition that indigenous people, indeed all people, engage in ongoing analysis of their own social processes, although they often do so from a different set of presumptions than the anthropologist does. Bringing that knowledge into dialogue with anthropological knowledge is vital to creating decolonized research relationships.

In the ethnohistorical research in Nicolás Ruiz, community leaders had a direct role in defining, in dialogue with the anthropologist, what it would be useful to know and how we should go about gaining that knowledge. In multiple interactions, we debated the documentary and oral evidence, as well as the emerging analysis, with community members. This allowed the community members to contribute to the development of the analysis itself. This collaboration allowed me to make explicit my commitment to the community where our goals overlapped and to incorporate the community in the definition of what knowledge should be produced and for what purpose. Moreover, this process enabled me to recognize and give weight to their analysis of the social processes and to ensure that this informed the final analysis. This did not happen in seamless fashion. Dialogue from vastly distinct perspectives and in unequal relations of power is not always, perhaps not ever, an easy undertaking. But the tensions and contradictions that such dialogues can raise can provide new understandings for both parties. Below, I consider this assertion in further detail.

Essentialism, Legalism, Dialogue. Above, we examined Brown and Haley's (2002) assertion that legal activists, focused on the exigencies of constructing winning cases, may be complicit in reducing, essentializing, and rendering static particular cultural identities. We may do so consciously, understanding such essentialisms as strategically necessary for winning specific cases that might offer significant advances in terms of gaining rights for particular groups—a sort of "strategic essentialism," in Spivak's well-known sense (Spivak 1988).[18] What Brown and Halley are concerned about is a failure to maintain a critical analysis of the larger picture of power relations and how rights are working within them. As various analysts have noted, rights struggles regularly reduce all justice issues to legal ones, which may be more manageable by states. One of the ways that they are rendered manageable is through delimiting, restricting, and reducing them by definition in laws and regulations (Brown 1995; Gledhill 1997; Hale 2002; Postero 2001). Identity and culture are essentialized (e.g., in the idea that indigenous people have a special relationship to the land) and fixed in law for the purposes of creating both regulations and precedent for future cases. Indigenous people—although this may be applicable to any number of groups—with their cultural particularities may find it difficult to meet those definitions and thus "qualify" for rights, creating authorized and unauthorized Indians and even generating a self-policing of indigenous identity.

In my work in Nicolás Ruiz, this issue came up precisely in relation to the above question of who has the authority to define indigenous culture and identity, though it did not come up in the way Brown and Halley would have expected. As an anthropologist trained in social constructionism and antiessentialism and cognizant of the critiques of legal rights struggles, I could see the pitfalls of an essentialized presentation of Nicolás Ruiz's cultural identity. I worked to find a way to define their indigenousness that continually emphasized the fluid and changing nature of culture and cultural identity without ceding the critical importance of that identity in lived experience and as the basis of claims to rights. I argued that culture, identity, and tradition are all continuously being reinterpreted in light of the experience at any particular historical moment. With this definition, I attempted to legitimize their claim without losing the historically constructed and unfixed nature of cultural identity.

Unfortunately, people in Nicolás Ruiz did not necessarily agree. They viewed their culture as unified and tended to emphasize continuity over change. Emphasizing change, in their view, made little sense in terms of the case and did not resonate with their own perceptions. Thus, although anthropologists might understand identity as inherently unstable and unfixed (Lowe 1991), we may have to confront the fact that indigenous groups often find such cultural fluidity contrary not only to their goals but also to their very understanding of themselves and their cultures.

When I first began to explore issues of reemergent indigenous identity in Nicolás Ruiz, I marveled at the fluidity: once indigenous, then campesino, then indigenous again. This confirmed and demonstrated all of my own anthropological notions of identity and culture. However, when I began trying to get at what people believed constituted their indigenous identity (important for the ILO representation and my own ethnohistorical analysis), I found that in fact their own notions of culture were far more stable than I had imagined. In fact, they largely staked their identity on that stability of form. The *comuneros* I spoke with argued that they had maintained a distinct social organization and political practice, which included communal landholding, collective decision making by consensus of the adult males, and of course, descent (expressed through demonstrating that their forefathers and mothers were Tzeltal). Note that these are much closer to the current discourse based in international law's emphasis on self-ascription and descent, than to the long-standing Mexican discourse in which language and dress, and even residence in rural community, are the primary traits identifying an indigenous person. When we discussed their distinct practices, their emphasis was on the continuity of these practices, not their fluidity and changeability. Perhaps this was not surprising, since the basis of their claim to indigenousness was precisely this continuity. I do not mean that they did not believe in it—that it was somehow strategic. In fact, their entire understanding of their history is tied to narratives of continuity, the continuity of their land ownership and of their land struggle.

Even as I understood this, I struggled with how to represent it. In one discussion, I ventured a query. "But things have really changed, haven't they? For example, isn't the way you do politics different since 1995 [when the *comuneros* left the PRI party and began to ally with the Zapatistas]?" The *comuneros*' response seemed equivocal, though it was expressed with confidence and certainty: "Yes of course, it has changed." One man elaborated: "What has changed is our relationship with the PRI, with the government. But the community functions in the same way [as before], through the assembly."[19] This man thus emphasized both the continuity of collective decision making as the *comuneros*' form of political participation (a key element of their cultural identity) and change in its interactions with the state and its ruling party (also an important force in shaping community identity). I tried again. "What about the *priistas*?" There were chuckles from the *comuneros*. "Well, they are the ones who are doing things differently, not us. They didn't attend the assembly, and that's why we took their land away."[20] Here the *comuneros* again emphasized the consistency of their position, arguing that those who had changed were the ones who had provoked the problem and thus had merited punishment.

In a different context, I asked a Zapatista leader about the community's radical realignment from *priista* to *zapatista*. He responded: "When we began to walk with the organization [the EZLN], we began to link our own struggle to that of others, many others who had similar struggles, with the *pueblos indígenas*. But it was the land struggle that brought us to the organization, the same struggle as always."[21] Like the man quoted above, he at once acknowledged the significance of the shift in their politics, now associated in their minds and consciously aligned with other struggles, including indigenous ones, *and* emphasized continuity, "the same struggle of always."

In a conversation with one of the Nicolás Ruiz's *defensores*, I struggled to articulate my concerns about the portrayal of the community in essentialized form. "The problem will be that if *indigenous* is defined so narrowly, later Nicolás Ruiz may have difficulty proving that it fits that definition," I said. Granted, this was not the best explanation of the problem. But his response is worth pausing to consider: "That's the situation we already have, that the government wants to leave us in [referring to the limits of language as a criterion]. If we get them to recognize our *usos y costumbres*, then there is not a problem. The proof is there—our *usos y costumbres ahí están, siempre los hemos tenido* [our customs and traditions are there, we have always had them]."[22]

Clearly, the *comuneros* viewed recent events through a very different lens than I, the activist anthropologist, did. Steeped in the antiessentialism of my discipline, I had tended to focus on change and fluidity in their situation. Cognizant of the critiques of legal activism, I was also concerned about contributing to essentialist portrayals of indigenous people that might become fixed in law or precedent and potentially do more damage than good in the medium term if we won. The *comuneros* came from a collective memory of struggle to recover their land. The origin story of that struggle was the founding of the community by Tzeltales and the *títulos primordiales* that documented it. And, as they reasserted their indigenousness, they reinterpreted "traditional" practices as proof of their cultural difference. From their perspective, emphasizing change alone detracted from the weight of their claim and made little sense.

The popular anthropological notions of cultural fluidity and of strategic essentialism were both poor fits for the reality of identity in Nicolás Ruiz. The people I talked to in Nicolás Ruiz simultaneously emphasized change and continuity in their identity. This was not problematic for the *comuneros*, whose identification processes were not bound to such categories. They acknowledged the historical construction of their identity through their ongoing land struggle and certain political and social practices, even as they recognized shifting identities and understanding of their practices in relation to changing social contexts. These shifting identities and the cultural traditions were at once strategic, offered as "proof" of their claims to rights, and "real," meaning that people did understand them to be manifestations of their difference. The defensor's statement that "our customs and traditions are there, we have always had them" at once suggests an essentialized notion of cultural continuity, a clear vision of customs and traditions' strategic mobilization, and a heartfelt claim about their significance. Identity is an ongoing process in Nicolás Ruiz, not something that the inhabitants change like a hat when it suits their purpose or something that is endlessly fluid and unbound.

Whether or not we resolved the questions, in the Nicolás Ruiz case we did spend time debating them; undoubtedly both my understanding and that of the community members I worked with were altered in the process. My own understanding of local cultural identities was greatly enriched by this engagement. It is hard to know and impossible to measure what we would have known had our research experience and learning process been different. But having to deal with the questions in the way that we did for the case brought me to my current understanding of how identity and identity formation were working in Nicolás Ruiz.

Does Collaboration Work?

We will also never know if the portrayal of indigenous culture that went into the ILO representation would have made an effective legal argument: the ILO did not issue a recommendation to the Mexican government but instead refused to consider the case. This did not necessarily mean that the case was not compelling. The Mexican government challenged the legality of the submission by the Frente Auténtico de Trabajo, on the grounds that it was not an "official" state labor union, and requested dismissal of the case on technical grounds. Though we responded with the obvious argument that if only state-controlled labor unions were permitted to submit representations, it was unlikely that any would ever be submitted. However, the ILO was unwilling or unable to override this challenge. The case did not achieve the return of Nicolás Ruiz's lost lands, nor did it garner recognition by the Mexican government that Nicolás Ruiz is an indigenous community.

However, this does not mean that our collaboration failed. I am wary of "practical effectiveness" criteria as a basis for evaluating the worth of activist research, both because it suggests a certain positivist nostalgia for notions of controlled studies and measurable results and because it seems to place demands on activist research that are rarely placed either on anthropological research or on political activism alone. In political activism, the immediate benefits are often hard to see and impossible to measure. Rarely is this interpreted to mean that they do not exist. Insisting on definable and demonstrable positive results for the community or group involved can be a circular drive difficult to exit. Who defines a "positive result," and how? How immediate must it be to be identified as a product of the activist research collaboration? Might not an outcome that seems negative in the short run contribute to a situation that generates a positive result in the medium or long run (or vice versa for that matter)?

Perhaps a better criterion for evaluating the success of activist research undertakings would be to ask ourselves whether they address the critical questions directed at the discipline. Do they address neocolonial power dynamics in our research processes? Do they seek to engage rather than to analyze our research subjects? Do they maintain a critical focus even as they make explicit political commitments, thus creating a productive tension in which critical analysis meets (and must come to terms with) day-to-day political realities? Might we gain more robust analyses as a result?

TOWARD A CRITICALLY ENGAGED ACTIVIST ANTHROPOLOGY

For most anthropologists, field research and analysis entail a significant engagement with the communities that are the subjects of our research. But should this engagement be explicitly activist? The tension between political-ethical commitment and critical analysis is always present in activist research, alongside numerous other tensions: those of power relations between researcher and researched and of short-term pragmatics and longer-term implications. Yet such tensions are present in all research. The benefit of explicitly activist research is precisely that it focuses on those tensions and maintains them as central to the work.

Critiques of anthropological authority and feminist standpoint theory have given us a heightened awareness of the socially situated nature of our knowledge production. Understanding the inherent inequalities of research relationships, we have reached some consensus in anthropology of the importance of "situating ourselves"—incorporating a reflexive consideration of how our positioning affects the knowledge that we produce. This includes considerations of our power and authority in the relationship with our research subject. Charles Hale (2004) argues that formulating explicitly activist research alliances, making our political commitments explicit up front, and keeping the social dynamics of the research process open to an ongoing dialogue with the research subjects are simply taking "positioning" to its logical conclusion. Critical analysis that is informed by an explicit politics has to grapple with those politics overtly rather than cede to the tendency to downplay their role. Critical analysis is continually drawn back to political grounding, whereas political strategy is continually challenged and potentially strengthened by the insights of critical analysis.

In the Nicolás Ruiz case, this dialogue between critical analysis and political commitment was key to anthropological insights I took away. I was challenged to rethink some of my own most deep-seated notions about identity and its fluid nature. Of course, identity, traditions, and culture are constantly changing. That is demonstrable by looking at them comparatively at different points in time. Yet for the people involved their manifestations at any particular point in time are concrete and are meaningful in that concreteness. In thinking about Nicolás Ruiz, I reflected on this in terms of my own complicated mixed-blood Native American identity, which I am continually rethinking in light of new experiences, new ideas, new contexts. My identity does change and has changed over time, yet it is fixed in terms of its meaning for me at any point in time. I came to believe that the same was true of Nicolás Ruiz and its community identity.

Anthropology may have some way to go in terms of theorizing identity and culture in a way that simultaneously recognizes both fluidity and the value and meaning of identity in specific moments. The concept of strategic essentialism went some distance in this direction, but with its emphasis on the strategic it stopped short of grasping the "real" effects of any strategic mobilization. Putting any identity category into play (as in a legal struggle) entails a new experience, which in turn has effects on one's understanding of history, culture, and identity. Those new understandings are every bit as correct and authentic as any that preceded them, and cannot be understood simply as strategy.

In Nicolás Ruiz, indigenous identity reemerged in the context of dialogic interactions with nonlocal actors who valorized indigenousness. Much as I (and all of us?) do, they reimagined themselves in light of new experiences and changing contexts. Our ILO case undoubtedly suggested strategic reasons for self-ascription as indigenous given their particular goals but also undoubtedly played a role in strengthening that reemergent identity by giving external valorization and providing information about international law that supported their self-ascription. Nevertheless, from their perspective what made them indigenous was essential to their community and was both real and unchanging.

I certainly cannot claim to have generated a new theoretical framework for understanding the relationship between fluidity and fixity in indigenous identity. But this particular activist engagement allowed me new insight into the complexity of that relationship. My own critical theorizing, which could certainly have told a pretty and anthropologically acceptable story about cultural fluidity, was forced to grapple with different perspectives and value them equally with my own "expert" notions. While my analysis is undoubtedly less neat as a result, it is potentially more insightful.

To the extent that research drawing critical analysis and political commitment into dialogue is possible, it will never be without contradictions. An explicitly activist engagement, when maintained in tension with critical reflection, forces us to address these contradictions, even if the conclusions generated are always partial, contingent, and subject to debate (as they are in all research). It is precisely the contingent and "subject to debate" aspect of the activist commitment that, rather than letting anthropologists off the hook, instead requires us to acknowledge power relations up front, deal with tensions as they arise, and find solutions in dialogue with our research subjects. Maintaining critical analysis and political pragmatics in tension pushes us to continuously acknowledge and grapple with the contradictions inherent in such a project.

I have focused in particular on critiques of rights and "left legalism," which argue that we may inadvertently support state efforts to define identity groups in ways that are limiting and undermining of their force as movements of resistance to oppression. I believe that critically engaged activist research is vital to addressing (though not resolving) the inherent tension. Members of specific groups may have understandings of their own identity that are complex and contradictory and that do not meet anthropological categories of understanding culture. If we keep a critical analysis that focuses on these larger structures of oppression, as an anthropologist is trained to do, definitions are more likely to be negotiated out before they make it into case law. This is not to say that the anthropologist's role is to tell members of a group that their understanding of their culture and identity is wrong—far from it. Rather, it means engaging in a respectful dialogue with members of a group with whom the anthropologist is allied in a common struggle and reaching mutual understandings about legal strategies and their short- and long-term effects, both for the group involved and for others like them. Although mutual understandings may not always emerge, a critical dialogue based on shared commitment is a good way to keep the tension between critical analysis and political pragmatics ethically viable and productive.

In today's anthropology, collaborative, dialogic engagement with our research subjects is ethically and practically warranted. The kind of research proposed in this chapter is not appropriate for all researchers or all research situations. However, for those who have a commitment to decolonizing our discipline, it may offer one path. This path is situated firmly on the terrain of research practices, not in the realm of the textual or of critique alone. On this terrain, a collaborative dialogue toward shared goals respectfully engages our research "subjects" and makes their own analysis a fundamental part of the process of knowledge production. It merges cultural critique with political commitment toward creating knowledge that is empirically grounded, theoretically innovative, and mutually beneficial. It also makes use of productive tensions, grapples directly with unproductive ones, and strives for more just relations in our discipline and our world.

NOTES

I am grateful for the comments of Miguel Angel de los Santos, Kathleen Dill, Melissa Forbis, Mark Goodale, and Charles Hale. Research was supported by the Social Science Research Council—MacArthur Foundation, the Ford Foundation–Mexico, and a Mellon Faculty Research Grant of the Lozano Long Institute of Latin American Studies at the University of Texas at Austin.

1. One aspect of these critiques was a challenge to the term *research subject*. The term carries other meanings than *subject* as in "topic"—including "subject of power," which adds to the sensitivity about the hierarchically structured power relations between researcher and the researched. I use the term purposefully in this text to remind us of the problematics of those power relations, although without the cumbersome quotation marks often used around the term to denote the author's recognition of the term's negative implications.

2. Social conflict was not born in Chiapas with the 1994 uprising; however, the presence of the Zapatista movement and the governmental response to it have shaped politics and political conflict at the community level in many areas of the state, including Nicolás Ruiz. Although open combat with the Mexican Army lasted only twelve days, political polarization, militarization, paramilitarization, and low-intensity warfare (not to mention continued social injustice) have all contributed to ongoing social conflict in the state.

3. The history of Nicolás Ruiz in this section is drawn from primary sources, including documents in the possession of the community in the municipal archive and in Bienes Comunales, documents in the Archive of the Diocese of San Cristóbal de las Casas, and documents in the Archive of the Registro Agrario Nacional in Tuxtla Gutierrez, Chiapas. A more complete history of the community is elaborated in Speed (2006).

4. Oral histories abound, and those collected by the author are presented in Speed (2006).

5. As early as 1900, census records show that there were no speakers of Tzeltal in Nicolás Ruiz. However, in 1998 older adults told me that their parents had spoken Tzeltal, and these people would clearly have been alive after 1900. As recently as 1998, there were still several very elderly Tzeltal speakers.
6. From my field notes of July 1999. Notes of these and other conversations cited below are in my possession.
7. Recounted to me by authorities of Nicolás Ruiz in August 2000.
8. Women do not hold land or participate in the assembly.
9. Rus (1994) has demonstrated how indigenous communities in highlands Chiapas were transformed into "revolutionary institutional communities" (after the ruling party's name, Revolutionary Institutional Party) as their local leaders and political processes were integrated into the corporatist state through clientelism, ensuring the party's hegemony in Chiapas for decades.
10. From a conversation with me in March 2002.
11. Although one might be tempted to interpret this as the government's fulfilling its role of protecting the rights of individuals to choose their political allegiances, it is extremely unlikely that the government would have intervened on behalf of supporters of an opposition party.
12. Project ILO 169 was headed by attorney Alvaro Reyes with funding from the Echoing Green Foundation.
13. A complaint regarding a violation of an ILO Convention by a signatory state is called a representation and is presented only through an established labor union. The Defenders' Network worked in coordination with the Frente Auténtico del Trabajo (Authentic Labor Front, or FAT by its Spanish acronym) to present the representation on behalf of Nicolás Ruiz.
14. Nicolás Ruiz does not seek the return of lands lost to *ejidal* grants, recognizing that the communities established on them have now lived there for decades and have a right to remain.
15. *Comunero* speaking in community assembly, June 2001.
16. *Comunero* speaking in community assembly, June 2001.
17. The ILO Complaint was prepared by attorneys Alvaro Reyes and Lisa Glowacki, in collaboration with Rubén Moreno Méndez and Herón Moreno Moreno, representatives of Nicolás Ruiz in the Defenders' Network.
18. Hale (2006) critiques this process in the important Awas Tigni case before the Inter-American Court.
19. *Comunero* in conversation with me, July 2000. All names are pseudonyms, and the translations of quotes are my own.
20. *Comunero* in conversation with me, July 2000.
21. In conversation with me, March 2002.
22. Defensor in conversation with me, June 2002.

REFERENCES

Brown, Wendy. 1995. *States of Injury: Power and Freedom in Late Modernity.* Princeton: Princeton University Press.
Brown, Wendy, and Janet Halley. 2002. *Left Legalism/Left Critique.* Durham: Duke University Press.
Clifford, James. 1988. *The Predicament of Culture: Twentieth-Century Ethnography, Literature, and Art.* Cambridge, MA: Harvard University Press.

Clifford, James, and George Marcus. 1986. *Writing Culture: The Poetics and Politics of Ethnography.* Berkeley: University of California Press.

Denzin, Norman. 2002. "Confronting Anthropology's Crisis of Representation." *Journal of Contemporary Ethnography* 31 (4): 478–516.

Gledhill, John. 1997. "Liberalism, Socio-Economic Rights and the Politics of Identity: From Moral Economy to Indigenous Rights." In *Human Rights, Culture and Context: Anthropological Perspectives,* edited by Richard Wilson, 70–110. London: Pluto Press.

Gordon, Edmund T. 1991. "Anthropology and Liberation." In *Decolonizing Anthropology: Moving Further toward an Anthropology for Liberation,* edited by Faye Harrison, 149–67. Washington, DC: AAA Association of Black Anthropologists.

Gurguha, Francisco. 2000. "Nicolás Ruiz: Tierra sin Ley" [Nicolás Ruiz: The Lawless Land]. *Areópago* 275 (March 6): 6–9.

Hale, Charles R. 2002. "Does Multiculturalism Menace? Governance, Cultural Rights and the Politics of Identity in Guatemala." *Journal of Latin American Studies* 34 (3): 485–524.

———. 2004. "Reflexiones hacia la práctica de una investigación descolonizada, presentado a la reunión de la 'red de investigación indígena.'" Paper presented at the Center for Latin American Social Policy (CLASPO) conference, La Paz, Bolivia, June.

———. 2006. "Activist Research vs. Cultural Critique: Indigenous Land Rights and the Contradictions of Politically Engaged Anthropology." *Cultural Anthropology* 21 (February): 96–120.

Haraway, Donna. 1988. "Situated Knowledge: The Science Question in Feminism as a Site of Discourse on the Privilege of Partial Perspective." *Feminist Studies* 14 (3): 575–99.

Harrison, Faye Venecia, ed. 1991. *Decolonizing Anthropology: Moving Further toward an Anthropology for Liberation.* Washington, DC: AAA Association of Black Anthropologists.

Lowe, Lisa. 1991. "Heterogeneity, Hybridity, Multiplicity: Marking Asian American Differences." *Diaspora* 1 (1): 24–44.

Lyotard, Jean-Francois. 1984. *The Postmodern Condition: A Report on Knowledge.* Minneapolis: University of Minnesota Press.

Marcus, James, and Michael M. J. Fischer. 1986. *Anthropology as Cultural Critique.* Chicago: University of Chicago Press.

Merry, Sally Engle. 1997. "Legal Pluralism and Transnational Culture: The *Ka Ho'okolokolonui Kanaka Maoli* Tribunal, Hawai'i, 1993." In *Human Rights, Culture and Context,* edited by Richard A. Wilson, 28–48. London: Pluto Press.

Messer, Ellen. 1993. "Anthropology and Human Rights." *Annual Review of Anthropology* 22:224–25.

Mutua, Kagendo, and Beth Swadener. 2004. *Decolonizing Research in Cross-Cultural Contexts: Critical Personal Narratives.* New York: State University of New York Press.

Postero, Nancy Grey. 2001. "Constructing Indigenous Citizens in Multicultural Bolivia." www.geocities.com/tayacan_2000/paperpostero.html ?2006264. Accessed February 2006.

Price, David. 2000. "Anthropologists as Spies." *Nation* 271 (16): 24–27.

Rappaport, Joanne. n.d. "Beyond Writing: The Epistemology of Collaborative Ethnography." Unpublished manuscript.

Rus, Jan. 1994. "The 'Comunidad Revolutionaria Institucional': The Subversion of Native Government in Highland Chiapas, 1936–1968." In *Everyday Forms of State Formation: Revolution and the Negotiation of Rule in Modern Mexico*, edited by Gilbert Joseph and Daniel Nugent, 265–300. Durham: Duke University Press.

Said, Edward. 1978. *Orientalism*. New York: Pantheon Books.

Scheper-Hughes, Nancy. 1995. "The Primacy of the Ethical: Propositions for a Militant Anthropology." *Current Anthropology* 36 (3): 409–20.

Speed, Shannon. 2006. *Lucha por la tierra y identidad comunitaria: La etnohistoria y etnopresente de Nicolás Ruiz, Chiapas*. [Land Struggle and Community Identity: The Ethnohistory and Ethnopresent of Nicolás Ruiz]. Tuxtla Gutierrez: CONECULTA.

Spivak, Gayatri. 1988. "Can the Subaltern Speak?" In *Marxism and the Interpretation of Culture*, edited by Cary Nelson and Larry Grossberg, 271–315. Chicago: University of Illinois Press.

Tuhiwai Smith, Linda. 1999. Decolonizing Methodologies: Research and Indigenous Peoples. Berkeley: Zed Books.

9. Community-Centered Research as Knowledge/Capacity Building in Immigrant and Refugee Communities

Shirley Suet-ling Tang

> We are ready for change
> Let us link hands and hearts
> together find a path through the dark woods
> step through the doorways between worlds
> leaving huellas for others to follow,
> build bridges, cross them with grace, and claim these puentes our "home"
> si se puede, que asi sea, so be it, estamos listas, vámonos.
>
> Now let us shift ...
>
> GLORIA E. ANZALDÚA, "now let us shift ... ,"
> in *this bridge we call home: radical visions for transformation* (2002)

In the essay "(Un)natural Bridges, (Un)safe Spaces" in *this bridge we call home: radical visions for transformation* (2002b, 1), Gloria Anzaldúa, writer, cultural activist, and recipient of the American Studies Association Lifetime Achievement Award, wrote, "Bridges are ... passageways, conduits, and connectors that connote transitioning, crossing borders, and changing perspectives. Bridges span liminal (threshold) spaces between worlds, spaces I call nepantla, a Nahuatl word meaning tierra entre medio. Transformations occur in this in-between space, an unstable, unpredictable, precarious, always-in-transition space lacking clear boundaries.... Most of us dwell in nepantla so much of the time it's become a sort of 'home.'"

Nepantla, the space in between, is a dynamic place of transformation within which American studies and ethnic studies scholars have increasingly positioned themselves. In his 2001 American Studies Association presidential address, George Sanchez reflected on the nature of this interface and pointed to what George Lipsitz (2001) has referred to as "dangerous crossroads," or, in Sanchez's own words, "the crossing of disciplinary boundaries which . . . creates the intellectual excitement of American Studies" (Sanchez 2002, 7). He went on to emphasize that a significant border to cross in the post-9/11 era is the one that "separates the academic community from the wider public." "American studies and ethnic studies have a long history of public engagement which should be celebrated and built upon," he noted. "Even in moments of difficulty, we need to encourage each other to persist in these interventions in public discourse, working closely with local communities to learn from them and transmit alternative ways of looking at the world based on our scholarly research and teaching" (7, 11). Sanchez's call for boundary crossing into the public arena resonates well with Anzaldúa's exploration of epistemologies, which stresses the importance of actively linking one's "inner reflection and vision" with "social, political action and lived experiences to generate subversive knowledges—or what she described as "the path of conocimiento . . . inner work, public acts" (Anzaldúa 2002a, 542, 540). The word *conocimiento*, she wrote, "derives from cognoscera, a Latin verb meaning 'to know' and is the Spanish word for knowledge and skill. I call conocimiento that aspect of consciousness urging you to act on the knowledge gained" (577 n. 2).

Inspired by the commitment of scholars in American studies and ethnic studies to public engagement, and building on the insights of Gloria Anzaldúa's powerful metaphors about "knowing" and "acting," I have organized my work in the last few years to respond to the critical challenges and directions charted by scholars and critics in my fields. My central concern is how we develop research and writing in ways that are responsive and accountable to community struggles over capacity building and community development. Specifically, I explore research methods that underscore community production of knowledge to support community efforts in self-representation and self-advocacy. In this chapter, I discuss *why* practitioner knowledge matters and *how* a community-centered research process can draw out hidden and overlooked sources of knowledge that, in turn, enhance capacity and knowledge building in immigrant/refugee communities. First, I will discuss my role and responsibilities at the University of Massachusetts at Boston (UMass Boston) and a personal experience to demonstrate how my community and teaching commitments have influenced my research priorities and directions. I will then discuss a research methodology that I developed and employed in my research with two Khmer (Cambodian) American communities in Massachusetts. The research process will be described in detail, not as a "how-to" guide for readers, but as a way to trace how bilingual and bicultural community practitioners have become knowledge producers. Finally, I will reflect on my academic journey and explain why I consider nepantla, the space-in-between, to be a habitat for my research, political activism, and intellectual positioning. As I hope the following sections will show, it is important for us to begin our work with the understanding that grassroots community knowledge has been systematically marginalized and to stay mindful of how this has had a significant impact on the kinds of analytical frameworks and sources that we consider valid or important for scholarly research and teaching. The conscientious efforts of community practitioners to become active knowledge producers—and the wide-ranging impact of community knowledge production—are, however, unmistakable and imperative. It is, therefore, respectful of their commitments and contributions that I reflect on my subjective choice to make bilingual/bicultural community practitioners' acts of knowledge production matter. This intended focus on the state of "doing" knowledge/capacity-building work within communities complements other chapters in this volume that address a broad spectrum of issues and challenges in relation to activist scholarship.

FRAMING RESEARCH PRIORITIES

At UMass Boston, our institutional obligation and responsibility to engage with urban places, people, and issues and their complex local and global connections have consistently reminded us of the need to transform traditional functions of the university—teaching, research, and service. Teacher-scholars at UMass Boston's ethnic studies programs are what Anzaldúa has called *las Nepantleras:* moving within and between different institutional structures, different disciplines, different cultures, and different publics and using this movement to "facilitate passage between multiple worlds" and to create more inclusive, culturally responsive, and academically relevant learning communities. Indeed, the boundary-crossing, overlapping nature of this kind of publicly engaged academic activity has been characteristic of my work since 2001. I offer the following example to highlight my own positioning in relation to the communities that we serve.

In September 2003, as I planned for a vigil and healing ceremony on Revere Beach, I was working with community leaders and members who had long been sharing their knowledge and resources with me about urban history and what really matters—on the ground—in "doing" research that focuses on race/ethnicity, (im)migration, and development. This ceremony brought together different generations of local residents in the Revere-Lynn–East Boston region, including a younger group of Khmer (Cambodian), Latino, Black, and white residents, as well as teachers, religious leaders, community organizers, and activist artists in this multiethnic community. The healing ceremony was organized and attended by primarily young adults in the community, including nearly two-thirds of all the Khmer American students attending UMass Boston, to collectively respond to the violence and loss after a shooting that had caused the death of a Khmer American young man on Revere Beach. A four-sentence newspaper brief reported the killing and described the motive as gang member rivalries. But the victim was not a gang member, and those who knew him wanted his story to be told more fully and accurately. Given my own research and teaching commitments, I developed a range of semester-long research projects with relevant content to directly respond to the crisis, while also convincing the *Boston Globe* to assign a reporter to do a new story and providing the reporter with sociohistorical analysis and different community-based perspectives based on my continuing research in local immigrant/refugee communities. The dominant public and academic discourse on community violence in urban neighborhoods emphasizes gangs and juvenile delinquency. But increasingly, American studies and ethnic studies scholars are generating new evidence and developing new ways of understanding that challenge these preconceived notions about urban lives and environments.

The young man who was shot to death was Gift Chea, a Khmer American young man whom I had been recruiting to UMass Boston, and whose struggle and determination to attend and finish college remind us of the many first-generation, immigrant/refugee, and working students at our urban, public university. Gift's mother is, in fact, a UMass Boston alumnus and had been a bilingual teacher in Lowell for years until a 2002 statewide ballot initiative financed by California businessman Ron Unz successfully eliminated bilingual education in Massachusetts. Gift had just completed his GED and was planning to meet with me to talk about possible courses he might take in the future. Then suddenly, on a Friday night, he was shot to death by another Asian American man on Revere Beach. The tragic death of Gift brought confusion and guilt to a community, including some of our UMass Boston students, who asked themselves what they were going to do to "live" and whether the knowledge they were acquiring in educational institutions could lead to progress in any meaningful sense. At the healing vigil, they stood together as a community, trying to make meaning of their realities. Gift's friends told stories of how he had fostered enduring friendships with people from different backgrounds in a neighborhood struggling against lasting legacies of war, trauma, racism, poverty, and the daily realities of language and cultural barriers. Others urged the community to recognize the historical connections between interethnic violence and school failure in the 1990s and the violence against Asians associated with arsons, murder, car vandalism, and racial harassment during the early years of Southeast Asian refugee resettlement throughout the 1980s. Still others, the youngest generation of the youth who showed up at the vigil, carried banners filled with words and drawings of both protest and hope.

I reflect on this example to illustrate how I see my role in advancing and acting upon scholarly areas in ways that are directly and holistically integrated with critical intervention projects in our communities, especially those that are underserved and under-researched. Despite all the efforts to enable the reporter to excavate this wealth of knowledge embedded in the community, the second *Boston Globe* article still failed to capture the multilayered story of Gift's death. Nor did it offer any vision for change. Teacher-scholars, including myself, need to act more upon the primary mission of the academy—the advancement of knowledge—to support what Angela Davis and others (see, e.g., Davis 2005; Alexander 2004) refer to as "communities of struggle" in uncovering their grassroots knowledge and in building their research capacity for long-term development. As the following sections will show, my work aims at engaging with these challenges by explicitly and consistently linking research to community-centered initiatives. My research activities shape community-centered interventions as much as they are shaped by them. Specifically, I have utilized and extended the methodological skills in my fields to develop a community-centered methodology for conducting culturally responsive research, particularly in relation to public health and community development, in various immigrant and refugee communities, including the Khmer American communities discussed in this chapter. As I increasingly position myself within the space of nepantla, the space-in-between, I have also gauged my own research efforts not only by their level of original contribution to my fields (for example, gathering original data in under-researched and underserved groups that have not been at the center of systematic analysis in American studies and ethnic studies) but also by the level of public engagement in communities before and after. I begin here with the importance of practitioner knowledge in the process of "doing" community-centered research.

CENTERING PRACTITIONER KNOWLEDGE

In *Vital Difference: The Role of Race in Building Community,* a report published by MIT's Center for Reflective Community Practice, Ceasar McDowell and his colleagues argue that the growing demand for data-driven results by funders and policy makers misses much of what community practitioners know. "The problem," they state, "is not the demand for data; the problem lies in the over-reliance on quantitative measures as a means of representing practitioners' knowledge" (Amulya et al. 2004, 9). In respecting many innovative forms of knowledge production, they make the case that the stories, experiences, and voices of people working or living in the communities are essential to understanding how those communities of struggle work. They call this "developmental knowledge," or knowledge "formulated by those who do community work over time and integrating context, history, politics, culture, and place, [without which] we lack a critical source of learning needed to build healthy and just communities" (39).

My own research in immigrant/refugee communities is grounded in the belief that community members and practitioners who are involved in the work of neighborhood building have vital and powerful knowledge that has grown out of their own experience. Immigrant/refugee community practitioners often apply their multilingual/multicultural skills to strengthen others' research about their communities, yet such research processes typically do not provide them with opportunities and structures to enhance their own competencies and developmental pathways. Despite the value and potential of their involvement, community practitioners are often relegated to instrumental positions in which their voices and visions are marginalized, misused, or completely neglected. When the research is over, their contributions are "forgotten" within those communities being "studied"—not unlike the "places" that Ruth Wilson Gilmore refers to in chapter 1 of this volume. This is particularly true for immigrant and refugee communities and communities of color that do not have direct access to networks and resources enabling the practitioners to design, implement, and monitor their own research projects and to integrate their personal, professional, and community commitments more holistically in relation to capacity building and long-term community development.

Recognizing this reality, the next few sections examine ways in which community-centered research in immigrant/refugee communities is developed explicitly to draw on as well as to build the capacity of bilingual/bicultural community members through a collaborative research process. At the core of this theory/practice is the enabling of people from communities of struggle to have direct control and full power over how to explore and use their knowledge, skills, and capacities to imagine and build community. In addition, my work takes into account the immigrant/refugee community's specific history, including the complex, uneven ways it has developed over time. The design of effective community-centered research, then, not only produces fresh, meaningful knowledge but also benefits and contributes directly to the community's unique capacity-building and development process. This work contributes to both activist scholarship and the field of community building.

DEVELOPING TOOLS FOR SELF-REPRESENTATION AND SELF-ADVOCACY

Practitioner knowledge has the potential to inform and support healthy and just community development that is grounded, over time, in the direct experiences and insights of community members. While some community practitioners already have the "tools" to engage in the critical analysis of social relations and the theoretical exploration of the work they do—perhaps in collaboration with scholar activists who are seeking new forms of knowledge to advance their academic work—others simply do not have or prefer such tools. Those without such tools need to create, develop, and refine methodologies for advancing their own indigenous knowledge systems and for becoming better positioned and empowered to represent and advocate for their communities.

For example, in the Khmer (Cambodian) American communities of Lowell and Lynn, Massachusetts—the second- and fifth-largest Khmer American communities in the United States respectively—violence and trauma through war and genocide, combined with the disintegration of the traditional agrarian, social-cultural-spiritual system of Cambodia and their forced migration and displacement through refugee resettlement, have had long-term effects on individuals and intergenerational dynamics. Populations in both cities include those who were resettled here as refugees escaping from Cambodia's killings fields in the early 1980s, together with more recently arrived immigrants, younger generations who were born and raised locally, and a segment that has moved from other cities within Massachusetts or other states (Pho, Gerson, and Cowan, 2007; Smith-Hefner 1999; Nou 2006; Chan 2003, 2004). In Lynn, despite having more than two decades of history and being the largest Asian ethnic group in the city, Khmer Americans have surprisingly little public voice, access to resources, or organizational capacity. In Lowell, too, inadequate schools, ineffective health care, lack of affordable housing, and racism have represented critical challenges for the community. At the same time, historic victories related to bilingual education, the successful campaigns of Mr. Chanrithy Uong as Lowell's first nonwhite city councilor—the first Khmer American elected official in U.S. society—and specific examples of cultural development have distinguished Lowell's profile from Lynn over the past two decades (see, e.g., Chea 2003; Massachusetts Advisory Committee 1998; Kiang 1996).

In conducting research with the Khmer American communities in both Lowell and Lynn, I have noted that the majority of these communities' leaders/practitioners share personal migration stories of resettlement as refugees in the United States during the mid- to late 1980s or early 1990s. Many currently work as "frontline" staff in mainstream agencies or community-based organizations but also serve as critical, bilingual/bicultural resources wherever they work. They typically take on many roles beyond their job descriptions and often outside their own personal or professional interests. They are engaged in the difficult work of (re)constructing community in U.S. society—"helping people," as they would call it. They work tirelessly, looking for solutions to meet the urgent demands and complex realities in their communities. In the process, however, these frontline practitioners often find themselves marginalized and excluded from decision making about resources that affect their communities. Therefore, they need to develop, articulate, and assert their own critical, cultural, and analytical perspectives so that resources and strategies can be developed and allocated more fairly and creatively. In many settings like the Khmer American communities in Lynn and Lowell, this capacity for engaging in knowledge production and challenging decisions about resources needs strengthening.

With this in mind, I have developed a knowledge/capacity-building process to support and sustain the work of building systematic bodies of practitioner/community knowledge through collaborative research. This process, described below, aims at providing opportunities for community practitioners to be trained in skills of collecting, validating, interpreting, and translating community data and in using collaborative research methodologies while making central and visible their own on-the-ground experiences and capacities as bilingual/bicultural leaders. Moreover, the process emphasizes the goal of producing knowledge individually and institutionally across multiple arenas, including research, public policy, philanthropy, and, most importantly, communities at the grassroots level—all of which have important roles to play in the course of long-term community development. The following section offers a detailed description of the knowledge/capacity-building process to highlight the efforts of community practitioners to become knowledge producers—and how I, as an external investigator, helped to facilitate that process. I also share some insights drawn from the knowledge generated by community members who were involved in these research projects.

ENGAGING COMMUNITY PRACTITIONERS AS KNOWLEDGE PRODUCERS AND CAPACITY BUILDERS

The needs assessments discussed in this chapter were each commissioned by a community organization. In 2000, Massachusetts Asian and Pacific Islanders for Health (MAP for Health, formerly known as Massachusetts Asian AIDS Prevention Project or MAAPP)—a nonprofit organization that "promotes health, HIV and sexuality awareness, and access to care in Massachusetts Asian, South Asian, and Pacific Islander communities"—launched a state-funded needs assessment project that explored the state of HIV/AIDS prevention in the Khmer American community in Lowell (Tang 2001) In 2004, the Khmer Association of the North Shore (KANS)—a newly formed community organization whose mission is to "foster and promote the civic, economic and social sufficiency of the greater Lynn Khmer and Southeast Asian Community"—conducted a needs assessment focusing on the challenges and barriers faced by the Khmer American community in Lynn (Tang 2004). In both cases, I was invited to serve as the external principal investigator. Drawing on my own experience as a frontline community organizer in Southeast Asian American communities as well as my interdisciplinary training in American studies and ethnic studies, I used these unique research opportunities to support community processes not only to uncover and articulate the knowledge that they possess but also to make their knowledge accessible to others locally and nationally.

Both needs assessments involved the collective efforts of the external principal investigator, community practitioners/leaders, and other community members. Selected community practitioners were trained by the principal investigator as co-researchers to conduct bilingual/bicultural focus groups while drawing on their own experiences as immigrant leaders. Co-researchers with extensive community networks recruited community members who received incentives (cash stipends) for their participation in a series of focus groups.

The knowledge/capacity-building process began with my visits to the local community. Through MAP for Health's networks in Lowell, I met staff and community members affiliated with the Lowell Community Health Center, the Cambodian Mutual Assistance Association, and Southeast Asian Bilingual Advocates Inc.—some of the oldest organizations serving Southeast Asian American populations in Lowell. Most community practitioners in Lowell were Khmer American and had previously collaborated on a number of community projects, including the annual Khmer New Year Celebration, the annual Lowell Southeast Asian Water Festival, and many public health projects. These collaborations, often co-sponsored by mainstream social service and government agencies, had enabled a critical mass of bilingual/bicultural community leaders to emerge. Indeed, this emergence of a significant number of Khmer American community practitioners in the late 1990s signified a major advancement in the community's capacity to develop effective community responses and had tremendous impact on the level of readiness among these practitioners to co-lead collaborative research.

In Lynn, KANS was initiated by local community leaders and service providers in response to the demise of Cambodian Communities of Massachusetts (CCM)—the oldest Khmer American community organization in Massachusetts—and the obvious unmet needs for both services and advocacy on behalf of the city's rapidly growing Khmer American population. On the one hand, the emergence of KANS as a new organization offered a significant opportunity for renewed investment, community development, and collaboration, both internally and externally. On the other hand, decades of a resource-poor institutional environment had resulted in a leadership void and an overwhelming workload for a newly formed organization. The initial priority for KANS, therefore, was to clarify its mission by identifying the most urgent problems/needs in the community through a community needs assessment, while investing fully in the existing capacity of the organization so that new initiatives would become possible. Though the Khmer American community practitioners in Lynn did not have the same history of collaboration as their counterparts in Lowell, they shared the same level of commitment to the work of community building, including the needs assessment research and documentation process.

Confronting Research as an "Academic Enterprise"

The initial meetings were intended to share the knowledge/capacity-building approach, emphasizing the importance of generating knowledge that is embedded within the community among people who are living or working in it. This included introducing the role of "co-researchers" in a collaborative research project and providing an orientation to the goals of learning for individual co-researchers, the organization, and the community as a whole. The repeated naming and elaboration of the role of "co-researchers" at these initial meetings demystified the work of research as an "academic enterprise" and motivated community practitioners not only to take ownership and responsibility over the knowledge production process but to view and embrace the research process as a "critical practice." Moreover, these meetings enabled me to explain my role as the external investigator, working closely with the organization to design and implement the research project and supporting the co-researchers step by step.

From these conceptual frameworks, we then outlined logistics and concrete concerns. The co-researchers and I collectively decided on specific budget items for the project, underscoring the particular needs of community members, including transportation, child care, and refreshments. We also discussed incentives for participants who would be involved in the project. Here is an example of how bilingual/bicultural capacity matters. Community practitioners used their "insider" knowledge to determine that cash stipends (rather than vouchers) should be used as incentives for community participants because the participants could actually use the cash to shop for food and daily necessities in neighborhood ethnic stores without having to travel out to a mall or a market that they felt was outside their familiar territory or comfort zone. Even though I had worked as a community organizer in a similar Khmer American community before and was familiar with the socioeconomic backgrounds of people and such needs in the neighborhoods, it was through discussions of such particulars of the research process with community practitioners that I gained a current understanding of the deep sense of isolation and persistent marginalization that Khmer Americans were experiencing. The gathering of these community practitioners also opened up much-needed spaces for co-researchers to share with each other—their personal, professional, and community commitments, as well as the daily struggles and dilemmas they faced as leaders with multiple responsibilities. These conversations became important sources of knowledge about both community and organizational challenges that we used to frame our research projects.

At the end of these initial meetings, I developed a structure detailing every single step of the research process. This detail-oriented structure was intended to serve two goals. First, given that resources were limited and practitioners were already working on many projects, the structure was developed to provide the co-researchers with a list of research activities and accompanying deadlines, with the understanding that flexibility would be necessary to maintain a truly supportive learning environment. Second, I used this structure to "bargain" time and support with the supervisors of the frontline workers/co-researchers by highlighting the level of commitment required for completing the research project. I found this strategy extremely necessary and useful, especially with predominantly white supervisors who were used to research projects that mainly engaged their frontline workers in roles such as recruiting community members, passing out surveys, getting ethnic food, and, of course, cleaning up after meetings! For me to be accountable to community struggles over self-representation and self-advocacy means, in part, using my academic privilege to clear away potential obstacles that might discourage community practitioners from taking on the challenge of community knowledge production. Needless to say, as empowered, knowledgeable participants, community practitioners also advocated for themselves, so my role was to mobilize attention to their demands. The basic structure of the collaborative research process is described in the next sections.

Experiencing Research as Critical Practice

Because not all community practitioners had experience in conducting research, the collaborative research design process drew on an experiential learning model, beginning with a facilitated dialogue in which co-researchers shared specific moments when *they* saw/heard/felt an urgent need/problem that was facing Khmer people in the community. (In the Lowell needs assessment the discussion was focused more specifically around the state of HIV prevention.) Co-researchers were given specific question prompts to "tell the story." This dialogue created opportunities for community practitioners to draw on their own perspectives and, through a story-sharing process, to generate knowledge about their community. It also modeled a method for them to facilitate their own focus groups with community members, using the dialogue/story-sharing process with similar question prompts. Furthermore, the stories, insights, and analysis gathered during these dialogues were later used for preparing the final product of the research project.

In deepening their understanding of the knowledge/capacity-building framework, community practitioners were asked to think critically about a set of questions, and through a joint discussion we developed a shared understanding about the purpose, scope, and methods of the needs assessment. These questions included the following:

- What is the context or background of the study? What prompted you to conduct the needs assessment?
- Who is interested in the study results? Why do they want the information? What might those individuals do with the results?
- Who should be involved in the research and in what role(s)? What perspectives can these individuals and programs/organizations/agencies offer to the needs assessment? What can they learn from the needs assessment?
- What research methods would best motivate community members to engage fully in the research project?

Using the ideas and insights generated in the dialogue, individual co-researchers worked with me to develop group-specific questions for the focus groups (or community conversations, as some practitioners would prefer to call them). In the process of finalizing the questions I compared and connected the issues/problems/needs that co-researchers had identified to existing information, wherever appropriate. The research team then made decisions about the needs assessment tools, including all the questions being used, and set up a schedule for workshops on how to conduct focus groups.

Building Research Skills and Using Bicultural/Bilingual Capacities

The efforts of co-researchers created the conceptual and logistical groundwork for conducting research in their communities. In addition, co-researchers participated in skill-building workshops to resolve questions concerning reporting, transcription, and translation. Both groups of co-researchers discussed samples of summary reports and transcripts and made informed decisions about how to document their findings from the focus groups. The Lynn research team gave more attention to discussing the whole process of conducting focus groups, from logistical details (e.g., getting tape recorders ready) to facilitation skills (e.g., how to facilitate a discussion with talkative or quiet participants) to writing summary reports. Knowing that only a few of the co-researchers in Lynn had prior research experience, I also developed a set of detailed guidelines for writing focus group reports.

The Lowell research team, with participants who had led other focus groups and community forums in the past, had a different kind of discussion that enabled us to develop research materials that were culture, language, gender, and age specific. The male and female co-researchers were involved in debates over certain pointed questions about sexuality and HIV. After reviewing a draft of focus group questions, the men's group was concerned about the cultural appropriateness of engaging adult men in discussing sexual behaviors. The women's group, however, thought that those were exactly the questions that would yield important insights about community interventions. In the end, the team members agreed that the questions being used for the focus groups needed to be gender and age specific. The men's group decided not to ask specific questions related to sexual experiences (see the section "Reclaiming Grassroots Cultural Knowledge," below, for interesting findings in the men's group). The Lowell team also discussed recent developments of HIV/AIDS education in Cambodia and highlighted the transnational realities and connections in Khmer American communities and the impact of these connections on translating HIV-related materials in the United States. They agreed that ensuring the consistency of Khmer language usage in both countries was a priority, and they translated the needs assessment materials accordingly.

Co-researchers formed teams of two people for each focus group. These teams were formed such that cultural norms and expectations were taken into consideration (particularly around the age, gender, language, and educational status of community members who would be involved). In some cases, co-researchers with prior research experience were paired with those without. This pairing structure—together with the joint analysis of findings described in the next section—maximized the use of bilingual/bicultural resources and thus the validity of "findings" to be collected, interpreted, and recorded. In addition, co-researchers discussed the consent process, developed follow-up questions for the various focus groups, and practiced facilitation skills with one another.

Research Process and Joint Analysis of Findings

Co-researchers facilitated focus groups/community conversations at local community organizations. I provided additional support to the groups that were facilitated by co-researchers who had little or no prior experience with research (e.g., I was physically present to help set up some focus groups). I did not participate directly in any focus group in order to make space for the co-researchers to facilitate an open and honest dialogue with the community members—most of whom had agreed to participate in the focus groups because they had relationships of trust with the co-researchers.

Following the focus groups, the co-researchers prepared full transcripts or summary reports highlighting powerful stories that were shared in each dialogue as well as their own critical analysis and insights about the community. A point person in each group met with me to make sure that the stories and issues being captured in writing were clearly articulated and explained. Through these one-on-one discussions, co-researchers began to reflect more deeply about the research data and then further contributed to the process of co-interpreting the data with me. The co-researchers then selected excerpts (quotes by community members) and edited these excerpts with my assistance. On the basis of this in-depth joint analysis and writing, I prepared a first draft of the findings and sent it out to the co-researchers for their review.

The co-researchers and I then met again as a team. I began with a presentation of my analysis, followed by a feedback session and a stimulating discussion about issue-based community responses as well as broader visions for community development. These discussions with a range of co-researchers were particularly beneficial to me as the one crafting the report because they allowed me diverse on-the-ground perspectives of each community. Throughout the research process, my role as an "external principal investigator" necessarily made me an "outsider." Even though I was deeply involved in developing and implementing the research process, I did not facilitate any of the focus groups. At the same time, in the final analysis, I drew substantially on the community practitioners' critical insights and analytical perspectives generated in our joint analysis and writing.

Follow-up discussions, feedback sessions, reflection memos, and writings all provided opportunities for co-researchers to reflect critically about issues in their communities, to develop a shared understanding across different perspectives, and to craft effective solutions together. Each and every co-researcher was intensely engaged in the knowledge/capacity-building process, reflecting deeply about their roles and responsibilities in their work and in life and contributing significantly to the knowledge being produced about their communities.

Dissemination and Continuing Reflections

From there, the co-researchers became prepared to act as "bridges" of knowledge in a number of different settings, using the final written report that I had written to continue to facilitate dialogue beyond those directly involved. Through their extensive social and professional networks, for example, our reports were distributed widely throughout local agencies, community organizations, and other institutions in Lowell and Lynn. In most situations, the co-researchers not only passed out reports but created opportunities for dialogue and discussion with other community members and practitioners. The co-researchers defined a fresh role for themselves in community-based research: not simply to document, analyze, or present the needs/problems of the community but, in the process of uncovering knowledge about their community, to initiate dialogue and further reflections with other community members as well.

The reports were also widely presented at local, national, and international conferences. For example, presenting the Lowell needs assessment project at a statewide conference organized by the Massachusetts Department of Public Health AIDS Bureau in 2000 led to a cross-cultural dialogue between the Khmer American co-researchers and health practitioners in local Haitian and Latino communities. Similarly, the Lynn research team's presentation of their report at the 2004 conference of the National Association for the Education and Advancement of Cambodian, Laotian, and Vietnamese Americans (NAFEA) enabled the co-researchers to engage with refugee/immigrant practitioners from throughout the country. Co-researchers' participation at these conferences brought community-grounded perspectives and analysis to the fields of public health, education, and ethnic studies. Reciprocally, community practitioners gained greater access to policy makers, funders, and other decision makers with resources—some of whom then followed through with specific invitations for collaboration.

Furthermore, like many diasporic populations, Khmer American communities are deeply engaged across national and cultural borders as individuals and organizations seek to rebuild familial, social, cultural, political, economic, and spiritual relationships in their homeland. In an attempt to bridge the local and the global, I organized a poster presentation focusing on the knowledge/capacity-building framework and community-based methodology at the 2004 International AIDS Conference in Bangkok, Thailand. I used this international gathering to facilitate a discussion about the opportunities and challenges of this kind of capacity-building work with health practitioners throughout the world, particularly Southeast Asia and other countries worst affected by the epidemic. A compelling moment occurred during the dialogue when a Kenyan researcher in the health sector reflected on the problem of "brain drain"—the migration of trained practitioners from resource-poor countries to countries that offer higher-paid jobs and better working conditions. The issue of "brain drain" underlined the important roles, and demanding expectations, of transnational, bilingual/bicultural Khmer Americans (and community practitioners in other immigrant/refugee communities) as co-researchers and capacity builders in the global community. This perspective also probed the significance of community-centered research to nurture, train, and mentor new "layers" of bilingual/bicultural co-researchers. As people with skills and vision often move between jobs, issues, and even state lines or national borders, depending on their assessments of needs, opportunities, resources, personal interests, and timing, the intentional capacity-building component of our work becomes even more crucial.

RECLAIMING GRASSROOTS CULTURAL KNOWLEDGE

> People who are expert[s] . . . cannot think that they are [able] to change or better the community. . . . People won't share and trust you if you don't know about their religion or culture. You are not going to become an effective supporter if you lack these experiences.
>
> Khmer American co-researcher in Lowell

> From the beginning of the research process through the end, I personally have a chance to use my personal and cultural background and the lessons I have learned from my previous work experience [as a physician in Laos] to apply to this research. . . . I also learned that this kind of research is not only useful for Southeast Asian communities but will be helpful for me in the future to work with other communities. I will apply this research method to develop needs assessments among other communities in the U.S. and around the world.
>
> Lao American co-researcher in Lowell

> From the first time of recruiting for participants to the time of focus group meetings, we saw the spirit of "community" greatly moved and empowered people to help each other. For instance, they helped us to recruit people for the meetings. . . . When time came for the meetings, some of them volunteered to pick up people who did not have transportation, and during the meetings they

tried to comfort and encourage one another to overcome obstacles in their daily life. This spirit of community is not just existing at this time, but it has been for many thousand years back in our country of origin and it is still with us in the new country.
Vietnamese-Khmer American co-researcher in Lynn

The different views and experiences addressed in the focus group had motivated me to look at things from more perspectives.
Khmer American co-researcher in Lynn

The grassroots knowledge produced through our collaborative, community-centered research projects is essential for understanding community problems/needs in their complexity. While quantitative research studies often provide important data, our community-centered research methods not only generate vital knowledge and rich possibilities for theory building but also model change-oriented relational practices. Dominant data-based, discipline-centered approaches typically fail to acknowledge how (or why) research frameworks and methodologies can be culturally relevant and how (or, again, why) the process of research can be used creatively for building or reconstructing community. However, the bilingual/bicultural co-researchers' reflections clearly converge in highlighting that research methods and processes *need* to be culturally and linguistically connected and that they *are* valuable opportunities for community practitioners to integrate more holistically their personal, professional, and community commitments through visions of knowledge/capacity building and long-term community development.

Community practitioners have, for example, transformed focus groups into culturally vibrant and community-spirited sites in which research participants become highly engaged with each other as the audience and producers of knowledge. Community practitioners revive a story-sharing tradition, taking on roles resembling those of a respected storykeeper while at the same time being aware of potential risks characteristic of hierarchical relationships that exist between researchers and the researched within more traditional research frameworks. Story sharing has the capacity to capture multiple perspectives and contradictory views that emerge in group discussions, especially when they are carefully facilitated by indigenous bilingual/bicultural community practitioners living or working in the communities. The process of story sharing opens up spaces where different meanings and emotions flow toward and influence each other, thus creating spaces and connections for new ideas and insights to be constructed. Through story sharing, community members involved in our projects talk openly about their experiences with each other. As the dialogue deepens, they begin to reflect more on their usual ways of thinking and, in some cases, even consider modifying their ways of being or doing accordingly.

The specific insights, analysis, and positions generated through community knowledge production shed light on change interventions and community-building efforts that might otherwise be hidden or unnoticed. In Lowell, for example, our story-sharing process produced critical evidence about deeper, unresolved contradictions within the community, reflecting the larger cultural-historical context by which Khmer self-definitions as "refugees" are intersecting with and challenging those of "citizens," "minorities," and "Americans." These multifaceted identities and self-representations complicate the evidence yielded about evolving communities. In the case of HIV/AIDS, our inquiry touched on two highly sensitive taboo subjects at once—death and sexuality—and thus raised questions of ethics within a "traditional" community. But our evidence sharply contradicted preconceived notions of Khmer Americans' knowledge, attitudes, beliefs, and behaviors (the data on which were largely based on a formulaic evaluation model typically used in the public health field), particularly in assuming widespread "silence" and "fear" toward discussions of HIV/AIDS and other sex-related topics. In fact, the majority of participants in our focus groups explicitly stated how they had been seeking culturally relevant opportunities to gain knowledge about HIV and other health issues. Moreover, we had witnessed how the story-sharing process mobilized the adult male participants to talk openly with each other about men's sexual behaviors (even though specific questions on sexual behaviors were not used in the men's group), work their way through the conversation, and come to some conclusions about HIV/AIDS—and themselves—that were surprising and inspiring to us. Through the story-sharing process, these men resumed a cultural responsibility to model healthy behaviors for the young generation and suggested that a new framework of HIV/AIDS education should enable participants to think deeply about their cultural roles and responsibilities. These voices and views, generated through the story-sharing process, were essential for (re)framing the issue in its complexity and for developing distinctive conceptual frameworks to address these contradictions more directly, as the example in the following section clearly illustrates.

Community/cultural knowledge *has* the capacity to transform our understanding and craft new solutions. Unlike most quantitative research conducted in the field of public health, the Lowell needs assessment proceeded from a root cause analysis and capacity-building framework that recognized the complex, reciprocal relationship between public health and community development. Even so, it was the Venerable at the Lowell Buddhist temple who best articulated this transformative vision of reciprocity and connection. In response to our question regarding what HIV/AIDS prevention strategies were available at the temple, the Venerable reframed the question and transformed it by offering, instead, a vision of Buddhism in the following terms: "Buddhism is education.... A person needs to immerse him/herself in the environment to become educated.... HIV/AIDS education is not in conflict with the teachings of Buddha.... The monks need to learn about HIV/AIDS, so do the lay people." Before citing specific strategies, the Venerable first turned to the interconnectedness of Buddhism and education and shifted the frame of reference into one of spirituality and holistic health. This holistic approach acknowledges the threat of HIV/AIDS in the community while embracing the larger realms of spirituality and community health for ultimate solutions. The Venerable's response thus offers a transformational framework that has lifted the collective understanding and vision to another level.

Yet to fully understand and respond to current needs in the communities, our research design must also be linked to the specific history of development of the community as well as to the roles, values, and commitments of community practitioners. Critical differences between the research practices in Lowell and Lynn, for example, reveal and reflect the striking contrast in terms of capacity and resources available to these two Khmer American communities. In Lynn, co-researchers recognized that KANS, as a new organization with no staff capacity, urgently needed resources. While conducting the research and reporting process, they actively explored how various sectors of the city, county, region, and state could support their continued capacity building and development. The research team's presentations at local and national conferences then generated important new funding opportunities. History influences the research process; it is also shaped by research that intentionally builds capacity so that places do not become forgotten over time (see chapter 1 of this book and Kiang and Tang 2006).

REFLECTIONS ON POSITIONING

My experiences in "doing" collaborative community-centered research, combined with my interdisciplinary training in American studies and ethnic studies and my community organizing experiences, have helped me see that both academics and practitioners have much to learn from each other. To produce new forms of knowledge, activist scholars use approaches of participatory action research, collaborative writing with community activists, and other models that are explored in this collection. But I believe that the work becomes even more powerful if also connected to a radical examination of academic privilege and standards—including what kind of "knowledge" is being valued and what is not—as well as to support and capacity building with community practitioners/members who are already deeply engaged with the difficult work of social activism. If "activist scholarship" is about excavating and generating *usable* knowledge, then it requires new research methodologies and processes, not just for the activist-minded "scholars," but also for the people whose daily lives and realities are most directly impacted by the work of knowledge production.

My choice to develop alternative research methods that engage directly with bilingual/bicultural community members is shaped by my own journey in academia. I did not come to the United States until 1991, when I entered an interdisciplinary PhD program in American studies at the University at Buffalo (UB)—having completed my undergraduate education in the proud Cantonese-speaking environment of Chinese University of Hong Kong. As the first person in my family to attain a higher education degree, I had little knowledge of what graduate training was about. I came to UB's Department of American Studies because of its explicit intention to work with international students, whose relative unfamiliarity with U.S. society was being viewed as a valuable resource for reimagining American life and building local-global linkages for students and faculty on campus. I found this perspective fresh, this attitude welcoming, and the invitation extended to "newcomers" to contribute to a field that had traditionally been ethnocentric and nationalistic particularly appealing. So I moved across national borders and assumed that what I had to offer would somehow matter.

The commitments of UB's American Studies Department to comparative and international/interethnic approaches were quickly affirmed by the department's decision to invest in efforts to help foster an Asian American academic community during the 1990s. By that time, American studies at UB, which was founded at the height of the civil rights movement in 1968, included an intercultural studies program, a women's studies program, and two ethnic studies programs (Native American studies and Puerto Rican studies); the department also worked in conjunction with the Department of African American Studies on campus. Having sponsored an independent study class focused on Asian American experience that was initiated and facilitated by undergraduate students, my advisor at the time, the late Professor Lawrence Chisolm, then observed that it was time for Asian American studies to be developed at UB. He advised me and other graduate students to establish a study group that helped to position Asian American studies as a generative site for producing and advancing knowledge of challenging and complex issues central to the changing landscape of the United States and the world: U.S. nationalism, racialized exclusion, anti-immigrant nativism, gendered stratification, labor exploitation, global economic restructuring, and so on. Professor Chisolm also emphasized active learning through such practical work as teaching and direct participation in community organizing. He recruited and mentored a group of Asian Americans—including immigrants—to develop and teach Asian American studies at UB. Thus, over a five-year period at UB in the mid-1990s, I developed and taught a series of courses in Asian American studies. Most of the students who took my classes were from immigrant backgrounds and living in New York, and later I also had international graduate students from Japan. As an Asian living in the United States, I felt that I could relate to many of my students' experiences, in a way that they could perhaps relate to mine. It was an unspoken connection; it was empowering; it was a strong though unarticulated sense of solidarity; and despite obvious language barriers, I never doubted my ability to teach Asian American studies classes.

I made certain decisions in teaching Asian American studies based on my own "international" background at the time. In some "Asian American Experience" classes, I encouraged bilingual/bicultural immigrant students to speak both languages. In teaching about Chinese diasporic experience, I also used Chinese materials (in translation) as course texts. Sometimes I did the translation myself (including literature from Hong Kong and Taiwan). Working on my own and without institutional status in Buffalo, I never shared these decisions to teach diasporically with anyone else in the field of Asian American studies. In looking back, I see that my own bicultural/bilingual background and, most importantly, the fact that I was encouraged to teach (an explicit acknowledgment of my intellectual capacity and skills) and to make critical decisions for Asian American studies at UB were key to such transformations—especially in terms of multiple languages used in the classroom as well as the development of international and comparative perspectives. In addition, I was joined by others with similar commitments to teach Asian American studies. Zhou

Xiaojing, an immigrant scholar who was hired as an adjunct to teach Asian American literature, and Margo Machida, a New York–based art curator and artist who was then entering American studies as a PhD student, both developed and taught new courses that helped to further energize Asian American studies at UB during this period.[1]

These first five years were also a time when I began to my grapple with my identity in the United States. As an international student, I was by definition not here to stay and was excluded from certain rights and obligations in this country. During these years I became acquainted with a range of reasons for "disqualification"—of which "You are not a citizen of the United States" remained constant—when I searched for national fellowships in academia, considered voting in government elections, or was summoned for jury duty. I never talked about these issues with anyone either, never shared my feelings about "disqualification," and never published my personal experiences in writing, even though they were painfully Asian American experiences that shaped my academic choices and life journey. The boundaries of language and immigration/citizenship status, even for those crossing national borders to be here, were not so easy to navigate. UB's American studies and Asian American studies programs, however, were for me a counterpoint experience, a saving grace.

Yet the mid-1990s was also a time of severe budget cuts in the State of New York and major restructuring at UB. As the Department of American Studies was being forcibly dismantled—a decision that the historian Michael Frisch critiqued more fully in his 2000 presidential address to the American Studies Association (Frisch 2001)—a group of undergraduate and graduate students, mostly politically active Latino and Asian American immigrant student leaders, formed the Coalition for Latino and Asian American Studies (CLAAS), through which they mobilized diverse undergraduate and graduate students to support the establishment of Asian American studies and Latino studies within the Department of American Studies, organized forums to educate high school students of color in the Buffalo area about access to higher education, protested incidents of racial stereotyping on campus, and convened workshops for students and faculty about the histories of Asian Americans and Latinos. In 1997, this group of students organized a series of demonstrations on campus and a sit-in outside the Office of the Dean of Arts and Letters.

While I supported and participated in almost all the organizing activities led by CLAAS, I did not look forward to the day on which the sit-in was planned. On my way to the dean's office that morning, I was overwhelmed by a mix of emotions. I felt appreciative that these student leaders, most of whom had taken classes with me before, were taking to heart the social movements they had learned and written about in ethnic studies and initiating political activism on their own campus. I was inspired by the clarity and strength demonstrated by students who had long been involved in immigrant organizing in New York City and who now applied their skills in the UB campaign. At the same time, however, I was feeling extremely vulnerable about my own situation as an F-1 status international student who needed an assistantship to cover my tuition and living expenses. I was directly confronted, for the first time, by institutional power and my limitations as an international student within the Asian American/Latino student movement. Was the dean going to take away my teaching assistantship? How would I pay for my tuition? Where was I going? With my F-1 status, where could I go, after all? The activist founding principles of Asian American studies, then, posed serious challenges to me regarding my own values very early in my academic life and in my teaching in the United States.

Most members of the Asian American Graduate Student Study Group organized or came to support the sit-in. Everyone knew that I was in a very vulnerable position given my international status, but I felt I was still expected to do something. My conscience did not allow me to leave my students and my peers alone, despite my analysis that it was not the right decision for me as an individual. I walked with the protesters all the way to the dean's office. I went into the office and sat in at the meeting. Later, I was told that because of budget cuts the funds for my teaching assistantship were unavailable.

The faculty in my department defended me, but American studies at UB was facing its own institutional challenges. With nobody in the national Asian American studies field aware of the situation or offering support, I chose to exit from Buffalo before being asked to leave by the administration. Later, I did wonder why I had risked my own international student status. But I did what I felt was right because I believed in the community-centered spirit of ethnic studies. At the same time, my lived experience had enabled me to recognize very clearly immigrants' and their allies' shared commitments to ethnic studies—as they, too, believed in that same spirit as I did. I have carried this experience with me ever since, while learning firsthand about the meaning of subject position from that vulnerable (disad)vantage point as an instructor with international student/graduate student status.

After stopping out from UB at that critical moment, I became a street outreach worker in a community organization in Massachusetts that agreed to sponsor my work visa. Soon I was immersed in the Khmer community of Revere—a residential and commercial community settlement of Cambodian refugees in the Boston area that preceded and later remained connected to those of Lowell and Lynn. The next three years of intense street work with Khmer American girls and young women amid outrageous poverty, inequality, and trauma as well as vision, love, and responsibility eventually gave me reason and motivation to return to UB to complete my PhD and to begin to shift and recraft my subject position in academia as both teacher and community-centered researcher (Tang 2002).

As I reflect on my community-centered research projects in the last few years, I am very much aware that there is more than one way to respond to my fields' basic calls for public engagement. Indeed, the very diversity of our work in knowledge production, given all our disciplinary strengths and combinations, advances the definitions and meanings of "activist scholarship." I have always felt that the most intellectually stimulating and challenging place to carry out my publicly engaged work is not at the center of dominant academic and public discourses but rather in those in-between spaces of nepantla and constant transformation. In continually crossing disciplinary boundaries and connecting academia and wider publics, nepantla itself is a bridge, an always-in-transition space, a place where different sides and multiple perspectives can be simultaneously seen and heard. Concrete accomplishments and sacred promises are shared in this place of transformation, so much so that, over time, this also becomes a place to call "home."

It has been powerful and rewarding to root myself in this nepantla space—in my program of historical research on race, (im)migration, and community development located at the intersections of Asian American studies, ethnic studies, comparative race/ethnicity/culture studies, and urban cultural history; in my teaching that emphasizes the integration of theory and practice; and through a structured joint appointment in American studies and Asian American studies. In this chapter, I have focused on one set of research projects that, I think, most clearly demonstrates my active commitments to public engagement. The grassroots-level cultural knowledge that I have gained through these research projects has become the foundation upon which I build my study of Khmer American community/cultural development in the North Shore region of Massachusetts. But, as Gloria Anzaldúa (2002, 574) has cautioned, bridges are also "the most unsafe of all spaces." "You don't build bridges to safe and familiar territories, you have to risk making *mundo Nuevo* (new worlds), have to risk the uncertainty of change," she adds (574). During my years thus far at UMass Boston, I have successfully mentored numerous undergraduate and graduate students and have recruited five Khmer American students from the North Shore and other regions where I previously worked as a community practitioner, at times engaging them in community-centered research projects (like those described above) to continue to build capacity among the younger generation; yet I have also watched even more people stop out of my university to deal with overwhelmingly challenging and unpredictable obstacles in their lives. At the end of the day, then, I have to ask myself: What is a good teacher? During this same period, I have devoted significant energy to conducting scholarly research, publishing academic articles, and participating in professional conferences, knowing that this also means giving relatively less time to attend to the daily lives of people whom I have counted on most for productive dialogue about my research. Thus I have found myself often wondering about a second question that also seems central: What is a good scholar?

I know that the changes in my role and responsibilities have come with my transformation to be a teacher-scholar at an urban, public, and research-intensive university. However, I want to emphasize that nepantla has been, and is, the critical space for me where change happens. I hope I can continue to work with my colleagues in both American studies and ethnic studies (Asian American studies) and other fields to find and claim our own crossroads, to collectively build and rebuild bridges, and to leave *huellas* (footprints) for ourselves, our students, and others who are on their journeys home.

Now, let us shift...

NOTE

1. Zhou Xiaojing is now an associate professor of English at the University of the Pacific, and Margo Machida is an associate professor of Art History and Asian American Studies at the University of Connecticut.

REFERENCES

Alexander, Leslie. 2004. "The Challenge of Race: Rethinking the Position of Black Women in the Field of Women's History." *Journal of Women's History* 16 (4): 50–60.

Amulya, Joy, Christie O'Campbell, Ryan Allen, and Ceasar McDowell. 2004. *Vital Difference: The Role of Race in Building Community. A CRCP Practitioner Knowledge Report*. Cambridge, MA: MIT Press.

Anzaldúa, Gloria E. 2002a. "now let us shift . . . the path of conocimiento . . . inner work, public acts." In *this bridge we call home: radical visions for transformation*, edited by Gloria E. Anzaldúa and Analouise Keating, 540–76. New York: Routledge.

———. 2002b. "(Un)natural Bridges, (Un)safe Spaces." In *this bridge we call home: radical visions for transformation*, edited by Gloria E. Anzaldúa and Analouise Keating, 1–5. New York: Routledge.

Chan, Sucheng. 2003. *Not Just Victims: Conversations with Cambodian Community Leaders in the United States*. Urbana: University of Illinois Press, 2003.

———. 2004. *Survivors: Cambodian Refugees in the United States*. Urbana: University of Illinois Press.

Chea, Phala. 2003. "Effects of Cultural and Ethnic Identity on Academic Performance and Self-Esteem of Cambodian Adolescents." PhD diss., University of Massachusetts Lowell.

Davis, Angela Y. 2005. *Abolition Democracy: Beyond Empire, Prisons, and Torture*. New York: Seven Stories Press.

Frisch, Michael H. 2001. "Prismatics, Multivalence, and Other Riffs on the Millennial Moment: Presidential Address to the American Studies Association, 13 October 2000." *American Quarterly* 53 (June 2001): 193–231.

Kiang, Peter N. 1996. "Southeast Asian and Latino Parent Empowerment: Lessons from Lowell, Massachusetts." In *Education Reform and Social Change: Multicultural Voices, Struggles, and Visions*, edited by Catherine E. Walsh, 59–69. Mahwah, NJ: Lawrence Erlbaum.

Kiang, Peter N., and Shirley S. Tang. 2006. "Electoral Politics and the Contexts of Empowerment, Displacement, and Diaspora for Boston's Vietnamese and Cambodian American Communities." *Asian American Policy Review* 15:13–29.

Lipsitz, George. 2001. *American Studies in a Moment of Danger*. Minneapolis: University of Minnesota Press.

Massachusetts Advisory Committee to the U.S. Commission on Civil Rights. 1998. Civil Rights Briefing, November 6.

Nou, Leakhena. 2006. "A Qualitative Examination of the Psychosocial Adjustment of Khmer Refugees in Three Massachusetts Communities." Occasional paper, Institute for Asian American Studies, Boston, August. *Journal for Southeast Asian American Education and Advancement* 1. http://jsaaea.coehd.utsa.edu/index.php/JSAAEA/issue/view/1.

Pho, Tuyet-Lan, Jeffrey N. Gerson, and Sylvia Cowan, eds. 2007. "Southeast Asian Refugees and Immigrants in the Mill City: Changing Families, Communities, Institutions—Thirty Years Afterward." Lebanon, NH: University Press of New England.

Sanchez, George. 2002. "Working at the Crossroads: American Studies for the 21st Century. Presidential Address to the American Studies Association, 9 November 2001." *American Quarterly* 54 (March): 1–23.

Smith-Hefner, Nancy J. 1999. *Khmer American: Identity and Moral Education in a Diasporic Community.* Berkeley: University of California Press.

Tang, Shirley S. 2001. *Community Development as Public Health/Public Health as Community Development: A Report of the Needs Assessment on HIV/AIDS among Cambodian Americans in Lowell, Massachusetts.* Boston: Massachusetts Asian AIDS Prevention Project.

———. 2002. "'Enough Is Enough!': Struggles for Cambodian American Community Development in Revere, Massachusetts." PhD diss., State University of New York at Buffalo.

———. 2004. "An Assessment of Khmer American Community Needs in Lynn, Massachusetts." Lynn, MA: Khmer Association of the North Shore.

10. Theorizing and Practicing Democratic Community Economics

Engaged Scholarship, Economic Justice, and the Academy

Jessica Gordon Nembhard

Sitting with my two-month-old grandson on my lap, I realize I am a scholar activist not just because I believe in human agency and engaged scholarship but also because I believe in the future. I believe that people can make positive change and that things will change for the better. I believe that a better world is possible and that I and my work can be a part of creating that better world.

I study political economy because I believe that we can fashion economies that are transformative, liberating, democratic, and equitable—rather than limiting, oppressive, and reinforcing of archaic hierarchies and inequalities. Informed proactive people are the agents of such change. Engaged scholarship and transformative economics are catalytic tools. Grassroots economic organizing and democratic ownership are some of the mechanisms to effect such change.

Why do I and why should we explore alternative economic solutions? Significant economic progress in the twenty-first century will require that our economic values more closely reflect our humanitarian values and ethics, as well as ecological priorities. I believe that more and more of us are coming to understand the limitations and the consequences of both human exploitation and the exploitation of our natural resources. If the twentieth century was an era in which rapid economic progress occurred at the expense of human and natural resources, the twenty-first century will be an era in which economic progress can continue only if we protect those resources, nurture the harmonies, and create and accumulate wealth based on the principles of caring community, sustainable development, and people-centered economics.

Most traditional economic models analyze and address the activities and needs of an elite, or one segment of a population, but leave out and behind many other people and activities. Additional strategies are needed in the twenty-first century to broaden the analysis and find models that provide economic options, stability, and prosperity for all. Marginalized subaltern communities left behind by market failures, traditional economic development, and gentrification, for example, need new, more democratic economic opportunities and new democratic forms of industrial organization to provide stable, sustainable, wealth-creating, and egalitarian economic development. Economic self-betterment requires a change in paradigm. We know a lot about the ways to do this. We need comprehensive strategies that empower people to control more resources and engage in a wider variety of productive and collaborative activities in order to create wealth and thus prosperity. Economically just community economic development also requires that people continuously learn and experiment in order to participate meaningfully. It will also require more strategies that allow community members to combine their energy and willingness to work together with unconventional and alternative resources, and to pool those resources, so that they can dream of, as well as implement and manage, needed programs and economic activities.

I worry particularly about economic inequality, racial/ethnic discrimination, and ways to attain sustainable equitable economic development. My research focuses on subaltern populations—populations that are not mainstream, that are subordinate to a dominant class or ruling group.[1] Subaltern peoples have historic identification with territory controlled by the dominant group and share important commonalities with the dominant group but simultaneously are distinct and oppositional to the mainstream—usually because of their race or culture. My research addresses the economic marginality of subaltern people and explores economic empowerment strategies practiced by exploited and underserved populations (see, e.g., Gordon Nembhard 2004a). I chronicle the enduring strength and persistence of grassroots democratic economic organizing and the necessity of better understanding it. My research and analysis also contribute to our finding policies and practices to strengthen and promote such development.

My previous experience studying international development and international finance provides good background knowledge and a fresh perspective on community and urban economic development. Coincidentally, scholars in the United States are beginning to apply international development theory and strategies to U.S. domestic economic development. To the emerging field of democratic community economics I bring knowledge of a variety of economic theories and practices; knowledge of the relationship between international development and finance, and between international development and domestic development; interdisciplinary training and knowledge orientation in African American studies; and training and experience in urban minority education and curriculum development. My interdisciplinary background is particularly helpful because the most innovative and consequential aspects of the research require a scholar to balance market with nonmarket analyses, economic factors with political and social components, and academic perspectives with practical considerations and needs, as well as to understand historic, cultural, and institutional dimensions and relationships, particularly race, class, and gender dimensions. The variety of capacities I have developed over my career uniquely position me to contribute to the development and advancement of this field of study.

This chapter reflects on my multipronged exploration to further develop the theory of democratic community economics; to document more of its historic and current practices, particularly in communities of color; to work with practitioners and community activists to engage in scholarship that helps them to evaluate, strengthen, and promote democratic community-based economic enterprises; to disseminate this information and my analyses to my academic peers as well as to grassroots activists, communities of color, and policy makers; and to teach democratic community economics to both college students and community groups.

To establish a common understanding, I begin this chapter by providing definitions of *economics, political economy, democratic community economics, community economic development,* and *cooperative economics*. I then discuss my research in the area of democratic community economics and how we can understand and study it in practice. I introduce the concept of subaltern cooperative economic development and provide examples of non-White communities who have used cooperatively owned businesses to achieve economic independence. I then delineate and describe the growing number of principles and values that characterize democratic community economics and become discernable from this analysis. In the final section, titled "Engaged Scholarship and Scholar Activism," I discuss the necessity of working closely with practitioners and utilizing participatory research. I discuss ways that I use my activism to deepen my scholarship and use the research to enrich my activism. I conclude with a reflection on the challenges both inside and outside the academy to doing this kind of work.

POLITICAL ECONOMY AND THE NON-NEUTRALITY OF ECONOMICS

> The more we collectively become mutually supportive communities—the more we'll realize that economics is essentially about organizing our interdependence with our neighbors and nature.
> TOM ATLEE, "Y2K and Sustainability"

Economics can be and is a transformative discipline. It is a tool for both understanding and orchestrating change. I define *economics* as the study of human relationships, processes, and institutions as they relate to production, service, and commerce (exchange of goods and services). Economics is first and foremost a social science: the study of the organization of social and financial interactions for the production and exchange of goods and services and the study of the management of human reproduction, economic activity, and exchange. An economy is a tool, an instrument, for effecting social reproduction, improving the quality of life, and facilitating prosperity.

Political economy describes the interactions between and among economic activity and the institutions and sociopolitical relations surrounding that activity. Political economists recognize that economies do not exist in a vacuum apart from social and political (and even cultural) forces and tensions. Political economists focus on the consequences of the decisions and choices that are made and on who controls this tool—the economy—and for what purposes. From the perspective of a political economist, an economy is a system of chosen relationships—a tool to effect a certain way of life. Choices and assumptions are made about the way interactions will occur and what models will be used to design the interactions and evaluate the outcomes. Some person or some group decides on the rules of the game, and the values upon which the options are based—but this is hidden.

Assumptions are made but are often presented as canons or tenets, even natural laws, that must be followed or that always apply. Scarcity, for example, is not a given but an assumption, based on an ideology that creates a set of theories and models to promote and perpetuate economic activity based around that notion—that there is not enough for all. Modern mainstream economic theories exalt the market as the only mechanism that properly manages scarcity. Political economic analysis exposes scarcity as a false constraint. The notion is perpetuated by an elite group who benefit materially from modeling the economy as a "zero-sum game" with limited resources and thus limited distribution options: that is, there must be winners and losers. Political economy helps us to understand and challenge the hegemony of neoclassical theory in economics. I briefly discuss this set of theories, mostly to better explain democratic community economics afterward.

Neoclassical economics focuses on individual needs and wants and individual profit making in a world of scarcity. Such economic values are concerned with maximizing individual utility (wants and preferences), given budget constraints, and achieving "economic efficiency" based on minimizing private costs and maximizing private individual profits. Public costs, social welfare, and ecological preservation are rarely factored in, and public benefits are at best an afterthought or used as a political pawn. Neoclassical economists argue that the market reinforces and rewards individual initiative and free exchange, which they insist are necessary for the optimal functioning of an economy. Their models attempt to justify and legitimize the pursuit of profits above all else and a system whereby only an elite can be prosperous—and deserve to be (since they have worked hard, sacrificed, and delayed gratification, as "anyone" can do).

Modern neoclassical economists have put their energies into discovering and designing mathematical equations and relationships that reflect the assumption that the sum of the parts of individual greed add up to the common good (i.e., "the invisible hand"). To use mathematical equations they have had to design economic models that abstract from most of the realities of human and economic interactions and hold constant all the dynamics of those interactions. Rather than the reality of market failures and imperfect information, for example, they model the unreality of full information and perfect market clearing. Rather than multiple outcomes and solutions, they model "stable equilibria."[2] Rather than recognize the heterogeneity of the population and the power of group identity and collaboration, they model the single representative agent, identical to all others, operating alone (unless involved in an illegal cartel). Conventional economists model short-term interactions and ignore long-term balances or imbalances and consequences. They assume that private optimality is the same as social optimality, in which case there is no significant difference between social costs and private costs. Social benefits are only vaguely recognized. They calculate no costs or consequences for using up human or natural resources or polluting the environment, only the individual costs of accumulating human capital and extracting and transporting labor and natural resources. The exploitation of human beings and nature, particularly keeping costs down (and often undermining social reproduction), actually contributes to higher profits in these models. We should not then be surprised by high poverty levels, wealth inequality, and ecological devastation in societies with economies developed along this model.

A political economic analysis helps us understand that markets are actually imperfect because those who exchange through markets come to the marketplace with unequal endowments and unequal power. Some have more money and resources to use to influence and dominate market transactions; some have previous experience and knowledge or privileged information that helps them better navigate through and use the marketplace to their own advantage. Some have racial and cultural advantages or disadvantages. Because markets reflect these disparities and can be hijacked, they are not neutral or necessarily benevolent.

A flaw in using the individual as the unit of analysis is that in neoclassical models returns to production and investment go to individuals (and applied economists use the family or household as the unit). Political economists understand that this does not recognize the positive as well as negative influences, and power, of collective activity—which is what helps some people survive and gives some corporations an advantage. A political economic analysis also understands that businesses are not developed by one individual alone, and that wealth is not accumulated by one individual, without help from family, employees, public education, public infrastructure, and more. A deeper analysis of wealth accumulation reveals that wealth building is a collective activity and that net worth is the result of intentional and unintentional collective action. Wealth should be valued and remunerated in our economy as a collective tool for achieving well-being. Not only is the neoclassical conceptualization of wealth faulty and counterproductive, but the focus on income masks the importance of wealth (though this latter problem is beginning to change). Traditional economic models use income rather than wealth as a major indicator of economic health, while asset ownership, wealth accumulation, and net worth (or their lack) prove to be more consequential to well-being—and to better explain economic inequality (and economic power). A perspective on wealth, and on wealth building as a collective activity, helps us to accept a wealth-based vision of the good society (caring community) that guides democratic community economics.

Those of us who study the economy from the grassroots, from the point of view of the "have nots," and of sustainability, are learning that a commitment to economic empowerment and economic justice is essential to long-term economic stability, particularly the revitalization of depressed areas and the protection of our physical environment. We are learning that a better understanding of collective assets and nontraditional resources contributes to finding and implementing alternative strategies that reach and benefit those that "the market" has failed. We are also finding that practicing economic justice is necessary to the maintenance of democracy. If we want affluent communities of people living dignified, happy lives, creating sustainable wealth for all, and participating positively in civil society, then we need a new economic paradigm—a revaluation of our economic principles, goals, and practices.

DEMOCRATIC COMMUNITY ECONOMICS

> It must be quite clear, then, that our economic program for a cooperative democracy . . . is one in which the economic improvement of the country will be the economic improvement of the whole people, an improvement that is to result most from their own united and organized efforts. It is, above all else, a program that provides the necessary conditions for the development of real individual initiative and healthy personalities in a more humane society with a definite reason for being, and one that demonstrates its care for all.
>
> CHANCELLOR WILLIAMS, "The Economic Basis of African Life"
>
> It is now our business to give the world an example of intelligent cooperation. . . .
>
> If leading the way as intelligent cooperating consumers, we rid ourselves of the ideas of a price system and become pioneer servants of the common good, we can enter the new city as men and women and not mules.
>
> W. E. B. DU BOIS, "Where Do We Go from Here?"

I am a political economist pioneering a branch of knowledge that I call democratic community economics. This field focuses on the study of people-centered local economic development that is community based and controlled, collaborative, and democratically or at least broadly owned and governed through a variety of structures. These structures include worker, producer, and consumer cooperatives and credit unions; community land trusts; democratic Employee Stock Ownership Programs (ESOPs); and other forms of worker ownership and self management. Other structures include collective not-for-profit organizations involved in social entrepreneurship; community-controlled community development corporations; and community-controlled development planning and community development financial institutions.[3] Cooperative enterprises, workplace democracy, collective ownership, and collaborative asset building are growing practices around the world. Many of these practices have spontaneously emerged from historic indigenous, grassroots experimentation in several countries, including the United States. Others have been consciously crafted and developed by groups seeking to decrease economic marginalization and increase income, wealth, and economic participation and decision making. There is an increasing number and variety of such economic entities and experiments, and increasing attention to studying them.

Democratic community-based enterprises operate according to a set of principles encompassing equality of participation, collaboration, profit sharing, and cultural and ecological sensitivity (more below). The value added from democratic economics is economic stability at a high quality of life for the greatest number of people. The means are democratic participation and self-management, grassroots empowerment, community-based asset development, and wealth creation. Within democratic community economics I also include the theoretical and applied study of how and why such alternative structures are economically viable; public policies that are supportive of such development; and ways to document and measure their traditional and nontraditional economic, social, and political outcomes and impacts.

Democratic community economics develops out of political economic analysis applied to problematics in community economic development, economic welfare, and democratic studies. It also parallels the growing fields of asset development and community-based entrepreneurship and enterprise development that are being pioneered at universities and research centers around the country and internationally and practiced in communities everywhere. The term *community economics* is often used to describe the study of community economic development (CED) and is often used alongside *regional economics*—as in "regional and community economics." Regional economics is the study of the economy of regions and economic interactions within regions or metropolitan areas. Community economics is thus a similar study of a smaller jurisdiction. *Community economic development* is "a term for the processes of change through place-based economic activities, controlled by, or at least oriented toward, local residents for their betterment," and focused on "activity that is local, indigenous, grassroots; centered on people, and a variety of stakeholders (residents, workers, business owners, policy makers, and civic and political organizations, etc.)" (Gordon Nembhard, forthcoming). Community control, economic stability, financial independence, and prosperity are the goals of both community economics and community economic development.

Community economics is broader than CED because it covers not just local economic development activities and who controls them but also a total understanding of economic activity and economic relations on a small scale, within a prescribed community, even at the neighborhood level, and the impact of outside forces such as corporate globalization on a locality. It is more complex than family economics—the ways that families handle and plan production and exchange, reproduce themselves economically, budget for and exchange goods and services, and prosper. Community economics is the study of the theory and practice of local economic activity.

Democratic community-based enterprises are businesses that offer commercially viable products and services for exchange or distribution and that create and retain jobs in the local community. They strive to be socially responsible, sustainable, and environmentally sensitive enterprises that provide the following benefits to their communities:

1. They create and anchor capital, businesses, and jobs in the community, institutionalizing local income generation and wealth accumulation, while increasing and stabilizing the community's tax base.
2. They utilize a mix of public and private assets and capital and can reduce local dependence on external capital and externally-owned enterprises.
3. They have multiple owners, who share resources, risks, profits, and governance.
4. They are privately owned, or feature some combination of public and private ownership, and exist in a variety of sectors: agriculture, grocery, procurement and marketing, child care, health services, maintenance and janitorial services (commercial and residential), catering and baking, temporary services, utilities and telecommunications, auto and bicycle repair, printing and copying, credit and housing.

5. They exercise entrepreneurial leadership and innovation in building consensus and obtaining the support of key stakeholding groups and individuals in the community, by addressing their goals as well as those of the enterprise.
6. They involve owners, managers, and workers in decision making and workplace governance, and they practice labor-management cooperation and sometimes self-management.
7. They contribute to reducing the gap between rich and poor by more equitably distributing opportunities, assets (including wealth and income), and the benefits of business ownership, governance, and entrepreneurial leadership skills among all groups in the community, irrespective of their race, ethnicity, gender, national origin, culture, and socioeconomic status.
8. They often lead their industries in wages and benefits, production, flexibility, and innovation.[4]

DEMOCRATIC COMMUNITY ECONOMICS IN PRACTICE

While there are a variety of alternative economic structures and institutions, such as municipally owned enterprises, family-owned businesses, microbusinesses, and ESOP businesses, a smaller subset are democratically owned and governed (and often managed under a less hierarchical process). Many of the alternative structures have the potential to be democratic as well, depending on how they are incorporated, managed, and governed. Below I discuss first cooperatively owned businesses as one of the best examples of democratic community-based enterprises and then the methodologies that are and can be used to assess this sector.

Cooperative enterprises, and worker-owned businesses in particular, tend to exemplify the eight principles delineated in the section above. Co-operatives, particularly worker-owned co-ops, are one form of democratically owned economic enterprises that allow members to control their own income and wealth and be change agents in their local sphere. Cooperatives are companies that are owned by their members (the people who use their services) and created to satisfy a need—a needed good or service at an affordable price or an economic structure to engage in needed production or distribution. Cooperatives may be consumer owned, producer owned, or worker owned (or some combination of the above). Cooperatives are characterized by pooling of resources, joint ownership, democratic governance, and sharing risks and profits in the production, distribution, and/or acquisition of affordable, high-quality goods and services. Cooperative businesses operate according to a set of principles that include democratic participation ("one member, one vote"), open membership, returns based on use, continuous education, and concern for community (see International Co-operative Alliance 2006; National Cooperative Business Association 2007). Cooperatives often develop and survive as a response to market failure and economic marginalization (Fairbairn et al. 1995).

Worker-owned cooperatives and other democratically owned businesses are being found to be some of the most innovative and empowering methods to bring together labor and capital equitably to meet a demand and create an affordable quality product or service. Cooperative economic development, while not a well-known or well-practiced strategy, is proving to be successful in urban as well as rural areas for poverty reduction as well as income generation, and sometimes wealth production, around the world. The United Nations and the International Labor Organization, for example, have recognized the potential of cooperative enterprises for economic development (Birchall 2003; International Cooperative Alliance n.d.; International Labour Conference 2002). Some of the issues that cooperatives help resolve are local development in an increasingly globalizing world; community control in an age of transnational corporate concentration and expansion; social and community entrepreneurship, particularly when business development is increasingly complicated and especially risky; pooling of resources and profit sharing in communities where capital is scarce and incomes are low; and increased productivity, superior working conditions, and high worker satisfaction in industries where work conditions may be poor and where wages and benefits tend to be low. Cooperatives develop out of the wealth of cultural and social capital in communities whose diverse residents often have strong social networks and few options but to work together.

Cooperative financial institutions such as credit unions provide financial services to underserved populations, make affordable financing available, and keep financial resources circulating in the community. Credit unions are some of the most numerous, widely used, and successful of the consumer cooperatives. Cooperative housing makes home ownership affordable and stable. Cooperative retail enterprises provide high-quality goods at affordable prices. Natural food grocery stores and rural electric and energy cooperatives are some of the most successful examples. Worker-owned businesses provide economic security, income and wealth generation, and workplace democracy (Gordon Nembhard 2004b, 2002a; Haynes and Gordon Nembhard 1999). Cooperative Home Care Associates in New York City increases the quality of home care workers and their working conditions, wages, and benefits. ChildSpace in Philadelphia increases the quality of day care providers and provides them with a variety of benefits, including Individual Development Accounts (IDAs) to increase employee/owners' savings. Rainbow Grocery in San Francisco has pioneered personnel orientation, in-service training, and meeting facilitation techniques that have increased the level and efficiency of democratic participation in management and production. Rainbow Grocery's members also now serve as the much-needed experts in meeting facilitation for the fledgling U.S. Federation of Worker Cooperatives (established in 2004). Equal Exchange, outside Boston, has made fair trade in coffee a viable business, connecting socially responsible workers and community activists in the United States with small coffee cooperatives around the world (and now expanding into tea and chocolate). These are all vibrant, growing, democratically owned and governed companies that provide multiple benefits to their communities.

METHODOLOGY AND RESEARCH FINDINGS

Why study democratic community economics? What do we learn from focusing on democratically owned, community-based enterprises? The economic problem I am most concerned about is how to bring economic empowerment and prosperity to underdeveloped, marginal, and underserved communities, particularly communities of color. My research also explores how to measure the effectiveness of such strategies. Using the lens of democratic community economics, I am able to explore a variety of ownership structures, the ways businesses operate under different ownership and management structures, asset building through such ownership structures, and a variety of ways such enterprises are effective and profitable to their owners, as well as their families and communities. I document the myriad ways that democratically owned businesses benefit their member-owners and their communities.

I have been finding that job creation, buying from and outsourcing to other local businesses, development of affiliated businesses, increased skill levels of members and/or employees, higher wages, and affordable, high-quality products and services are outcomes that are fairly easy to measure, particularly once we associate them with cooperative businesses (Gordon Nembhard 2004b). Other studies have found that productivity and flexibility increase in democratically run businesses.[5] Others benefits of cooperative ownership for communities are consumer and member education, democratic participation, meaningful work, asset ownership, leadership development, civic participation, and general community economic stability. At the same time, cooperatives do face many challenges and have suffered failure over the years. While they tend to survive longer than traditional small businesses, start-up is often more costly and slower, and cooperatives need even stronger business plans than traditional businesses, but also more strategic planning about how to address their socioeconomic mission and objectives at the same time that they meet the business requirements. Cooperatives, especially those serving low-income members, sometimes suffer from lack of adequate capitalization, specialized management training, adequate cash flow, and effective business and/or strategic planning. Financing is extremely important at start-up and often for maintenance, especially for cooperatives that are in low-resourced communities, have high capital costs, or are trying to keep wages and benefits consistently high. Training and education are also extremely important assets to develop and maintain. Cooperatives in communities of color and/or in emerging innovative industries are often the most vulnerable. My research on the history of African American cooperative ownership, for example, finds that Black co-ops have suffered and continue to suffer from sabotage and racist violence and attack. White businesses have often physically threatened Black-owned businesses and their owners or have used financial sabotage to undermine the businesses by increasing rents, taking away needed insurance or other infrastructure, and/or denying lines of credit and other financial services to Black-owned cooperatives. In addition, throughout U.S. history the White plantocracy (and more recently corporate agriculture) has blocked supportive policies for African American co-op development, particularly in the South (see Woods 1998 for an example).

Many of the impacts, outcomes, and benefits from cooperative ownership are not recognized or measured in mainstream economic analysis, often because the definition of "economic efficiency" does not include such aspects and/or the unit of analysis is not inclusive enough. Traditional economic analyses measure profit margins, how many people are employed, total assets and revenues, and perhaps taxes paid. While important, traditional economic analyses ignore or miss other kinds of interactions between businesses and their members and communities, such as democratic economic participation and governance, increased local economic interactions, "sweat equity," volunteer work, teamwork, and leadership development. More research is needed on how to identify and quantify these impacts, outcomes, and benefits as indicators/measures of economic achievement as well as economic and civic well-being. More research is also needed to better analyze the failures and delineate the lessons learned.

The methodology required to identify such indicators, design survey instruments to assess them, and collect the data for more detailed evaluation is interdisciplinary, using mixed methods (in the broadest meaning of that phrase). This analysis requires methodologies borrowed from most of the social science disciplines (and some in the humanities). This methodology is emerging and changing but is based on historical analysis, community organizing, industrial organization, and ethnographic and participatory research methods, in addition to more traditional statistical and demographic analyses. I combine theoretical analysis of economic development strategies with historical analysis of what has worked in the past, under what conditions and for what populations. I combine exploration of community needs with analyses of community organizing efforts, institutional development, organizational management, and business performance. I examine businesses' income and loss statements (total assets, total revenues, liabilities, member accounts, etc.), dividend returns, employment rates and benefit profiles, member and/or employee orientation programs, in-service training, and contributions to community. Ways that community-based businesses use social capital, cultural capital, human capital, and capacity building inside and outside the enterprise are also important dimensions to incorporate.

In addition, I contact and join the professional, trade, and community organizations that represent and serve existing democratic community-based enterprises in order to engage in participatory action research as another approach. Through interviews and discussions with and observation of co-op members in their workplaces and during conference workshops, panel presentations, and co-op research meetings, I compile data on the issues facing and practices of cooperative enterprises. I have spent years cultivating relationships among researchers, practitioners, co-op developers, advocates, and member-owners of these enterprises and their organizations in order to learn the issues, share my theories and research, and earn the trust of the people with whom I will work and whom I will interview. All this takes time and slows down the traditional research trajectory. Such a rich and complex methodology, in addition to the variety of information, takes longer to process. The assessment of their enterprise often takes more time, as does the process of finding enterprises and people to interview, earning their trust, compiling the necessary information, and evaluating the results. Many of the people in these enterprises are wary of being "evaluated," do not want to "tell their story" too often (especially to people who do not retell it correctly), have not had the luxury to think about the issues in the way the questions are asked (or from this kind of perspective on the business), and/or are too busy keeping the business going to take time to think about some of these issues or even answer questions about it. Consequently, conducting and completing this kind of research is a longer and more difficult process.

I plan to further explore ways to calculate what I call a "cooperative multiplier"—the "multiplier effect" of the circulation (recirculation) of money and economic activity within a community through cooperative enterprises and community-based ownership. We do not have good measures of this multiplier effect—the ways local businesses anchor capital and recirculate dollars in the neighborhood and community. Most cooperatives and community-based businesses, however, often deliberately buy locally, hire locally, and even borrow locally as part of their mission and principles of operation—and to be good neighbors and citizens. These are all activities that recirculate dollars around the community (Gordon Nembhard 2004b). In contrast, multinational corporations, and their branch offices and franchises, tend to export capital and resources from a community—they usually do not buy locally, often do not hire many neighborhood residents, and seldom invest or bank locally (see Fairbairn et al. 1995).

I am becoming one of the few experts in identifying and measuring the variety of economic, social, and political impacts of democratic economic enterprises and the spillover effects on civil society created and catalyzed by these democratic economic activities (Gordon Nembhard 2004b; Gordon Nembhard and Blasingame 2002). In one such study (Gordon Nembhard and Blasingame 2002), we conclude:

> Studies are also finding that the democratization of workplaces enhances the political learning and governance experience and skills that are necessary for greater participatory democracy in the wider society. These enterprises are "training grounds" that develop transferable skills and capacities in their members. Greater employee control over one's own work is positively correlated with political participation. Cooperatives create social efficiencies derived from the democratic participation of all, self-help, self-management, and concern for community principles which guide them. Cooperatives encourage interaction, team work, inter-cooperation and giving back to one's community. They also develop social ties among members and between members and the

community—i.e., social capital—so that networking and working together become the norm, and the skills to facilitate this are developed in all members. Cooperatives develop and empower young people to become involved both in the cooperative and outside (more research is needed in this area). Co-op members and employee owners become used to the transparency and accountability in their own organizations (open book policies, one member one vote, shared management, etc.). They come to expect transparency and accountability and help recreate this in civil society and political arenas. Many members become more active in their communities in general, take on leadership roles both in their co-ops and in voluntary and community organizations (this was found especially with women members and in communities of color). They even run for elected office in local, state and national races. In addition, organizing citizen activism and advocacy can often be effective countervailing forces which increase democracy and participation. (375)

SUBALTERN COOPERATIVE ECONOMIC DEVELOPMENT

I have also formulated a concept that I term *subaltern cooperative economic development* to describe the process and strategy through which members of subaltern populations use strong group identity and concern for community to develop productive, collaborative, cooperative economic enterprises (see, e.g., Gordon Nembhard and Haynes 2002). I study ways that subaltern populations take control of their economic lives instead of remaining passive victims or dropping out of the formal economy because they choose to engage in alternative activities for their economic survival. I study the way members of marginalized populations use their sense of cultural or racial/ethnic solidarity to work together on economic development activities and in economic enterprises. I find that strong group identity, concern for community, pooling of resources with family and community members, desire for self-determination, and democratic participation all create a basis for sustainable economic development through cooperative structures. Sometimes these are informal, unincorporated structures that mainstream economic indicators miss or obscure. In other instances, formal, legally recognized cooperative businesses are incorporated.

Cooperative enterprises are a particularly effective and responsive way for subaltern populations to participate economically. Because subaltern peoples are discriminated against in mainstream labor, capital, and housing markets, they often have to rely on one another and work together in alternative institutions. Subaltern populations often accumulate little personal wealth and are excluded from much of mainstream prosperity and economic stability. The market system does not often work for many members of subaltern groups.

Recent research, for example, shows that disparate and inferior economic outcomes are the norm for subaltern populations throughout the world, no matter in what country they reside. In a preliminary study of international economic ethnic and racial intergroup disparity, Darity and Gordon Nembhard (2000) find that subaltern status is typically associated with negative economic consequences in countries with both large and small populations, those experiencing relatively rapid economic growth as well as those with slow growth, countries with high and low levels of general inequality, and rich as well as poor countries. These findings also reveal persistent and pervasive labor market discrimination throughout the world. In the United States in the 1980s and early 1990s the labor power of men of color declined dramatically. In addition, women of color and their children have remained the poorest populations around the world, even though in the United States Black women have made gains in the labor market compared with White women over the past thirty years. In a time of dwindling economic opportunities for women of color, and with many poor women in the United States reaching the five-year time limit for public assistance, for example, understanding how cooperative business ownership and other forms of democratic enterprises help women of color become entrepreneurs, control their own income, and stabilize their economic lives will increase our policy tools for viable economic development.

Subaltern groups have a history of solidarity, working together because of their common culture or ethnic identity and their common experience of exclusion from the dominant culture and economy. *Subaltern cooperative economic development* is a term that describes this conception of cooperative economic development as a strategy for the economic empowerment and self-reliance of subaltern peoples. Examples such as the Mondragón Cooperative Corporation in northern Spain illustrate the economic power of the combination of ethnic solidarity, democratic ownership and participation, and interlocking economic activities (Gordon Nembhard and Haynes 2002).

The Mondragón Cooperative Corporation is a complex of more than 150 industrial, financial, distributional, research, and educational cooperatives, mostly worker owned, in northern Spain. The corporation is rooted in grassroots networks of cooperative businesses owned by Basque nationalists originally mobilized during the Franco era. These Basques, in the face of war, chose the more peaceful road of cooperative enterprise development to assert their need for economic independence (Gordon Nembhard and Haynes 2002). The first cooperative was a worker-owned and -managed innovative ceramic heater factory, started in 1956 by graduates of a community-run "polytechnic" high school founded by a priest who taught cooperative economics and worker ownership. Other enterprises developed around this, in particular a credit union that has continued to supply financing, technical assistance, and research and development for future cooperatives. Other schools and a university were eventually established to support the growing worker-owned factories in the network. The expanding complex of cooperatives also established their own social security system early on, when the government of Spain would not allow the member-owners to participate in the national system because they were considered to be self-employed. The association grew into a multi-billion-dollar cooperative network of manufacturing, service, educational, financial, and distributive enterprises.

Trends continue to show progressive levels of growth in assets, sales, and workforce. In 2001, for example, total sales for all the companies exceeded U.S. $7 billion; total assets were greater than U.S. $12 billion.[6] The fifty-year success of this cooperative holding company and its affiliated companies can best and most fully be explained when the myriad economic, social, cultural, and political market and nonmarket forces involved are analyzed.

In the process of developing this conglomerate, organizers and members identified existing individual and community assets, harnessed concern for community and desire for self-determination, and utilized these as economic resources to build successful businesses. They formalized and institutionalized networks of cooperation, self-help, and community development that recognized their common culture and values. They continue to identify their company as a Basque organization and to describe themselves as a business group of grassroots cooperatives: "The Mondragón Corporación Cooperativa is a socio-economic business organisation with deep cultural roots in the Basque Country. It was created by and for people and is based on the Basic Principles of our Co-operative Experience.... Furthermore, it is based on a firm commitment to solidarity, and uses democratic organisational and management methods. [It] promotes the participation and involvement of its worker-members in the management, profits and ownership of its companies, which strive together for harmonious social, business and personal development" (Mondragón Cooperative Corporation 2001, 39).

There are examples around the world and within the United States (though smaller) of successful cooperative organizations that have organized themselves on the basis of cultural and social solidarity as well as economic need and affinity. Freedom Quilting Bee in Alberta, Alabama, is one such example (Freedom Quilting Bee 2002). In the mid-1960s, a group of African American women in sharecropping families in Alabama formed a craft cooperative to pool their resources to produce and market quilts to supplement their families' earnings. Sharecropping was a system of debt peonage, and in the 1960s it was becoming politically unfeasible, since landowners were evicting Black families from the land if they tried to register to vote or were involved in civil rights activity. Freedom Quilting Bee helped the women buy sewing machines and other supplies, provided a place for them to quilt together, and marketed and distributed the quilts around the country, including through the Sears Roebucks Catalogue. The cooperative was so successful that they bought land, built a small sewing factory, started a day care center, and by 1991 were the largest employer in the town. In addition, they were able to use the land they bought to help sharecropping families relocate and eventually buy their own land, especially after they were denied access to their traditional farmlands because of their political activity. The income earned also was an important supplement to the meager income their families made from farming. In 1967 Freedom Quilting Bee became one of the founding members of the Federation of Southern Cooperatives—a predominantly African American nonprofit organization supporting cooperative development and land retention, with agencies in six southern states.[7]

Analysis of the successes of such cooperatives and their benefits to their communities allow us to identify a set of principles and characteristics of democratic community economics.

PRINCIPLES OF DEMOCRATIC COMMUNITY ECONOMICS

From my research I am able to identify a set of basic economic values, principles, or characteristics that underlie democratic community economics and formulate a new paradigm for economic development. While democratic community economic principles are dynamic and continue to grow and change, they encompass the following: common social and economic values; just, nonexploitative relationships and sustainability; the dignity of work; responsible, active participation; democratic decision making; diversity and equity; invisible productivity; control of capital; asset ownership and wealth accumulation; human-made and dynamic processes; no neutrality of influence and effects; and self-regulation.[8]

1. *Common Social and Economic Values.* Communities and societies prosper or fail depending upon economic relationships and activities between and among people and institutions. How we structure our relationships to each other around economic questions is the ultimate measure of what we value and believe about the worth of each human being and our relationship to the environment. Economics does not have a separate ethics or morality.

2. *Just, Nonexploitative Relationships and Sustainability.* Economic relationships and activities should be judged by their communal, cooperative, ethical, cultural, environmental, sustainable, and antipoverty effects as much as (or more than) by their productivity, efficiency and ability to make a profit. The pursuit of social and economic justice requires a vision and a concrete plan for how to restructure social and economic relations between ourselves, our communities, society at large, and our natural environment. Economies must be able to sustain their communities and to persist and deliver over the long run without damaging or exploiting other human beings or mother nature.

3. *Responsible, Active Participation.* We are all economic agents, participants in ongoing, daily economic activities. We constantly make economic choices and economic decisions. We each have a stake in how economic activity is arranged and valued. We should be aware of what values are expressed through the economic decisions we make. We have a responsibility to be conscious economic actors, responsible to our neighbors, communities, and ecosystems.

4. *Democratic Decision Making.* As conscious economic actors we have the responsibility to participate in economic decision making and be advocates for democracy. Democratic decision making puts us in control of our income generation and wealth accumulation and in control of our lives as workers and consumers. Participating democratically in economic activity allows us to create and operate democratic structures at all levels. Action is necessary to ensure that democracy is expanded so that communities have the power, the right (by law with clear enforcement), the provisions, and the resources to participate equally. Communities participate as equal partners in making economic decisions that will affect them

and the lives of their residents. When we practice democratic decision making in economic environments, we develop and practice skills that are transferable to all other aspects of our civic and social lives.

5. *Diversity and Equity.* Economic agents are heterogeneous (diverse) and bring a range of perspectives, assets, and skills to any activity. Diversity is a strength—like ecological and genetic diversity, actually a necessity. Equity, even more than diversity, is essential. This requires that economic agents, their relationships, activities, and institutions, be monitored and regulated according to humane principles, social values, and equality of outcome. Opportunity is not enough. Responsible actors must commit to end discrimination (by race, ethnicity, nationality, gender, class, disability, and sexual orientation).

6. *The Dignity of Work.* All work is valuable and measurable and should be rewarded. All work should be meaningful and viewed as productive. Democratic economic organizations are based on the dignity of work and the sovereignty rather than the subordination of labor. Particularly in the global postindustrial economy, very good jobs are more and more scarce; sometimes any job is scarce. Many jobs do not provide "living wages" or the necessary benefits, and most do not include asset ownership and the chance to accumulate wealth. Why is it acceptable that a person can work full time and remain poor, that an illness can put someone in bankruptcy and poverty, and that a corporation can pay a manager four hundred times what it pays its average worker? Democratic economic organizations give priority to work and those who do the work. Many observe "wage solidarity" and keep the difference between the highest-paid member or employee and the lowest paid to a minimum.

7. *Invisible Productivity.* Productive activity has value even when not formally or officially recognized or exchanged. Child rearing, nurturing, home care activities, household work, volunteer work, and protection of the environment all have value—economic value—whether formally compensated (paid for) or not. Democratic economic organizations recognize the value of a variety of activities. Ways to measure and reward such work should be elaborated.

8. *Control of Capital.* Since capitalization of businesses is necessary for their success, and since communities generally need capital to attract and maintain economic activity, the control of capital and the democratization of capital are important components of economic development. Financing needs to be accessible and financial services available; therefore community development financial institutions and alternative financing

are necessary. The ability to direct capital to the kinds of support and programs that will benefit the community most is crucial. Business and financial support and reinvestment help enterprises stay in business and expand, help in the training of members and employees, and increase development activities. Keeping the control of capital in the hands of democratic enterprises ensures autonomy.

9. *Asset Ownership and Wealth Accumulation.* All economic activity should contribute to asset ownership and wealth accumulation, which are essential to stability and well-being. This requires the development or recognition of nontraditional as well as traditional assets and their wealth creation possibilities. Ownership with democratic participation is found to be the best combination for increased productivity (Levine and Tyson 1990). We understand that wealth is crucial to economic well-being, stability, and quality of life.

10. *Human-Made and Dynamic Processes.* Economic processes do not operate by immutable or unchangeable laws but depend on interdependencies between and among people and between people and nature. An economy is made by human beings for human betterment. Economic laws do not supersede a society's values and objectives—they should reflect and effect a society's highest values. There are no economic activities and relationships that cannot be reevaluated or changed to better meet human and environmental needs.

11. *No Neutrality of Influence and Effects.* Economics is not apolitical. Economic processes are not neutral: they reproduce and can reinforce prevailing inequalities, have unequal effects and consequences, and can be manipulated by political processes. Economic processes depend on and reflect existing power relationships, unequal information, and previous and unequal exchanges. Some economic systems and relationships are more exploitative, oppressive, and discriminatory than others. Some depend more on competition and inequality than others. Some depend more on cooperation, concern for community, and reciprocity. Economic systems can be created to intervene in, mediate (regulate), or eliminate inequalities and injustices.

12. *Self-Regulation through Democratic Participation.* Democratic participation and equitable relations act as regulating mechanisms in democratic economics. Markets are imperfect and need intervention and regulation. Governments and other human institutions are also imperfect and need to be held accountable to humane and just values. Governments and markets are regulated by fully participatory, democratic, and coopera-

tive governance, engaged in by diverse, empowered, and knowledgeable participants from every level of society. Democratic governance requires and facilitates transparency and accountability.

These principles provide a basis for us to study, measure, and evaluate economic enterprises and their efficacy.

ENGAGED SCHOLARSHIP AND SCHOLAR ACTIVISM

I have written about the need for comprehensive community economic development strategies that take into account existing community strengths, attachments, and resources; utilize values of self-help, concern for community, collaboration, and democratic participation; and have significant benefits and asset-building potential for community residents (see, e.g., Gordon Nembhard 1999, 2000; Haynes and Gordon Nembhard, 1999). I have theorized and written about how cooperative economic development can be a strategy for urban community development and economic development for subaltern populations such as African Americans (Gordon Nembhard 2004a). I continue to document, and look for examples to document, such activity and develop theory to help support and explain such activity.

Much of what I have been learning about these organizations, how they operate, their principles and successes, has come from participatory community-based research—community engagement—combined with traditional applied economic analysis. Evaluation and outcome measurement of democratic community-based economic development strategies is a perfect tool to use to engage community/practitioner participation and combine rigorous scholarship with applied and participatory research in communities. This kind of engaged scholarship—working closely with community businesses and cooperatives, relevant professional and trade organizations, and community activists—increases my knowledge about and deepens my understanding of the mechanisms involved in democratic community enterprises, the issues facing them, and these enterprises' development and growth.

The connections I have developed expose me to a variety of practitioners and researchers in the United States and Canada with whom I can share ideas and learn. They also provide me with social and personal contacts necessary for my qualitative and ethnographic research. They keep my ideas fresh, keep me grounded in the real-world problems that need solving, and help me understand the consequences and actions of the economic activity I study. While I believe that new and effective economic activities and enterprises must be developed, implemented, and supported, I also recognize that alternative forms of business and industrial organization already exist and are being continuously transformed. One way to study and promote changes in our economic paradigm is to study existing forms and evaluate them according to the principles listed above. A good part of my research, therefore, is the engaged scholarship that puts me in touch with and enables me to observe existing examples and share in the creation of knowledge.

In addition, I work with community activists to disseminate the knowledge I am gaining to people and communities where it can be of help, to promote equitable development policy, and to provide models for how it can be achieved. I am a member, for example, of the ONE DC Equitable Development Initiative (EDI) in Washington, D.C. This is an organization led by a local activist community development corporation and composed of D.C. residents (originally in the Shaw neighborhood) who see gentrification in the area as hostile to long-term low-income residents and essentially a "Negro removal" process. We work with city agencies and private developers to ensure that community benefit agreements are included in any new development packages. The benefits we advocate are affordable housing for the lowest income families (under $25,000 and $50,000); a majority of wages livable for local residents and a majority of short and long-term jobs targeted to them; support for small resident-owned businesses and local business development; and a community development fund to support educational, cultural, and recreational activities in the neighborhood (see ONE DC, n.d.). Other community benefits agreements also include ecological guidelines.

Minor victories have been won. One of our greatest obstacles, however, in addition to our concern with marginalized, mostly invisible people, is that our definition of *affordable housing* does not match the definition used by the city and the developers from HUD (the U.S. Department of Housing and Urban Development). HUD uses traditional economic models and formulas based on an understanding of average family incomes that does not take into account existing income and wealth gaps or racial gaps that make the experiences and level of affordability substantially differ by race and class. Recent studies, for example, have found that over the past twenty years incomes for the top fifth of the population in D.C. have increased by 81 percent (from $87,300 to $157,700) and for the middle fifth have increased by 31 percent, while the incomes of the bottom fifth of the population have increased by only 3 percent (from $12,300 to

$12,700) (Lazere 2006, 1). If we use the current average or even median incomes of the city or the neighborhood, we are not reflecting the status of the people our group wants to make sure can afford to stay in the neighborhood. The skyrocketing incomes of the upper-level earners mask the very low stagnant incomes of the target population. Using the normal average or median would mean that affordable housing would be targeted to those making between $30,000 and $50,000 at best (and in some calculations those earning up to $75,000 or $100,000 if working families were being considered), and not those making under $25,000 (one of EDI's targets). In addition, Black and White incomes in the Shaw neighborhood are quite different (the White incomes are much higher). Further, these figures do not include measures of wealth (or lack of wealth), which also make a big difference in who can or cannot afford certain levels of housing. Wealth gaps are increasing locally, nationally, and internationally. Finally, the development models advocated by the city and the private developers are based on attracting large outside corporations, giving them tax breaks, and then attracting suburbanites back into the city to live and shop. This model increases housing values and property taxes for those trying to remain and removes economic development from community control, ignoring the needs of the existing low-income residents. Even job creation through such models often does not trickle down to the existing longtime residents.

As a scholar activist developing a specialized, not well-known or respected, branch of knowledge, I am often pushed and pulled in a variety of directions—to advance knowledge and theory in this area, conduct research and evaluation studies, advise practitioners, and convene meetings and conferences. This is often overwhelming and unrealistic, particularly for a junior faculty member. On the other hand it is almost impossible to focus just on a narrow traditional research agenda, since most of my research depends on interaction and engagement with, and reflection on, economic practice.

The field of economics does recognize and embrace applied economic analysis (although I was trained mostly in economic theory), but more as a mathematical exercise engaged in by a detached outsider manipulating numbers. Industrial organization is probably the subfield that has a well-defined ethnographic methodology for such work; traditional, mainstream neoclassical economics focuses more on the application of reified mathematical models. While industrial organization develops important methodologies, it tends not to study community-based business organization. This means that there are few economic scholars with whom I can collaborate, few who understand or see the relevance of my work as part of a defined economic canon, and few economic journals in which to publish my research.

My academic department is African American studies—which is much more supportive of engaged scholarship, innovative methodologies, and interdisciplinary work. However because African American studies departments tend to be less respected in the academy, they are often professionally conservative. African American studies also has traditionally been based more on cultural and intellectual studies, history and literature, political science and sociology. Economics is not as well defined a subject area, and community economics is addressed by few African American studies scholars. Neither economics nor community economics is well represented in African American studies journals.

Pathbreaking and pioneering research and engaged scholarship in this area are not well rewarded in the forms universities recognize and prefer when determining tenure and promotion. This kind of work is best undertaken by senior scholars who can afford to stray from the beaten path. It is very difficult to be tenure track and know that even though my scholarship and commitment depend on my social justice activities and teaching, the tenure decision will be based on everything but that—and may suffer as a result.

There are political as well as scholastic challenges to this work. There are contradictions within the academy that both halfheartedly makes space for me to do such work and at the same time constrains my ability to pursue it creatively and comprehensively. There are also reactionary forces outside the academy that underfund, subvert, and undermine existing and potential efforts. At a time when universities want and need their faculty to be "entrepreneurial" and bring in big grants, it is easier to gain funding for more traditional research. What would facilitate my work would be more support in terms of scholars to engage with, funding of the research, and academic credit for the activism and engaged scholarship I do. A university that supports and rewards social justice scholarship and teaching (academically, monetarily, and in promotions) would help sustain me and would sustain an environment that would enhance this kind of scholarship and teaching. It is important to be in the academy in order to more fully develop the theory behind this research, to conduct "third-party" evaluations, to legitimize this scholarship, and to teach and train students in this area.

In conclusion, economic democracy does not work if people do not see a role for themselves in the economy and in the change process and if they do not believe or understand how economic relations and economies can change (see Gordon Nembhard 2002b). Economic democracy must start with people's agency. It also requires an understanding of paradigms and how paradigms shift. That requires exposure to and an understanding of a variety of paradigms and successful models. This leads back to my research—why we need to document examples of economic democracy and models of change, to evaluate the strengths and weaknesses of the different models and enterprises, and to explain how and why they work or do not work. Such scholarship should be shared with scholars and practitioners. It must be accessible and applicable to a wide variety of audiences—hence the need to combine academic scholarship and engaged scholarship and publish in a variety of media. I hope that my scholarship has chronicled and will chronicle the enduring strength and persistence of grassroots democratic economic organizing and the necessity of better understanding it. I also hope my scholarship will help find ways to strengthen and promote the development of democratic community-based enterprises.

NOTES

1. I use the concept and definition of *subaltern* as described in Gordon (1997).
2. For a more detailed comparison and discussion of these differences, see Gordon Nembhard (1996, 31–35).
3. See Democracy Collaborative (2005) for explanations and examples of these kinds of enterprises and organizations. Also see Gordon Nembhard (2006) and McCulloch (2001).
4. Thanks to Nancy S. Bordier, PhD, for working with me in 2002 to best describe these attributes as we refined a joint proposal for an Institute for Community-Based Enterprise Development (for which we were never able to raise funds).
5. See Gordon Nembhard (2000) for a summary of the findings; Krimerman and Lindenfeld (1992); and Levine and Tyson (1990). Also for the latest data on this, see Logue and Yates (2005).
6. See www.mcc.coop (calculations from Euros to U.S. dollars are my own).
7. See Federation of Southern Cooperatives/Land Assistance Fund (2002, 1992); also, I discuss both the federation and the Freedom Quilting Bee in Gordon Nembhard (2006, 2004a) and provide a case study of the federation's successes in Gordon Nembhard (2004b).
8. Thanks to Ka Flewellen, who worked with me on an earlier version of these principles when we were both with the Preamble Center in Washington, D.C. I summarize them in Gordon Nembhard (2002b).

BIBLIOGRAPHY

Atlee, Tom. 1999. "Y2K and Sustainability." *Co-op America Quarterly* 47 (Spring): 22.
Birchall, Johnston. 2003. *Rediscovering the Cooperative Advantage: Poverty Reduction through Self-Help*. Geneva: Cooperative Branch, International Labour Office.
Curl, John. 2003. "A History of Worker Cooperation in America." www.redcoral.net/WorkCoops.html. Accessed March 6, 2003.
Darity, William A., Jr., and Jessica Gordon Nembhard. 2000. "Racial and Ethnic Economic Inequality: The International Record." *American Economic Review* 90 (May): 308–11.
DeMarco, Joseph. 1974. "The Rationale and Foundation of Du Bois's Theory of Economic Cooperation." *Phylon* 35 (March): 5–15.
Democracy Collaborative [Steve Dubb]. 2005. *Building Wealth: The New Asset-Based Approach to Solving Social and Economic Problems*. Washington, DC: Aspen Institute, Nonprofit Sector Research Fund.
Du Bois, W. E. B. 1907. *Economic Cooperation among Negro Americans*. Atlanta: Atlanta University Press.
———. 1971. "Where Do We Go from Here? (A Lecture on Negroes' Economic Plight)." Address delivered at the Rosenwald Economic Conference, Washington, DC, May 1933. In *A W. E. B. Du Bois Reader*, edited by Andrew G. Paschal, 146–63. New York: Collier Books.
———. 1975. *Dusk of Dawn*. Millwood, NY: Krause Thompson.
Fairbairn, Brett, June Bold, Murray Fulton, Lou Hammond Ketilson, and Daniel Ish. 1995. *Cooperatives and Community Development: Economics in Social Perspective*. Rev. ed. Saskatoon: University of Saskatchewan Center for the Study of Cooperatives.
Federation of Southern Cooperatives/Land Assistance Fund. 1992. *25th Anniversary Annual Report, 1967–1992*. East Point, GA: Federation of Southern Cooperatives/Land Assistance Fund.
———. 2002. *Thirty-fifth Anniversary Annual Report—2002: Learning from Our History as We Plan for Our Future*. East Point, GA: Federation of Southern Cooperatives/Land Assistance Fund. www.federationsoutherncoop.com.
Feldman, Jonathan M., and Jessica Gordon Nembhard, eds. 2002. *From Community Economic Development and Ethnic Entrepreneurship to Economic Democracy: The Cooperative Alternative*. Omea, Sweden: Partnership for Multiethnic Integration, National Institute for Working Life.
Freedom Quilting Bee. 2002. "Freedom Quilting Bee: History, Activities, Plans." www.ruraldevelopment.org/FQBhistory.html. Accessed September 30, 2002.
Gordon, Edmund T. 1997. "Cultural Politics of Black Masculinity." *Transforming Anthropology* 6 (1/2): 36–53.
Gordon Nembhard, Jessica. 1996. *Capital Control, Financial Regulation, and Industrial Policy in South Korea and Brazil*. Westport, CT: Praeger.

———. 1999. "Community Economic Development: Alternative Visions for the 21st Century." In *Readings in Black Political Economy*, edited by John Whitehead and Cobie Kwasi Harris, 295–304. Dubuque, IA: Kendall/Hunt.

———. 2000. "Democratic Economic Participation and Humane Urban Redevelopment." *Trotter Review* 12:26–31.

———. 2002a. "Cooperatives and Wealth Accumulation: Preliminary Analysis." *American Economic Review* 92 (May): 325–29.

———. 2002b. "Education for a People-Centered Democratic Economy." *GEO Newsletter*, no. 53–54 (July–October): 8–9.

———. 2004a. "Cooperative Ownership in the Struggle for African American Economic Empowerment." *Humanity and Society* 28 (August): 298–321.

———. 2004b. "Non-traditional Analyses of Cooperative Economic Impacts: Preliminary Indicators and a Case Study." *Review of International Co-operation* 97 (1): 6–21.

———. 2006. "Entering the New City as Men and Women." In *The Urban Black Community*, edited by Lewis Randolph and Gail Tate. New York: Palgrave Macmillan.

———. Forthcoming. "Community Economic Development." In *International Encyclopedia of Social Sciences*, 2nd ed. Farmington, MI: Macmillan Reference USA (Thomson Gale).

Gordon Nembhard, Jessica, and Anthony A. Blasingame. 2002. "Economic Dimensions of Civic Engagement and Political Efficacy." Working paper, Democracy Collaborative-Knight Foundation Civic Engagement Project, University of Maryland, College Park, December.

Gordon Nembhard, Jessica, and Curtis Haynes Jr. 2002. "Using Mondragón as a Model for African American Urban Redevelopment." In *From Community Economic Development and Ethnic Entrepreneurship to Economic Democracy: The Cooperative Alternative*, edited by Jonathan M. Feldman and Jessica Gordon Nembhard. Omea, Sweden: Partnership for Multiethnic Integration, National Institute for Working Life. Excerpted from "A Networked Cooperative Economic Development: Mondragón as a Model for African American Urban Redevelopment," working paper, 2002.

Haynes, Curtis, Jr. 1993. "An Essay in the Art of Economic Cooperation: Cooperative Enterprise and Economic Development in Black America." PhD diss., University of Massachusetts, Amherst.

———. 1994. "A Democratic Cooperative Enterprise System: A Response to Urban Economic Decay." *Ceteris Paribus* 4 (October): 19–30.

Haynes, Curtis, Jr., and Jessica Gordon Nembhard. 1999. "Cooperative Economics: A Community Revitalization Strategy." *Review of Black Political Economy* 27 (Summer): 47–71.

Hoyt, Ann. 2001. "The 21st Century Case for Urban Cooperative Development." *Journal of Cooperative Development* 2 (Spring): 1, 17.

International Co-operative Alliance. 2006. "Statement on the Cooperative Identity." www.ica.coop/coop/principles.html. Accessed May 14, 2007.

International Co-operative Alliance and International Labour Organization. n.d. (ca. 2005). "The Global Co-operative Campaign against Poverty: Co-operating out of Poverty." Geneva, Switzerland. www.ilo.org/coop.

International Labour Conference. 2002. "Recommendation 193: Recommendation Concerning the Promotion of Cooperatives." www.ica.coop/outofpoverty/documents/summarycampaign.pdf. Accessed August 23, 2006.

Kaswan, Jacques. 1999. "Cooperatives as a Socioeconomic Alternative to the Mainstream: Are We Ready?" *Grassroots Economic Organizing Newsletter*, no. 38 (September–October): 2–3, 12.

Krimerman, Len, and Frank Lindenfeld. 1992. *When Workers Decide: Workplace Democracy Takes Root in North America*. Philadelphia: New Society.

Lazere, Ed. 2006. "Income Inequality Grew Dramatically in DC over the Past Two Decades." DC Fiscal Policy Institute, Washington, DC, January 26. www.dcfpi.org/?p=112. Accessed May 14, 2007.

Levine, David, and Laura D'Andrea Tyson. 1990. "Participation, Productivity and the Firm's Environment." In *Paying for Productivity: A Look at the Evidence*, edited by Alan Blinder, 183–237. Washington, DC: Brookings Institute.

Logue, John, and Jacquelyn Yates. 2005. *Productivity in Cooperatives and Worker-Owned Enterprises: Ownership and Participation Make a Difference!* Geneva: International Labour Office.

McCulloch, Heather. 2001. *Sharing the Wealth: Resident Ownership Mechanisms*. Oakland, CA: PolicyLink.

Megson, Jim, and Janet VanLiere. 2001. "The Role of Worker Cooperatives in Urban Economic Development." *Journal of Cooperative Development* 2 (Spring): 2 and 18.

Mondragón Cooperative Corporation. 2001. "A History of an Experience." February. www.mcc.coop/ing/quienessomos/historiaMCC_ing.pdf. Accessed January 31, 2006.

National Cooperative Business Association. 2007. "About Cooperatives." www.ncba.coop/abcoop.cfm. Accessed May 14, 2007.

ONE DC. n.d. "About EDI." One DC, Washington, DC. www.onedconline.org/EquitableDevelopmentInitiative.htm.

Shipp, Sigmund C. 1996. "The Road Not Taken: Alternative Strategies for Black Economic Development in the United States." *Journal of Economic Issues* 30 (March): 79–95.

———. 2000. "Worker-Owned Firms in Inner-City Neighborhoods: An Empirical Study." *Review of International Cooperation* 93 (March): 42–46.

Six Nations Politechnic. 2002. *A Co-operative Entrepreneurship Curriculum*. Ontario, Canada: Six Nations Politechnic.

Stewart, James B. 1984. "Building a Cooperative Economy: Lessons from the Black Community Experience." *Review of Social Economy* 42 (December): 360–68.

Williams, Chancellor. 1961/1993. "The Economic Basis of African Life." Chapter 9 of *The Rebirth of African Civilization*, 151–81. Chicago: Third World Press.

Woods, Clyde. 1998. *Development Arrested: The Blues and Plantation Power in the Mississippi Delta*. London: Verso Press.

PART IV

Making Ourselves at Home

11. Crouching Activists, Hidden Scholars

Reflections on Research and Development with Students and Communities in Asian American Studies

Peter Nien-chu Kiang

At a symposium convened by the New England Resource Center for Higher Education (NERCHE)—one of the premier networks in the nation working to transform higher education—Alison Bernstein (1998), vice president of the Ford Foundation, asked those assembled to support and mobilize "a community invasion" to revitalize the mission and life of the university. Within academia, I have often assumed that I am on deep-field operations as part of the long-range reconnaissance team preparing for that community invasion. Having successfully infiltrated ivy walls and ivory towers with internalized orders to claim voice, space, and resources for underserved communities, I can say with clarity and confidence that my core qualification and legitimacy to teach in and direct an Asian American studies program has little to do with my doctoral training but rather comes from and has been sustained by my years of community organizing in Boston Chinatown and with various immigrant communities of color. And frankly, if I consider any of the significant or meaningful challenges that I have responded to in academia—whether winning over resistant graduate students in courses on multicultural education or moving interdisciplinary program proposals through rigid bureaucratic structures and skeptical governance bodies or articulating my own cases for tenure and two promotions while questioning the arbitrary and inauthentic fragmentation of service, teaching, and scholarship as separate categories—I have consistently turned to skills, methods, and conceptual frameworks developed through my community-organizing experiences rather than my learning from graduate school and academic life.

When I began teaching Asian American studies courses in the early 1980s, I had no institutional status as either a faculty member or a graduate student. Following my graduation from college, I had lived on food stamps while working/volunteering to establish the Asian American Resource Workshop (AARW), a grassroots educational resource center in Boston Chinatown where we produced bilingual slideshows and developed curricula on Asian immigrant issues for adult ESL classes, trained community members in video production for cable television access, organized coalitions to protest anti-Asian racist violence and police brutality, convened conferences and professional development workshops for teachers about stereotypes and Asian American history, and more. Our goal was nothing less than making fundamental social change through the development of Asian American awareness, pride, and unity—a mission with revolutionary intentions that funders and mainstream agencies never truly grasped but that still continues today, nearly thirty years later.

By the mid-1980s, growing numbers of Asian American students at many schools "East of California"[1] were asserting new demands for Asian American studies courses and programs. During that crucial growth period, those of us planting the Asian American studies field on the East Coast—like braceros and coolie contract laborers following the crops from season to season—rode buses and trains throughout the week, migrating from campus to campus to provide students with what might be their only opportunity to experience Asian American studies at their school. In spring 1988, for example, I taught three days at the University of Massachusetts at Boston (UMass Boston), one night at Boston University, and one day at Yale (Kiang 1995, 1988).

My invited course at Yale on Asian American community development attracted several leaders of the campus Asian student organizations and motivated others to become more involved in campus issues related to ethnic studies, university investment policies, and labor disputes. Although I had been told initially that my lecturer contract would be renewed if the course were well received, I later heard indirectly about administrators' concerns that my teaching was "too political" and students were becoming "too active." In explaining to students why they did not invite me to return to Yale for the following semester, however, the department chair simply stated that I lacked a doctoral degree.

Yale's decision to not renew my contract helped to clarify my understanding of politics and elitism in higher education. If I intended to continue "teaching to transgress" (hooks 1996), then I needed a doctorate for protection and legitimacy. Until then, I had refused to enter a doctoral program, always believing that my community-organizing experience in Chinatown represented my strongest qualification for teaching Asian American studies. Why wasn't community-based practitioner knowledge recognized or valued by universities? Certainly it was more relevant and applicable than my master's degree program at Harvard, where Asian American perspectives were completely absent from every course I took and where there had been no Asian American faculty to work with. My professors had not discouraged me from pursuing Asian American topics in my own research and writing—which I did in every course—but my passions were marginal, at best, within the larger institution. Imagining the frustrations I would face in a traditional PhD program dedicated to narrow disciplinary training without attention to issues of pedagogy or curriculum design, I chose to complete an EdD degree—despite its low status within academic hierarchies—in order to focus on the transformative power of learning environments in Asian American studies (Kiang 2000).

By then, I was teaching as a part-time instructor at UMass Boston—an urban, public, commuter university—and had already engaged in "activist scholarship" through a multifaceted project with students from several Boston-area schools to provide documentation and direct support for a group of Chinese immigrant women garment workers who, after being displaced by plant closings and ignored by government agencies, were fighting for and eventually won job retraining rights, extended health benefits, and unprecedented decision-making control over the funding, design, and evaluation of their language and occupational retraining programs. Throughout a two-year period, Asian American students provided much-needed legal research, documented the workers' organizing efforts in print and photographic media, and distributed petitions and conducted outreach to schools throughout the region to build support. In turn, the garment workers' struggle became the subject of at least four undergraduate term papers, two undergraduate theses, graduate papers at MIT, Harvard, and Brown University, and a collaborative student/community-produced bilingual video documentary that presents the issue of garment worker displacement and documents the organizing process and personal transformation of the garment workers—from hardworking but humble immigrant women to united and empowered community labor leaders (Kiang and Ng 1989; Lowe 1992).

Though nearly all the college students who participated in the garment workers' support committee were Asian American, they came from different schools and also from differing cultural and class backgrounds. In reflecting on lessons from the struggle, an out-of-state student from one of Boston's elite private research universities noted, "I guess I was genuinely outraged at the lack of justice these Chinese garment workers received. Earlier, I felt that after raising a wrong, it would be corrected immediately. Boy, was I naive! It turned out to be a real drawn-out process." In contrast, when the video documentary about the garment workers' struggle was screened for the first time in an Asian American studies class at UMass Boston where many students from the local communities attend, one class member exclaimed shortly after the opening scene, "Hey, that's my mom!" The striking differences in outlook and life experience of these two students point not only to complex challenges of organizing with Asian American students and communities but also to the stratification of higher education institutions that greatly affects the work of both students and faculty, even in relatively open fields such as Asian American studies, where some of us have intently cultivated academic space to feed activist scholarship and advance community invasions.

STRUCTURAL REALITIES AND SYSTEMIC CHALLENGES

In their paper "Curriculum Development in Asian American Studies," presented at the second national Asian American Studies Conference in 1973, Lowell Chun-Hoon, Lucie Cheng Hirata, and Alan Moriyama predicted that "at some point, the lines between action and education, individual service to students and collective responsibility to communities may easily diverge.... It is a logical result of an attempt to create, within the structure of one of the dominant institutions of existing society, a form of education that is aimed at specific advocacy rather than mythical objectivity; that tries to be accountable to groups traditionally unrepresented in the university structure and oppressed by society-at-large." These pioneers in the Asian American studies field correctly identified what has continued to be the central contradiction facing ethnic studies praxis in U.S. higher education after more than three decades of development: simply stated, schools and universities reflect and reproduce the structure and culture of inequality that define U.S. society, while providing space and resources that still allow for the development of revolutionary visions and modest transformative practices. This structure/culture of inequality refers, for example, to the segmented structure of U.S. higher education, in which resources, status, and influence are asymmetrically allocated (and culturally assumed) such that elite private Ivy League and large Research I institutions are top tier, while working-class state universities and community colleges are counterpositioned as bottom tier. That same hierarchy of inequality then defines the day-to-day structuring of faculty work across and within institutions through differential teaching loads and the valuing of research/scholarship over teaching or service in faculty personnel reviews and hiring decisions. The organization and method of doctoral student training also effectively reproduce this structure/culture in the preparation of future faculty.

A clarifying example for me took place at a 1993 Ford Foundation conference in Los Angeles that focused on diversifying the university curriculum. In the wake of the previous year's riot/rebellion in L.A., a panel of nontenured Latino and African American faculty from local institutions were venting deep frustration with their experiences in responding to relentless demands by communities, government agencies, and the media to provide analysis and assistance during that crisis period and then discovering that their interventions counted for little in their annual reviews. Penalized by the traditional reward systems of their institutions, they had each grown cynical about their own roles in the academy, while distancing themselves from the issues and communities that had beckoned to them with such urgency during the previous year.

As the only person in the room from an Asian American studies program, I suggested the possibility of finding greater individual support as well as more productive precedents of community-university collaboration within their schools' ethnic studies programs. The panel remained skeptical, though, and the ensuing discussion enabled me to see potential connections with the agendas of several national networks pursuing higher education reform in domains ranging from service learning and general education to the restructuring of faculty roles and rewards. The efforts of visionaries such as the late Ernest Boyer in placing applied scholarship at the center of many institutions' commitments to overhaul tenure criteria resonated deeply with all of us (Glassick, Huber, and Maeroff 1997; Boyer 1990). Similarly, Boyer's close associate, the late Ernest Lynton—a UMass Boston colleague who was then formulating methods to evaluate faculty professional service activities in communities—also addressed the dysfunctional institutional structures that were disciplining and punishing not only the panel but most of us in the room (Lynton 1995).

In challenging these systemic structural and cultural realities of higher education during the past decade, many innovative models, resources, and frameworks were being developed through activist and feminist scholarship, educational ethnography, service learning, university-community collaboration and civic engagement, and community-based curriculum development (Calderón 2003; Zou and Trueba 2002; Vo and Bonus 2002; Padilla 1999; Eyler and Giles 1999; Hirabayashi 1998; Fong 1998; Gamson 1997; Auerbach 1994). Broader conceptualizations of higher education reform, particularly as articulated by Boyer and Lynton, provided language and methods with which to transform how scholarship can be defined and assessed (Boyer 1990; Glassick, Huber, and Maeroff 1997; Lynton 1995). Inspired in part by Boyer's legacy, the sustained commitments of several national professional associations have, since then, improved the conditions for community-centered practitioners to conduct and disseminate activist scholarship in the academy. Examples include the Association of American Colleges and Universities' efforts to expand diversity and democracy in the curriculum, the Carnegie Foundation's investments in pedagogical practice through the Carnegie Academy for the Scholarship of Teaching and Learning, and Campus Compact's leadership related to service learning and civic engagement (American Colleges and Universities 2007; Carnegie Foundation 2007; Campus Compact 2007). Regrettably, though, too few colleagues in ethnic studies and Asian American studies have been directly involved in any of these national networks or initiatives.[2] This has been a weakness of those national, predominantly white networks and a reflection of what higher education researcher Mitch Chang (1999) and others refer to as the disciplining of Asian American studies—a process I witnessed firsthand.

DISCIPLINING THE NATIONAL ASIAN AMERICAN STUDIES FIELD

During the late 1980s and early 1990s, I served in national and regional leadership positions for the Association for Asian American Studies (AAAS), the field's national network and leadership body. An important question facing the AAAS national board during the late 1980s was how to collaborate strategically with more established professional associations in order to gain greater presence and legitimacy for the field. Some urged a continuing coalition with other ethnic studies associations such as the Puerto Rican Studies Association and the National Association of Chicano Studies. This approach included an occasional presentation at each other's national conferences and eventually a coordinated joint convention in the Bay Area with colleagues in Black studies and Chicano studies.

Others proposed joint sessions with mainstream scholarly organizations such as the American Studies Association and, more recently, the Asian Studies Association. Still others, including myself, were inspired by the effort in 1989 by Paula Bagasao and Bob Suzuki to publish a special issue of *Change* magazine focusing on Asian Americans in the academy. At the time, I argued that national higher education networks like the American Association of Higher Education (AAHE), which institutionally sponsored *Change*, and others such as the Association of American Colleges and Universities (AAC&U) and the American Council on Education (ACE), not only commanded resources and influence that our field lacked but, more importantly, shared aspects of an agenda to reform, if not transform, higher education institutions to become more diverse and democratic.

Though these three approaches were not mutually exclusive, the AAAS lacked the capacity to pursue all three actively. While individuals followed personal commitments, the AAAS organizationally began to invest its collaborative energies with mainstream scholarly associations. Soon, for example, the AAAS began convening annual invited sessions at conventions of the American Studies Association. Similarly reflecting this orientation, active Asian American caucuses or subdivisions within disciplinary professional associations such as the American Psychological Association, the Modern Languages Association, and the American Political Science Association also emerged over time. The success in "mainstreaming" and "disciplining" the field, for both better and worse, contributed to and benefited from the growing stature of the field's senior scholars and the entry of many more graduate students with Asian American interests, particularly at elite public and private research universities.

The field's increased presence and acceptance in mainstream scholarly associations greatly aided some individuals to develop their own scholarly agendas inside their departments and traditional disciplines without having to sacrifice Asian American content in their presentations and publications. To some extent, this level of acceptance also made Asian American studies program development more viable at many institutions by legitimizing the possibilities of joint appointments with discipline-based departments.

On the other hand, analysis in terms of the field's founding intent to transform higher education to serve students and communities leads to the inescapable conclusion that the dominant structure and culture of higher education have transformed the Asian American studies field far more than the field has transformed higher education. This is understandable, given the AAAS's strategy to align with professional associations whose missions focused simply on advancing their own scholarly areas rather than challenging the multiple inequities inherent within the system of higher education. In fact, the role played by the mainstream scholarly associations in reflecting and reproducing the highly stratified structure of U.S. higher education and the elitist, individualistic culture of faculty life deserves a much fuller critique.

The primary institutional impact of Asian American studies within higher education, then, has been to diversify aspects of the academy's content. This is by no means an "empty prize," despite the large promises to communities that have gone unfulfilled (Nakatsu 1973). But even in the domain of content, the field is still far from transforming higher education. For example, in a review of undergraduate course catalogues for nineteen public higher education institutions in Massachusetts (eleven community colleges, four state colleges, and four state universities), Kiang and Wong (1996) counted a total of 15,318 courses offered. Of that total, we identified 180 as Asian studies—mainly language and literature classes—and 116 as multicultural studies courses that might include Asian Pacific American content. Only eight courses of the total (0.05 percent) could be considered explicitly as Asian American studies courses, and nearly all were offered at UMass Boston. A more recent catalog-based counting of Asian American studies courses that included major private as well as public universities locally (Yu 2002) found that UMass Boston offered more than twenty courses, compared with Wellesley, Harvard, and MIT, which listed seven, five, and three courses respectively, and Boston College, Boston University, Northeastern University, Tufts University, and UMass Lowell, which listed two courses or fewer. These data from Massachusetts describe a reality in which Asian American studies courses are completely or nearly absent from the formal curriculum of most public and private colleges and universities across the state. Related research shows that there is also little Asian American content included within the K–12 state curriculum frameworks and their closely aligned high-stakes tests that are now required nationally as part of federal No Child Left Behind legislation (Kiang 2004b).

RECOGNIZING INEQUALITY WITHIN THE ASIAN AMERICAN STUDIES FIELD

Within the Asian American studies field, there is undeniable inequality and marginalization as well. For example, in contrast to the growing presence of "underrepresented" Korean American, Indian American, and *hapa* (mixed-race) scholars and content that are emerging in Asian American studies through pathways with access to the academy based on traditional qualifications, pervasive and powerful systems and structures of exclusion and inequality effectively constrain the development of other, more marginalized and under-resourced populations such as Cambodian, Lao, Hmong, and to some extent Vietnamese Americans (Kiang 2004a). Despite the field's inclusive social-political intentions and clear theoretical articulations about racialization and pan-ethnicity, this is evident from an analysis of the AAAS annual conference programs for the years 1995 to 2000, where only one Lao American, five Cambodian Americans, five Hmong Americans, and eighty-five Vietnamese Americans out of a total of 2,162 presented (see Table 1). Moreover, in terms of content presented, in a total of 1,610 papers and roundtable discussions, regardless of the presenter's ethnicity, one was Mien focused, two were Lao focused, three were Cambodian focused, nine were Hmong focused, fifty-two were Vietnamese focused, and nine were focused generally on Southeast Asian topics (see Table 2).

Admittedly, simple counts do not provide meaningful measures of equity. Nor do they offer explanations about why this is the case. But I offer these examples to show that both Southeast Asian American content and participation remain marginal within the national, pan-Asian American studies field, especially for Cambodian, Hmong, and Lao American populations, even though more than a quarter-century has passed since the early years of refugee resettlement. I view this reality as unacceptable, not only because of baseline principles of representation, but more importantly because these are, overall, the most under-resourced Asian communities in the United States. They should, therefore, be the highest priorities for intervention by the Asian American studies field and other facets of the Asian American movement that have articulated commitments to equity, justice, and social/institutional transformation (Louie and Omatsu 2001).

TABLE 1. Selected Ethnicity of Presenters at AAAS National Conferences, 1995–2000

	1995 SF	1996 DC	1997 Seattle	1998 Hawaii	1999 Philly	2000 Utah	% of yearly total	% of overall total
Lao	0	0	1	0	0	0	1	0.05
Cambodian	1	1	2	0	1	0	5	0.2
Hmong	0	0	1	1	1	2	5	0.2
Vietnamese	9	8	17	15	19	17	85	3.9
Indian	13	15	9	14	42	30	123	5.7
Filipino	28	18	55	47	42	37	227	10.5
Korean	20	44	41	47	49	39	240	11.1
Japanese	47	46	86	77	61	59	376	17.4
Chinese	94	123	128	106	117	112	680	31.5
Other	66	52	65	84	63	90	420	19.4
TOTAL	278	307	405	391	395	386	2,162	100.0

NOTE: All five Hmong presenters were different individuals. The five Cambodian presenters were three individuals, two of whom presented in two different years. The eighty-five Vietnamese presenters represented the participation of fifty distinct individuals—eleven of whom presented at three or more conferences and accounted for thirty-nine of the total. The "Other" category includes ethnicities such as Chamorro, Hawaiian, Pakistani, Thai, and non-Asian Americans.

Thus, even if Asian American studies has succeeded in transforming what is taught and, to a lesser extent, who teaches in universities, the operating structure and institutional culture of the academy have been little affected by Asian American studies as a field. This, in turn, has made the fulfillment of revolutionary promises to students and communities nearly impossible for programs to sustain, initiate, or even imagine. I offer this critique to show how difficult it is to carry on transformational work, including activist scholarship, within the context of U.S. higher education, even within relatively open spaces such as Asian American studies, which, itself, is marginalized, under-resourced, and disrespected by the academy at large.

TABLE 2. Southeast Asian American–Focused Papers Presented at AAAS National Conferences, 1995–2000

	1995 SF	1996 DC	1997 Seattle	1998 Hawaii	1999 Philly	2000 Utah	% of annual total	% of overall total
Mien	1	0	0	0	0	0	1	0.06
Lao	0	1	1	0	0	0	2	0.1
Cambodian	0	1	2	0	0	0	3	0.2
Hmong	1	0	2	3	1	2	9	0.6
Vietnamese	10	1	15	8	5	13	52	3.2
SE Asian	2	2	1	1	1	2	9	0.6
Total SE Asian Am	14	5	21	12	7	17	76	4.7
Total not SE Asian	167	211	272	305	290	289	1,534	95.3
TOTAL	181	216	293	317	297	306	1,610	100.0

PLANTING FIELDS WITHIN A PROGRAM

As the direction of the AAAS and Asian American studies field became more aligned with a process and outcome of academic professionalization during the 1990s, I withdrew from the national scene, believing that the students and communities served by my own under-resourced institution would benefit more fully from comparable investments of care and attention. Today, many years later, I continue to focus my own commitments locally, though with explicit expectations to develop and sustain a programmatic model that the revolutionary founders of ethnic studies would still recognize and support. Perhaps because of UMass Boston's realities as an urban, working-class, public school where we are rich in vision but pathetically poor in material resources, the original principles of ethnic studies—to empower students and communities and to transform schools and society—still resonate here.

Survival and persistence are ongoing realities for our students, many of whom are the first in their families to attend college and most of whom work between half and full time while also managing heavy responsibilities within their immigrant families. The immediate Boston neighborhood next to our campus (known as Fields Corner, Dorchester) is home to the largest concentration of Vietnamese residents, organizations, and businesses in the Northeast and the fifth largest in the United States. The second and fifth largest Cambodian communities in the United States are nearby in Lowell and Lynn, as are new Chinese/Vietnamese residential and commercial areas in Quincy and Malden and the 130-year-old Boston Chinatown. By grounding our curriculum, teaching, and applied research in the realities of these dynamic local communities and by respecting the knowledge and bilingual/bicultural skills that many of our students bring to the classroom, we create powerful learning environments for all students to gain critical understandings of the struggles, contributions, and voices of diverse Asian populations over time in the United States.

Our curriculum accounts for 75 percent of all Asian American studies courses offered throughout the entire system of public higher education in Massachusetts (Yu 2002; Kiang and Wong 1996) and should be understood, in part, as a systemic commitment to build the organizing, documentation, and research capacities of local Asian American communities. Enabling students, many of whom come from those communities, to engage in relevant Asian American community research and activist scholarship is an important component of this explicit capacity-building commitment. Rather than viewing our engagement with communities as "outreach"—a relationship that places the university at the center—we have framed the question differently by considering the communities as the defining center of the relationship. From that vantage point, we continually ask: What are the roles and resources represented by the university—and our Asian American Studies Program specifically—that can support the healthy, long-term development of Asian American communities and the ecological well-being of the larger urban environment?

Given an institutional reality of three-course teaching loads each semester, one necessary and compelling way to support faculty commitments to activist scholarship has been to connect such projects collaboratively with students through Asian American studies courses. Since UMass Boston is a commuter university without dormitory residences, our students are themselves community members with multiple strengths of culture, language, and lived experience that directly contribute to the research process. Student/faculty projects have focused on a wide range of subjects—some defined by students, others suggested and structured in collaboration with community-based organizations and/or former students who are active in local communities—from analyses of voting patterns and health insurance coverage in specific ethnic and geographic communities to profiles of community-based farming projects and Asian-heritage language schools to mural design projects and bilingual oral histories with immigrant owners/workers in ethnic small businesses.

Often the most exciting and original projects are those in which students effectively connect meaningful questions and appropriate methods with their own community-based social networks, cultural understandings, and bilingual skills. For example, a deeply insightful study about Khmer youth gang involvement was produced in this course by a Cambodian American woman whose boyfriend was, at the time, a leading gang member. Her interviews, observations, and critical analysis presented a range and depth of data that other researchers simply could not produce. Similarly, an extensive and nuanced analysis of political dynamics in the local Vietnamese community was produced in this course by a student in his late fifties who had been an elite commando in the South Vietnamese army and a political prisoner in Vietnam for over twenty years. Because of his age, rank, and status, he was able to reach and interview every important leader of every political faction within Boston's Vietnamese community and offer his own comparative, critical, bilingual analysis of their various platforms. Outside researchers, including most Asian American studies students and faculty, simply cannot gain comparable access to these populations. At the same time, insiders with direct access also cannot produce such powerful work unless they are trained in ethnic studies community research methods and stance.

Through continued curricular and program development in Asian American studies, therefore, we have developed a range of individual tactics and shared strategies within our particular institutional context in order to:

- facilitate socioculturally responsive and academically relevant learning communities that support student persistence, mentoring, and connection at our urban, working-class, commuter university;
- document significant issues, needs, and interventions in local Asian American communities and on campus, recognizing that our own students and alumni are themselves members and participants within local neighborhoods, workplaces, and community-based institutions;
- develop scholarly resources in our fields and research capacities in local Asian American communities through connecting ethnic

studies methods, stance, and analytic frameworks with students' indigenous social networks and cultural/linguistic knowledge; and

- sustain faculty engagement with community research and activist scholarship through the curriculum, particularly by supporting the work of applied research teams as core commitments of regular faculty teaching loads over multiple semesters.

In addition to creating and sustaining collective space for activist scholarship by faculty and students within specific Asian American studies courses, we have implemented a second set of strategies and tactics that involves collaboration with multiple units on campus to seed research and development in relevant fields such as Vietnamese diaspora studies, where, as noted above in the critique of the national Asian American studies field, interventions can make a critical difference. With campus partners that include the William Joiner Center for the Study of War and Social Consequences, the East Asian Studies Program, the Institute for Asian American Studies, and the Asian American Studies Program, and with multiyear funding from the Rockefeller Foundation, we have supported not only individual scholars but also collective networks that are bringing together a younger generation of emerging bilingual or English-speaking scholars completing their PhDs and working in traditional academic environments with an older generation of mainly Vietnamese-speaking scholars who work outside the academy. Importantly, we have needed to create participatory structures for those individuals who do not have flexibility in their job situations to be away for the extended periods of time that typically characterize traditional residency programs in academic settings. For example, a brilliant historian writing in Vietnamese simply could not take a "leave" from his position to be "in residence" because his daily immigrant, working-class reality on an electronics assembly line in Southern California did not allow it. In addition, as should be expected from activist scholarly work that challenges embedded ideological commitments and/or structures of power, attacks against this effort—specifically anticommunist protests by some individuals and groups in Vietnamese communities locally and nationally—have been pointed and relentless through the duration of the project thus far.[3]

"Planting fields," then, refers to the development not only of Asian American studies but also of emerging fields such as Vietnamese diaspora studies, in which good questions, meaningful methods, coherent theoretical frameworks, and effective systems of scholarly collaboration are still in the initial stages of "seeding" and "planting," in part by drawing on interdisciplinary insights from a variety of fields that span ethnic studies, area studies, cultural studies, gender studies, trauma studies, development studies, and so on through shared dialogue and collective learning. A second meaning of "planting fields" refers to the words of a Vietnamese peasant recorded in Peter Davis's 1974 historic documentary film *Hearts and Minds,* in which he asserts that his country will survive the war by continuing to plant rice fields, even though bombs are dropping daily. Though not as dramatic, our own collective planting of fields while surviving numerous attacks during the past several years resonates with this image as well.

In Ang Lee's Oscar-winning film *Crouching Tiger, Hidden Dragon,*[4] the story begins as Li Mu Bai (Chow Yun Fat) and Yu Shu Lien (Michelle Yeoh), two of the most highly skilled and disciplined warriors of the Wudan School, rejoin each other. While seeking peace in each other's company, they are forced, separately and together, by both circumstance and desire to confront Jen (Zhang Ziyi), the self-centered, aristocratic daughter of the local governor who has secretly developed fierce fighting skills herself. Upon meeting Yu Shu Lien for the first time, Jen gushes, "It must be exciting to be a fighter, to be totally free! I've read all about people like you. Roaming wild, beating up anyone who gets in your way!" Yu Shu Lien replies quickly to correct Jen's naive assumption: "Fighters have rules too: friendship, trust, integrity.... Without rules, we wouldn't survive for long.... Writers wouldn't sell many books if they told how it really is.... No place to bathe for days, sleeping in flea-infested beds.... They tell you all about that in those books?" Jen deceives and later arrogantly challenges Li and Yu in separate confrontations after stealing Li's powerful sword. Weary of fighting himself, but still looking for someone from a new generation to mentor, Li Mu Bai effortlessly parries Jen's attack, and offers: "You've got potential. You've studied the Wudan Manual but you don't understand it. You need a real master.... Real sharpness comes without effort. No growth without assistance. No action without reaction. No desire without restraint. Now give yourself up and find yourself again. There is a lesson for you.... You need practice. I can teach you to fight.... I've always wanted a disciple worthy of Wudan's secrets."

At the beginning of the film, when Li Mu Bai and Yu Shu Lien initially reunite, Li describes a critical moment from his recent retreat with their masters at Wudan Mountain: "During my meditation training ... I came to a place of deep silence.... I was surrounded by light.... Time and space disappeared. I had come to a place my master had never told me about." When Yu Shu Lien asks him if, at that moment, he experienced enlightenment, Li responds, "No. I didn't feel the bliss of enlightenment. Instead ... I was surrounded by an endless sorrow. I couldn't bear it. I broke off my meditation. I couldn't go on." Later when alone again with Yu, his comrade and soul mate, Li Mu Bai sighs, "Gong Wu [the Martial Arts World] is a world of tigers and dragons, full of corruption.... I tried sincerely to give it up but I have brought us only trouble."

Certainly, the director, producer, and co-writers of this Chinese film had no intention to comment on U.S. higher education. Yet academia itself is often also a world of tigers, dragons, and corruption. Moreover, in the film, a spoiled, self-serving younger generation has learned through books and privilege rather than disciplined practice, while an older generation of dedicated warrior-comrades longs for but is unable to find rest or peace. Similarly, a generational rift within Asian American studies has displaced the field's founding values with ambitions to achieve professional status. Interestingly, only through the character Lo, a Mongolian minority-nationality young man with the pure spirit of the desert and the highly developed survival skills of a bandit leader, does it seem possible to connect the older generation values and training of Li Mu Bai and Yu Shu Lien with the visions of a new generation, even though Lo has neither the resources nor the attraction that Jen commands. In introducing himself, Lo explains: "The Hans [Chinese majority] call me Dark Cloud. I'm not that tall or big, but I'm quick as lightning.... Out here [in the desert], you always fight for survival. You have to be part of a gang to stand a chance. Slowly, your gang becomes your family. All that Dark Cloud stuff is just to scare people and make my life easier." Lo's modesty, realistic assessment of his material conditions, and collective view of struggle and development all remind me of the strengths and weaknesses of my own program and institution, especially when I consider the commitments that my colleagues and I have made to activist scholarship. Though faculty at many universities engage in passionate, purposeful activist scholarship, they typically do so as individuals, without the coordination, coherence, or collectivity that ethnic studies programs were originally intended to provide. My own research agenda has been primarily qualitative, with commitments to supporting the development of Asian American students, families, and communities, especially among Vietnamese, Cambodian, and Chinese refugee/immigrant populations in relation to K–12 schools, universities, and community settings. Examples of activist scholarship have focused on Southeast Asian and Latino parent organizing and coalition building in Lowell, Massachusetts (Kiang 1996, 1994) and Asian American youth development, particularly in response to racist violence in schools (Kiang 2001, 1998) as well as the Chinese immigrant women garment worker struggle described at the beginning of this chapter. I have also been committed to the development of grounded theory in much of my work with Southeast Asian American college students (Kiang 2002). Most importantly, though, my scholarly work has both informed and evolved from my commitments to construct and expand collective spaces for Asian American studies teaching and program development.

Indeed, under-resourced institutions like UMass Boston—or others such as community colleges that have even less prestige and flexibility—are critical sites for powerful and generative activist scholarship. Though these institutions lack the resources and status of either the private liberal arts colleges or the public and private Research I universities, they nevertheless are the primary sites in higher education where the community invasion proposed by the Ford Foundation's Alison Bernstein has already taken place. Ironically, the working-class and immigrant/refugee students who are critical to the success of our models of community research will most likely not gain access to major research grants or PhD programs or publishing opportunities because their backgrounds do not match well with the crouching norms and hidden priorities of resource-rich foundations, research universities, and academic presses. This is a great injustice and loss, not only for those who deserve such opportunities, but for the fields of study that continue to go uninformed by their compelling and original contributions to research and development. But just as demographics do not dictate destiny, invasions—even those with revolutionary intentions—do not promise development. To sustain and support activist scholarship and related commitments of Asian American studies programs, we have to continue to plant fields that can sustain collective work, while also taking far greater collective responsibility to become serious partners with others who are deeply engaged in the broader, long-term institutional transformation of U.S. higher education.

NOTES

1. The term *East of California* is used both informally and officially within the national Asian American studies field to challenge assumptions that curricular content, pedagogical strategies, programmatic models, and research agendas

within Asian American studies must follow the traditional paradigms and practices of California-based universities, where the field has been historically institutionalized.

2. Notable exceptions who have bridged these worlds of higher education innovation and ethnic studies praxis include José Calderón, Nadinne Cruz, Evelyn Hu-DeHart, Gregory Yee Mark, and Daniel Teraguchi.

3. For examples of attacks and responses, see William Joiner Center (2003).

4. Written by Wang Hui Ling, James Schamus, and Tsai Kuo Jung; based on the novel by Wang Du Lu.

REFERENCES

American Colleges and Universities. 2007. "Diversity." www.aacu.org/issues/diversity/index.cfm. Accessed October 5, 2007.

Auerbach, Elsa. 1994. *From the Community to the Community: Community Training for Adult and Family Literacy Project Final Report*. Boston: Boston Adult Literacy Fund.

Bagasao, Paula Y., and Bob H. Suzuki, eds. 1989. *Change*. November–December.

Bernstein, Alison. 1998. "Community Building: An Agenda for Higher Education and Its Communities." Keynote address, New England Resource Center for Higher Education, Boston, November 12.

Boyer, Ernest L. 1990. *Scholarship Reconsidered*. Carnegie Foundation for the Advancement of Teaching. San Francisco: Jossey-Bass.

Calderón, José Zapata. 2003. "Partnership in Teaching and Learning: Combining the Practice of Critical Pedagogy with Civic Engagement and Diversity." *Peer Review* 5 (3): 6–9.

Campus Compact. 2007. "Initiatives." www.campuscompact.org/initiatives/. Accessed October 5, 2007.

Carnegie Foundation. 2007. "CASTL" [under "Program Areas: Undergraduate Education"]. www.carnegiefoundation.org/programs/index.asp?key=21. Accessed October 5, 2007.

Chang, Mitchell J. 1999. "Expansion and Its Discontents: The Formation of Asian American Studies Programs in the 1990s." *Journal of Asian American Studies* 2 (2): 181–206.

Chun-Hoon, L., L. Hirata, and A. Moriyama. 1973. "Curriculum Development in Asian American Studies." In *Proceedings of National Asian American Studies Conference II*, edited by George Kagiwada, Joyce Sakai, and Gus Lee, 83–90. Davis: University of California at Davis.

Eyler, Janet, and Dwight E. Giles. 1999. *Where's the Learning in Service Learning?* San Francisco: Jossey-Bass.

Fong, Timothy P. 1998. "Reflections on Teaching about Asian American Communities." In *Teaching Asian America: Diversity and the Problem of Community*, edited by Lane Ryo Hirabayashi, 143–50. Lanham, MD: Rowman and Littlefield.

Gamson, Zelda F. 1997. "Higher Education and Rebuilding Civic Life." *Change*, January–February, 10–13.

Glassick, C. E., M. Taylor Huber, and G. I. Maeroff. 1997. *Scholarship Assessed*. Ernest L. Boyer Project of the Carnegie Foundation for the Advancement of Teaching. San Francisco: Jossey-Bass.

Hirabayashi, Lane Ryo, ed. 1998. *Teaching Asian America: Diversity and the Problem of Community*. Lanham, MD: Rowman and Littlefield.

hooks, b. 1994. *Teaching to Transgress: Education as the Practice of Freedom*. New York: Routledge.

Kiang, P. N. 1988. "The New Wave: Developing Asian American Studies on the East Coast." In *Reflections through Windows of Shattered Glass*, edited by Gary Y. Okihiro, Shirley Hune, Arthur Hansen, and John M. Liu, 43–50. Pullman: Washington State University Press.

———. 1994. "When Know-Nothings Speak English Only: Analyzing Irish and Cambodian Struggles for Community Development and Educational Equity." In *The State of Asian America: Activism and Resistance in the 1990s*, edited by Karin Aguilar-San Juan, 125–45. Boston: South End Press.

———. 1995. "From Different Shores Again." In *Revisioning Asian America: Locating Diversity*, edited by Wendy L. Ng, Gary Y. Okihiro, Soo-Young Chin, and James S. Moy, 207–11. Pullman: Washington State University Press.

———. 1996. "Southeast Asian and Latino Parent Empowerment: Lessons from Lowell, Massachusetts." In *Education Reform and Social Change: Multicultural Voices, Struggles, and Visions*, edited by Catherine E. Walsh, 59–69. Mahwah, NJ: Lawrence Erlbaum.

———. 1998. "*We Could Shape It:* Organizing for Asian Pacific American Student Empowerment." In *Struggling to Be Heard: The Unmet Needs of Asian Pacific American Children*, edited by Li-Rong Lilly Cheng and Valerie Ooka Pang, 243–64. Albany: SUNY Press.

———. 2000. "Wanting to Go On: Healing and Transformation at an Urban Public University." In *Immigrant Voices: In Search of Educational Equity*, edited by Enrique T. Trueba and Lilia I. Bartolomé, 137–66. Lanham, MD: Rowman and Littlefield.

———. 2001. "Pathways for Asian Pacific American Youth Political Participation." In *Asian Americans and Politics: Perspectives, Experiences, Prospects*, edited by Gordon H. Chang, 230–57. Stanford: Stanford University Press and Woodrow Wilson Center Press.

———. 2002. "Stories and Structures of Persistence: Ethnographic Learning through Research and Practice in Asian American Studies." In *Ethnography and Schools: Qualitative Approaches to the Study of Education*, edited by Yali Zou and Henry T. Trueba, 223–55. Lanham, MD: Rowman and Littlefield.

———. 2004a. "Checking Southeast Asian American Realities in Pan-Asian American Agendas." *AAPI Nexus: Policy, Practice and Community* 2 (1): 48–76.

———. 2004b. "Linking Strategies and Interventions in Asian American Studies to K–12 Classrooms and Teacher Preparation." *International Journal of Qualitative Studies in Education* 17 (2): 199–225.

Kiang, P. N., and M. C. Ng. 1989. "Through Strength and Struggle: Boston's Asian American Student/Community/Labor Solidarity." *Amerasia Journal* 15 (1): 285–93.

Kiang, P. N., and K. Wong. 1996. "The Status of Asian Americans in Public Higher Education in Massachusetts: Asian American Studies in the Curriculum." Unpublished paper, Institute for Asian American Studies, University of Massachusetts, Boston.

Louie, S., and Omatsu, G., eds. 2001. *Asian Americans: The Movement and the Moment.* Los Angeles: UCLA Asian American Studies Center Press.

Lowe, Lydia. 1992. "Chinese Immigrant Workers and Community-Based Organizing in Boston: Paving the Way." *Amerasia Journal* 18 (1): 39–48.

Lynton, E. A. 1995. *Making the Case for Professional Service.* Washington, DC: American Association for Higher Education.

Nakatsu, P. 1973. "Keynote Address." In *Proceedings of National Asian American Studies Conference II,* edited by George Kagiwada, Joyce Sakai, and Gus Lee, 5–9. Davis: University of California at Davis.

Padilla, Felix M. 1999. *The Struggle of Latino/Latina University Students: In Search of a Liberating Education.* New York: Routledge.

Vo, Linda Trinh, and Rick Bonus. 2002. *Contemporary Asian American Communities: Intersections and Divergences.* Philadelphia: Temple University Press.

William Joiner Center. 2003. "Rockefeller Fellowship: The Vietnamese Diaspora." April 7. www.joinercenter.umb.edu/Programs/Education%20 Progams/Rockefeller%20Fellowship/Rockefeller%20Fellowship.htm. Accessed October 5, 2007 (typo "Progams" is actually in the link).

Yu, Amanda. 2002. "Asian American Studies Course Offerings in Massachusetts Colleges and Universities." Unpublished paper, University of Massachusetts, Boston.

Zou, Yali, and Henry T. Trueba, eds. 2002. *Ethnography and Schools: Qualitative Approaches to the Study of Education.* Lanham, MD: Rowman and Littlefield.

12. Theoretical Research, Applied Research, and Action Research

The Deinstitutionalization of Activist Research

Davydd J. Greenwood

Activist research in academic institutions is rare. A powerful set of forces, external and internal to universities, are arrayed against it. Tayloristic academic institutional management structures basically make the necessarily multidisciplinary work of activist scholars impossible by organizing daily work life in a way that ties academics to their campuses. Under these circumstances, sustained interactions with the nonacademic world are extremely difficult. Academic professional organizations ostracize activist scholars through a combination of self-policing censorship and the imposition of intellectual frameworks inimical to activist scholarship. External forces including state and federal governments who provide funding and thus regulate behavior and private sector interests selectively discourage activist work and police activist scholarship when it approaches issues those in power would prefer to leave unexamined.

The above statements probably sound like the complaints of a marginalized professor with paranoid tendencies, but this is not the case. I am a senior and successful insider at an elite university, the holder of an endowed chair in anthropology with a long list of publications, grants, and awards and with decades of experience as an academic administrator. So I offer this critique and analysis from a position of power and privilege within the existing system. I am a current stakeholder in this system who has learned a great deal about its workings over the course of a thirty-six-year professional career.

To substantiate the claims I make requires a compressed essay because the argument has many necessary components. I must offer a general presentation of the poorly understood contours of activist research.[1] I must briefly describe the purging of activist research from the academy.

Since this purging generally has been justified on the grounds that activist work cannot be "scientifically meaningful," I must address this criticism by showing that activist research, if anything, has greater potential for meeting the standards of scientific knowledge creation than does conventional social science. I do this by reviewing a set of distinctions between three types of knowing, *epistêmê*, *tékhnê*, and *phrónêsis*, Aristotle's three-part epistemic framework, and showing that activist research necessarily privileges *phrónêsis*. I provide epistemic and empirical justification for my assertion that action research produces results that are far more likely to be "valid" precisely because they are "engaged" directly in transformations of the phenomena they study. This directly undermines the self-serving academic falsehood that activist research cannot make significant contributions to knowledge generation. Finally, I briefly describe how the promotion of action research would require fundamental changes in university structures, in the disciplines, and in the ways in which research and teaching are organized. Though such changes are difficult to enact, I close with a review of the changes in the relationship between universities and society under way now and the claim that this unsettled moment might offer important opportunities to reintroduce activist research into the academy.

FROM REFORM TO PROFESSIONALIZATION AND "BACK"?

That activism now has to be treated as a topic to be given separate consideration in the social sciences is the outcome of a long-term process: the domestication of the social sciences through the elimination of the reformist ideals that caused them to be founded in the first place. What follows is a very brief overview sprinkled with a few references for further reading. When you delve into the history of the social sciences in the United States, you are confronted with a process by which reformist political economy (both neoclassical and Marxist) was subdivided into hermetic disciplinary minicartels and deactivated as a reform activity. The subdivision of political economy first into economics and the rest in the 1880s and then into economics, sociology, psychology, anthropology, and political science by 1905 is a story of the creation of a group of academic professions attached to the growth of specialized doctoral education in the United States. But it is more than that. By breaking up political economy in this way, the Tayloristic academic division of labor made it impossible for the so-called social sciences to contribute integrated or actionable knowledge to the solution of social problems. Breaking society into an arbitrary set of pieces was a growth industry for universities, and it also created the self-regarding and self-generating academic fiefdoms whose internal networks and ranking systems are the focus of activity of most conventional social scientists.

To the extent that some few social scientists failed to toe the line and retained an interest in social reform, they were punished by being fired from tenured positions, denigrated in the academic professional societies to which they belonged, and later systematically purged by the FBI and CIA (Ross 1992; Furner 1975; Price 2004). To add insult to injury, eventually even the memory of their presence at the founding of these academic professions was eradicated (see Madoo Lengermann and Niebrugge-Brantley 1998 for an exposé of the case of sociology).

The domestication of social science has been a continuous process, with high points during the Haymarket Riots, the labor unrest in Homestead, Pennsylvania, the Great Depression, the McCarthy era, the coercion of Southeast Asia scholars during the Vietnam era, and smaller incidents like Camelot. Through experience, most social scientists internalized the lesson that they should focus on building theory, being "objective," writing mainly for each other in a language of their own creation, building professional associations, and staying away from political controversies.

In anthropology, activist researchers like as Margaret Mead, Elsie Clews Parsons, Zora Neale Hurston, and Sol Tax never gained control of the agenda of American anthropology or the American Anthropological Association any more than Jane Addams, Charlotte Perkins Gilman, and Marianne Weber did in sociology or Richard Ely, Thorstein Veblen, and John R. Commons did in economics. In the case of anthropology, even after the initial purges were over, there was so much tension between theorists and practitioners that in 1941 the Society for Applied Anthropology was founded as a reaction to the disdain for applied anthropology demonstrated by the "pure" anthropologists who ruled the American Anthropological Association.

The role of applied anthropology in the history of American anthropology is poorly understood. Most younger anthropologists are unaware that anthropologists have worked in the Bureau of Indian Affairs that they contributed to the war effort in World War II, and that nearly half of the postgraduate degree holders in anthropology currently work outside the academy in applied jobs. I have met few people who know that the Cornell University Department of Anthropology was founded as an applied anthropology department by Alan Holmberg and Lauriston Sharp in 1948 with a Carnegie Foundation grant covering faculty salaries, administrative support, and even furniture for seven years. It quickly became the world leader in this field. Yet by 1970 any hint of a faculty member's interest in applied anthropology was cause to question the seriousness of his or her academic commitments, and students with such interests were not admitted to the graduate field. Their applications were shunted off directly to the Department of Rural Sociology (now Development Sociology) in the College of Agriculture and Life Sciences without the courtesy of a reading.

George Stocking's interesting essay on Sol Tax includes a great deal of information about Tax's characteristically energetic attempts to create an "action anthropology" in the 1950s and to anchor this at the University of Chicago, an effort that also failed after a few years (Stocking 2000). In subsequent generations, the emergent reformist fields of science and technology studies, women's studies, and ethnic studies were also purged and gradually converted into domesticated academic departments that now look and operate much like the disciplinary departments against which they revolted (Messer-Davidow 2002).

While activist research has been purged from the conventional social sciences, the form of activist research called action research is found scattered through some business schools and in the fields of organizational development, human resource management, environmental studies, and adult education. Action research is a powerful and prestigious practice in Norway, Sweden, Denmark, Finland, the Netherlands, Colombia, Mexico, and Australia. For a time, it was highly regarded in England, with efforts centered on the Tavistock Institute for Human Relations and the work of the reformers Eric Trist and Einar Thorsrud but with no anchor in the higher education system. It was also briefly made popular in the United States through the work of Kurt Lewin at MIT in the 1940s.

While in Europe anthropologists and sociologists (particularly in Scandinavia) have played some role in this form of activist scholarship, U.S. anthropologists and sociologists have ignored it, with the exception of occasional involvement in action research activities in Latin America and Africa. To become trained in action research, it is necessary to focus on the literatures in organizational development, European social psychology, and adult education, where such perspectives are, if not dominant, at least commonplace.[2]

I don't point this out to be dismissive of the conventional social sciences but to make the case that the overall historical trajectories of the conventional social sciences make it clear that activist research was purged from all of them to an equal degree. This history, aside from raising interpretative questions, takes me to the practical point that it makes little sense to try to reintroduce activist research into these conventional social sciences one social science at time. The history reveals a much broader and deeper system problem in the political economy of the social sciences themselves. Such problems cannot be addressed by half-measures.

Before anyone would want to listen to my arguments in favor of activist scholarship, they would need to be persuaded that activist scholarship is "real" scholarship capable of producing significant social science understandings. I turn to this issue now and then will return to the issues surrounding the reinstitutionalization of the social sciences.

APPLIED RESEARCH, ACTION RESEARCH, AND WHY THE CONVENTIONAL AND APPLIED SOCIAL SCIENCES CANNOT BE "SCIENTIFIC"

The attempt to move ahead on the issues of activist research is hamstrung by conventionally imposed divisions of social science activity into theoretical and applied work. Operating with this radical dichotomy, produced by the historical domestication of the reformist social sciences, makes anything deserving the name *social science* impossible. It creates a language game and a system of power relations by which theoreticians take full ownership of academy and exile the activists, despite the self-evident point that theory without practice is not theory at all but merely useless speculation.

To create a space for a more nuanced discussion of these issues, it is necessary to move philosophically back through the neopragmatists to the pragmatist philosophers and ultimately to Aristotle's distinctions between *epistêmê*, *tékhnê*, and *phrónêsis*.[3] These Aristotelian distinctions have been revitalized in the work of Stephen Toulmin and Bjørn Gustavsen (1996), Olav Eikeland (2006), Hans Joas (1997), and Bent Flyvbjerg (2001). As they and I have written a good deal about this elsewhere, I propose here to say only enough to anchor the rest of this essay (Greenwood and Levin 1998a, 1998b, 2006).

It is useful to begin the discussion with the observation that the social sciences, including anthropology, are rife with punishing dualisms that make activist research unthinkable. Among these dualisms are theoretical versus applied social science; theory versus practice; pure versus engaged social science; participant observer versus partner or advocate; and informant or subject versus co-subject.

Theoretical versus applied social science. The theoretical/applied dualism is found throughout the social sciences. As often happens with such dichotomies, the inhabitants of each side are quite certain that they are the superior side, the theorists resting their sense of superiority on being "theoretical" and the "applied" social scientists feeling superior because they are "making a difference" in the world. This dualism, however, does not express an egalitarian relationship. For example, I am fascinated by how many applied anthropologists accept without question their inferior intellectual status in relation to theoreticians and somewhat sadly yearn for greater recognition from their theoretician colleagues (see Hill and Baba 2001).

Pure versus engaged social science. The distinction between pure social science and "engaged" social science is increasingly widespread. In the past couple of years, both the American Sociological Association and the American Anthropological Association have themed their annual meetings to highlight the public and applied character of their fields. Of course, the term *pure* is rarely used self-referentially, but use of the term *engaged* as an adjective before the name of a particular social science (e.g., engaged anthropology, engaged sociology) is common. The unmarked noun in such a dualistic framework generally occupies the power position; so "pure" (like "white" in racial classifications) is the tacit ideal state of professional being. However, in this particular language game, the "engaged" social scientists are more aggressively self-confident, pepper their discussions with critiques of the "academics," and assert the ethical rightness of their engagement vis-à-vis elitist university faculty.

Participant observer versus partner or advocate. Though anthropologists are the most likely social scientists to use the term *participant observer* to distinguish themselves from other kinds of onlookers and participants in social change processes,[4] there are participant observers in sociology and social psychology, as well as in the applied social sciences. The concept of participant observer is a particularly intriguing professional fiction because participant observers claim to be authentically present in a situation and thus cannot and do not deny the impact of their own presence on the world they observe. Yet as participant observers they still manage to refuse to see themselves as "engaged" with their subjects in any proactive way. This is generally accomplished by rejecting any formal responsibility for the consequences of the engagement other than following norms of confidentiality and informed consent.

Participant observers often assert high levels of personal involvement with local people and reminisce about meaningful relationships created in the fieldwork process, and I have no reason to doubt the sincerity of their feelings. But what they choose to observe, how they observe it (within the limits of local norms), how they interpret what they see, and how they write about it are all decisions they reserve for themselves. Thus they participate only as a data-gathering strategy and not for the purpose of creating relationships of mutual obligation and collaborative learning.

Informant or subject versus co-subject. Another common dualism distinguishes between the "informant" or "subject" and an unspoken other pole that could be rendered as "co-subject" or even "colleague/friend." This time, the academic end of the dichotomy is marked. The people social scientists study are constructed as "informants" or "subjects." They only exist academically insofar as the information they provide is valued and interpreted by academics. This way of thinking assumes that the informant/subjects are capable of "informing" the professional researchers only in response to expert questioning techniques and systems of professional academic knowledge. At the extreme, these human subjects are made to appear incapable of generating scientifically meaningful knowledge on their own. By contrast, a co-subject or friend/colleague is someone on a more equal footing with the professional researcher, a full person who has a right to structure research relationships to meet his or her own interests and to demand reciprocities from the professional researchers in return for collaboration.

There are more such dualisms, but I have said enough to make it clear that all parts of this dichotomous universe set the professional social researcher firmly apart from the informant/subject. Such a radical separation has the consequence of making "engagement" with the subjects unscientific, personal, and unprofessional, even if engagement is considered to be a meaningful ethical and human response to life in the company of our fellow humans. This procrustean model dichotomizes "pure" and "applied" research and makes it impossible by definition for applied research to have any scientific or professional value beyond some personal contribution to the amelioration of significant human problems.

EPISTÊMÊ, TÉKHNÊ, PHRÓNÊSIS

A three-part scheme derived from Aristotle breaks up this dualistic mode of thinking in a useful way, one that could help us revise the terms of internal management in the social sciences and that provides the basis for both pragmatist philosophy and action research.⁵ The Aristotelian distinctions I use, following Eikeland, Toulmin, Gustavsen, and Flyvbjerg,⁶ are those between *epistêmê, tékhnê*, and *phrónêsis*. The scheme distinguishes three kinds of knowledge where conventional social science normally distinguishes only two. Of these three, no one form is superior to the others; all are valid forms of knowing in particular contexts and for particular purposes. They are most powerful in combination. This perspective clashes harshly with conventional social science's privileging of *epistêmê*.

Epistêmê comes close to matching our commonsense definition of theory. It focuses on contemplative ways of knowing centered on the eternal and unchangeable operations of the world. *Epistêmê* arises from many sources—speculation, analysis, logic, and experience⁷—but focuses on the generalities lying beyond particular situations. What makes *epistêmê* complex is its theoretical constructions via elaborate definitional statements, logical connections, and the building of models and analogies. While *epistêmê* obviously is not a self-contained activity, it aims to remove as many concrete empirical referents as possible to achieve the status of general truth. *Epistêmê* is evaluated by professional peers, and thus the most common form of engagement in work centering on *epistêmê* is with a group of like-minded theorists who are similarly situated professionally, as in the case of intraprofessional dialogues and peer reviewing.

While the meanings of *epistêmê* correspond roughly to the everyday use of the term *theory, tékhnê* and *phrónêsis* do not map on the current intellectual landscape so easily. *Tékhnê* is knowledge that is action oriented and socially productive. It focuses on what should be done in the world to increase human happiness, and it requires experiential engagement in the world to design the way to achieve "what should be done." Thus *tékhnê* cannot be translated merely as "technique" or as the application of theoretical knowledge. *Tékhnê* is a mode of knowing and acting in its own right. The development of *tékhnê* involves the creation and debate about ideas of better designs for living that will increase human happiness.

Typically, practitioners of *tékhnê* debate ideal ends, strategize about the contextualization and instrumentalization of these ends, and then work on the design of activities that improve the human condition. *Tékhnê* is not the mere application of *epistêmê*; it arises partly from *epistêmê* and partly from its own sources in moral/ethical debate and visions of an ideal society. It is a realm inhabited by professional experts, and it is evaluated through impact assessments developed by the professional experts themselves. The evaluations aim to decide whether their projects have enhanced human happiness and, if not, why not.

Practitioners of *tékhnê* do engage with local stakeholders, power holders, and other experts. Often they are contracted as consultants by those in power to attempt to achieve positive social changes. Their relationships to the subjects of their work are often close and collaborative, but practitioners of *tékhnê* seek to retain their status as outsiders and professional experts who do things "for" rather than "with" the local stakeholders.

Phrónêsis is not well known or understood because the contemporary social sciences have lapsed into an oversimplified dualism between theory and practice whose principal function has been the separation of university social science from the everyday life world. *Phrónêsis* can be understood as the design of problem-solving actions through collaborative knowledge construction with the legitimate stakeholders in the problem. The sources of *phrónêsis* are collaborative arenas for knowledge development in which the professional researcher's knowledge is combined with the local knowledge of the stakeholders in defining the problem to be addressed. Together, they design and implement the actions to be taken on the basis of their shared understanding of the problem. Together, the parties develop plans of action to improve the situation together, and they evaluate the adequacy of what was done. If they are not satisfied, they recycle the process until the results are satisfactory to the parties.

Phrónêsis involves the creation of a new space for collaborative reflection, the contrast and integration of many kinds of knowledge systems, the linking of the general and the particular through action and analysis, and the collaborative design of both the goals and the actions aimed at achieving them. It is a practice that is deployed in groups in which all the stakeholders, research experts and local collaborators have legitimate knowledge claims and rights to determine the outcome. Thus *phrónêsis* involves socially solidary engagement across knowledge systems and diverse experiences. *Phrónêsis* is the basis for action research. It is rarely an element in any form of applied research.

Phrónêsis is not anti-*epistêmê* or anti-*tékhnê*. Many *phrónêsis*-based projects derive significant utility from the kinds of generalized knowledge and understandings of the consequences of methodological choices that prevail in *epistêmê* and debates about the ideal outcomes of change projects that prevail in *tékhnê*-based work. However, in *phrónêsis*-based projects, knowledge gained through *epistêmê* and *tékhnê* is joined with the knowledge and experiences of the stakeholders in a more solidary and dialogical mix.

Why do these distinctions matter to a discussion of activist research in the academic social sciences? These distinctions show the inadequacy of the split of social science into pure and applied or theoretical and applied. Philosophers like Dewey (1990), Rorty (1981), Gadamer (1993), and Habermas (1992) have all made it clear that any kind of activity that makes claims to the legitimacy of the term *science* must cycle constantly between theorization and application as a way of developing and testing understandings, regardless of its intentions about social change. In the social sciences, as in most of the physical and biological sciences, theory without practice cannot be considered theory; it must be viewed as speculation, even if it is not idle speculation.

Not surprisingly, this argument is quite unattractive to most academic audiences. For many positivists, the notion that they should have to "test" their models by examining their impact on the problems they are studying is an unacceptable pressure to cross the boundary from their academic safe havens into the messiness and risks of a complex and dynamic world. For them, a factor analysis or a regression analysis is a sufficient "test" (as determined by peers who behave in the same way), even if the cost of this preference is that their theories neither are deployable in practice nor produce the known outcomes.

Many of my colleagues satanize positivists, generally advocating "qualitative" research and constructivist positions. They routinely condemn positivist social science as nonsensical both epistemologically and methodologically. But qualitative analyses, no matter how beautifully manufactured, still must to be checked for fit against the world of experience. Otherwise, the choice of explanations also is only an exercise in logic. The approval of these logical games by colleagues is a confirmation not of their validity but rather of the coherence of networks of professional peers within the disciplines.

Applied researchers are not much more careful. What they did to promote positive changes, why it worked or failed, and what should be done differently in the future are usually laid out in narrative form and judged mainly by their applied colleagues and by those who hire them as consultants. While there is some testing in action, this kind of applied knowledge remains resolutely a professional monopoly and is rarely commented on by the objects of the application.

To be blunt, neither the theoretical nor the applied parties allow themselves to be held accountable to the standards of the scientific method for confronting concepts with observations and examining the fit cyclically. Social scientists cannot have it both ways. Unless we are willing to abandon the claim to be social "sciences" (perhaps by calling ourselves "social studies," "civics," or "cultural studies" instead), we cannot escape the requirement of specifying the relationships between ideas, methods, and data.

The problem of the social sciences is not a problem, as is often lamented, of their being too obsessed with being scientific. Rather, the problem is that they are innocent of the training to follow the scientific method in any way. They are far too happy with armchair speculation and basically unwilling to find out if their concepts work in practice.

To summarize, rather than one major modality of engagement in the everyday world, that of *tékhnê*-based "applied social science," there are two—one, *tékhnê*, that is expert dominated and hierarchical and the other, *phrónêsis*, that is collaborative, dialogical, and built around joint praxis and evaluation. Using these distinctions permits us to see that applied social science, which is principally dominated by *tékhnê*, is not the "application" of theoretical social science. Rather, it is a relatively independent form of expert knowledge based on the imposition of professional authority.[8] *Phrónêsis*, the intellectual basis of action research, is not the mere application of theory either. Rather, it is a democratizing form of context-specific knowledge creation, theorization, analysis, and action design in which the goals are democratically set, learning capacity is shared, and success is collaboratively evaluated. As such, it is radically different from applied social science.

WHAT IS ACTION RESEARCH?

For an activity to be action research, it must meet a number of criteria. It must involve collaboration between experts in social research methods and legitimate local stakeholders (community members, coalition members, organization members) in setting the agenda for a collaborative project. Subsequently, it must involve an effort to see that all the relevant classes of stakeholders are able to participate and contribute their knowledge and actions to the process. Once the topic of the work is collaboratively set, a research design and training process is undertaken that must prepare the local participants to play an active role in their own action research project. Together, the insiders and outsiders must design and conduct the research, interpret the results, design the actions that can improve the situation, implement the actions, and evaluate their effectiveness. If the results are not satisfactory, they must cycle through the process again, assuming there are sufficient resources and energy in the group.

This process is built, not just on democratic commitments, but on the belief that no one, no matter how much social science training and professional authority he or she has, is as much an "expert" in the lives of the local stakeholders as the stakeholders themselves. Local knowledge is broad and deep and is an essential part of the process. At the same time, the collective knowledge of the research community is also relevant, both in terms of findings from other relevant work and in terms of the effective use of concepts and models drawn from *epistêmê* and *tékhnê* and the careful choice of methods. It is also important for the action researcher to be a skilled process facilitator capable of assisting in the construction of a democratically functioning group in which differences are treated as assets rather than obstacles to be overcome.

From this, it should be clear that action research is neither a theory nor a particular set of methods. It is a way of orchestrating combined research and social change activities to pursue collectively desired outcomes. Action research uses theories and methods from a wide variety of sources. A key part of the role of the professional researcher in action research is to understand and explain to the local stakeholders the numerous theoretical and methodological options that exist in any particular action research situation. Thus action researchers must meet a high standard of theoretical and methodological competence, high enough to facilitate the choice of theory and methods with local stakeholders and to train them in their use.

One of the common justifications for action research is its political/moral goodness. While I am glad to emphasize the importance of the democratic commitments built into action research processes, there also are powerful epistemological and methodological reasons for doing action research. Since my coauthor Morten Levin and I have gone to considerable trouble to make an epistemological and a methodological argument for the superiority of action research as an approach to social science (see Greenwood and Levin 1998a), I will only briefly rehearse the argument here.

The scientific method demands an ongoing confrontation between theoretically structured expectations about how certain phenomena or processes will work under a particular set of conditions. The principal reason for the development of the scientific method is to discipline this process through ongoing confrontation between theorization and results in a cyclical form that aims to produce reliable knowledge. In the social sciences, the causal networks are more complex, in the sense of our having to deal with physico-chemical causal structures and logico-meaningful ones that are complexly interwoven. At the same time, this difficulty is partly overcome by the intersubjective interactions possible between researchers and research subjects.

In action research, the problem focus is defined by people who live with the problem every day, in collaboration with social researchers. The amount of knowledge local stakeholders have about the genesis, configuration, and dynamics of the problem, though often not framed in academic language, is great—something all anthropologists would probably agree with. What constitutes a meaningful approach to the problem—empirically, theoretically, methodologically—is negotiated openly among the participants, and the local stakeholders are trained in the relevant research methods. They deploy these methods, judge their effectiveness, and collaboratively interpret the results. From here they move to defining courses of action based on the causal analyses that have been arrived at. The actions are taken and the results are compared with their expectations and hopes. If the results are found wanting, the actions are redesigned or the interpretative framework is altered until the actions produce the desired outcome. While anyone familiar with the philosophy of science knows that such an outcome does not "prove" the validity of the analysis, surely this process produces more reliable knowledge than can a group of hermetic professional social scientists who unilaterally engage in all phases of the process and judge the results, not by the degree to which problems have been solved, but by the degree of agreement among peers about the way they did the work.

Put another way, action research, unlike conventional social science, to use John Dewey's term, issues "warrants for action" where the interested and at-risk parties gain sufficient confidence in the validity of their research results to risk harm to themselves by putting them into action. In my view, this is a "real" significance test. I very much doubt that conventional social scientists would be willing to risk their own health, homes, or domestic economies on the "validity" of work they have done from an *epistêmê* or a *tékhnê* point of view, work that has never confronted a test of action.

Despite these benefits, action research involves a host of inconveniences. There is no guarantee that a group of local stakeholders will define an issue for action research that is "anthropological" or "sociological." Human problems do not come in disciplinary packages; they generally are multiparty, multicausal, complex, and dynamic, and research professionals have to help find the relevant academic knowledge and expertise where it lies, regardless of their own training. Again, most conventional social science is built around defining problems to match disciplinary solutions, not the reverse. This is the "If I am a hammer, everything I see is a nail" approach to research. Thus the behavioral and organizational changes that action research requires of the researchers are considerable.

ACTIVISM AND ENGAGEMENT

Given the distinctions made above, it turns out that terms like *activism* and *engagement* are too imprecise. They can apply to both *tékhnê*-based and *phrónêsis*-based work despite the profound differences between them. Further, among both applied social scientists and action researchers there are many variants, ranging from top-down application to collaborative work in industry, government, and development agencies and including mobilization and liberation work in oppressive situations.

The vast majority of anthropologists and sociologists who are interested in acting on the world around them view *tékhnê*-based work as the main option for engagement. There is little breadth of discussion about the diverse meanings of engagement, least of all about the ethical and methodological implications of engaging collaboratively with co-subjects in the manner of *phrónêsis*-based action research.

To make matters worse, there is a tendency for activism and engagement to become simultaneously fashionable and disengaged. Over the last few years, I have had the opportunity to examine the personal statements of many anthropologists who describe themselves as professionally interested in "activism." While I am not criticizing their intentions or projects, I do note that one discursive thread involves repayment to the people with whom they have done conventional fieldwork. They often seek to make this repayment by becoming either expert witnesses for local causes or in some other way trying to be helpful to the community they worked in. They generally take pains to present this activity as clearly separate from their conventional fieldwork and their "academic" activities, as moral commitments taken on voluntarily and extraprofessionally. This discursive machinery reproduces the *epistêmê/tékhnê* distinction within the anthropologists' own professional work while conserving intact their position of professional authority based on *epistêmê*.

The other main thread I have discerned is a perverse desire to become *epistêmê*-based students of "activism." These students of activism study the agency of others from an *epistêmê* viewpoint and refer to the *epistêmê*-based literature almost exclusively. However, their only agency is *epistêmê*-based work. This converts activism into yet another deactivated intellectual product. These anthropologists seem to feel that they are meeting their ethical obligations to their "informants" merely by showing an interest in the subject of activism itself.

None of these approaches satisfies action research's principles of engagement. The terms of engagement, the ways of studying the issues, and the ownership of the actions and the intellectual products are not negotiated democratically with the legitimate local stakeholders. The expert model prevails.

If the arguments in this essay are persuasive, then we are left with an institutional puzzle. If action research is so clearly superior to the alternatives, why is it so poorly represented in academia generally and almost not represented at all in anthropology? There are many barriers to this approach, and I have devoted the last six years to analyzing and writing about them. I recently completed a four-year project funded by the Ford Foundation on the future of the social sciences in "corporatizing" universities. Among other things, such as discovering just how truly dim the future of the conventional social sciences really is, this project analyzed the declining support for the conventional social sciences and the structural impediments in universities and the social science professions to altering social science research in the direction of action research.

My colleague Morten Levin and I have written a series of analytical essays on the obstacles to deployment of action research in university settings (1999, 2000a, 2000b, 2001a, 2001b), and now we are at work on the larger project of the increasingly uncertain fate of the conventional social sciences under the immense fiscal pressures that contemporary higher education faces. Our arguments have three dimensions, two of which have already been laid out in this essay: the purging of the reformist elements in the social sciences; the hermetic professionalization of the social science disciplines, making them inward-looking and self-regarding; and the creation of a work-life organization that is incompatible with action research.

After the purges and the professionalization processes, we now face an organization of social science work life on most campuses that is incompatible with any form of activism. Teaching schedules, faculty meetings, college and university committees, and research mainly done in the summers and on leaves taken every six or so years at wealthy institutions make up the work life of most faculty. The research is concentrated in time and then followed by months or years of writing up the results.

This work system is completely incompatible with conducting any form of activist or action research. To engage seriously with external stakeholders, the researcher must be flexibly available to them and must be able to work with them when they need support, not only when the researcher has a leave, does not have a faculty meeting to attend, does not have to hold office hours, and so on. In other words, a system of work organization has been created that is inimical to any meaningful form of *phrónêsis*-based engagement.

These institutional patterns do not arise from immutable natural laws; they are administrative creations that support the purging of activism and the coercive control of the academic professions over the lives of social scientists. Because universities saw important financial benefits in supporting the sciences and engineering, scientists and engineers have had flexible work schedules for many years. They can attend to their research and work with external constituencies with relative ease. Social scientists and humanists cannot.

These work organizations can be changed, should the will exist to change them. There are ways to second multidisciplinary teams of faculty to external projects and to reorganize project and extension work at universities to make *phrónêsis*-based work possible. But thus far U.S. universities have shown little interest in having their faculty engaged in action research and in managing the complexity that such engagements bring.

In Norway, Sweden, Finland, and Denmark, a number of action research programs have been mounted through the administrative creation of action research teams connected to external stakeholders. PhD training programs in action research have been built by my colleague Morten Levin at the Norwegian University of Science and Technology. In these programs, multidisciplinary teams of faculty and students have been seamlessly involved in both off-campus projects and on-campus course work.

Of course, unlike the United States, Norway makes social and academic policy by creating agreements between the government, the employers' federations, the labor unions, and higher education institutions. Put another way, the Norwegians use action research to support and strengthen the programs of their welfare state systems. One looks in vain for a similar set of institutional supports in the United States. So the problem of doing action research at universities is as much a problem of the national social agenda as it is of the organization of the activities of the social sciences.

Despite the clearly unfavorable national political and social environment in the United States, relatively few forces here prevent at least tenured faculty from teaching activist perspectives. In my own experience at Cornell University, I was able to mount two quite successful action research courses and to create a program for undergraduates to combine community service with action research training (Greenwood et al. 1997; Greenwood et al. 2004). My colleagues have had similar successes, including courses in city and regional planning, nutrition, and education and programs of urban action research (e.g., Reardon 2005). Thus there is little question that we can teach these courses, supervise undergraduate and graduate students, and create successful and dynamic programs.

But three decades of this work have not actually made my university a more activist institution. So long as these programs are individual initiatives that do not press for changes in the existing Tayloristic organization of the university, they are tolerated. During the same period that these various activist efforts have surfaced, universities like mine have withdrawn even more from public work than before. Nationally famous and vanguard programs such as the Field and International Study Program in the College of Human Ecology and the Program for Employment and Workplace Systems in the School of Industrial and Labor Relations Extension Division have been shut down and the staff fired. In a behavior that can only be described as self-destructive, as state and federal subsidies to the university have decreased, the senior administrators have responded by weakening programs aimed at serving the public.

Cornell is the land grant university of the State of New York and thus statutorily required to provide teaching, research, and public service to the people of the state. Yet instead of focusing attention on the ways this can be done, most current administrative thinking aims at substituting private sector funds, alumni gifts, and increased tuitions for the lost public revenues. This is a clear race to the bottom. As the university serves the people of the state less and less, the people of the state are less and less ready to subsidize the operation of the university.

At the same time, we are moving into a period of unprecedented demands for public accountability and quality assurance in higher education. This movement began during the Thatcher era in the United Kingdom with her decision to convert the polytechnics into universities and then to do a "Research Assessment Exercise" to evaluate all professors individually, sum the scores for their departments, and compare these departments to all the other departments in these fields in the country. According to the score received, departments then received a portion of the national funding for research in their areas. In addition, a Quality Assurance in Teaching evaluation scheme was created to evaluate teaching on a national scale. These exercises have been repeated a number of times and have created havoc in the British system, hollowing out the social sciences, closing down whole fields at individual universities, and ultimately consolidating the grip of the elite universities on national funding (Rhind 2003).

Despite the deleterious results of this process (the RAE is going to be terminated now that the damage is done), the Bologna Process, involving the creation of uniform degree, credential, and teaching evaluation systems across most of Europe, has imposed many of the same procedures on a huge array of European universities (see Bologna Secretariat 2007), erasing national differences, unique programs, and sources of individual excellence everywhere.

Now this accountant's dream scheme has made its way across the Atlantic to our shores in the guise of the Spellings Commission report (Commission on the Future of Higher Education 2006). This report, the fruit of a long and publicly acrimonious process, articulates strong demands for public accountability of higher education and public quality assurance standards for teaching as well. Though the report is less than a month old as of this writing, the Department of Education, a notoriously slow-moving institution, has already set up six regional accreditation commissions to restructure the U.S. higher education accreditation system in line with these concepts of accountability. We know from the European experience that these systems reinforce academic Taylorism and short-term autopoetic disciplinary behavior and that they are radically incompatible with action research or other activist work that is necessarily multidisciplinary and long term. This is clearly a neoliberal move in which conservatives demand that all units of public universities justify themselves in terms of the value for educational dollar spent. The accountability scheme sets up the accounting agencies as defenders of the "public interest" through these coercive schemes.

Few U.S. academics seem to have noticed how much their world is about to change, and it stands to reason that these changes will not fall evenly on the different groups. The scientists and engineers are already engaged with external constituencies in many projects of the sort that will meet these kinds of accountability criteria. The humanities are usually given a "pass" on such matters because most people, particularly conservatives, view the humanities as inherently useless or at best "ornamental" activities. But the social sciences are headed directly into a major crisis.

The new accountability will demand a demonstration of value for the dollar of the sort that the conventional social sciences simply cannot provide. Having cut themselves off from the study of socially relevant problems and from the engagement with external constituencies that might value their work, they have nowhere to hide. They have exiled *tékhnê* and *phrónêsis* and now have to face the consequences of their choices.

Despite the origins of this accountability system in neoliberal conservative policies, I do agree that university social scientists have a public obligation. Universities, even private ones, are both tax-exempt and tax-subsidized institutions. This means that they are publicly supported. But in return for what? We have done such a poor job of giving anything back to the public that is meaningful to them that they now have lost their respect for us and their belief that what we do is worth funding. These kinds of pressures will force many more social scientists to consider applied research and will eventually rearouse all the issues about activism that both the conservatives and the social scientists have worked so hard to suppress.

While this could be viewed as a dismal scenario, in my view these could be interesting times for strategically minded activist researchers. Action research that mobilizes the social science and other expertise of universities collaboratively with external stakeholders for their mutual benefit may well be a viable response to these accountability pressures. While it is a dangerous game to take reforms created by conservative activism and attempt to turn them into significant support for social reform, it is a game that action researchers could play effectively while subverting the conservative purposes that gave rise to the accountability system in the first place. When university administrators, starved for funds and under attack by state and federal authorities over their high costs of doing business, their high tuitions, and their disregard of the needs of the public, see a form of social science work that promises to deal constructively with the public, perhaps the time will be right to attempt again to convert individual activism into institutional activism.

NOTES

1. I will focus on action research, a form of activist scholarship all but ignored in anthropology. While I am personally pleased to be an anthropologist and have

found what I have to offer because of my training to be of value in action research projects, I long ago gave up on the AAA and its publications as a venue for my work. For example, four of the five books I have published since 1990 have been outside anthropology, and I have not submitted any of the scores of articles I have published to anthropology journals in the United States (though some have been published in anthropology journals in Spain). This is not a boycott of anthropology but grows from a desire to be published without receiving incompetent peer reviews and to put my work before people who actually are interested in using it.

2. The first clear sign of a change is the seven-volume *Ethnographer's Toolkit*, in which action research is presented as a methodological alternative alongside all the other methods (Schensul et al. 1999).

3. No one reading what follows will confuse me with a trained philosopher. This is an extremely complicated subject on which a great deal has been written. Aristotle has been used and misused by generations of thinkers to justify their positions. However, there has been an interesting recuperation of Aristotle for action research recently. Olav Eikeland is probably the leading expert on this subject; he has published an immense book on these issues in Norwegian and is now trying to bring out a synthesis of the arguments in English in the next year or so. Though he bears no responsibility for what I write here, my judgment has been influenced by the drafts of his Aristotle papers that I have read recently.

4. Elsewhere I have written a comprehensive critique of the ambiguities of the concept of participant observation (Greenwood 2000).

5. This section is adapted from a presentation on this topic made at the Sociedad Española de Antropología Aplicada meetings in Granada in November 2002 under the title "La antropología 'inaplicable': El divorcio entre la teoría y la práctica y el declive de la antropología universitaria." My discussion owes a great deal to the work of Olav Eikeland (2006), Stephen Toulmin and Bjørn Gustavsen (1996), Bent Flyvbjerg (2001), and Shen-Keng Yang (2000).

6. Although I have drawn from all of these authors, Eikeland, a trained philosopher who is also an action researcher, has written the most comprehensive and in-depth analysis of these concepts, and I refer any interested reader to it (Eikeland 2006).

7. It is worth highlighting that, in the Aristotelian framework, theory is not independent of data drawn from experience.

8. Despite this, I find it interesting how few applied anthropologists take responsibility for their own theorizations, often preferring to subordinate themselves to their "theoretical" colleagues (See Hill and Baba 2001)

REFERENCES

Bologna Secretariat. 2007. "Welcome to the Bologna Secretariat Website." www.dfes.gov.uk/bologna/. Accessed May 10, 2007.

Commission on the Future of Higher Education. 2006. "A Test of Leadership: Charting the Future of U.S. Higher Education." www.ed.gov/about/bdscomm/list/hiedfuture/index.html. Accessed May 9, 2007.

Dewey, John. 1990. *The School and Society* and *The Child and the Curriculum*. Chicago: University of Chicago Press.

Eikeland, Olav. 2006. "Phrónêsis, Aristotle, and Action Research." *International Journal of Action Research* 2 (1): 5–53.
Flyvbjerg, Bent. 2001. *Making Social Science Matter: Why Social Inquiry Fails and How It Can Succeed Again*. London: Cambridge University Press.
Furner, Mary. 1975. *Advocacy and Objectivity: A Crisis in the Professionalization of American Social Science*. Lexington: University of Kentucky Press.
Gadamer, Hans Georg. 1993. *Truth and Method*. 2nd ed. New York: Continuum.
Greenwood, Davydd. 2000. "De la observación a la investigación-acción participativa: Una visión crítica de las prácticas antropológicas." *Revista de Antropología Social* 9:27–49.
Greenwood, Davydd, Nimat Hafez Barazangi, Melissa Grace Byrnes, and Jamecia Lynn Finne. 2004. "Evaluation Model for an Undergraduate Action Research Program." In *Learning and the World We Want*, edited by Budd Hall, 152–59. Victoria: University of Victoria.
Greenwood, Davydd, Johan Elvemo, Lisa Grant Mathews, Ann Martin, Aleeza Strubel, and Laurine Thomas. 1997. "Participation, Action, and Research in the Classroom." *Studies in Continuing Education* 19 (1): 1–50.
Greenwood, Davydd, and Morten Levin. 1998a. *Introduction to Action Research: Social Research for Social Change*. Thousand Oaks, CA: Sage Publications.
———. 1998b. "The Reconstruction of Universities: Seeking a Different Integration into Knowledge Development Processes." *Concepts and Transformation* 2 (2): 145–63.
———. 1999. "Action Research, Science, and the Co-optation of Social Research." *Studies in Cultures, Organizations and Societies* 5 (1): 237–61.
———. 2000a. "Reconstructing the Relationships between Universities and Society through Action Research." In *Handbook of Qualitative Research*, 2nd ed., edited by Norman Denzin and Yvonna Lincoln, 85–106. Thousand Oaks, CA: Sage Publications.
———. 2000b. "Recreating University-Society Relationships: Action Research versus Academic Taylorism." In *Educational Futures: Shifting Paradigm of Universities and Education*, edited by Oguz N. Babürglu and Merrelyn Emery and Associates, 19–30. Istanbul: Sabanci University Press.
———. 2001a. "Pragmatic Action Research and the Struggle to Transform Universities into Learning Communities." In *Handbook of Action Research*, edited by Peter Reason and Hilary Bradbury, 103–13. Thousand Oaks, CA: Sage Publications.
———. 2001b. "Re-organizing Universities and 'Knowing How': University Restructuring and Knowledge Creation for the Twenty-first Century." *Organization* 8 (2): 433–40.

Greenwood, Davydd, and Morten Levin. 2006. *Introduction to Action Research: Social Research for Social Change*, 2nd ed. Thousand Oaks, CA: Sage Publications.

Habermas, Jürgen. 1992. *Moral Consciousness and Communicative Action*. Cambridge, MA: MIT Press.

Hill, Carole, and Marietta Baba, eds. 2001. *The Unity of Theory and Practice in Anthropology: Rebuilding a Fractured Synthesis*. Washington, DC: NAPA Bulletin 17.

Joas, Hans. 1997. *The Creativity of Action*. Chicago, University of Chicago Press.

Madoo Lengermann, Patricia, and Jill Niebrugge-Brantley. 1998. *The Women Founders: Sociology and Social Theory, 1830–1930*. New York: McGraw-Hill.

Messer-Davidow, E. 2002. Disciplining Feminism: From Social Activism to Academic Discourse. Durham: Duke University Press.

Price, David H. 2004. *Threatening Anthropology: McCarthyism and the FBI's Surveillance of Activist Anthropologists*. Durham: Duke University Press.

Reardon, Kenneth. 2005. "The Cornell Urban Scholars Program: Cultivating New York City's Next Generation of Leaders." *Journal of Higher Education Outreach and Engagement* 10 (2): 127–39.

Rhind, David. 2003. "Great Expectations: The Social Sciences in Britain." www.city.ac.uk/vco/davidrhind/expectations.html. Accessed May 9, 2007.

Rorty, Richard. 1981. *Philosophy and the Mirror of Nature*. Princeton: Princeton University Press.

Ross, Dorothy. 1992. *The Origins of American Social Science*. Cambridge: Cambridge University Press.

Schensul, Jean, Margaret LeCompte, et al., eds. 1999. *The Ethnographer's Toolkit*. 7 vols. Walnut Creek, CA: Altamira Press.

Stocking, George, Jr. 2000. "Do Good, Young Man: Sol Tax and the World Mission of Liberal Democratic Anthropology." In *Excluded Ancestors, Inventible Traditions*, edited by Richard Handler. Madison, University of Wisconsin Press.

Toulmin, Stephen, and Björn Gustavsen, eds. 1996. *Beyond Theory*. Philadelphia: John Benjamins, 1996.

Yang, Shen-Keng. 2000. "Issues of Practicability of Comparative Education Knowledge in the Postmodern Age." www.ntnu.edu.tw/teach/messboard/doc/20000903.

13. FAQs

Frequently (Un)Asked Questions about Being a Scholar Activist

Laura Pulido

Dear Potential Scholar Activist,

I am taking this opportunity to write an open letter to all those contemplating or in the early stages of an academic career and wondering if and how they can negotiate the seemingly disparate demands of political engagement and academic performance. I decided to do so because I am routinely asked—generally by activist graduate students whom I don't know—about how I reconcile the two. To be perfectly frank, I rarely know how to respond. I often answer in generalities, such as "You need to follow your heart," which, while certainly true, does not begin to address the complexities involved. Accordingly, I thought I would use this chapter to answer some of the most frequently asked questions that I receive, as well as some questions that I am *not* asked but that any person considering becoming a scholar activist would do well to consider.

Before I get into the substance of the letter, I will share a bit about myself, since most of you have never met me and some background will hopefully provide a context for my comments. I am a professor at an aspiring research university in Los Angeles, the University of Southern California (USC). I have a joint appointment in geography and American studies and ethnicity, and most of my research centers on questions of race, political activism, social movements, Chicano/Latino studies, and environmental justice. I identify as a Chicana and native Angeleno—facts that shape a good deal of who I am as a scholar, activist, and human being. While I have always had strong political views, it was not until I entered graduate school in the 1980s that I became politically active. The impetus to get involved stemmed from several sources, including my eagerness to understand how people transform the world, as well as my own commitment to antiracism, workers' rights, and anticapitalist politics. I do not recall when I realized that I needed to *both* study political activism and be politically active myself, but that notion has been a central part of who I have been since graduate school.

Needless to say, there are many different ways to pursue oppositional scholarship and politics. The form of my own practice and the focus of this letter is what Ruth Wilson Gilmore (1993, 73) calls "organic praxis." Gilmore has identified several tendencies among oppositional scholars, including individual careerism, romantic particularism, luxury production, and organic praxis. Both individual careerism and luxury production emphasize theory production at the cost of disconnection from larger movements for social change. There is nothing wrong with such work, and its practitioners have made many contributions to our understanding of how the world works. Indeed, universities are all too happy to promote this type of scholarship, especially among scholars of color. Romantic particularism, another tendency within oppositional work, is distinctly counterhegemonic but hesitates to portray the marginalized in all their complexity, a serious omission. Both rigorous scholarship and committed action demand that we identify and analyze the contradictions that are present in all social formations. The final tendency, which I will be referring to throughout this letter, is organic praxis. Gilmore defines oppositional work as "talk-plus-walk: it is [the] organization and promotion of ideas and bargaining in the political arena" (71). What distinguishes organic praxis is "the walk," or more specifically, political bargaining. Whether the bargaining takes place on campus or in the larger community is irrelevant; the point is that the scholar is somehow connected to oppositional action beyond that of writing for academic audiences.

Over the course of my career, I have been involved in several different movements and organizations primarily in Southern California. These include labor, environmental justice, and social justice groups. I have never been the leader of a major organization, nor am I an academic star: I am an average-performing academic who has tried to keep one foot firmly in academia, the other grounded in community struggles and institutions—in addition to trying to maintain some semblance of a personal life (the latter being a more recent development).

Certainly there is nothing exceptional in what I do, but for several reasons students have identified me as a scholar activist and frequently ask for my advice. One reason I am queried about such matters is that I come from a relatively small discipline, geography, where activists readily stand out. Likewise, I come from an exceedingly white discipline, where vocal people of color attract attention. Also, some young scholars are genuinely curious as to how I negotiate the challenges posed by conducting ethnographic work with people I am politically involved with. While there are many other academics operating within such a framework, I realize that the potentially dehumanizing process of graduate education results in many students eager for role models and alternative ways of being.[1] Consequently, I hope that this chapter will be a small contribution toward helping scholars and activists think through some of the implications of being a scholar activist.

I have structured the letter around six major questions and themes. Topics range from the very practical, such as how to balance the competing demands of academia, to the more abstract, including negotiating the ethical minefields of ethnography, to the personal, such as the need to be honest with yourself. While such an approach is less than ideal in that it may appear scattered and incoherent, I trust my instincts and experience that these are some of the key things that graduate students and newly minted PhDs need to be aware of as they go about the business of building their academic and political lives.

Question 1: How does your department/university respond to your political work?

ANSWER: This is easily the most frequently asked question that I receive. Clearly, people *assume* that institutions oppose counterhegemonic activist and scholarly work. Indeed, many are genuinely surprised when I explain that for the most part I have not faced any real problems from my administration. It is not that I happen to teach at some enlightened institution; rather, a variety of circumstances, both fortuitous and deliberately chosen, have provided me with the space necessary to be a scholar activist. I will discuss three of the factors that have contributed to this situation: colleagues, a solid publication record, and my sense of self.

For the most part I have been blessed with colleagues who, though they may not always agree with what I do and how I do it, respect the notion of academic freedom (if not the actual work that I do). The scope of appropriate academic activity has been defined broadly in my fields of geography (partly because of its connection to planning) and American studies and ethnicity (because of the activist roots of ethnic studies; Omatsu 1994), providing me with ample room to be a scholar activist. While I am certain that some colleagues disagree with my politics, they have for the most part been professional and respectful. Moreover, I have several senior colleagues who are also scholar activists in their own right, and I suspect that they have been instrumental in paving the way for more junior colleagues to pursue such a path. They have set a high standard of both scholarship and social commitment, showing that the two are not mutually exclusive, and this, in turn, has made my life much easier. While there is an element of luck to my situation regarding my colleagues—I know many who are not so fortunate—the truth is that I carefully considered it when I first began searching for a new job. I was not interested in the most prestigious university or the best geography program; rather, I was looking for a place that was in Los Angeles *and* that would allow me to flourish as a scholar activist. Because of the reputation of some of my senior colleagues, I thought that USC would be a potential fit, and I was right: not only was I fortunate, but I chose well.

A second reason that I have not encountered serious problems from my institution is that I have maintained a steady publication record, which, regardless of what anyone says, is the primary thing that academics get evaluated on at research universities (Goldsmith, Komlos, and Schine Gold 2001, ch. 7). Mine is not a great record—certainly I publish far less than some of my more "productive" colleagues—but it is solid and entirely acceptable. I strongly suspect that had I not published on terms satisfactory to the institution, I might well have encountered far greater problems. Thus, to a certain extent, the publication record has served as a shield of sorts. Though a strong publication record will not protect you if the institution is intent on getting rid of you, it is the first line of defense. If the publication record is "weak," however that is defined by the powers that be, that will be the first and potentially easiest way for the institution to eliminate you (Winkler 2000, 744). This applies to all scholar activists, but particularly to scholars of color, who often publish in journals deemed "marginal to the discipline" by hostile forces. Knowing this, I consciously built a solid publication record so that the university would have a relatively hard time dismissing me.[2]

A final factor contributing to my limited experience of institutional conflict stems from my own perception of the situation. A strong sense of self, clarity of purpose, and knowledge of my priorities have helped buffer me against institutional pressures. I realize that this factor is much more subjective than the first two mentioned and that it edges toward relativism. But upon surveying my own experience as well as that of others, I am convinced that my sense of purpose and identity—my knowledge of who I was, who I wanted to be, and how that translated into particular behaviors—has helped minimize my experience of institutional conflict.

This does not imply that conflict doesn't exist, only that I do not experience it as an acute problem.

A telling moment came when I was up for tenure. At that time the janitorial and food-service workers on my campus had become deeply embroiled in a contract stalemate with the administration. The main issue was subcontracting, and the unions, both of which were composed of low-wage workers of color, initiated community-based campaigns to pressure the administration into accepting a more favorable contract. I, along with several other faculty, became deeply involved in the campaign. I routinely brought the workers and union organizers to my classes; I organized class research projects around the issues; I encouraged students to organize and get involved; I was part of a small group that tried to get other faculty to pressure the administration; I participated in marches, rallies, and civil disobedience actions and eventually helped organize and participated in a campus-wide fast in support of the workers. These activities began approximately two years before I was up for tenure and continued until the year after I received it. Because of the timing, the university had the perfect opportunity to get rid of me. I knew that I was in a vulnerable position, but I also knew that I could not refrain from involvement—What kind of person would I be? I would not be the person that I wanted to be or saw myself as. Could I live with myself? I reached two important conclusions that helped me chart a course of action: I decided, first, that I had to be involved, and second, that I deserved tenure. For me, convincing myself that I deserved tenure was a bigger hurdle than actually getting it. Once I was clear on those matters, I could readily identify my fears, assess their significance and meaning for me, and, eventually, move beyond them. In this instance, the worst-case scenario was my not getting tenure, but what it *meant* for me had changed—I no longer interpreted tenure denial as a negative judgment of me or my performance. I knew that such an act would be politically motivated and not a true reflection of my record and abilities. I could live with that. I decided that if I was denied tenure I would fight it in court. Once I understood the objective forces arrayed against me, my various options, and the emotions driving those choices, my course of action became not only apparent but comfortable.

I do not wish to imply that all or even most problems scholar activists face are due to their own perceptions of the problem. I have seen and heard all too many instances when administrators go after faculty in the most brutal fashion. So let's be clear—witch hunts and retaliation do exist. But there is a sizable gray area between such hostile actions and how individuals choose to experience the situation. This gray area is shaped not only by circumstances over which we have no control but also by our identity, sense of purpose, and ability to be honest with ourselves. Rest assured, as a scholar activist you *will* be tried, but if you are clear in your convictions, then the crisis will not be quite so traumatic; it becomes just an episode, though a potentially difficult one. If, on the other hand, deep down inside you are less than sure of what you are about, then that event may indeed become a crisis forcing you to acknowledge the truth of who you really are.

Question 2: How does one combine scholarship and activism?

ANSWER: Although such a question may appear to be relatively straightforward, in reality it is anything but. This is because how you combine scholarship and activism is linked to how you construct your life. In my case, building an integrated life has been a key part of being a scholar activist.

Allow me to begin with an often overlooked issue that has emerged as crucial to me: place. Perhaps because I am a geographer I have realized the need to deal with the reality and limitations imposed by space. Place figures two ways in my life. First, I do not traverse space particularly well, and, second, I am passionate about the place where I live, Los Angeles. Such a confluence of circumstances, while seemingly mundane, has made it relatively easy for me to build an integrated set of research, teaching, and political activities centered in one geographical location. This, in turn, has provided a convenient framework for my life as a scholar activist.

I did not initially consider space to be a relevant issue in shaping my political and academic work, but over time I discovered its importance. My dissertation research, which explored environmental activism among working-class Chicanas/os, focused on two specific places, northern New Mexico and central California. I realized quickly the conflict between my life as a researcher and my life as a political activist: if I wished to work with and become a committed member of those communities, this would entail a particular type of energy expenditure that was especially difficult for me—traveling. As much as I like seeing new places and meeting new people, travel is stressful on my body and usually results in some illness afterwards. For a long time I denied this fact and pushed myself, insisting that this was simply what politically committed academics did. Indeed, travel has essentially become a job requirement for all scholars. Eventually I acknowledged that traveling was not sustainable for me, and I began to locate most of my activities at home. Of course, there are many ways I *could* have been a scholar activist from a distance, including doing applied research, advocacy work, and fund-raising, for example. While I was not averse to doing such things, such an arrangement would have precluded me from being part of the *everyday* life of an organization or movement, which has been paramount to me (more on that later).

Thankfully, not everyone feels this way. I have known many scholars who are intimately involved with communities beyond their backyard as well as halfway across the globe (Sangtin Writers and Nagar 2006; Routledge 2003; Gilmore and Gilmore 2003). Such individuals negotiate the physical and social distances between the various parts of their lives, facilitated increasingly by rapidly evolving technology. Indeed, if it were not for such people, the geographic distribution of scholar activists would be more skewed than it is, leaving large swaths of the globe without the benefits and resources, however meager, that committed academics can bring to marginalized communities.

The question of geography may appear to be mundane or irrelevant to your particular situation. That's okay. The point is to encourage you to think about your basic character, your likes and dislikes, and how you want to live your life. As this example illustrates, seemingly irrelevant issues can play a major role in how you develop as a scholar activist. Obviously, there is no right way to decide which communities you will work with and what kind of relationship(s) you will construct. The goal is to find a situation that works for you in which you are able to grow, contribute, and find meaning.

Just as space is important to the development of scholar activists, so too is time. Do you prefer long-term, short-term, or sporadic relationships with activist communities? I have a strong preference for long-term relationships, but there are merits to each, provided the proper context. One of the reasons I tend toward long-term commitments with activist groups is that I have seen numerous academics rush into a community ready to contribute, do their thing, and leave. This is not necessarily bad, as sometimes organizations and movements are in dire need of some quick assistance and such a strategy serves a need,[3] but it is not a model I am comfortable with because it pays scant attention to the ongoing needs of the community and issues of reciprocity. In my case, partly because I lack the kind of skills typically associated with critical short-term assistance (see Question 5), and also because of my scholarly interest in social movement activism, I have sought to build long-term relationships with activists who share my political interests and commitments.

You may consider issues of space and time to be fairly abstract, but in reality they provide the foundation for more concrete matters. Identifying such key issues has facilitated my ability to integrate my research, teaching, university service, and political activism. The first three, research, teaching, and service, constitute the pillars of any academic career. Although universities usually view these domains separately, many scholar activists, myself included, manage to weave them together so that they perform "double duty" in terms of university requirements. For example, much of my research and many of my publications have been based on my community "service." More recently, I have tried to create the same kind of symbiosis pedagogically. Over the last seven years or so, I have designed most of my undergraduate courses so that they are centered on a community-based research project. My motivation was largely pedagogic, as I had come to realize that students are far more apt to remember and be transformed by what they *do* than by what they hear and read. At the same time, I realized that this was a way to contribute to and strengthen my relationship with local community groups. Fortunately, the university has either supported such activities or, more often, simply not blocked them, even when they were critical of the institution (see, e.g., Houston and Pulido 2002). While this has been my experience, I know that faculty have been disciplined both formally and informally for engaging students in research critical of their employers. In such cases, scholar activists would do well to study their institution in advance in order to assess how it might respond to critical projects. At the very least you can hopefully make an informed decision about how you want to proceed.

In short, by integrating my research, teaching, and political activities as much as possible and keeping them in all one place, I feel that I have been able to sustain myself as a scholar activist and contribute in various ways to causes I am committed to. The specifics of how you choose to be a scholar activist will differ for everyone, but what is important is that you are clear on your particular needs and how that will inform your political and academic life.

Question 3: What kind of scholar activist should I be?

ANSWER: There are many different ways of being a scholar activist, each of which has its own merits and makes a particular contribution. For example, there are public intellectuals along the lines of Howard Zinn (1999), those who see their theoretical work as directly contributing to activism (Riedner and Tritelli 1999), those who engage in advocacy research (Hondagneu-Sotelo 1993), and those who practice "militant ethnography" (Juris 2005). In addition to the type of activism one might choose, there is also the question of site. Will you direct your energies toward transforming the campus, the local community, the country, or the world? To further complicate matters, within each of these categories there is considerable variation. In terms of community activism, for example, some scholar activists may assume positions of leadership (Kobayashi 1994; Meagher 1999), while others may contribute as rank-and-file members. Indeed, an individual may move through these various categories over time, as Alan Wald has shown (Tritelli and Hanscom 1999). What is important is that you are aware of *how* you wish to be a scholar activist, the reasons for such a decision, and how that choice may change over time. Whether one is drawn to a specific form of activism or simply thrust into a particular role (a surprising number of people "stumble" into activism; Pulido 2006, ch. 3), it seems to me that one of the key issues is negotiating change. Not only is change often difficult for people, but we need to consciously decide what direction we wish to move rather than just letting life happen to us. In short, how does one evolve as a scholar activist, and how can one facilitate that process? The business of becoming an activist and an individual's trajectory of activism are the products of both larger political events, what might be called external factors, and one's personal dynamics, what I refer to as internal factors (Pulido 2003). By understanding both the external and the internal, we can appreciate how individual changes occur at the nexus of both.

External events are larger shifts in the political climate, organizing opportunities/obstacles, and other situational changes that usually are beyond your control. These are developments that you must respond to. I'll provide an example of one such instance. I recently completed a project on the Third World Left in Los Angeles. This was a comparative study of African American, Asian American, and Chicana/o activists in which I examined the extent to which differential racialization led to distinct forms of radical politics. As part of the investigation, I explored the early politicization of activists, particularly the circumstances that had led to their politicization. Although there were some interesting variations among members of the various racial/ethnic groups, across the board all activists traced their early political involvement to two key events: the antiwar movement and the Black civil rights struggle. These events were so profound and pervasive that they forced individuals to respond to them and take a position. Both are examples of external events—they provide the larger historical backdrop that shapes our lives.

The internal, in contrast, is a vast terrain that includes such things as one's personality, temperament, moral compass, and stage in the life cycle.

These are factors that will greatly influence what activities we decide to pursue at a given time. At one point, for instance, I was deeply involved with a local organization, the Labor/Community Strategy Center. Until then I had largely eschewed campus activism for community engagement (I will admit to not only preferring community activism but also seeing it as more "authentic" than campus work, an admittedly problematic distinction). However, when the worker conflicts on my campus arose, I was soon called upon to get involved, and I felt, given my position as a faculty member, that my participation was essential. I quickly learned, however, that I could not maintain two spheres of political work very well. I felt very scattered and did not feel that I was able to give my best to either struggle. Moreover, it was at a time when I began experiencing some health problems and wanted to simplify and streamline my life somewhat. For these reasons, I decided to focus on the campus labor struggles—a decision very much driven by internal factors. Upon the conclusion of the labor campaigns, the campus itself had changed considerably, and I became increasingly immersed in campus activism. Not only had the campus changed, but *I* had changed, and I began to see and enjoy the possibilities of campus activism in a new light.

I realize that I have articulated a somewhat artificial distinction between the external and the internal, but I have found this to be a useful device insofar as it illuminates distinct spheres of influence. Of course, the reality is that internal and external are always in dynamic conversation and shape the overall tapestry of one's life, as can be seen in my decision to concentrate on campus activism. The point, as always, is to pay attention to what is going on both outside and inside as you negotiate changes in your trajectory as a scholar activist.

Question 4: As a scholar activist, how should I approach community work?

ANSWER: Two fundamental issues should guide how scholar activists approach community work: accountability and reciprocity. Both are shorthand for a series of important relations, including how individual scholars view themselves as activists, how they see themselves in relation to other activists, and the kinds of relationships they build. When all is said and done, what kind of scholar activist you are and the amount and type of work that you produce are secondary to the issues of accountability and reciprocity. In my experience, these are the criteria by which you will be judged and remembered.

Accountability refers to the fact that scholar activists are not lone mavericks. Indeed, the idea of a scholar activist operating alone is something of an oxymoron. The whole point of being a scholar activist is that you are *embedded* in a web of relationships, some of which demand a high level of accountability to a community or other group of individuals. It is accountability that will hopefully ensure the relevancy of your work in the effort to create social change. Accountability requires seeing yourself as *part* of a community of struggle, rather than as the academic who occasionally drops in. As longtime activist Lisa Duran, the executive director of Rights for All People (RAP), recently explained, "One of the problems with scholar activists is that they're just not useful because they are not sufficiently rooted in the community so that they don't have a sense of where their time should be spent. Being clear on how the effort being put forward is short term, long term, or medium term and its connection to the larger goal is not just an idea—it's rooted in struggle" (interview, July 2, 2004, Los Angeles).

It has become commonplace to hear activists and community residents complain about academics who act as if they are not accountable to anyone but rather privilege their own work and agenda. This is understandable, as academia is all about the individual: one's research, teaching, service, promotion, and evaluation all focus on the individual abstracted from a larger social context. In contrast, activism is very much a collective process (or at least effective activism usually is). Thus, if you are serious about becoming a scholar activist, at some point you need to decide how you will reconcile your own personal desires with that of a larger community. And while I see many students and faculty who genuinely want to work with others, being held accountable is another story. I know this to be true because I have been one of those persons (see below).

Closely related to but distinct from accountability is reciprocity. *Reciprocity* denotes a mutual give and take and is something that scholar activists must always be attentive to. Just as activists and community residents resent academics who are not accountable, so too do they resent those who swoop in, collect what they need from a community, and then move on, having enriched themselves but not necessarily provided anything of substance to the community in question. Academics often rationalize that they are providing an important service simply by telling the story of a subordinated or otherwise marginalized group. While some may buy this (certainly, conventional academic norms encourage such thinking), do not be fooled. Writing about a community's plight or struggle should *not* be confused with reciprocity. Consider for a moment what the scholar is getting out of the arrangement. If a student, the scholar is most likely earning a graduate degree. If the scholar has already graduated, then the data collection and analysis will lead to either tenure or a promotion, an enhanced reputation, further academic opportunities, and perhaps some modest level of fame, if not fortune. How does the community benefit? Their story gets told to a particular audience. Though it is certainly true that a subordinated group's story must be told if the situation is to improve, there is ample evidence that simply telling that story will not lead to any substantive change. In fact, university libraries are filled with accounts of how aggrieved communities, nations, and workers struggled and resisted, but in no way did these stories contribute to a shift in power relations. Activists and residents of well-studied communities, such as northern New Mexico, the Mississippi Delta, Appalachia, and South Central Los Angeles, are quite aware of the unequal power dynamics embedded in research initiatives and of who bears the actual costs. For this reason, many communities are wary of sharing their experiences with new scholars, as experience has taught them to be cautious.

The need for reciprocity does not imply that every scholar activist should engage in participatory or advocacy research. Rather, it means looking for ways to reciprocate. Below I offer some examples of how this may or may not work. In the first case, I draw upon my own experience to illustrate a failure of accountability and reciprocity, and in the second, I share the success of my friend and colleague Pierrette Hondagneu-Sotelo, who has reciprocated in some innovative ways.

My own story of failing to reciprocate stems from my dissertation fieldwork in northern New Mexico. As stated earlier, the project centered on how working-class Chicano/a communities in California and New Mexico mobilized around environmental issues (Pulido 1996b). The New Mexico case study centered on Ganados del Valle, a community-based organization dedicated to sustainable development. I was deeply sympathetic to and fascinated with the local community and its struggle, but I was also on a mission—to complete my dissertation. Besides thinking that I could not afford to be "sidetracked" by giving of myself in a substantive way, I lacked confidence in my research skills and did not see how they might be helpful. As a result, although I did make some offers of assistance, they were vague and not particularly fruitful. In addition, the fact that I was not rooted in the community and was unwilling to make a long-term commitment to the region (as this would have required traveling) all worked against my forging a respectful and viable relationship with the group. In short, I was simply not willing to make the necessary investment of time and energy, despite my good intentions.

The situation was complicated by identity politics. Although other scholars were also studying Ganados del Valle, I was one of the few Chicanas/os. Our shared heritage added a layer of ethnic confusion to the picture: not only did I sense (correctly) that the white researchers thought I had a different relationship to the community, but also I was uncertain about the meaning of my identity in the research process. Did I have a greater connection because of our ethnicity, despite the significant differences between an urban Chicana and rural New Mexicans? If so, did I also have a greater responsibility? Finally, because I was already a political activist of sorts, I assumed that I would produce politically relevant and useful work. However, I was still under the illusion that simply telling a story was a politically useful act. In short, although I was a political activist in Los Angeles, and although I identified as a scholar activist, the reality was that I was not yet one, as I did not understand fully what being one meant.

Being accountable would have required me to perhaps stay longer and/or make numerous repeat trips to the region; it would have necessitated shifting from my narrow dissertation focus to develop related projects and activities that were of more direct use to the community. Instead, regardless of the reasons, I operated as a scholar—certainly a very sympathetic one—but not a scholar activist. As can be seen, accountability requires flexibility, the ability to give of yourself, and willingness to step outside yourself, regardless of how "oppositional" your research might be. While I am not exactly proud of how I handled myself in this situation, the episode was important insofar as it made me realize that I *needed* to figure out how to be a scholar activist.

Fortunately, I did figure it out over time. However, for an entirely different reason, I now once again find myself in a situation of not being able to reciprocate and be held accountable. Three years ago I became a mother, and while this has brought me great joy, I have had to scale back my political work. Given the centrality of reciprocity to me, however, this has meant a change in research focus, as I would not feel comfortable writing on community organizing and activism without everyday participation. Not only would this limitation result in inferior scholarship, but such a practice would violate my code of reciprocity, as I lack the time and energy to give back to any communities. Consequently, I am currently pursuing archival and popular education projects (see "A People's Guide to Los Angeles," www.pgtla.org). Hopefully, when my children are older, I can return to a life of intense political engagement and writing about my passion, social movements.

In contrast, my friend and colleague Pierrette Hondagneu-Sotelo understood early on what being a scholar activist entailed and how reciprocity worked. For her dissertation, Hondagneu-Sotelo conducted extensive fieldwork among Mexican immigrants in Northern California, exploring how gender relations were transformed through the migration process. On the basis of the data she gathered, she wrote her dissertation, received a PhD, and eventually turned it into an award-winning book (Hondagneu-Sotelo 1994). Although Hondagneu-Sotelo benefited immeasurably by tapping into the lives, stories, and experiences of these Mexican immigrants, she also understood the power dynamics at play and was not content to simply take from her subjects. Upon completing her fieldwork she moved to Southern California, where she became involved with a group called Coalition for Humane Immigrant Rights, Los Angeles (CHIRLA). Initially, she simply asked CHIRLA how she might be of service—always a good first move. Eventually it was decided that the group would create a series of *fotonovelas* to be used for popular education purposes among Latino immigrants. Hondagneu-Sotelo's research led specifically to the development of a *fotonovela* focused on the rights of domestic workers (Hondagneu-Sotelo 1993), which has been widely used. In this case the researcher reciprocated, not directly with the individuals she had investigated, but rather with the same class or group of people. The fact that she had moved to another part of the state did not hinder her commitment and sense of responsibility to the community in question; instead, she found innovative ways to maintain accountability and to reciprocate.

Question 5: I want to be useful to the "community." What kind of work should I do?

ANSWER: This is a very common question, as it gets to the heart of what most scholar activists desire: to be of service and to change the world. While there are many ways to alter the existing social formation, many hope that their research will be of direct use to those actually engaged in counterhegemonic struggle. In reality, however, the production of such research raises a host of issues concerning how activists operate as researchers. I will begin by discussing the kind of research that social change organizations often need and will then present alternatives one might consider if one lacks the requisite skills outlined.

There is, admittedly, something very compelling about conducting research of direct use to activists. Outside the classroom, there are few venues where academics can really feel that they make a difference and see concrete change result from their work. Seeing one's research put to such productive ends creates a deep sense of satisfaction. Although scholars of all disciplines engage in such research, it is performed most by social scientists—given that field's supposed goals of addressing societal problems. If you harbor such aspirations, I would recommend honing your quantitative, technical, grant-writing, and policy skills. In my experience, this is what many social change organizations need when it comes to research: people who can conduct sophisticated quantitative and/or technical analyses; people who can challenge both policy makers and right-wing think tanks on their own turf; and people who can help organizations grow and/or fund new projects. Quantitative skills are always in demand, as are people who know how to make maps using GIS, digest an Environmental Impact Report (EIR), or decipher a state budget. Such research skills, though often devalued in theoretically driven fields, can make a tremendous difference to a community struggle. For example, several years ago Los Angeles–area researchers employed by Justice for Janitors (Service Employees International Union [SEIU] 399, now 1877) produced a study entitled "A Penny for Justice" (SEIU 1995), which documented the extent to which the public subsidized low-wage janitors via health care costs. Researchers argued that employers, by contributing an additional penny per hour, could provide janitors with health insurance and thus no longer burden the public with such costs. This was a terrific piece of activist scholarship that was debated in city council, resonated with the public, and ultimately helped the janitors secure a better contract (Merrifield 2000).

Unfortunately, I am not one of those scholars. I have a very limited set of quantitative skills, and my passion is really for history and talking to people about their experiences and stories. I have found, however, that such products are of far less use to those communities I am interested in working with. Accordingly, I have had to think through this skills mismatch problem. My research on environmental justice provides a clear example. *Environmental justice* refers to the disproportionate exposure of people of color and low-income communities to environmental degradation (Bullard 1993). Environmental justice emerged as a topic while I was a graduate student; thus, not surprisingly, I became involved with the movement. Activists welcomed me as an academic, but it was quickly apparent that I did not have the skills that they really needed. Certainly they needed researchers who could tell the stories of struggling communities to a larger audience and who could challenge the hegemonic nature of Western science, as well as attend rallies and lick envelopes—all of which I was happy to do. But what they *really* needed was someone who could identify various sources of pollution, map them, and conduct a rigorous demographic analysis of the data. This I could not do. To be honest, I could have retooled and learned these skills, but ultimately I was not willing to do so. I was not willing to put the movement's immediate needs ahead of my own because I knew I would have been miserable. I was much more interested in documenting the history of community struggle and exploring how the racial formation affected organizing efforts, as well as how discourses of race were operationalized within environmental justice politics and research (Pulido 2000, 1998, 1996a). While these topics were certainly of interest to the larger movement, they were not considered urgent or of immediate use.

I handled the problem in two ways. First, I did my best to connect the organizations in question with people who had the requisite skills. Although I lacked the specific research skills, I knew and had access to people who did. Sometimes this meant coaxing colleagues to help out, encouraging graduate students to get involved, or, in some cases, conducting preliminary assessments myself. Though this was a relatively small effort on my part, it was deeply appreciated by community residents and activists. As academics we often take for granted the resources available to us, resources that may be difficult for poor and working-class constituencies to access.

The second thing I did was to consciously contribute in other ways. While some scholar activists prefer to function primarily as researchers, I tried to be a reliable supporter/member who could provide whatever assistance was needed. Sometimes this required setting up tables and making phone calls, while at others it meant utilizing my legitimacy as a university professor to provide testimony, for example, at public hearings. Although I couldn't conduct specific forms of analysis, I could produce and contribute to a number of other projects that were useful to the overall struggle, including helping to write/edit newsletters, giving lectures on relevant topics, organizing class research projects that generated basic data, and developing popular education materials.

Despite being generally happy to contribute either as a researcher or as a general member, I am somewhat critical of the way that I have handled the situation. While I reject the model of the academic "expert," in retrospect I could have leveraged more of my "social capital" to greater effect. One reason I hesitated to do so was my discomfort with the distance between myself and the community in question. Feminist scholars have problematized the space between researchers and subjects (Behar 1993; Gilbert 1994; England 1994), arguing that this distance, regardless of how uncomfortable, must be acknowledged, as it is the result of uneven power relations. While I know this intellectually, I have had a harder time incorporating the knowledge into my attitudes and behavior. This is partly because I come from a working-class family: My parents are "those people" who don't understand EIRs and budgets and policy analyses. As a result, for a long time I did not wish to set myself apart from them and was uncomfortable with the status conferred by the PhD and my professorial position. This, coupled with my disdain for those who related to working-class communities *only* as the academic expert, led me to bend over backwards not to be like them, but at a price. Had I been more comfortable with my "in-betweenness," I might have been able to do a better job of contributing more fully to the communities and struggles that I was committed to (see also Question 3).

Question 6: What kinds of ethical problems might I confront as a scholar activist?

ANSWER: Scholar activists will inevitably encounter a range of ethical dilemmas. This can catch them by surprise, as they sometimes have romantic visions of the "beloved community." Among progressives there is a deeply entrenched narrative that confers a nebulous moral authority upon nonelites (Joseph 2002). While such beliefs are entirely understandable given hegemonic values, subordinated communities can also be sites of unethical conduct and/or political disagreement (Nagar 2000). Contradictions may become more apparent and potentially problematic the closer one is to a community. Scholar activists often seek closeness, as it facilitates access to events, materials, and members of the community (which may contribute to scholarship) and produces a sense of political efficacy (which feeds the activist). As you become more integrated into a group, however, the boundaries between the scholar and activist may become muddied, and responding to conflicting demands increasingly difficult. Such conflicts may be fraught with ethical challenges, including conflicts of interest, questions of representation, and questions of one's commitment to the community (versus the university, discipline, etc.). While at first glance these may appear to be political issues, I frame them as ethical ones. I do so because progressive scholars and activists routinely overlook the ethical dimensions of political activism. If we define ethics as the exploration of how we should best live our lives, it will become apparent that ethical commitments underlie most political positions. If we wish to fully understand the dynamics informing our political work—which I believe is essential—then we must consider the role of ethics. The world of the scholar activist is filled with ethical dilemmas, and although I only discuss two examples, I hope that this brief discussion will encourage you to be cognizant of the many ethical issues in your life.

My first example centers on a political disagreement I had with a labor union in which my actions did not reflect my beliefs. In short, I was not truthful to myself. It is important to understand that *ethics* does not refer solely to how we treat others; it also encompasses how we act in relation to ourselves. As previously mentioned, I developed relationships with union locals who were considered quite progressive and at the forefront of "social movement unionism." Social movement unionism is a form of unionism in which labor unions are politically relevant to working-class people and address a range of important issues, not just narrow bread-and-butter concerns (Scipes 1992). The goal of social movement unionism is for labor to actually become a vibrant social movement, rather than merely being defined as a "special interest" group (Milkman 2000; Bernstein 2004; Merrifield 2000). The political goals and energy of the locals led me to participate in numerous campaigns, not just ones related to USC. Workers and organizers alike could count on me to attend events, provide needed contacts, participate in mass civil disobedience, or whatever was required. For the most part, I felt good about my participation: I learned a great deal and felt confident that I was assisting workers who were struggling not only for a decent livelihood but also for a better union movement.

While there were certainly small things that I disagreed with, there was significant political agreement between me and one local until the issue of Indian gaming arose. Over the past decade, California, like many other states, has allowed Indian tribes to operate gambling operations on sovereign land (Morain 2004). This has become a highly profitable enterprise. Given the money involved, as well as the fact that a protected minority is at the center of the debate, there has been an explosion of legislation surrounding the issue. When the matter first came before the California electorate in 1998, the union actively opposed Proposition 5. It argued, along with environmentalists and others, that the proposed law would authorize unregulated gambling in the state, something that organized labor, understandably, challenged on a number of grounds.

In California, Latinas/os constitute a significant portion of the Indian gaming workforce, and serious questions have been raised regarding wages, working conditions, and unionization. By opposing Proposition 5, which legalized the expansion of Indian gaming, a progressive labor union, was, in effect, pitted against Indian tribes. Regardless of the pros and cons of Indian gaming, I disagreed with how the union advocated its position. Although Indian gaming is not without its problems, I felt that native peoples should be allowed sovereignty to the extent possible. Moreover, given the genocide, displacement, and poverty they have suffered and continue to endure, I hesitate to categorize indigenous people as just another special-interest group, as I believed the union was doing. I agreed that questions of workers' rights and wages needed to be addressed, but through political negotiation. Given that two marginalized groups were at the heart of the conflict, I hoped that both parties would be committed to working out an acceptable solution.

Instead, the union waged an all-out war against Proposition 5, assuming that once I was "educated" on the matter I would get on board, as I had with other issues. The local invited me to speak at events, distribute pamphlets, and get other people involved in the cause. I could not do so, however, because my heart was not in it. Perhaps I was somewhat naive in my hope that the matter could be resolved outside the legislative arena, but what is important is that I disagreed with the union's approach and lacked the courage to say so. I did occasionally try to complicate the situation, question the union's strategy, and point out various contradictions, but I did not systematically explain my position and why I could not actively participate in this campaign. This was a low point for me in my experience as a scholar activist: I felt great pressure from the union but could not speak my truth. In retrospect, I believe that most union members would have accepted my decision and respected it as simply a political disagreement, but I was too afraid to test the waters, too afraid of somehow having my commitment questioned. Given where I am at today, I am confident that I would handle the situation differently, as I have a greater ability to stand by my convictions. But I also understand that this particular event helped me reach that point. Ethical dilemmas and political disagreements, however difficult, are valuable opportunities that allow us to clarify our beliefs and how we wish to act upon them, which is all part of the process of political development.

The second ethical conflict I wish to address involves representations of scholarly work, particularly differing interpretations and narrations of activism and activists and how they are represented in texts. Although volumes have been written on the question of representation from various perspectives, my intent is to discuss how I have experienced this problem as a scholar activist. Although I present one instance, I have encountered this problem in every major research project in which I have used a large interview set. Moreover, numerous other scholar activists have discussed this problem with me, suggesting that it is a common problem for those engaged in ethnographic and qualitative fieldwork.

As previously mentioned, I recently completed *Black, Brown, Yellow, and Left: Radical Activism in Los Angeles* (Pulido 2006). The project was essentially based on archival sources as well as many interviews with African American, Asian American, and Chicana/o activists. Since I sought to interview people outside my own racial/ethnic group and with whom I did not necessarily have a history, my reputation, or the willingness of others to vouch for me as a reliable academic, was key in getting those I did not know to talk with me. Many former activists were hesitant to discuss this part of their lives. Not only did they feel betrayed by previous academics whom they felt had misrepresented them, but they also had fears of state surveillance. Because of these concerns, my activist "credentials" were crucial in enabling me to secure interviews and also offered some hope to activists that their stories would be appropriately told. Needless to say, I took this confidence seriously and did my utmost to convey the stories I gathered with respect and accuracy, not only because they are the memories and experiences of real people, but also because I cared deeply about these movements and struggles and wished to portray them in all their richness and complexity.

To do so, I needed to develop a process for working with my interviewees. This was relatively easy, since feminist scholars have pioneered various collaborative research models, which, in turn, have been embraced by an array of critical scholars. For example, researchers such as Diane Fujino (2005), Mario García (1994), Maurice Isserman (see Healey and Isserman 1993), and Richa Nagar (see Sangtin Writers and Nagar 2006) have pursued relatively collaborative, nonhierarchical models of knowledge production in which the subject and researcher work together on the project at every step. Most scholars, however, employ a modified approach in which the subjects are consulted, invited to review drafts, and asked to comment but are not necessarily engaged in every decision.

In my case, I conducted the interviews, transcribed them, and sent them to the interviewees for comments. Although few actually commented, this strategy generated some valuable feedback and, perhaps more importantly, provided interview subjects with a transcript, which many found useful. Upon completing a draft of the manuscript, I sent copies to most of the interviewees for comments and incorporated a number of their suggestions. Certainly these exchanges lengthened the process, but these are common practices among those seeking to address the power imbalance inherent in contemporary social science research.

During the course of *Black, Brown, Yellow, and Left*, I did a series of interviews with Asian American activists and wrote an account of one Japanese American organization. This was a difficult history to reconstruct, as there were few written records; I had to piece together a narrative based largely on individuals' memories. Not only are memories notoriously faulty, but more importantly, they reflect distinct experiences—which differed radically in this case. As usual, I sent the manuscript to all the interviewees; this led to a collective conversation among them and prompted another former activist to ask to be interviewed late in the process. I happily obliged, thinking the new material might add greater accuracy to the text. And in fact the informant was extremely helpful in identifying shortcomings and helping to clarify the organizational account. However, she differed radically from the other members in her analysis of the group's gender relations. While most interviewees described the organization as patriarchal and sexist, she insisted that it was not. When confronted with the evidence that other interviewees had presented, she often dismissed the other female informants as being "weak" on gender issues or simply not recalling things accurately. She continued to communicate with me over several months through e-mails explaining her perspective on the organization. Typically, these e-mails were also sent to the other interviewees, a correspondence that allowed me to glimpse not only the differing interpretations of gender relations but also how members interacted with each other. The reality was that the activists were continuing to play out the dynamics of an earlier period, including issues that had not yet been resolved. Unfortunately, being part of this process was extremely time consuming and emotionally draining, as I was under intense pressure from the various parties to portray their experience and interpretations as *the* organizational experience. I felt as if I had walked into a quagmire of difficult personalities and unresolved issues to which there was no easy answer or exit. After several months of intense interactions, and after I had taken firm positions with the various parties, I invoked the press deadline as one way of concluding the dialogue. Ultimately, I decided to depict the organization as patriarchal (though far less so than its Chicana/o and African American counterparts), but with clear acknowledgment that not all parties agreed on this interpretation. Although this experience is hardly uncommon, it was nevertheless difficult and raised several ethical concerns: To what extent should one accommodate the needs and desires of one's research subjects?

What are the political and ethical implications of privileging particular narratives? Where does my responsibility to the informant end and my role as researcher take precedence? Certainly the answers to these questions will depend on both the individual and the circumstance. Indeed, it is not my intent to offer any ready solutions. Rather, I wish to illustrate the kinds of ethical challenges I face in the course of my research—issues that you might very well confront yourself.

Upon the conclusion of such research I am usually so drained that I often follow a major ethnographic project with an archival or theoretical study requiring minimal emotional energy. Such work, I find, restores me, and inevitably whets my appetite to go back into the field again.

I have tried to address the most frequently asked questions, as well as those that seem pertinent for anyone considering becoming a scholar activist. Although I have tried to cover a sizable terrain in this letter, I would like to highlight some key themes and lessons. The first is simply recognizing that being a scholar activist is not always easy but is immensely rewarding. You will inevitably find yourself having to make difficult professional, ethical, and political choices and having to live with the consequences. This is never easy, but it is part and parcel of a rich life. Second, it is of the utmost importance that scholar activists pay attention to the rules and requirements of academia. It is imperative that you be fully aware of what is expected of you and that you make fully informed choices. You may decide that some institutional requirements are worth challenging, or you may decide to comply and direct your energies toward other goals. What is important is that *you* make the decision and that it is not made for you, or worse, that you were unaware of the expectations. There is certainly nothing wrong with deciding to leave academia (as a number of brave souls have done), but it is far preferable to leave on your terms.

A third lesson, which applies to all spheres of life, is the importance of living a life of reflection. Because becoming a scholar activist entails making difficult choices and acts of courage—particularly the determination to live your truth—it is essential that you be attentive to your emotions and thoughts and consider how they affect your attitudes, values, and behavior. Clarity in your actions will spare you a great deal of grief and allow you to be more open and direct with colleagues and comrades. Finally, as suggested above, the life of the scholar activist is not for the fainthearted, weak, or nominally committed. The truth is that it takes fortitude and wisdom to live such a life. Fortitude is required to make unpopular decisions, to challenge both the powerful and the disenfranchised; and wisdom is necessary to ensure that you have weighed your options, understand the consequences, and are creating a life that you can be proud of. Living the life of the scholar activist not only helps to change the world but also provides an avenue to change yourself.

In Solidarity,
Laura Pulido

NOTES

Many thanks to Charlie Hale for his helpful comments. I remain responsible for all shortcomings.

1. For instance, the recently published *Chicago Guide to Your Academic Career* does not even mention political activism and in fact advises junior faculty to refrain from engaging in institutional politics (Goldsmith, Komlos, and Schine Gold 2001, 146–49).

2. I do not mean to suggest that the current "standards" of evaluation are fair, reasonable, or appropriate. In fact, they are extremely problematic and contradictory (Domosh 2000), and, thankfully, other scholar activists are challenging them. I have chosen not to take on this particular battle—perhaps if I had my story would be quite different.

3. One could argue, however, whether this is in fact scholar activism, as there is an absence of commitment, reciprocity, and accountability.

REFERENCES

Behar, Ruth. 1993. *Translated Woman: Crossing the Border with Esperanza's Story.* New York: Beacon Press.
Bernstein, Aaron. 2004. "Can This Man Save Labor?" *Business Week*, September 13.
Bullard, Robert. 1993. *Confronting Environmental Racism: Voices from the Grassroots.* Boston: South End Press.
Domosh, Mona. 2000. "Unintentional Transgressions and Other Reflections on the Job Search Process." *Professional Geographer* 52 (4): 703–8.
England, Kim. 1994. "Getting Personal: Reflexivity, Positionality, and Feminist Research." *Professional Geographer* 46 (1): 80–89.
Fujino, Diane. 2005. *Heartbeat of Struggle: The Revolutionary Life of Yuri Kochiyama.* Minneapolis: University of Minnesota Press.
García, Mario. 1994. *Memories of Chicano History: The Life and Narrative of Bert Corona.* Berkeley: University of California Press.
Gilbert, Melissa. 1994. "The Politics of Location: Doing Feminist Research at 'Home.'" *Professional Geographer* 46 (1): 90–96.

Gilmore, Ruth Wilson. 1993. "Public Enemies and Private Intellectuals: Apartheid USA." *Race and Class* 35 (1): 69–78.

Gilmore, Ruth Wilson, and Craig Gilmore. 2003. "The Other California." In *Globalizing Liberation: How to Uproot the System and Build a Better World*, edited by David Solnit, 381–96. San Francisco: City Lights.

Goldsmith, John, John Komlos, and Penny Schine Gold. 2001. *The Chicago Guide to Your Academic Career*. Chicago: University of Chicago Press.

Healey, Dorothy Ray, and Maurice Isserman. 1993. *California Red: A Life in the Communist Party*. Urbana: University of Illinois Press.

Hondagneu-Sotelo, Pierrette. 1993. "Why Advocacy Research? Reflections on Research and Activism with Immigrant Women." *American Sociologist* 24 (Spring): 56–68.

———. 1994. *Gendered Transitions*. Berkeley: University of California Press.

Houston, Donna, and Laura Pulido. 2002. "The Work of Performativity: Staging Social Justice at the University of Southern California." *Environment and Planning D: Society and Space* 20:401–24.

Joseph, Miranda. 2002. *Against the Romance of Community*. Minneapolis: University of Minnesota Press.

Juris, Jeff. 2005. "Practicing Militant Ethnography within Movements against Corporate Globalization." www.euromovements.info/html/jeff-juris.htm. Accessed April 19, 2006.

Kobayashi, Audrey. 1994. "Coloring the Field: Gender, Race and the Politics of Fieldwork." *Professional Geographer* 46 (1): 73–80.

Meagher, Sharon. 1999. "The Academy on the Front Stoop: Theory, Community and Resistance." *Minnesota Review* 50/51:75–86.

Merrifield, Andy. 2000. "The Urbanization of Labor: Living Wage Activism in the American City." *Social Text* 18:31–53.

Milkman, Ruth. 2000. *Organizing Immigrants*. Ithaca: Cornell University Press.

Morain, Dan. 2004. "California on Path to Becoming Nation's Gambling Capital." *Los Angeles Times*, August 25, A1, A24.

Nagar, Richa. 2000. "Mujhe Jawab Do [Answer Me]: Feminist Grassroots Activism and Social Spaces in Chitrakoot India." *Gender, Place and Culture* 7 (4): 341–62.

Omatsu, Glenn. 1994. "The 'Four Prisons' and the Movements of Liberation: Asian American Activism from the 1960s to the 1990s." In *The State of Asian America*, edited by Karin Aguilar-San Juan, 19–69. Boston: South End Press.

Pulido, Laura. 1996a. "A Critical Review of the Methodology of Environmental Racism Research." *Antipode* 28 (2): 142–59.

———. 1996b. *Environmentalism and Economic Justice: Two Chicano Struggles in the Southwest*. Tucson: University of Arizona Press.

———. 1998. "Development of the 'People of Color' Identity in the Environmental Justice Movement of the Southwestern U.S." *Socialist Review* 96 (4): 145–80.

———. 2000. "Rethinking Environmental Racism: White Privilege and Urban Development in Southern California." *Annals of the Association of American Geographers* 90 (1): 12–40.

———. 2003. "The Interior Life of Politics." *Ethics, Place and Environment* 6 (1): 46–52.

———. 2006. *Black, Brown, Yellow, and Left: Radical Activism in Los Angeles.* Berkeley: University of California Press.

Riedner, Rachel, and David Tritelli. 1999. "Writing, Pedagogy, and Activism in the Human Sciences: An Interview with Stanley Aronowitz." *Minnesota Review* 50/51:101–11.

Routledge, Paul. 2003. "Rivers of Resistance: Critical Collaboration and the Dilemmas of Power and Ethics." *Ethics, Place and Environment* 6 (1): 66–73.

Sangtin Writers and Richa Nagar. 2006. *Playing with Fire: Feminist Thought and Activism through Seven Lives in India.* Minneapolis: University of Minnesota Press.

Scipes, Kim. 1992. "Understanding the New Labor Movement in the Emergence of Social Movement Unionism." *Critical Sociology* 19 (2): 81–101.

Service Employees International Union, Local 399. 1995. "A Penny for Justice: Janitors and L.A.'s Commercial Real Estate Market." Working paper, SEIU, Los Angeles.

Tritelli, David, and Sharon Hanscom. 1999. "The Formation of an Activist Scholar: An Interview with Alan Wald." *Minnesota Review* 50/51:125–42.

Winkler, Julie. 2000. "Faculty Reappointment, Tenure, and Promotion: Barriers for Women." *Professional Geographers* 52 (4): 737–50.

Zinn, Howard. 1999. *A People's History of the United States: 1492–Present.* New York: HarperCollins.

Afterword

Activist Scholars or Radical Subjects?

Joy James and Edmund T. Gordon

In the introduction, Charles Hale discusses the prickly issue of "shared political sensibilities" among scholars involved in activist research, claiming "a shared commitment to basic principles of social justice that is attentive to the inequalities of race, gender, class and sexuality and aligned with struggles to confront and eliminate them." He further posits a strong, necessary connection between the authors' progressive politics and their chosen activist methodologies. Authors in this volume also reference the contradictions of "institutionalizing" activist research within academic institutions that situate and discipline.

Clearly, contributors have a shared desire to translate academic skills and positions into vehicles of passion for transformative social change and human liberation. However, the tentativeness that runs through the collection regarding this desire stems in part from the self-policing (against [nonelite] radicalism) that results from our participation in corporate academe. Such sites are at best liberal-reformist in their institutional politics and at worst complicit with the global military-industrial, and consumer-commercial, complex that enforces and/or regulates the marginalization and impoverishment of the majority of the world.

Reform might be the best that some can realistically hope to accomplish through engaged scholarship (of course, some engaged scholarship is explicitly reformist). Yet most of the authors here would agree that as world citizens and as activist scholars who work as academics we search for a transformative political agenda.

Shared desire for change is likely to be shaped by some affinity (no matter how tepid) for revolutionary struggle. Seeking *collectivities*—that is, communities shaped by egalitarian sociality that reject dominance and concentrations of power—a revolutionary is guided by love (as Ché Guevara famously stated). Love and outrage over injustices are motivations and sustaining emotions in revolutionary collectivities. The *guerrero del amor* becomes a warrior lover who understands struggle and battle as expressions of commitment, loyalty, sharing of self—a selflessness that is not sacrifice but fulfillment through collectivity. The unfolding of self within the collective, just as the self develops in its individuality, is likely to be the foundation for radical subjectivity.

Love functions as a counternarrative and alternate reality to narcissism. By *narcissism* we mean the self-absorption, competitiveness, and careerism characteristic of the "normal" academic. We are arguing for activist scholarship not as therapeutic but rather as a radical, potentially revolutionary, alternative to the corporate university. Thus, in considering an alternative, we have to examine three issues for struggle raised by Hale and volume contributors. First, is it possible to open up our institutions in order to create "more supportive space for the particular kind of research that we do"? Second, do the rewards and operating principles of these institutions force us into "elitism and hierarchy" expressed as narcissism and conformity? Third, will our mere presence and participation within elitist institutions make us complicit in the subjugation of subaltern communities? Concerning "supportive space" in the academy, higher education depends upon the continued support of elites, given that it is a leading sector of the global North whose governing principles include the management and control of disenfranchised communities. Institutions of higher education have a vested interest in keeping scholarship "objective" (mystifying), "nonpolitical" (nonsubversive), and "academic" (elitist)" and in continuing to reserve the most advanced technical training for that small portion of the world's population who will manage the rest, as well as consume or control its resources and political economies. Unless elite educational institutions are transformed, activist research will never reside within the academic mainstream as an entity that produces a revolutionary, or even radical, counternarrative and practice.

Antonio Gramsci writes that academics are the organic intellectuals of the bourgeoisie. As noted in many of the preceding chapters, incentives offered by the academy reward those whose knowledge production contributes to elite power. This plays to our narcissistic conformity. That same system diminishes the production of potentially transgressive political knowledge by questioning its "objective" status or "scientific" value. (Dis)incentives channel the dissemination of potentially radical knowledge into journals and books where its usefulness to the dominated becomes increasingly marginal and its commodification creates currency for antiradicals. Our continued participation in these institutions strengthens them by allowing them to make hegemonic claims to fostering "academic freedom," a "marketplace of ideas," and rational neutrality, but we are not inherently handmaidens to the reproduction of control.

THE ACADEMIC ARENA: APPEARANCE, DISCOURSE, PERFORMANCE

We insert into the academy at three points: appearance, communication or discourse, and performance on the staged arena of academic life. Progressives maintain the continuity of systems of dominance at the first two points of entry and have the potential for disrupting them at the third point: that is, we can exit the staged arena. We can be organic intellectuals of formations other than the academy—that is, relevant radical subjects—if, and only if, we reject the sites of entry and performance as *final destination points for activist politics* for social justice.

Let us consider the implications of the three points of our entry (and the possible point for our departure). First, there is physical entry into the academy itself. The notion that mere appearance of progressives in institutionalized learning constitutes a disruption of the normative reproduction or the continuity of repression seems shortsighted. Just to have women, queers, and people of color in academe is insufficient, in and of itself, for social change. Second, there is the entry point of communication and political rhetoric through academic discourse. The view that writing or teaching in a "radical" vein, or building progressive units within the academy, transforms educational institutions also seems myopic. Neither entry nor communication is sufficient to incite transformation. Radical ideas can easily be commodified to accommodate hegemonic institutions in their claims of impartiality that mask their facility to reproduce or enable dominant social structures.

But the third entry point, of the staged arena, can actually function as an exit point from the academic machinery. Our work with marginalized communities as a destination point for our intellectual and political selves requires that we connect to radical collectives embedded in communities struggling for social justice. They exist identifiably as marginalized minority formations seeking radical change in ways similar and dissimilar to the formations of radical academics. As does the larger society, the academy functions as an identifiable aggregate that harbors collectives that are conservative, liberal, or radical (the last being marginal). Radical-minded groups are not trapped in their respective spheres if they seek like groups in other sites. We are handmaidens to the bourgeoisie until we exit the academic arena in search of these radical collectivities.

All of those who define work as academics by progressive agendas will not necessarily exit. Those who define their teaching and publications of critical thinking (antiracist, feminist, queer, Marxist, anti-imperialist) as inherently radical are likely not to exit. The predictable stressors of the "safe" environment of conservative-liberal academe foster less aversion than radical praxes emanating from sites that elites do not control.

Skepticism regarding the intellectual powers and leadership of radical sectors within nonacademic communities is an equal-opportunity affair among ideologically embattled academics. Progressive academics while besieged in the institution may also fight against radicals linked to collectivities. Dialogic warfare waged by progressives to control political discourse and meaning suggests that radicals loyal to the academy are not necessarily radical subjects.

Radical academics may point to the hegemony of the institution, and its dominant intellectuals, without challenging their own power and investment in these structures. Their "outsider" status mystifies the power and privileges of progressive activist scholars. Once truly outside the academy, academic-bound radicals may be unmasked as "insiders" aligned with institutional power. Stable identity constructs as "transformative" or "activist" scholars crumble—except for those who can reconstitute themselves as practitioners outside the academic arena. Those who can do so are no longer merely "outsiders" belonging to or within the academy. In the shell game that is academe, they are able to break a losing streak in a rigged game by locating the mark: the mark only materializes outside. Leaving the academy and embedding ourselves in collectivities, we act beyond conventional society. This is one of the true hallmarks of the radical subject, a sign that distinguishes him or her from the activist scholar.

With the academy as stage or arena, academics politically perform themselves. Even given the power differentials within the academy, we all share some of the spoils of war. Alexander Kojeve's *Introduction to the Reading of Hegel* (1980) posits a master-slave dynamic in which the slave is actually the more powerful, since the master is dependent on his or her labor. Academic-bound radicals, as slaves, despite their marginalization engender new thinking and analyses and through their very criticisms of the prevailing order function to revitalize that order. Some may recognize this "power" and become loath to relinquish the prerogative of a "slave."

The performative shapes the interdependency of academic radicals, liberals, and conservatives. One performs an ideological subject position. In the academy, conservatives and liberals dominate the contextual arena and the material ability to stage performance, providing structure to both props and script. Radical subjects, to construct and control the presentation of their own politics, need a departure, an exit from the arena. If they refuse to exit, academic-bound radicals reject radical subjectivity and validate the reproduction of hierarchies in which we function as powerful "outsiders." Consequently, academic-bound radicals more easily share the arena with liberals and conservatives than with radical subjects as activists.

THE RADICAL SUBJECT

Perhaps only the academic-bound radical or activist researcher possesses a coherent public persona in the academy. In contradistinction, radical subjects may have little or no coherence in the academic arena, and this encourages their search for an exit. Inside the arena, such subjects operate not from a stance of political or moral superiority but from the position of a fractured self. While academic-bound radicals posit a coherence that is intelligible (only?) in the academic arena, fractured subjects suggest a coherence shaped by political literacy emanating from communities confronting crisis and conflict. Both the academic-bound radical as "coherent" subject and the radical subject as the fractured self share similar fears and weaknesses: loss of status and respectability, diminishment of social stability and material resources. The fractured self can guard against its potential losses by entering on levels one and two mentioned above, appearance and communication: show up to work, teach class, publish, convene conferences, build programs. But entry will not protect it from other fears: those of irrelevancy and bad faith. *Furthermore, the radical subject is not a revolutionary subject given his refusal to accept the losses from nonparticipation in repressive institutions.*

Despite its political limitations, the fractured self of the radical subject desires what the academy cannot provide: relevancy and accountability to collectivities resisting domination. The radical subject rejects the arena provided by the academy to perform as center-stage spectacle or sideshow attraction. The desire for recognition and legitimization in a context other than that built by the academy is what fractures and pushes the radical subject outside, off stage. Radical subjects seeking activism outside the academy do not try to create a space inside as a final destination point or as an identity marker for radicalism.

We have argued that whereas the academic-bound radical enters the stage of performance and public recognition as another destination (after appearance and labor), the fractured self as radical subject exits. Therefore, we contest the viability of elite structures to reproduce themselves while reproducing repression and claiming our allegiance *in performance*. We do not contest our obligations (contractual agreements for material and emotional remuneration) to appear and communicate—to show up, teach, write, conference, workshop, build programs. We contest only the performance of the loyal outsider in Kojeve's master-slave dynamic.

Earlier we stated that our mere presence allowed elite institutions to make claims for themselves as encompassing diversity (of gender, color, ideology, sexuality) and therefore as being comprehensive and liberal in scope. We identified three categories in order not to conflate them, so that presence and communication are not inherently synonymous with performance. We have little control over the meanings given to our appearances or our words within the academy; we have agency only over our departure from the academic staging of our radicalisms.

The institution has the power to fix us in ways that valorize it. Still, to appear is not necessarily the same as to conform. To practice a radical activism, we seek an appropriate staging ground unavailable within the academy. The fractured subject is mobile, not stationary or stagnant.

Exploring political action unauthorized by the institution, we may find a level of "performance" that institutions will be forced to ignore because they cannot interpret activism within a totalizing, assimilating narrative. Imagine transport as mobility, mobility as potentiality. To be able to walk in and walk out, and to return, is a freedom wielded by the radical subject (to be able to act freely is an agency wielded by the revolutionary subject). There is likely to be a price to pay for this exercise of agency and independence. While most enter the staged arena, the radical subject may depart. It is in the departure from managed performance that fractured subjects—and their present and future collaborations with collectives of affinity, shared passions, revolutionary aspirations—can be located.

We seek spaces that constitute their own sites of struggle. So we leave academia to make connections with collectivities within which our very elitism is challenged and devalued. As radical rather than revolutionary subjects, we accept our engagement with academic institutions while asserting our responsibility to be more than mere performers. Hence we offer ourselves, and encourage our students, to labor for justice.

The meaning of our productivity cannot be determined by academia alone. Seeking the exit door, we search for meaning, value, and political relevance given that our institutions are incapable of providing the conditions for radicalism as anything other than performance. Resistance to violent and premature social and biological death requires that we as activist researchers change into radical subjects.

REFERENCE

Kojeve, Alexander. 1980. *Introduction to the Reading of Hegel*. Ithaca: Cornell University Press.

Contributors

JENNIFER BICKHAM MENDEZ teaches sociology at the College of William and Mary.

CRAIG CALHOUN is President of the Social Science Research Council.

RUTH WILSON GILMORE teaches geography at the University of Southern California.

EDMUND T. GORDON teaches anthropology and African American studies and is Director of the Center for African and African American Studies at the University of Texas at Austin.

DAVYDD J. GREENWOOD teaches anthropology at Cornell University.

CHARLES R. HALE teaches anthropology at the University of Texas at Austin.

JOY JAMES teaches political science at Williams College.

PETER NIEN-CHU KIANG teaches education and is Director of the Asian American Studies Program at the University of Massachusetts, Boston.

GEORGE LIPSITZ teaches American studies at the University of California, Santa Barbara.

SAMUEL MARTÍNEZ teaches anthropology at the University of Connecticut.

DANI WADADA NABUDERE directs the Afrika Study Centre in Mbale, Uganda.

JESSICA GORDON NEMBHARD teaches African American studies at the University of Maryland, College Park.

JEMIMA PIERRE teaches anthropology and African American studies at the University of Texas at Austin.

LAURA PULIDO teaches in the Department of American Studies and Ethnicity at the University of Southern California.

SHANNON SPEED teaches anthropology at the University of Texas at Austin.

SHIRLEY SUET-LING TANG teaches American studies and Asian American studies at the University of Massachusetts, Boston.

JOÃO H. COSTA VARGAS teaches anthropology and African American studies at the University of Texas at Austin.

Index

AAAS. *See* Association for Asian American Studies
AAC&U. *See* Association of American Colleges and Universities
AAHE. *See* American Association of Higher Education
AARW. *See* Asian American Resource Workshop
Abe, Kosuzu, 108
Abolition democracy, 96–97; power relations and, 98–99, 107
"Abriendo Brecha" Activist Scholarship Conference, 7
Academia: accountability in, 335–37, 353; activist scholarship in, 17–18, 24, 130–31, 257–58, 299, 303, 314–15, 319–20, 333–35; Black scholars in, 131–32; collaboration in, 304–5; dualisms in, 323–25; elitism of, 300–301; intellectualism of, 368–69; political engagement and, 341–46; radicalism and, 369–71
Accountability, 152; academic, 335–36; to communities, 350–51, 353–54
ACE. *See* American Council on Education
ACLU. *See* American Civil Liberties Union
Action research, 64, 334–35, 337–38nn1, 2; criteria for, 329–31; problems in, 331–32
Activism, activists, xiii, xx, 102, 116; academic, 117–18; anthropology and, 187–92; anti-prison, 41–42; Black academic, 131–32; contributions of, 354–57; organizations, 94–95; political, 164, 341–43, 363n1; professionalization of, 50–51; radicals, 371–72; and scholars, 91–93; scholar, 148–49; social movements, 108–9; in social sciences, 320, 321–23; students of, 332–33; textual representation of, 359–62
Activist scholarship/research: institutionalization of, 17–18; methodological rigor in, 4–5, 12–13; objectivity and subjectivity in, 10–12, 13–14; positivism in, 9–10; types of, 348–50
Advocacy, 302; vs. participant observation, 324–25
Africa, 71; history of, 68–69; participatory action research in, 69–70. *See also* East Africa; *various countries by name*
African Americans, 133n6, 166; cooperatives, 277, 283; in Ghana, 121–22, 126; identity issues, 169–70; politics of, 96–98
African American studies, 290
African Association of Political Science, 74
African studies, 127
Afrika Study Center, 14, 71–72; field-building projects, 73–74, 82, 83
Agency, 39–40, 70
Agriculturalists: East Africa, 72, 78–79
Agriculture, 52, 54, 56n3; indigenous knowledge about, 74–75
Aids/US, 90
Alabama, 95, 283
American Anthropological Association, 321, 324
American Association of Higher Education (AAHE), 305

377

American Civil Liberties Union (ACLU): and Coalition Against Police Abuse, 173, 179n3
American Council on Education (ACE), 305
American Political Science Association, 305
American Psychological Association, 305
American Sociological Association, 324
American Studies Association, 305
Ang Lee, 313
Anthropologists: as culture experts, 224–25; identity issues of, 219–20
Anthropology, xxi–xxii, xxviii8, 14, 25, 63, 124, 133n5, 207n5, 213–14; academic, 185–86, 206n2–3, 207n4; action, 322, 337–38nn1, 2; activist vs. academic, 202, 205–6, 207–8n11; applied, 321–22, 338n8; applied vs. activist, 186–92, 206n1, 207n3; and Black Americans, 170–71; collaborative, 164, 169–76, 192–96, 232–33; decolonization of, 224–25; methodology in, 183–84; participant observation in, 64–66; power relations of, 203–4, 215; public, xvii, 117
Antisweatshop movement, 142, 149
Anzaldúa, Gloria, 237, 261–62
"Appeal for the Recognition of Women's Rights, An," 104
Architects and Planners for Social Responsibility, 53
Aristotle, xxiii, 323, 338n3
Asian American Graduate Student Study Group, 260
Asian American Resource Workshop (AARW), 300
Asian American studies, 24–25, 299, 300, 302, 314–15, 315–16n1; disciplining of, 304–6; inequality in, 307–9; planting fields, 312–13; at UMass Boston, 309–12
Asian Studies Association, 305
Asset ownership, 286

Association for Asian American Studies (AAAS), 304, 305, 307, 308(table), 309(table)
Association of American Colleges and Universities (AAC&U), 304, 305
Audre Lorde Project, 90
Australia, 322

Basques: Mondragón Cooperative Corporation, 282–83
Bell Curve, The (Hernnstein and Murray), 47
Bello, Walden, 90
Bernstein, Alison, 299
Black, Brown, Yellow, and Left: Radical Activism in Los Angeles (Pulido), 360–62
Black Panther Party, 179n4; and Coalition Against Police Abuse, 165, 166, 173, 177
Black Americans, 166. See also African Americans
Blacks, 118, 125, 130, 167; academic activism, 131–32. See also African Americans
Bologna Process, 336
Bosnian Serbs, 200
Boston: Asian American communities in, 299, 300, 301, 310–11
Boston Chinatown, 310; community organizing in, 299, 300, 301
Boston University, 300
Bourdieu, Pierre, xix–xx, xxiv
Boyer, Ernest, 303
Brazil, 169
Bruce, Blanche K., 97
Bullard, Robert, 90
Bureau of Indian Affairs, 321
Businesses: cooperative, 274–75; democratically owned, 276–77; worker-owned, 275–76
Bush, Vannevar, xvii

California, 56n5, 91, 354; *desakota* concept in, 35, 36; Indian gaming in, 358–59; prisons in, 40–42, 45–52

California Department of Corrections (CDC), 45, 51–52
California Environmental Quality Act, 41–42
California Prison Moratorium Project, 40, 52, 53
California Supreme Court: on police abuse issues, 173, 179n3
Cambodia: refugees from, 243–44, 310, 311. *See also* Khmer Americans
Cambodian Communities of Massachusetts (CCM), 246
Campaign for Labor Rights, 142, 145
Campus Compact, 304
CAPA. *See* Coalition Against Police Abuse
Capital: control of, 285–86; transnational social, 145, 158n5
Capitalism, 39, 93; corporate, 99–100; global, 148, 156
CAR. *See* Criminal Alien Requirements III
Carnegie Academy for the Scholarship of Teaching and Learning, 304
Carnegie Foundation, 304, 322
Catholic Worker movement, xvi
CCDH. *See* Centro Cultural Domínico-Haitiano
CCM. *See* Cambodian Communities of Massachusetts
CDC. *See* California Department of Corrections
CED. *See* Community economic development
Center for Justice and International Law (CEJIL): Haitian immigrants, 195–96
Center for Research and Documentation on the Atlantic Coast (CIDCA), 5
Central America: garment industry, 142
Centro Cultural Domínico-Haitiano (CCDH), 193, 197, 198
Change (magazine), 305
Chatauqua movement, xvi
Chea, Gift, 240–41

Chevron, 41
Chiapas, 215, 224, 233n2; indigenous communities in, 216–17, 234n9; land rights in, 218–19; politics and identity in, 226–28, 234n11
Chicana/os, 346; environmental issues, 352–53
ChildSpace, 276
Chinese: as garment workers, 301–2
Chinese Exclusion Act, 97
CHIRLA. *See* Coalition for Humane Immigrant Rights, Los Angeles
Chisolm, Lawrence, 258
CIDCA. *See* Center for Research and Documentation on the Atlantic Coast
Civilian Police Review Board, 169
Civil War (U.S.): African Americans in, 96–97
CJM. *See* Coalition for Justice in the Maquilas
CLAAS. *See* Coalition for Latino and Asian American Studies
Class, 15, 39, 120
Coalition Against Police Abuse (CAPA), 7, 9–10, 90, 164, 165–67, 168, 179–80nn8, 10, 13; collaborative research with, 169–72, 173–76; critique of, 177–78; infiltration and spying on, 172–73, 179n3
Coalition for Humane Immigrant Rights, Los Angeles (CHIRLA), 354
Coalition for Justice in the Maquilas (CJM), 147
Coalition for Latino and Asian American Studies (CLAAS), 259–60
Coalitions, 142, 315; goals within, 153–54; social justice, 165–67; trade union, 145–48
COINTELPROs. *See* Counter-Intelligence Programs
Cold War, 10
Collaboration, 6; academic, 304–5; in anthropology, 172, 232–33; community, 229–30; designing research, 184–85; in knowledge production, 14, 22; with MUDHA, 185–86

Collectivities, 367–68
College of William and Mary: living wage campaigns at, 137, 144, 146–47
Colombia, 21, 63–64, 322
Colonialism, 63–64, 133n5
Commission for Racial Justice, 90
Commission on the Future of Higher Education, 336
Communication: with communities, 77–78
Communities, 33, 76, 90, 266; accountability to and reciprocity with, 351–54; activist research/scholarship in, 71–72, 350; in Chiapas, 217–19, 234n9; collaboration with, 229–30; cooperative economic development in, 280–83; democratic enterprises in, 272, 273–74, 277–79; economic revitalization, 54–55; ethnic studies programs, 239–40; identity and politics in, 226–28, 231–32, 233n5; immigrant/refugee, 238, 242–43; indigenous, 216–17, 221–22; international, 166–67; Khmer American, 243–53; knowledge production in, 77–85; local, 153–54; prisons and, 44–50; public engagement in, 241–42; and UMass Boston, 310–11
Community economic development (CED), 272, 273
Community Human Rights Defenders' Network, 220, 221–22, 234n13
Community in Support of the Gang Truce (CSGT), 164, 167–69, 177–78
Community practitioners, 254; research by, 247–48
Community Reinvestment Act, 90
Comuneros: indigenous identity of, 220, 221–22, 226–28; land use rights of, 217, 218–19
CONFITEA V. *See* Fifth International Conference on Education
Conflicts: ethnic, xiv, 5; localized, 72–73; in Chiapas, 218–19
Contrasida por la Vida, 90
Convite, 191
Cooper, Lauren, 105

Cooperative Home Care Associates, 276
Cooperatives, 274–76; research on, 277–80; subaltern economic development, 280–83
Co-researchers: in Khmer American community studies, 245–53
Cornell University, 321–22, 335
Corporations: globalization of, 138–39
Counterinsurgencies: in Chiapas, 216, 218–19
Counter-Intelligence Programs (COINTELPROs), 173, 175
Credit unions, 275
Crimes: by U.S. military, 103–5, 106–7
Criminal Alien Requirements (CAR) III, 46
Critical analysis, 232; in politics, 230–31
Crouching Tiger, Hidden Dragon (film), 313–14
CSGT. *See* Community in Support of the Gang Truce
CST. *See* Sandinista Workers' Central
Cultural-historical framework, 11–12

Dar es Salaam School, 68–70
Davis, Peter: *Hearts and Minds*, 313
Decision making: democratic, 284–85
Decolonization: of anthropological research, 224–25
Defenders' Network. *See* Red de Defensores Comunitarios por los Derechos Humanos
Delano (Calif.): prison planned for, 40, 41–42
Democracy: abolition, 96–98; economic, 291, electoral, 141, 158n2
Democratic community-based enterprises, 272, 273–74
Denmark: action research in, 322, 334
Denton, Nancy, 90
Desakota, 34–35, 38; California prison system in, 40–41, 49–50; community activism in, 48–49; economic revitalization in, 54–55; population movement to, 43–44

Development theory: international, 266–67
Dialogue, 70, 73, 76, 78; knowledge production and, 81–82
Diop, Cheikh Anta, 69
Discrimination: in Ghana, 119–20
Dominican Republic, 18; Haitian immigrants in, 185–86, 192, 193–200, 201, 207n7
Dorchester (Boston), 310
Drama: communication through, 78
Du Bois, W. E. B., 132; on abolition democracy, 96, 98
Duggan, Lisa: *The Twilight of Equality*, 100
Duran, Lisa, 351
Durban World Conference on Racism, 198
Dyson, Michael Eric, 89

East Africa: localized conflicts in, 72–73; oral tradition in, 68–70; participatory research in, 63, 64, 66; security research in, 78–79
East Asia–U.S. Women's Network Against Militarism, 106
East Los Angeles, 41
East Palo Alto, 41
Economic development, xiv, 168, 267, 272; subaltern cooperative, 280–83
Economics, 54, 268; alternative, 265–66; applied, 289–90; democratic community, 10, 267, 271–74, 276–77, 283–87; neoclassical, 9, 269–71; and social justice, 165–66
Economic values, 265–66, 284
Economies, 52, 122; *desakota*, 35, 54–55
EDI. *See* ONE DC Equitable Development Initiative
Education, xxiii, 95, 244; of African Americans, 96, 97; higher, 302–3; K–12, 93–94, 306; traditional vs. Western, 75–76. *See also* Higher education
Elite(s), 52, 119; in academia, xv–xvi, 300–301

Emil, Antonio Pol, 198
England. *See* Great Britain
Enterprises: cooperative, 274–76; democratic community-based, 272, 273–74, 277–79
Envio, 149–50
Environment, xiv, 79, 102; prison impacts on, 46–47; rural sector, 41–42
Environmental issues, 21; Chicana activists, 352–53
Environmental justice, 90, 355–56; anti-prison activism as, 41–42
Environmental reviews, 56–57n6; federal prison construction, 48–50
Epistêmê, 320, 323, 326–27, 330; activism as, 332–33
Epistemology, 21–22
Equal Exchange, 276
Esperanza Peace and Justice Center, 91
Essentialisms, 225–26
Ethics, 223; in activist scholarship, 357–62
Ethnic studies: and academia, 257–58; coalitions in, 304–5, 314–15; at UMass Boston, 239–40
Ethnography, 139, 164, 184
Ethnohistorical research, 225
Expatriates: in Ghana, 119, 33n2
EZLN, 90, 142

Fair-housing movement, 90, 168
Fair-wage campaigns, 18, 137, 144, 146–47
Fals-Borda, Orlando, 64
Farmworkers, xxiii, 41
FBI, 173
Federal Bureau of Prisons (FBOP): prison construction, 45–50, 57n8
Federation of Southern Cooperatives, 283
Feminism(s), 17, 22, 130; and activist research, 140–41, 155, 156–57; pan-Pacific, 105–6
Ferguson, Roderick, 90
Fernández, Leonel, 186, 195
Field-building projects, 6; Afrika Study Center and, 73–74; East Af-

rica, 72–73; knowledge production in, 75–85
Fields Corner (Boston), 310
Fifth International Conference on Education (CONFITEA V), 84
Filipina women, 105
Finland, 322, 334
Ford Foundation, 303
Fotonovelas, 354
Foucault, Michel, xix
Fourteenth Amendment, 97, 98
Freedom movement, 95
Freedom Quilting Bee, 283
Free market, 99–100
Free Trade Zone (Nicaragua): garment and textile industry, 145, 149
Freire, Paulo, 70; *Pedagogy of the Oppressed*, 63
Fresno, 41
Fresno County, 46
Frisch, Michael, 259
Fukumara, Yoko, 90, 108
Funding agencies: transnational movements, 150–51

Gabriela network, 105
Gaming: Indian, 358–59
Ganados del Valle, 352–53
Gangs, 167, 168, 311
Garment industry, 149; in Massachusetts, 301–2; unions in, 142, 145–47
Gedicks, Al, 91
Gender relations, xiv, 15, 102–3, 126, 129, 361–62
General History of Africa (UNESCO), 69
Georgia, 54
Ghana: race issues in, 21, 115–16, 117, 118–23, 124–26, 129–30, 133nn2, 3
Gifford, Kathy Lee, 149
Gill, Marcus, 103
Gilmore, Ruth Wilson, 90
Globalization, 34, 72, 136–37, 138, 158n1; information, 142–43; political movements, 141–42; power relations, 150–52, 156
Global justice movement, 137, 142

Global Security and Cooperation (GSC) program, 5–6, 72, 192
Global University System, 85
Gould, Stephen Jay: *The Mismeasure of Man*, 47
Gramsci, Antonio, 23
Great Britain, xiii, 42, 322; academic accountability, 335–36
Grossi, Francisco Vio, 67
Grossman, Zoltan, 91
Grundtvig, Frederick S., 71
GSC. *See* Global Security and Cooperation program
Guerrero del amor, 368

Haitian-Dominican Cultural Center (CCDH), 193, 197, 198
Haitians: in Dominican Republic, 185–86, 192, 193–200, 201, 207n7; in racial hierarchy, 126, 127
Harding, Vincent: *There Is a River*, 96
Harp, Rodrigo, 103
Healing ceremony: Revere Beach, 240, 241
Health: in Khmer American communities, 245, 248, 250, 252–53, 255, 256
Hearts and Minds (film), 313
Hernnstein, Richard: *The Bell Curve*, 47
Hierarchies: academic, xv, 302–3; racial, 14–15, 20, 22, 123, 127, 129
Higher education, 84, 93, 302; Asian American studies in, 305–6; public accountability, 335–37; reform of, 303–4
Historical materialism, 64
History: Dar es Salaam school, 68–70
HIV/AIDS, 78; in Khmer American communities, 245, 248, 250, 252–53, 255, 256
Holloway, John, 90
Holmberg, Alan, 322
Hondagneu-Sotelo, Pierrette, 354
Housing: affordable, 288–89; fair, 90
HUD. *See* U.S. Department of Housing and Urban Development

Human rights, 142, 149, 202, 223; Haitian immigrants, 192, 193, 194–200, 201, 207n7
Human Rights Watch, 196

IACHR. *See* Inter-American Court of Human Rights
ICE. *See* Immigration and Customs Enforcement
IDAs. *See* Individual Development Accounts
Identity, 38, 126; African American, 169–70; of anthropologists, 219–20; indigenous, 216–17, 221–22, 226–27, 228–29, 231–32, 233n5; politics of, 39, 180–81n14
ILO. *See* International Labor Organization
ILO Convention 169, 221, 234nn13, 17
Immigrants, immigration, xiii, xiv, xvi, 133n6, 158n5, 238, 242, 354; Chinese, 301–2; community activism of, 49–50; criminal, 45–46; Haitian, 185–86, 193–200, 201
Immigration and Customs Enforcement (ICE), 46, 52, 53
India, 142
Indian gaming, 358–59
Indigenous communities: in California, 358–59; in Chiapas, 216–19, 221–22; identity and culture in, 225–27, 228–29, 231–32, 233n5; knowledge production in, 224–25
Individual Development Accounts (IDAs), 276
Indonesia: place in, 34–35
Industrial organization, 289–90
Industries of last resort: activist opposition to, 50–51, 54–55
Inequality, 266; in Asian American studies, 307–9
Infiltration: of CAPA, 172–73, 175, 179n3
Information sharing, 191–92, 207n4
Information technology: globalization of, 141–43

Inner-city issues, 168–69, 179–80nn8, 9
Institute for Policy Studies and Global Exchange, 148
Intellectuals, xvii, 20; academics as, 368–69; general and specific, xix–xx; knowledge of, 89–90; in social movements, 6, 22–23
Inter-American Court of Human Rights (IACHR), 185; Haitian immigrant cases in, 195–96
International AIDS Conference, 252
International Criminal Tribunal for the former Yugoslavia, 200
International development theory, 266–67
Internationalism, 33–34
International Labor Organization (ILO), 215, 275; and Nicolás Ruiz, 221–22, 229, 231
International Peace and Security (IPS), 5, 6
Internet, 85, 158n6; social movement use of, 142–43; and labor movements, 145–47
IPS. *See* International Peace and Security
Iraq, 104
Italy: fascism in, 23

Janitors: activist research and, 355
Japan: and Okinawa, 102, 103, 104
Joining Forces, 40
Justice: organizational pursuit of, 42–43. *See also* Environmental justice; Global justice movement; Social justice
Justice for Janitors, 355

Kadena Air Force Base, 106
KANS. *See* Khmer Association of the North Shore
Karimata, Nobuko, 106
Kastely, Amy, 91
Kenya, 78, 79, 80
Khmer American communities, 15, 239, 240, 243, 261, 311; grassroots

knowledge, 253–56; knowledge/-capacity building, 244–53
Khmer Association of the North Shore (KANS), 245
Khmer New Year Celebration, 246
Kikuyu, 79
Kimambo, Asaria, 68
Knowledge, xvi, xxiii, 11, 79, 94, 149, 178, 243; Aristotelean types of, 326–27; community/cultural, 253–56; globalization and, 147–48; indigenous, 20, 73, 74–75, 83, 84, 224–25; intellectuals and, 89–90; traditional and indigenous, 70–71; traditional vs. Western, 75–76
Knowledge/capacity-building process, 244–45; in Khmer American communities, 246–53
Knowledge production, 9–10, 19, 20, 21, 69, 139–40, 239; action research, 330–31; in anthropology, 190–91, 223–24; collaborative, 14, 22; community-based, 75–85, 230–31, 238; in Khmer American communities, 244, 254–56; race and, 127–28
Kuhn, Thomas: *Structure of Scientific Revolution*, xviii

Labor: Haitian immigrant, 193–94; internationalism of, 142
Labor/Community Strategy Center, 90, 350
Labor organization, 56n5, 95, 142, 158n3; Indian gaming and, 358–59; knowledge, 147–48; women's, 137, 145–47
Land use rights: in Chiapas, 216, 217, 218–19, 221, 227, 233n8, 234n14
Language: community activism and, 48–50; education and, 75–77; knowledge production and, 77–78
LAPD. *See* Los Angeles Police Department
Laotian Organizing Project, 91
Leadership: in activist organizations, 94–95; power relations of, 98–99
League of Women Voters, 53

Learn As You Work Folk Institute, 71
Ledet, Kendrick, 103, 105
Legalism, 214–15
Levin, Morten, 334
Lewin, Kurt, 322
Living wage campaigns (LWCs), 137, 142, 143, 153; information politics, 144, 146–47
Living with Africa (Vansina), 68–69
Los Angeles, 48, 56n3; activist scholarship in, 303, 346–47, 355
Los Angeles Police Commission, 173, 179n3
Los Angeles Police Department (LAPD), 173, 179–80n8
Louisiana, 54
Lowell (Massachusetts), 315; Khmer Americans in, 243–44, 245, 246, 248, 250, 252, 255–56, 261, 310
Lowell Southeast Asian Water Festival, 246
Lutheran World Federation: indigenous solutions, 74–75
LWCs. *See* Living wage campaigns
Lynn (Massachusetts): Khmer Americans in, 243–44, 245, 249–50, 252, 261, 310
Lynton, Ernest, 303

MacArthur Foundation, John D. and Catherine T.: and GSC program, 5–6, 192
Machida, Margo, 259, 262n1
Macke, Richard C., 103
Malcolm X, 169–70
Malden (Massachusetts): Chinese/-Vietnamese in, 310
MAP for Health. *See* Massachusetts Asian and Pacific Islanders for Health
MAPP. *See* Massachusetts Asian AIDS Prevention Project
Maquila industry, 18; information politics in, 149–50; union activity in, 142, 145–47
Marcus Garvey Pan-Afrikan Institute, 71, 83–84

Maria Elena Cuadra (MEC), 145, 146; information politics, 149–50; internal politics, 154–55; NGO funding, 151–52
Marxism, 64
Masai, 79
Massachusetts, 306; Khmer American communities in, 239, 243–44, 261
Massachusetts Asian AIDS Prevention Project (MAPP), 245
Massachusetts Asian and Pacific Islanders for Health (MAP for Health), 245
Massachusetts Department of Public Health AIDS Bureau, 252
Massey, Douglas, 90
Matsuoka, Martha, 90, 108
MEC. *See* Maria Elena Cuadra
Megaprisons, 35
Mendota, 46, 47–50
Methodological rigor: activist scholarship, 4–5, 12–13
Mexico, 90, 142, 234n11, 322; ILO Convention 169, 221, 229. *See also* Chiapas
Midwest Treaty Network, 91
Military: United States, 101–2, 103–5, 106–7
Million Man March, 167
Miskitu Indians, 5
Mismeasure of Man, The (Gould), 47
Mississippi, 95
MIT: activist research at, 322
Modern Language Association, 305
Mondragón Cooperative Corporation, 281–83
Movimiento de Mujeres Domínico-Haitianas (MUDHA), 185–86, 193, 197–98; human rights issues, 195–96, 199
MUDHA. *See* Movimiento de Mujeres Domínico-Haitianas
Multiplier effect, 279
Mumbai Statement, 84
Murder: at Revere Beach, 240
Murray, Charles: *The Bell Curve*, 47
Myers, Richard, 104

NAFEA. *See* National Association for the Education and Advancement of Cambodian, Laotian, and Vietnamese Americans
Nakiroro road, 80
NARO. *See* National Agricultural Research Organization
National Agricultural Research Organization (NARO), 75
National Association for the Education and Advancement of Cambodian, Laotian, and Vietnamese Americans (NAFEA), 252
National Association of Chicano Studies, 304
National Coalition for Haitian Rights, 196
National Labor Committee, 142, 145
Needs assessments: in Khmer American communities, 245–46, 248, 252
Neoliberalism, 90, 103, 138
Neo-Marxism, 64
Nepantla, 14, 237–38, 239, 241, 261–62
NERCHE. *See* New England Resource Center for Higher Education
Netherlands, 322
Network of Central American Women in Solidarity with Maquila Workers, 148
New England Resource Center for Higher Education (NERCHE), 299
New Mexico: Chicana research in, 352–53
New Right, 173
New Sudan: security research, 78, 79
New York City, 90, 108, 276
NGOs. *See* Nongovernmental organizations
Nicaragua, 5, 18, 20; information politics, 149–50; NGOs and, 151–52; women's labor organization, 137, 145–46
Nichomachean Ethics (Aristotle), xxiii
Nicolás Ruiz, 233n2; and ILO, 221–22, 234nn13, 17; indigenous identity in, 216–17, 226–27, 228–29, 231, 233n5;

knowledge production, 224, 225, 231; land use rights in, 218–19, 233n8, 234n14; political affiliations in, 217–18, 227–28
Nongovermental organizations (NGOs), 6, 71, 141, 143, 158n4; in Dominican Republic, 192, 193, 194, 197; MEC funding, 151–52; politics of funding in, 150–51
Norway, 322, 334
Norwegian University of Science and Technology, 334

Objectivity, xiii, 8, 10, 63, 172, 213, 321; positioned, 13–14, 20–21; Weber on, 11–12
Observant participation, 175–76
Okinawa: U.S. bases on, 101–2, 106–7; U.S. military crimes, 103–5; and OWAAMV, 102–3
Okinawan Women Act Against Military Violence (OWAAMV), 90, 100, 108; male leaders and, 102–3; security and military issues, 101–2; on sexual violence, 103–5; and U.S. military bases, 106–7
Oliver, Melvin, 90
ONE DC Equitable Development Initiative, 288
Oral tradition, 70; East African, 68–70
Orange Grove, 46
Organizations: activist, 94–95; as local, 153–54; pursuit of justice, 42–43
OWAAMV. *See* Okinawan Women Act Against Military Violence

Palaez, Elofna, 90
Palaez, Eloina, 90
Pan-Africanism, 34, 121
Pan-indigenous movements, 142
Parsons, Talcott, 63
Participant observation, 64–66, 174, 175–76, 324–25
Participants, 4, 284; community practitioners as, 247–48
Participatory action research, 67, 69–70

Participatory research, 66, 67, 149
Participatory research approach (PRA), 63–64, 66–67
Partnership: vs participant observation, 324–25
Pasteur's Quadrant, xvii
Pastoralists, 72; agricultural practices, 74–75; security issues, 73, 78–79
Patriarchy, 20, 22; of community organizations, 177–78
Pedagogy of the Oppressed (Freire), 63
Penney, J. C.: antisweatshop movement, 149
"Penny for Justice, A," 355
Persecution, 10–11
Philadelphia: ChildSpace in, 276
Philippines, 90, 105, 142
Phrónêsis, xxiii–xxiv, xxvin7, 320, 323, 326–27, 329, 332, 334
Pierre, Solange, 193, 196, 198, 199, 207n7
Place(s), 18, 106, 346–47; abandoned, 35–36; defining, 34–35; forgotten, 31, 32–33
Police, 169; and CAPA, 172, 173, 174–75
Police abuse, 9–10; in South Central Los Angeles, 164, 165
Political economy, 265, 268–69; and social sciences, 320–21
Politics, 42, 63, 170; academic, 1–2; academia and, 341–46; activist research and, 7–8, 164, 363n1; African American, 96–98; in Chiapas, 217–18, 227–28, 234n11; critical analysis and, 230–31; of funding, 150–51; gendered, 102–3; globalization, 141–42; identity, 39, 180–81n14; information, 149–50; internal, 153–55; labor organization, 145–47; oppositional scholarship and, 341–43; transnational, 144–45
Population movement: in *desakota*, 43–44; voluntary and involuntary, 35, 36
Positivism, 8, 9–10

Postcolonial era: race, 123–24
Powell, Enoch: "Rivers of Blood" speech, 42
Power relations, 62–63, 81, 118, 352; in anthropology, 184, 203–4, 215; globalization and, 150–52, 156; leadership and, 98–99; sexual violence and, 200–201; social movements, 107–8
PRA. *See* Participatory research approach
PRI. *See* Revolutionary Institutional Party
Priistas: in Nicolás Ruiz, 219, 220
Prison-industrial complex, 21
Prisoners, 31–32, 50, 104
Prisons, 31–32, 33, 56–57n6; in California, 40–42, 45–50, 51–53, 57nn8, 9; impacts of, 44–45
Privilege, 10, 20; challenges to, 15–16; of researchers, 154–55; skin color and, 129–30; white, 14–15, 120–21, 125–26
Project Disagree, 108
Project ILO 169, 221, 234n12
Property rights: intellectual, 77, 83
Proposition 5: union opposition to, 358, 359
Public spheres: transnational, 144–45
Puerto Rican Studies Association, 304
Puerto Rico: rent strikes in, 108

Quality Assurance in Teaching evaluation, 336
Quincy (Massachusetts), 310

Race, xiii, xvi, 21, 39, 133n5, 170; in Ghana, 115–16, 118–23, 124, 125–26, 129–30; unearned privilege and, 15, 20, 120–21; in United States, 126–27
Racial hierarchies, 22, 123, 127, 129; privilege in, 14–15, 20
Racialization, 40, 50, 128–29, 133n6; in Ghana, 117, 122–23; in United States, 126–27
Racism, xiii, 36, 47, 198, 277; environmental, 42–43; in Ghana, 21, 115–16, 119–21, 129; on Okinawa, 106–7
Radicals: in academia, 369–71; as subjects, 371–72
Rainbow Grocery, 276
RAP. *See* Rights for All People
Rape, 200–201; by U.S. military, 102, 103–4
Reagan, Ronald, 173
Reciprocity: to communities, 351–54
Recognition of prior learning (RPL), 84
Red de Defensores Comunitarios por los Derechos Humanos, 220, 221–22, 234n13
Refugees: Khmer, 242, 243–44
Rent strikes: in Puerto Rico, 108
Research, xvi, 2, 4, 6; activist, 7–8, 12; community based, 77–78; community on, 238–39; community responses to, 79–81
Research process: in anthropology, 214, 215; in Khmer American community studies, 245–53
Research subjects, 4, 233n1; anthropological, 213, 214; commitments to, 223–24
Resistance: in Chiapas, 218; to slavery, 96–97
Resource management: traditional vs. modern, 74
Revere (Massachusetts), 261
Revere Beach, 239, 240
Revolutionary Institutional Party (PRI), 217–18, 234n9
Right for All People (RAP), 351
"Rivers of Blood" speech, 42
Rodriguez, Juana, 90
Roman, David, 90
RPL. *See* Recognition of prior learning
Rural sector, 33, 35, 42. *See also* Desakota

Sanchez, George, 238
Sandinista Workers' Central (CST), 145

San Francisco: cooperatives in, 276
San Pedro de Macorís, 193
School of Oriental and African Studies (SOAS), 68–69
Science: applied, xvii–xviii; and truth, xviii–xix
Scientific method: in action research, 330–31
Security, xiv, 6, 73; community, 78–79; OWAAMV on, 101–2, 103
Seed banks: community, 74
SEIU. *See* Service Employees International Union
Service Employees International Union (SEIU), 53
Settlement: rural-urban patterns, 34–35
Settlement house movement, xiii
Sexuality: and HIV/AIDS issues, 250
Sexual violence, 207n71; power relations and, 200–201; by U.S. military, 103–4
Sex workers: social networks, 105–6
Shapiro, Thomas, 90
Sharecropping, 283
Sharp, Lauriston, 322
Shaw neighborhood, 288, 289
Skin color, 170; in Ghana, 125–26, 129
Slaves: resistance of, 96–97
SOAS. *See* School of Oriental and African Studies
Social capital: transnational, 145, 158n5
Social change, xxi, 67–68, 156
Social justice, 2, 7, 17, 95, 100, 143, 220, 284, 355; CAPA, 165–67; scholarship in, 290–91
Social movements, 6, 21, 100, 141; activism, 95, 108–9; and NGOs, 150–51; and power relations, 107–8; and scholarship, 92–93
Social movement unionism, 142, 358–59
Social Science Research Council (SSRC), xiv, 2–3, 5, 72
Social sciences, xvi; academic dualisms in, 323–25, 328–29; accountability, 335–36; action research in, 329–32; activism in, 321–23; and political economy, 320–21
Social soundness analysis, 66
Social struggles, 22–23
Social transformation, 67–68
Society for Applied Anthropology, 321
Sociology, xiii; public, xvii, 25
Sophia, xxiii–xxiv, xxvin7
Sorghum: indigenous knowledge about, 74–75
Soto Monzón, Rodolfo, 217
South Africa: relocation townships, 36
South Central Los Angeles, 48; anthropology and, 164, 170; CAPA in, 165–67; CSGT in, 167–69
Southeast Asian Americans, 245, 307. *See also* Khmer American communities
Space: activist scholarship, 346–48
Spain: subaltern economic development in, 281–83
Spellings Commission report, 336
Spying: on CAPA, 172–73
Squatters' movements: in New York City, 108
SSRC. *See* Social Science Research Council
Standpoint theory, 9, 21
Stockton: women's prison near, 52–53
Stokes, Donald, xvii
Story-sharing process: Khmer American community, 248–49, 254–55
Structure of Scientific Revolution (Kuhn), xviii
Students: of K-12 schooling, 93–94
Subaltern groups: economic development, 281–83
Subjectivity, 11–12
Subject participation, 183, 325
Subjects: radical, 371–72
Suburbanization: Stockton area, 52
Sudan: security research, 78
Sugar industry: in Dominican Republic, 185–86, 194, 195, 196, 201, 207n7
Sweden, 322, 334
Sze, Julie, 90

Tai, Stephanie, 91
Tanzania, 68; participatory research, 63, 64, 66; security research, 78–79
Tavistock Institute for Human Relations, 322
Tax, Sol, 322
Teamsters Union, 142
Tékhnê, xxiv, 320, 323, 326–27, 329, 330, 332
Temu, Arnold, 68
Teopisca, 216
Teso, 75
Texas: Esperanza Peace and Justice Center, 91
Textile industry: women's labor movements, 145–46
There Is a River (Harding), 96
Third World, 17, 34, 56n2, 66, 140; and globalization, 138–39
Thorsrud, Einar, 322
Toxic wastes, 41, 48, 102
Trist, Eric, 322
Tulane University, 125
Turkana community, 80
Twilight of Equality, The (Duggan), 100
Tzeltal Mayans: identity as, 216–17, 222, 228, 233n5

Uganda, 71; agriculture in, 74–75; indigenous knowledge in, 75–85
Uganda National Council of Science and Technology, 85
UNESCO, 84; *General History of Africa*, 69
Union and Loyalty League, 96
Unionism, 144; Nicaragua, 145–46; social movement, 142, 358–59; United States, 146–47
Unions, xvi, 142, 158n3; coalitions, 145–47; and Indian gaming, 358–59
UNITE, 142, 145
United Church of Christ Commission for Racial Justice, 90
United Kingdom, 142; university accountability, 335–36
United Nations, 275

United States: abolition democracy in, 96–99; academic accountability in, 336–37; action research in, 334–35; activist scholarship in, 15, 322; Black neighborhoods in, 170–71; higher education in, 302–3; labor movement in, 95, 142; and Okinawa bases, 101–2, 103–4, 106–7; racialization in, 126–27; rural sector, 33, 42; schools and social movements in, 92–93. See also various cities; communities; states
U.S. Department of Education, 336
U.S. Department of Housing and Urban Development (HUD), 288
U.S. Federation of Worker Cooperatives, 276
U.S. military: on Okinawa, 101–2, 103–5; in Pacific, 105–6
U.S. Social Security system, xiv
Universities, 15, 18, 303, 335; activist research in, 23–24, 315; applied studies in, 290–91; as elite, xv–xvi
University of Buffalo: ethnic studies at, 257–60
University of Chicago, xiii
University of Dar es Salaam, 68
University of Ghana, 125
University of Massachusetts at Boston, 238, 239, 240; Asian American Studies, 300, 301, 302, 306, 309–12
University of Southern California, 341, 344, 345
Uong, Chanrithy, 244
UPS: strikes, 142
Urban sector, 33, 194

Vansina, Jan: *Living with Africa*, 68–69
Vargas, João Costa, 90
Veblen, Thorstein, xvi
Vietnamese: in Boston, 310, 311; diaspora studies, 312–13
Vietnam War, 106–7
Violence, xiv; in Chiapas, 218–19; sexual, 200–201; by U.S. military, 101, 103–4, 105

Virginia: living wage campaigns in, 144, 146–47

Wal-Mart, 149, 158n3
Ward, Lester Frank, xvii
Warfare: in Chiapas, 218–19
Washington, D.C.: affordable housing in, 288–89
Watts Gang Truce, 167, 168
Wealth, 90; accumulation of, 270–71, 286
Weber, Max, 11–12
Whites, 123; in Ghana, 125–26; unearned privilege, 120–22
White supremacy, 123, 127–28
Wisconsin: education projects, 91
Wolf River Watershed Education Project, 91
Women, 142; Chinese immigrant, 301–2; Haitian immigrant, 185–86, 196–200, 207n7; labor organization, 137, 145–46; prisons for, 51–52; sexual violence and, 104, 200–201; social activism of, 100–101, 102; social networks, 105–6
Women's Secretariat, 145
Workers' movement, 18, 20, 142, 144, 145, 153
Working and Unemployed Women's Movement, 145
Workplace: democratizing, 279–80
Workshops (*charrettes*): Stockton area prison, 53–54
World Anthropology Network, 17
World order: and race, 123–24
World Social Forums, 142
World Women's Conference, 102

Yale University, 300–301
Yiga Ng'okola Folk Institute, 71

Zapatistas: in Chiapas, 216, 218–19, 227–28, 233n2
Zhou Xiaojing, 258–59, 262n1
Zinzun, Michael, 7, 165, 169–70, 173, 178, 179n3; on police abuse, 174–75

www.ingramcontent.com/pod-product-compliance
Lightning Source LLC
Chambersburg PA
CBHW031959220426
43664CB00005B/69